IN LIBERATING STRIFE
A Memoir of the Vietnam Years

VOLUME I
THE TRACK OF A STORM

by
Steve Atkinson

Testimonials

In Atkinson's personal story of service, families will hear echoes of the stories their veterans will not tell; it is a story that will help historians understand why drafted men fought in a war they thought unconscionable.

—Joseph C. Fitzharris, Professor Emeritus of History, University of St. Thomas, St. Paul, Minnesota

Steve Atkinson has performed a minor miracle with his memoir, *In Liberating Strife: A Memoir of the Vietnam Years*. He has humped the same path as David Maraniss did in his prize-winning *They Walked in Sunlight: War and Peace, Vietnam and America, October 1967*. Maraniss, a stellar reporter for the *Washington Post*, focused on one battle in Vietnam that October and the burgeoning antiwar movement at the University of Wisconsin.

Steve Atkinson shifts the American perspective to Minnesota, where he was a university student. What sets Steve's book off from Maraniss's and others is that he was in-country in Vietnam for a year and writes from ground zero. In compelling, colorful detail, Steve lets us into his inmost thoughts and feelings. He does this through remarkable reporting, both by himself and his wife Bev. He saved their letters from their courtship during his two-year absence, half of it in Vietnam. From their literate correspondence, we can learn to be English majors. Steve captures the ordeal Bev and his own family endured back home as he grew into a unique manhood in various danger zones in Vietnam.

This is a book for ordinary people—the kind who forged some connection with the Vietnam War, Americans who have served since and—perhaps most important—reaching out to civilians who must still decide how they feel about boots on the sand in Iraq and Afghanistan.

—Mike Tharp, correspondent and bureau chief with the *Wall Street Journal*, *New York Times*, *Far Eastern Economic Review*, *U.S. News & World Report*, *People Magazine* and as a freelancer for AARP publications. He was a soldier in Vietnam and received an Honorable Discharge and a Bronze Star. As a civilian he has covered six other wars.

© Stephen Barrett Atkinson. 2017.

All rights reserved. No part of this publication may be reproduced, distributed, or transmitted in any form or by any means, including photocopying, recording, or other electronic or mechanical methods, without the prior written permission of the publisher, except in the case of brief quotations embodied in critical reviews and certain other noncommercial uses permitted by copyright law.

ISBN: 978-0-9987976-0-1 (print)
      978-0-9987976-1-8 (ebook)

Book Design: Patti Frazee

Published by
City Limits Press
Minneapolis, MN

*To Mom, Dad,
Bev, and Robert*

Contents

I. Prologue ... 1
II. Farewell to College Joys

Chapter 1
    The End of High School, De La Salle, 1963-64 ... 13

Chapter 2
    Freshman Year, University of Minnesota, 1964-65 ... 37

Chapter 3
    Sophmore Year, University of Minnesota, 1965-66 ... 51

Chapter 4
    Junior Year, University of Minnesota, 1966-67 ... 77

Chapter 5
    Senior Year, University of Minnesota, 1967-68 ... 95

Chapter 6
    Graduate School, University of Minnesota, 1968-69 ... 125

Photos ... 179

III. Trainees

Chapter 7
    Basic Training, March-May 1969 ... 215

Chapter 8
    AIT and Leave, May-July 1969 ... 295

Chapter 9
    AIT and Leave, July-October 1969 ... 341

Glossary ... 391

About the Author ... 395

O beautiful for heroes proved
   In liberating strife.

—*Katharine Lee Bates*
"*America the Beautiful*"

I.
PROLOGUE

Great is the power of memory, a fearful thing,
O my God, a deep and boundless manifoldness;
and this thing is the mind, and this am I myself.

—St. Augustine,
Confessions

It is a delicate thing to write from memory…
I cannot but reflect on scenes I have beheld.

—John Adams
Letter to John Quincy Adams;
April 2, 1803

We are always coming up with the emphatic facts of history in our private experience and verifying them here. All history becomes subjective; in other words there is properly no history, only biography.

—Ralph Waldo Emerson
Essays: First Series
"History"

I am fortunate enough to have few regrets about my relationship with my parents, but has anyone ever reflected on their growing years without being troubled by at least some nagging thoughts of opportunities forever lost? I certainly wish that I had asked them more about the earlier years of their lives. There is much that I will never know about the days of their courtship, the early years of their marriage, and their lives in Florida and California during World War II when Dad was in the Navy. Those are the years I most regret "losing" because the comparable events of my own life have taught me that love and war are certainly among the most emotionally wrenching human experiences.

Such times of stress and uncommon intensity, times of liberating strife on both the emotional and physical levels, bring out both the best and the worst in people; those are the situations when men and women become most interesting, the times that writers often choose for their subject. In his magnificent Nobel Prize acceptance speech in 1950, William Faulkner observed that his lifetime of dedication to the art of writing had taught him that "the problems of the human heart in conflict with itself…alone can make good writing because only that is worth writing about." Love and war happened simultaneously for me and I decided to write about those events because I always wished that Dad and Mom had done the same. I never received such a legacy, at least partially because I never asked for it, but my thought was that at least I could leave such a remembrance to those coming after me. And even more intriguing in such accounts than the events and scenes described are the thoughts and feelings of the people involved, especially the narrator.

That observation leads me to a question I will address out of courtesy to you, the reader. Who's talking? Who is the narrator? Since I have chosen memoir rather than fiction as my genre the obvious answer is "me," but that response is not as straightforward as it may appear because I write of these events over forty-five years after they occurred. Is it me at twenty talking or me at my current age of sixty-nine? A book I set out to write now narrated by a young man as he walked through this history nearly half a century ago would be fiction rather than memoir because he no longer exists even though, to echo William Wordsworth's felicitous and profound observation, he truly is the father to the older man I am today. That would require me to attempt to ignore how much I have changed in the years since then, not to mention turning a blind eye to all the facts about the war in Vietnam that have come to light in the last half century.

The fact is that those two men did not always get along all that well, but since they had no choice but to live together they attempted to bridge the gap between them with alcohol. I burned that bridge back in 1987 when I arrived at a point where I was forced to acknowledge it for what it really was: not just a bridge to nowhere but slow-motion suicide, the ultimate spiritual dead end. The two of them were forced to reconcile while sharing the journey of recovery and they get along just fine these days, well enough to collaborate on a book, in fact, which I would regard as a true acid test of any relationship.

The best answer then is that the narrative voice is a conversation between the two of them. The younger man, as is typical, has a good deal to say because he kept a journal for a time and I also saved all of the letters he wrote, as well as those he received. The older fellow cannot help but be amused at times by his cohort's youthful naïveté, but he always takes him seriously, even while attempting to balance out the point of view with a bit of whatever wisdom he may have acquired over the decades. The younger has the advantage of having observed events firsthand, but the older possesses more years of experience along with the almost god-like command of information afforded by the Internet. Once they got used to working together I think they made a pretty decent team. So that is the narrative voice and I have attempted to make it as reliable as possible, although I harbor no illusions about the existence of a hard-and-fast line between fiction and memoir because memory is a notoriously slippery thing.

I have attended school reunions where some classmates remember certain things whereas others recall different events. After listening to such an exchange one of my old acquaintances exclaimed "Was I even there?" That kind of situation is both disconcerting and amusing, but the ones I find even more intriguing are when two or more remember the same event but in dramatically differing ways. The resulting cognitive dissonance brings to mind the ironic adage known as Segal's Law: "A man with a watch knows what time it is. A man with two watches is never sure." My own observation over the years, and I do count myself among the observed, is that most people will continue to regard their own recollection as the accurate one. They resolve the dilemma by refusing their friend's offer of the second watch. As in Alexander Pope's earlier observation on such behavior, no two watches display exactly the same time but each owner believes that his is the correct one. So what really did happen? Often the only possible answer is that it depends on who you ask. That is an inescapable fact of human experience. Even major historical events can be seen quite differently by various observers all presumably attempting to be as objective as possible.

Conrad's concise description of the writer's goal is certainly as accurate as any and better than most because of its elegant simplicity: "My task is to make you see." He was referring to fiction, but the observation is equally appropriate to memoir, for my goal is to describe what it was like to live through the years of these recollections, to help you see that to the best of my ability. The writer of fiction is an artist who has tools at his disposal that the composer of memoir has deliberately foregone, such as the freedom to invent characters, dialogue, narrative threads, and situations. The novelist converts experience into fiction through the subtle alchemy of literary art, whereas the memoirist attempts to present those experiences unaltered by that rough magic.

And yet, here again, the line of demarcation between the two genres is less clear-cut than that distinction implies. For the writer of memoir is also an inventor in the sense that he must pick and choose which incidents and anecdotes to include in his account. James Joyce demonstrated definitively by writing *Ulysses* that the events of only a single day could easily fill the pages of a long novel, and the same is certainly true of a work of memoir.

Selectivity is essential and that, along with how the events are described, are the essential elements of the memoirist's art.

And even though I was always faced with the need to decide which of countless historical events to include, the task of selecting personal anecdotes was equally integral to the process. I chose events that I considered the most relevant for understanding what the people I included were experiencing, giving special attention to local happenings in the Twin Cities and at the University of Minnesota. I was considerably less selective with the personal anecdotes because those unique stories, even those that might at first appear irrelevant or mundane, contribute so heavily to the flavor of a work such as this. I was always reluctant to leave one out and when I did it was most often only in order to avoid the possibility of embarrassing one or more of the people involved, myself included.

The primary reason I had so many anecdotes at my disposal is that my wife Bev and I are both inveterate packrats. We wrote to each other frequently while I was away in the Army, usually more than once every week, and of course both of us saved all the letters we received. I come by that habit honestly because after my mom passed away in 1999 I found a great many things stashed away throughout her house, some dross and some gold. Among the items of value, at least to me, was a plain brown unmarked grocery bag that contained all the letters I had written home to my family while I was in the service. I eventually got around to collating these three sets of correspondence in chronological order and found that I had quite a comprehensive account of both my experiences in the military and what was happening in the lives of the folks back on the home front.

Without those invaluable aids to memory I never would have been able to write this account after all these years. In addition, I inherited from my dad a love of photography and I took several hundred pictures during my year overseas in the war zone. We also sent reel-to-reel tapes back and forth. A few of those survive and I found an outfit with the equipment to transfer them to CDs so that I could listen to them once again.

These primary sources are essential elements of this narrative, but I also discovered as I proceeded that they were often enabling me to recall additional things that had not crossed my mind in over forty years, memories that I believe are largely accurate rather than confabulations. As with the school reunion experiences, it was disconcerting to realize that I had totally forgotten some incidents.

But what I had not anticipated was that the intriguing process of reliving some of those incidents was sometimes more than a little disturbing. It had never occurred to me that I had not adequately processed some of the emotional turmoil of those years. I believe that I had felt guilty about facing up to that fact because so many soldiers in Vietnam experienced things much more terrible than anything I ever encountered or am even capable of imagining. Their plight is often on my mind, but as I thought and wrote I slowly came to learn that I had no need to feel guilt over my need to work through my own problems related to my military experience. That was yet another journey that sobriety gave me both the courage to undertake and the emotional maturity to complete. I am grateful to everyone who plays a role in this narrative for their part, passive though it was, in helping me work through those often-repressed feelings by reliving the experiences in order to relate them.

Archival microfilmed issues of Minneapolis newspapers from the years I write about were also valuable for descriptions of relevant events. Back issues of our University of Minnesota student newspaper, *The Minnesota Daily*, were especially useful for helping me recall those often-tumultuous times on a campus I was fortunate enough to call home for nine years as a student and thirty as an employee. Those *Daily* issues, of course, also helped me to fill in the gap in my firsthand familiarity with local and campus happenings during the time I was away in the Army. I am deeply grateful to my fellow students working on the paper back then who were clearly aware they were living in the midst of significant events and did such a fine job of chronicling many of the local reflections of those turbulent times. Then, now, and always, our society owes a great deal to journalists, both students and professionals, with the integrity and persistence required to discover, write, and publish the truth.

The national and international events I describe have been extensively documented in numerous sources, and since this narrative is not a scholarly work I felt no need to cite such materials. Indeed, a frequent source in such cases was my own vivid memory of events too significant, and often disturbing, to forget. I have, of course, properly credited all direct quotations and the original ideas of other writers.

But, in accordance with my firm belief that all history is ultimately personal, I have chosen to tell the story primarily through firsthand accounts unique to this narrative. A recollection from World War II by a friend of my parents is an example of the often unexpected emotional impact that a seemingly trivial personal anecdote can precipitate. She told me that during the war there was often a hushed and subdued atmosphere at places of public gatherings, almost as in a church. The example she mentioned was movie theaters: she recalled that the volume of the conversations among the audience members before the film began was far lower than either before or after the war, especially if there was a great battle underway in Europe or the Pacific. One reason for that may have been that they were anticipating the *News of the World* that usually preceded the feature film in those days, news that would almost certainly include coverage of battles where, win or lose, American boys were suffering and dying to preserve the freedom of those on the home front, including those in that very theater. I had devoted quite some time to studying the great war but somehow that brief anecdote from Lu Allen Green gave me an additional and poignant perspective that none of the history books had provided. The stories related by participants bearing witness to their wartime experiences are always intriguing to me, and such accounts are often pure gold for understanding what it was like to live through such unsettling but memorable days.

So picture this, if you will: A plane full of soldiers nearing the end of an eighteen-hour flight originating near San Francisco is flying over the South China Sea in early October 1969. Their craft is not a homely military transport but rather a sleek commercial jetliner chartered by the Department of Defense. Many of the men on board are not destined for combat but a sizable number are so fated, and I know this is true because I am one of them. Some of us spent the last few months together at an Army base in northern Alabama attempting to learn the rudiments of jungle warfare. A coastline slowly comes into view on the right side of the aircraft and soon we are over a land colored such a verdant shade of green that even a field of ripe corn back home would pale by comparison, a landscape almost aglow with the wild fecundity of the torrid zones, the tropics.

As we descend further shell craters, fire support bases, and large areas of red dirt where the vegetation was killed off by defoliants come into view: It is also a land scarred by the ravages of war. Before long we are flying over military bases of countless prefabricated wood and metal buildings, and soon we are touching down at one of the largest. A stewardess welcomes us to "beautiful downtown Vietnam." She and her colleagues are all pleasant young American girls, creatures that we will soon learn to call "round eyes" during our rare encounters with them over the next year.

Two indelible sensations mark our first steps across the tarmac: The enervating heat and the smell of burning shit mixed with diesel fuel. The latter is the pungent result of the standard method of disposing of the output of latrines in an area lacking a sanitary sewage system. But the knowledge that overwhelms even these potent assaults on our senses is that we are now in a place radically different from any we have ever inhabited before. It is indeed strange, exotic, and perhaps even beautiful at times, but that is not the all-consuming thought. No, that thought is the realization that now for the first time in our young lives we are in a place where countless people would like nothing better than to kill us, along with the virtual certainty that a year hence not all of us will be alive to ride one of the big planes back home. We are soldiers in a war zone, a situation few of us would have even dreamed possible just a few years earlier.

The story of the year of my tour of duty that began that memorable day in late 1969 is the heart of this narrative and I relate that in Volume 2, but some context is essential for any understanding of how this situation came to be. I believe the reader has a right to expect that, and I also know that I felt a strong need to attempt to arrive at such an understanding myself. Perhaps the "how" would lead to at least some perspective on the "why." Perhaps not, but I needed to at least make the attempt for my own peace of mind. I think of Vietnam every day in any case, so it seemed logical to try to put those ruminations to some constructive purpose. With that objective in mind, the calendar now turns back six years to late 1963 for the beginning of Volume 1.

II.
FAREWELL TO COLLEGE JOYS

It is with a pious fraud as with a bad action;
it begets a calamitous necessity of going on.
—Thomas Paine
The Age of Reason

Chapter 1
THE END OF HIGH SCHOOL
DE LA SALLE
1963-64

When I was a senior in high school one of the required classes was an updated version of the old standby, Civics, entitled "Problems of Democracy." It was a title ambiguous enough to seem somehow both dry and intriguing at the same time, but if the intent was to make the course appear more interesting to seniors already preoccupied with plans for life after De La Salle, such an incentive was really not necessary since the class was a requirement for graduation.

Our teacher was Frank Maroney, a stocky Irishman nearing his retirement years with a full head of silver hair brushed straight back and a fondness for bow ties. He had a stern demeanor that commanded respect and a well-deserved reputation as a no-nonsense guy. Unlike many of our other teachers, both Christian Brothers and laity, I never saw him lay a hand on a student, but I suspect that was because we had heard stories from students who had come before us that dissuaded us from trying anything that might provoke him. "Problems" was the only course he taught, filling out the rest of his schedule with various coaching assignments, keeping track of attendance, and overseeing the school maintenance program. It was rumored that he kept a bottle or two hidden away, but I never knew if there was any truth to that and, given the aggravations of his job and the meager salaries of Catholic school teachers, I certainly could not have begrudged him a few nips if he did in fact choose to indulge on the sly.

Mr. Maroney definitely ran a tight ship, but as the weeks of fall trimester, 1963, at De La Salle passed by I began to regard him with more respect than dread, and even developed a certain fondness for him. He began to seem less like a strict taskmaster and more like a crusty but fair grandfatherly type who expected us to act like adults and, if we did so, would treat us as such.

This atmosphere fit the subject matter of the course, which was a serious business even though the lessons and tests required less effort than our math and science college prep subjects. In spite of the frequent shenanigans in many of our other classes, we were in fact young men now who would be college students and eligible for the draft in less than a year, although the former would postpone the latter and, with no war being waged, it seemed unlikely that most of us who were college-bound would ever serve in the military unless we chose to do so. Nevertheless, turning eighteen would make us adults in some significant ways, and then at twenty-one we would be able to begin drinking legally and voting, so the lessons of Problems of Democracy on the functioning of our government and the responsibilities of citizenship seemed like things we would do well to take seriously. The class was an easy A, but I also ended up profiting from it more than I had expected at the outset.

As a part of "Problems" we each received a weekly copy of a magazine entitled *Senior Scholastic,* which dealt mainly with national and international affairs. This also made me feel more like a young adult because the publication seemed very similar to the serious mainstream news magazines such as *Time* and *Newsweek*. Maps were featured prominently in most issues, sometimes depicting countries or regions, but often the entire world. The political world map would always have a key to the various shadings of countries designating three great regions: the free world, the communist countries, and the third world. The graphic had the look of a sort of ultimate game of Risk, with two mighty players contesting for world domination by competing for control of countries in the third region. Unlike the board game, however, one player was good and one evil, with both possessing the ability to destroy the entire world at will.

The nuclear sword of Damocles had been weighing heavily over humanity for about fifteen years but young people seldom spend much time contemplating death, and I do not recall brooding very often over the possibility of Minneapolis being vaporized in the blink of an eye. This was in spite of the fact that one of the elementary school nuns who had taught us at St. Charles Borromeo had an obsessive dread of a nuclear doomsday, unless she just harped on that as a way of scaring us into keeping our souls free from sin in case a Russian missile suddenly transported us to the other side without the benefit of a soul-cleansing visit to the confessional.

This type of map was familiar to us because it was the same style that was often used in history books and television programs such as *Victory at Sea* to illustrate the progress of my parents' war, World War II. That conflict, the worst catastrophe in the often brutal history of humanity, was also America's greatest triumph, the fight where our parents rose to the challenge after over a decade of punishing economic depression, took on two regimes bent on using any means up to and including mass murder to achieve world domination, reduced both of them to unconditional surrender, and then offered proof of our essential decency and goodness by helping the people of postwar Germany and Japan establish stable economies and governments. The maps of that war depicted the stages of our march against the oppressors, with the Allied territories usually shown in white or a shade of gray and the Axis in a forbidding black.

In the European theater the situation was desperate in 1940, with the black ink forming a frightening blot over most of the continent and only gallant Britain remaining as a possible staging area for an Allied counterattack. Then, as America intervened, the blot slowly shrank as Allied forces drove through North Africa, Italy, Eastern Europe, France, Belgium, Holland, and finally Germany itself until the lighter color covered the entire land mass and surrounding seas.

In the Pacific theater the area of Japanese control began by covering Eastern China, French Indochina, and all the islands composing what is now Indonesia, but the most frightening graphic on this map was a sinister lasso representing the huge area of the Pacific controlled by Japanese naval and military forces. That map changed also as the grim war years ground on until eventually the home islands were the only area colored in black, and finally, instead of the dreaded invasion of Japan, the Pacific map was rendered entirely white and free in an instant by the two mysterious atomic bombs.

Since the war was the defining event of my parents' generation, and indeed of the entire twentieth century, it strikes me now as notable how little they talked of it around us kids when we were growing up in the 1950s. Certainly one reason for that was that my mother's only sibling, our Uncle Joe Ackerlind, lost his life in the Merchant Marine during the conflict when his ship, the *Maiden Creek*, foundered in high seas about seventy-five miles east of Long Island on December 31, 1942. This was so traumatic for both my mom and her mother, Catherine Ackerlind, who lived with us, that neither of them could ever bear to talk about it at any length. But I believe an even more fundamental reason for my folks' reticence about discussing the war was that they wanted to protect their children from the horrors of those years: all the beaches stained with blood and littered with the broken bodies of brave young Americans, the concentration camps with emaciated corpses stacked up like cordwood and awaiting the ovens, and finally a weapon that could incinerate tens of thousands of human beings in an instant. The topic of the war sometimes came up, and Mom and Dad certainly took great pride in all that their generation had endured and accomplished both on the battlefields and on the home front, but now they were living in a new world, a world they could only dream of during all those years of economic struggles and military conflict.

The center of that world was their children, the Baby Boomers, seventy-six million of us born between 1946 and 1964. My parents, Robert and Margaret Atkinson, did their part: I was born in 1946, the year after the war ended; my brother Dave in 1949; my sister Mary in 1955; my brother John in 1956; and my sister Jane in 1957. Dad was the sole wage earner in our household of eight and as the family grew he took a second part-time job as a teller at the Minneapolis Postal Employees Credit Union. He eventually moved into a full-time managerial position there and resigned from his job as a letter carrier, thus firmly rooting our family in the rapidly expanding post-war middle class. The pattern was typical: his grandparents had been farmers seventy-five miles west of the cities in Meeker County, his father had worn the blue collar of a letter carrier, and now Dad was wearing a white collar at the credit union where he eventually attained the position of president.

This was a period of unprecedented economic prosperity in America, and our parents were able to lavish all the good things modern life had to offer on us. The United States (US) ruled the world and the country was ready to celebrate after sixteen long years of depression and war. The money was there to throw quite a party, and we kids were usually the guests of honor. Every year there were more and more of us: There were five kids in our family and at one point there were fifty-two children on our block in Northeast Minneapolis. Every year there were higher and higher piles of gifts under the Christmas tree, and our parents took touching and obvious joy in showering us with all the things they had to do without during their own growing years. The long celebration that was the 1950s had no shortage of crazy, wonderful fads such as Hula-hoops, drive-in movies, and Davy Crockett everything. Adults, as well as us kids, reveled in all the new toys, such as television, hi-fi stereos, and pocket-sized transistor radios. In spite of all this incredible material largess, however, what I treasure the most from the 1950s is the memory of the unconditional love and support of our parents. They certainly took delight in spoiling us with all the toys and gifts they could afford, but there were also clear rules to be observed. We wanted to learn to behave properly in order to please the parents who loved us so much, but also because we were preparing to be the leaders of tomorrow. As important as our folks always made us feel, could we be destined for anything less?

There are good reasons why so many of us who came of age in that era love to indulge in nostalgia for all things associated with the 1950s. Show me an atomic clock, a blond step table, some turquoise boomerang-pattern Formica, a brightly colored piece of Fiestaware, or a kitchen set with chrome tubular legs and I'm right back there. Anything mid-century modern can unleash a flood of pleasant memories for me, and the warm glow of nostalgia combined with the precious gift of a happy childhood may easily induce me to pine for a time when so much seemed to be right with the world.

And that world was an exciting new one: We moved into our new house on the Minneapolis city limits on Stinson Boulevard on October 13, 1949, ten days after my third birthday. The freshly sodded lawns were a verdant green, the new sidewalks were bright white, and the colors of the newly painted houses almost seemed to glow with the brightness that subsequent recoatings can never quite match. The framing lumber and roof decking up in the attic were still redolent with the Christmas tree scent of newly cut pine. Most of the trees were fragile little saplings, but there were also clear signs that we were not the original pioneers in this lovely new world. Some large trees had been spared by the building contractors and across the street in St. Anthony Village was a small farm complete with horses, chickens, and pigs.

But like all eras this one had its darker elements as well. As children, we could never have fully understood that many of our parents paid a heavy price for the secure and loving homes they created for their offspring. The physical and psychic scars remaining from experiencing the horrors of the war were by no means the only burdens they bore while striving to conceal their problems and fears from the awareness of their kids. For our fathers, economic success might require accepting the soul-numbing conformity of the life of the organization man or the endless repetitive drudgery and frequent physical damage of the assembly line. For our mothers, the limited opportunities for women outside of the home allowed most of them to achieve only a fraction of their economic and creative potential, whereas the majority of them, women who made the postwar middle class American way of life possible by not working outside of their homes, were often dismissed as "just housewives." For kids crippled by polio or born with any sort of obvious physical or emotional problem life was anything but happy because this was an era of conformity when being "different" in any way was cause for pity and being ostracized, or perhaps even bullied. The shameful treatment accorded racial minorities carried a loud and clear message that the American dream was not for them. As for sexual minorities, we would have had no idea what that term even meant.

✳✳✳

The devastation of two Japanese cities by only two bombs in August 1945 had ushered in the Atomic Age and the effect on our national psyche was distinctly bipolar. The confidence in our international dominance and invulnerability based upon our sole possession of The Bomb was soon shaken to the core when the dreaded communists acquired the same ability. The terrible new weapon was mysterious and impossible for anyone but a brilliant scientist to even begin to understand and we were soon to learn that now both sides possessed something called a hydrogen bomb that was so many times more powerful than the atomic version that a single bomb could unleash one-third of the destructive power of all the explosives used during the entire course of World War II. This was not so much a weapon as the gateway to Armageddon.

Our dread of this incomprehensible threat to our very existence was reflected in the numerous science fiction films of the 1950s depicting huge and powerful monsters wreaking destruction upon our cities. Sometimes the creature would be a long-buried dinosaur reawakened from his eons of subterranean slumber by an atomic test blast. But often the rampaging beasts were actually created by the bomb: gigantic insects or spiders resulting from mutations caused by the radiation from the tests. The monsters would be destroyed eventually, ironically enough sometimes by atomic weapons, but there was usually an unsettling dénouement where the protagonist speculated on how there was no way for mankind to know what new threat might soon emerge in this brave new world we had unleashed upon ourselves.

    Atomic power also inspired awe and hope, however, as both scientists and the general public dreamed of all the possible benefits resulting from our ability to split the atom. Could there be any limits to the potential applications of harnessing the fundamental force of the Universe? A house could be powered and heated for years by a bit of atomic matter smaller than a pea, and certainly the same could be true for a car and other means of transportation. "Atomic" meant both "powerful" and "modern" and abstract depictions of the atom quickly became ubiquitous as manufacturers used them to convey the message that their products possessed these essential characteristics of the post-war consumer culture. Soon we could see the abstract image of a nucleus surrounded by orbiting electrons on any number of things around the house: wallpaper, ashtrays, fabrics, TV trays, and appliances ranging all the way from electric shavers up to ranges and refrigerators. With the atomic clock the item itself reflected the shape of its namesake with the clock face being the nucleus and the electrons projecting out of it on the ends of rods, looking like nothing so much as an oversized display of canapés on toothpicks. None of these items, of course, had anything to do with atomic power except that supposedly they were also the latest thing. Even our built-in oven had an atomic symbol on the control knob even though the only thing atomic about that gas appliance was that it was composed of atoms.

    Our international adversaries who now also possessed the secrets of the H-bomb seemed almost as impossible to understand as those instruments of ultimate destruction themselves. A mysterious evil known as monolithic communism festered and grew behind an Iron Curtain enclosing Eastern Europe and nearly all of Asia. We Boomers were also the Cold War kids. The communists were our sworn enemies, and their goal was to conquer the free world, robbing us of our freedom and our religion. In the Catholic schools we attended, we prayed for those unfortunate enough to be living under atheistic communist regimes. Books written by Dr. Thomas Dooley describing his work in a distant land called Vietnam were popular because he was a devout Catholic and a virulent anti-communist. His graphic descriptions of injuries and torture inflicted on hapless peasants and children by the fanatical Vietnamese communists depicted them as nothing short of evil incarnate. When he died of cancer at the age of only thirty-four during our freshman year at De a Gallup Poll reported that Americans regarded Dr. Dooley as the third most esteemed man on earth, second only to President Eisenhower and the Pope.

Among our leaders, the baleful glare of Secretary of State John Foster Dulles was more frightening than reassuring because here was a man whose belief in the tactics of brinksmanship and massive retaliation made him appear temperamentally incapable of compromise, but if the other side also took such a stance what might be the result? One miscalculation or mistake would be all it would take. The terrible weapon we had employed in the cause of freedom to end World War II was now aimed at America, and the only thing preventing our enemies from using it was the nightmarish prospect of "mutually assured destruction"—the end of the world.

At least as frightening as the threat of communism from nations across the oceans was the knowledge that here in our own country Americans could somehow become communists and then work to undermine our way of life from within. This seemed impossible to understand and yet we heard about it so often in the papers and on radio and TV that we felt there must be something to it. As the political unity necessitated by the war effort rapidly dissolved, the Republicans (GOP) began relying on the strategy of red-baiting in an attempt to regain their long-lost political dominance. I was too young to really comprehend what the Army-McCarthy hearings in 1954 were all about, and yet that is one of the first things I can recall my parents and grandmother watching on television. To add to the mystery of this ubiquitous threat, Senator McCarthy himself was finally revealed to be guilty of some incomprehensible offense called "character assassination." Was he truly an evil man or the victim of one of the nefarious communist plots he ranted about?

The nation's almost pathologically obsessive fear of communism, like nearly all important American ideas and events in the second half of the century, had its roots in the pivotal event of that century, World War II. The emotionally charged wave of joy and relief over the end of the great crusade in Europe was soon somewhat muted by what the liberating Allied troops had found when they arrived at the German death camps, for the extent of the horror promulgated by the Nazis was never truly known until after the end of the war when our soldiers returned and the firsthand accounts, especially the photographs, reached the home front. This certainly reinforced the nation's conviction that our cause had been truly just, but such a graphic demonstration of the depths of evil to which humanity could sink was a memory that even the great victory could never efface.

It had always been true that demented individuals sometimes committed multiple murders, and if such a person was in a position of power he might enlist underlings to assist him, but here was a case where an entire nation had become so deranged by mindless hatred that it had turned to mass murder on a scale that only modern industrial technology made possible. The consternation over such an unprecedented atrocity was compounded by the fact that Germany was a member of the "free world" rather than a communist dictatorship or one of the primitive and rather mysterious "third world" countries. If a supposedly "civilized" nation could descend into such brutality, what horrors could be expected from the ruthless dictators ruling the collectivist states? Stalin's purges in the Soviet Union had already answered that question, and there was little doubt after witnessing the deaths of millions following the establishment of the People's Republic of China in 1949 and the fanaticism of the Red Chinese troops in the Korean War that the leaders of that dictatorship were fully capable of equal cruelty.

Just as the unfolding truth of the Holocaust clouded the end of the war in the European Theater with a deeply disturbing pall, the atomic bomb added a troubling shade of ambiguity to the triumphant conclusion of the conflict in the Pacific. The hope that America would be able to retain its monopoly on this fearsome and mysterious weapon was a fragile one from the start and, combined with the Nazi's grim example of mankind's potential for unrestrained evil, the thought that our nation's enemies would almost certainly soon acquire the bomb was a truly sobering thought. Indeed, it was a national nightmare and when Julius and Ethel Rosenberg were found guilty of providing the Soviets with vital information on atomic weaponry they were both sent to the Sing Sing electric chair in 1953.

At the confluence of these two profoundly disturbing facts lies the source of the post-World War II national fear of communism and there is no doubt that, even though this obsession was often ginned up for political advantage, a significant share of this phobia was firmly rooted in grim reality. But difficulties would begin to emerge when our leaders' fixation on this threat led them to view all international problems through the lens of the free world's struggle against what they perceived as a monolithic international communist movement, ignoring the historical experiences, values, cultures, and aspirations of nations very different from our own.

Congressional hearings held little interest for a child of seven, but television itself was rapidly becoming an essential element in the lives of most Americans, including my own family. We enjoyed many of the classic early shows in their initial runs such as *I Love Lucy, Jackie Gleason*, and *Ed Sullivan*. I loved *Howdy Doody* as well as several of the locally produced children's shows of the era. Gabby Hayes was always a favorite, especially when he fired Quaker Puffed Wheat or Rice out of his cannon pointed directly at the camera. That never failed to send my younger brother Dave scurrying into his hiding place behind the couch. The sitcoms depicted a world where things that went wrong were all straightened out in some amusing way by the end of the episode each week, but the commercials were promoting their products by attempting to indoctrinate their viewers with an equally rosy and consistent vision of what life in the post-war suburban consumer society should be like.

It was a world where everyone belonged to a happy and prosperous family. If something interfered with this idyllic existence, such as a headache, stomach problems, or body odor, the solution was simple: Buy a product to take care of the problem. But what if the issue was more serious, such as a married couple disagreeing or a single person unable to attract a suitable mate? The answer was the same: Our product will take care of things and do it far more effectively than that of our competitors. The purpose was to sell things, but an insidious secondary message was also coming through loud and clear: If your world is not happy, tranquil, and well-supplied with all material needs and wants, something is wrong with you. The little 30- or 60-second dramas were depicting a world designed to make viewers feel unhappy, or at least unfulfilled, but they also offered a solution: Buy me. But what if folks followed this advice, made the purchase, and yet remained unhappy? The only solution the makers of commercials could offer was to buy still more and, indeed, that was their only purpose. That an equally probable result of their efforts was to instill anxiety, chronic discontent, and feelings of inadequacy in many of their viewers by depicting an impossibly perfect world that was unachievable by any means, least of all by soap, deodorants, or analgesics, was irrelevant to them.

In the first year of the decade, the Cold War turned hot in Korea, providing further proof that the communists' will to power could only be restrained by American military superiority. In fact, the celebratory atmosphere of the 1950s did not begin to emerge in full force until the carnage of that conflict finally ground to a halt with an uneasy truce in July of 1953 at Panmunjom, six months after President Eisenhower was inaugurated.

For a kid eight years is an eternity and it seemed to me that the rather bland but calm, competent, and reassuring Ike was president forever. In fact for a time I thought that "Eisenhower" was the presidential title. And so the great American military leader of World War II began his term in the White House by presiding over the end of the Korean War. Both conflicts bore painful witness to the virtually unrestrained brutality of modern warfare, for both civilians and the troops, but compared to the Allied triumph of "the big one" the end of Korea was strangely unsatisfying. America had lost 37,000 lives, but in the end Korea was divided at the 38th Parallel, the same line of demarcation as before the war.

Actually in one sense it had not been an American war at all, since we had never been attacked or declared war, but a United Nations police action. It was a proxy war because our true enemy had not been North Korea but Red China and the Soviet Union, the great communist powers that provided most of the troops, supplies, and air cover for the other side. We had stopped the advance of communism into one otherwise insignificant little corner of the world, but clearly the atmosphere of unease and ambiguity that already characterized the Cold War and the Red Scare had now enveloped the previously black-and-white world of military conflict as well.

Is it any wonder that we fell in love with shows like *Davy Crocket* and all of the TV Westerns, where it was unambiguous who was good and bad, and the good guys always won? Their victories were almost invariably wrought through violence, usually gunfire or the threat of it. Every week, a parade of evildoers would be brought to justice by the heroes of the frontier who were intent on bringing law and order to the Wild West, and their defeat was anything but ambiguous as they ended up dead or wounded in a hail of bullets, unless they were lucky enough to face Roy Rogers, who ended his confrontations by shooting the bad guy's six-shooter right out of his hand. As Sherriff Matt Dillon demonstrated weekly in the opening sequence of

Gunsmoke, on the frontier justice prevailed only if its advocate was also the fastest with a six-shooter. But somehow we knew that the reason he was the best with a gun was not simply because of his reflexes and dexterity. No, he prevailed because he was the righteous one.

Like Superman in our own time, these knights errant of the Old West stood for "truth, justice, and the American way." They were building the world that our families were enjoying today, and our duty was to follow in their footsteps by standing up to the current threat to our way of life, the Red Menace. Ambiguity and the "adult Western" had not yet intruded into our world of certainties and, as we learned from the generation that won World War II, America was always right, not because of our powerful military but because of the values our nation represented. These thoughts of justice prevailing through violence were always the core inspiration for the endless scenarios of conflict and victory we enacted with the small arsenal of cap pistols, rifles, and machine guns that were often included among our birthday and Christmas gifts. At one point, we even had a toy cap-firing hand grenade. Another favorite pastime was to divide our many olive-drab "Army guys" into two small armies and then take turns firing missiles from a plastic cannon at each other's forces until one side was all knocked down dead. We would deem the victorious side, with a few men still standing, to be the Americans.

★★★

The new decade brought exciting changes as our class of 1960 graduated from St. Charles Borromeo School. It was strange to leave a place where we had spent nine years, well over half of our young lives, but many of the guys would see more of each other as we were going on to De La Salle High School on Nicollet Island in downtown Minneapolis. Then that fall John F. Kennedy (JFK) was elected president. That he was a Catholic was cause for much excitement at our church and school, of course, but even more thrilling than our common religion was the man himself. He was vigorous and youthful with bold ideas for America, and his inaugural speech—both a stirring call to action and an eloquent pledge to stand firm against the enemies of freedom—seemed like the most inspiring thing we had ever heard.

His phrase "the New Frontier" meant to us that the dawning era he spoke of would be just as exciting and crucial to America's future as that in which our ancestors had settled the West, but he also made it clear that the new challenges would be at least as daunting as those of our country's past, and his description of our current situation as "a long twilight struggle" seemed particularly poignant for that is the time dominated by neither light nor darkness. He was a war hero who had risked his own life to save his men in the South Pacific, and soon a popular song, "PT 109," was filling the pop music airwaves to glorify this feat. As crucial as Ike's role in World War II had been, could anyone have ever have imagined writing a popular song about him? JFK also had a beautiful, stylish wife and two adorable children that the country quickly learned to love. We were only freshmen in high school but the pervasive sense of ennui that had gradually become a distressingly familiar fact of life for us as we entered adolescence during the last of the Eisenhower years now seemed like it might be a thing of the past. The goal that he set four months later of putting a man on the moon by the end of the decade was especially exciting after all the science fiction movies and TV shows we had enjoyed, and the astronauts would soon become the cowboys of our own time.

As our freshman class settled into the all-male environment of De La Salle we quickly learned that corporal punishment was a fact of life there, usually a hard whack to the head or slap to the face with an open hand. At the time we did not think of this as abuse, but it was really the next logical step upward from the emotional abuse practiced by some of the nuns at St. Charles as they regaled highly impressionable young children with nightmare-inducing threats of burning for all eternity if we should die in a state of mortal sin. They would ask us to recall the pain of burning your finger and then to imagine feeling that agony over your entire body for a time that would never come to an end.

The high school teachers then took over by assuring young men going through puberty that we were now capable of committing such sins and that those fires awaited anyone who touched a girl or even himself "impurely." The danger was multiplied exponentially by the knowledge that even harboring "impure thoughts" could be a one-way ticket to the burning nether world. And so, well-intentioned but ignorant and hopelessly naïve celibates passed along the same warped beliefs that had been instilled in them during their younger years. Rather than learning that our natural urges must be tempered by respect for ourselves and others in order to become the source of one of humanity's greatest joys, we were instead taught that such desires were our own version of the serpent in the garden, inherently evil and a potential ticket to eternal damnation unless held strictly in check, a source of shame and guilt. Some teachers appeared to view sex as an evil thing rendered necessary to perpetuate the species, something that had no legitimate place outside the institution of marriage.

The unwritten code of conduct at De for getting whacked was well understood: Guys who got hit were the ones who disrupted class or showed some other sign of disrespect toward the wrong teacher. Of course, you also had to be caught doing this to be punished, and one of the most frequent forms of entertainment, especially in boring classes, was for the bolder guys to see just how much they could get away with and remain unscathed while the rest of us egged them on. To perpetrate mischief without being caught was one of the surest ways of earning status with your peers. Then again, sometimes a teacher having a bad day would decide to ruin a student's day, or even entire subsequent life, by whacking him for no apparent reason. Few of us needed the threat of punishment to pay attention to our teachers because most of them were obviously serious-minded men dedicated to helping us learn, but it does seem remarkable to me now that this type of physical discipline was not recognized as abuse and was deemed perfectly normal and acceptable by both the school staff and our parents. Much of our lives over the coming years would be shaped by events that led us to challenge accepted beliefs and practices such as this, sometimes rendering utterly outrageous things that were taken for granted as facts of life only a few years before.

JFK's foreign policy got off to a rocky start only three months after his inauguration with the failure of the Cuban Bay of Pigs invasion, an ugly fiasco that led Castro to seek a closer alliance with the Soviet Union. Eighteen months later in October 1962, this association led to the Cuban Missile Crisis, and for two weeks the world stood on the brink of nuclear Armageddon as the strategy of brinksmanship was put to the acid test. We prayed for peace in school and at church, all the while wondering if today would be our last, the end of the world. I had read Nevil Shute's *On The Beach*, a horribly depressing novel describing Australian survivors of a nuclear war awaiting their inevitable death by radiation poisoning, and now we were confronted with the possibility that apparently that could happen to us at any time, maybe today. Would Minneapolis be another Hiroshima? Finally, the Soviets agreed to withdraw their missiles from Cuba and in return we agreed to move some of ours out of Turkey. As he had vowed in his stirring inaugural address, the President refused to back down when confronted with a grave threat from the communists, and the nerve-wracking episode seemed to demonstrate once again that the enemies of freedom could only be deterred by the threat of force.

That experience was seared into our memory because of its gravity, but as the early 1960s moved along it was clear that the crisis was only one of many important events that were occurring with greater frequency than would have seemed possible during the staid late 1950s. In 1962, Pope John XXIII convened the Second Vatican Council, and we were told that this synod could result in major changes in our church. We had always been taught in the Catholic schools that the church was the inerrant guardian of eternal truths, so what could it mean that it was about to change? In August 1963, we witnessed the March on Washington and Dr. King's "I Have a Dream" speech on TV. The significance of the event escaped me at the time because in our virtually all-white neighborhood and schools we never considered the plight of blacks in America. The prevailing attitude was certainly not one of hatred or prejudice, but indifference toward the people we referred to as "negroes." The proverb "out of sight, out of mind" would be an accurate description. To their great credit considering the era in which they were raised, I never heard my parents speak disparagingly of racial minorities, but there had been no black students or teachers at St. Charles. At De La Salle, which drew students from the entire Twin Cities metropolitan area, we had only one black student in our class of four hundred. The same year, Betty Friedan's *The Feminine Mystique* was published, but the proposition that our mothers might feel somehow suffocated and unfulfilled in their role as the keepers of our happy and secure homes seemed not so much radical to us as utterly incomprehensible. Change was in the air, but we still could never have guessed that within months we were to experience things that would irrevocably alter our lives and way of seeing the world.

In June 1963, newspapers and magazines printed a photograph taken in Saigon of a Buddhist monk burning himself to death as a protest against the oppression of members of his faith by the US-supported regime of the blundering and corrupt South Vietnamese President Ngo Dinh Diem. The holy man, whose colleagues had assisted him by soaking his robes with gasoline and then striking a lighter, is sitting in the street with his legs crossed and hands folded in the classic Buddhist position of repose. He is sitting in a large puddle of burning gas enveloped in flames that shoot up several feet above his head. What can be seen of his face is not contorted in agony, but appears strangely expressionless, perhaps even serene. The immediate message that Thich Quang Duc was sending by his suicide was that it was a grave injustice for the Catholic Diem to oppress Buddhists, but in hindsight his self-immolation could have been a prophetic warning to America: No earthly force, not even the most powerful military in the history of the world, will ever be able to break the will of a people and culture that could produce a man capable of an act such as this. Far from being able to conquer the Vietnamese communists, America's actions in that tortured land would make it clear in the years to come that we would never even be able to understand them.

On November 2, Ngo Dinh Diem, a strident anti-communist, was assassinated in Saigon by members of his country's army. The unrest caused by Diem's dictatorial rule had been increasing across South Vietnam throughout the year, especially since Quang Duc's dramatic suicide, and US advisors had informed Diem's generals that if they attempted a coup the US would not stand in the way. This clumsy US attempt at nation-building, like so many of our efforts over the next decade, only made matters worse as South Vietnam descended into chaos with only the prospect of further American support standing in the way of the feared communist takeover.

Such perspectives on these two crucial events, of course, do not reflect our viewpoint in 1963. By that time we were at least aware that there was such a place as Vietnam, but communist mischief seemed to go on all the time along the familiar borders on our world maps where the two great adversaries' territories came together, and assassinations and coups in small, unstable countries were nothing new either. Nuclear war was the big worry and if there ever was another confrontation involving conventional weapons we expected it to be in Eastern Europe, perhaps caused by a Soviet attempt to take over all of Berlin. The ambiguous outcome of the Korean conflict could have served as a warning, but even then that was largely "the forgotten war" and when we did pause to reflect on it the conflict seemed to reinforce the belief that communist aggression must be met with equally determined opposition.

We were high school seniors concerned with such things as producing the class plays, cheering on our champion basketball team, and preparing for graduation. Most of us planned to go on to college so the decision as to where to apply and the application process itself were also much on our minds. My choice was the University of Minnesota, a short bus ride from our home, and my tentative career plan was to teach high school English, a decision influenced partially by a favorite TV series about such a teacher, *Mr. Novak*, but primarily by admiration for my favorite high school teacher, Mr. James Elsenpeter. He had taught our sophomore English class much like a college course, and the erudite insights he provided into *The Scarlet Letter* began to open my eyes to the vast power of the art of literature. When he had us chant the words to Vachel Lindsay's "The Congo," we had to go over to a meeting room in the adjacent brothers' house so that our shouting and stomping on the floor would not disturb the other classes. Some of us actually imagined that the experience helped us to better understand the roots of black culture, although we still used the term "Negro" in those days.

***

One Friday afternoon in late November during our senior year, we were sitting in Mr. Miller's religion class when suddenly there was an unusual amount of activity out in the hall and students started whispering to each other. Something was up. Then Brother Mark, our principal, came over the PA system with the news that President Kennedy had been shot in Dallas. We prayed and sat quietly awaiting further news. Soon Mr. Roach came in and whispered something to Mr. Miller. I heard only two words clearly: "He's dead." No death up to that point in my life had touched me so deeply. My heart sank. The shock was unbelievable. This was quickly followed by fear. What did this mean? Would the Soviets take advantage of this moment of confusion to launch an attack? Before long, Brother Mark's voice came over the speaker again to tell us that classes were dismissed for the rest of the day and that we should listen to the radio over the weekend to find out when they would resume. Everyone says they remember exactly where they were when they heard the terrible news on November 22, 1963, and I can truly say that the memory is seared into my mind for life. I still think about it when I drive by the old school and look at the windows of the classroom where I heard the words, "He's dead."

The long, nightmarish weekend that followed was a tumult of all the emotions of the early stages of dealing with a terrible loss: denial, anger, fear, and uncertainty. The individual and communal grieving process was rudely disrupted by two additional murders as well. It began with the bus ride home on Friday afternoon, a glum silence replacing the usual chattering and horseplay. At home we were unable to leave the TV for long. Our need for more information was insatiable even though no new facts could restore our murdered hero or lighten the overwhelming burden of our grief. The great unanswered question was *why*, but that could not be answered until we knew *who*. The authorities answered that for us quickly as we learned that less than two hours after JFK's death an arrest had been made, but only after a Dallas police officer had been gunned down by the same suspect. Oswald's name meant nothing, of course, and he was certainly providing no answers.

Then there was the photograph of LBJ taking the oath of office on Air Force One with Jacqueline by his side still wearing her bloodstained suit, but this was not the same Jackie we had known for the last three years, so self-assured, beautiful, intelligent, and yet somehow also so warm and approachable. Instead we saw a woman slumped forward in abject sorrow, her beautiful face a pathetic frozen mask not so much of grief as of utter shock and incomprehension. We looked into her hollow eyes hoping for some sort of reassurance but all we saw was a reflection of our own despair. By early Friday evening, Air Force One, bearing JFK's body, Jackie, and our new president, was back in DC.

On Saturday, the president's coffin lay in state in the East Room of the White House. All the while, the newscasts kept breaking in with updates on Oswald's background, his repeated questioning by various authorities, and eventually his being charged with the two murders. On Sunday, the coffin was drawn to the Capitol on a horse-drawn caisson where it lay in state under the great dome of the rotunda while an estimated quarter-million mourners filed by to pay their respects. Again the nation's futile attempt to come to terms with our loss was interrupted by a news bulletin telling us that Oswald would be seen on live TV as he was transported between jails.

Despite our hatred for this man, we could not resist the need to see him, as if that might provide some understanding of his motivation. Then, just as he came into view in the basement of Dallas Police Headquarters, a stocky man in a dark suit and fedora stepped forward and shot him in the stomach, the first murder witnessed by millions as it happened. I was largely unsuccessful in resisting the sin of rejoicing at this bizarre turn of events, but our attention soon turned back to the live coverage of the endless procession winding its way silently through the Capitol.

On Monday morning, the caisson again carried the president's coffin back to the White House, and then on to St. Matthew's Cathedral for the funeral Mass. We thought our hearts would break when Jackie finally broke down briefly as a tenor sang "Ave Maria," the same singer and prayer as at their wedding Mass ten years earlier. Then the body was carried to the caisson one last time for the funeral procession through DC and across the Potomac to Arlington. If we had any tears left, we offered them up at the sight of John-John saluting his father's flag-draped coffin in front of St. Matthew's. It was his third birthday. The solemn drama of that procession is one of my most vivid memories of those horrible four days: the beautiful, riderless horse Black Jack with the empty boots backwards in the stirrups, the endless staccato beat of the drums, the mournful funeral marches played by the military band, the bagpipers, the flyover of fifty fighter jets followed by Air Force One, and finally the lighting of the eternal flame at the gravesite on the slope beneath the Custis Lee mansion.

On Tuesday, classes resumed at De La Salle, businesses reopened, and we began the process of trying to move on. I cannot say we resumed our normal routines because somehow things were not the same, even though we could not yet know how utterly they had changed. I was looking at the world with different eyes. The reason I stare at those classroom windows whenever I drive by the old school is because that is where the last vestiges of my childhood died, but hindsight also was to make clear that the hinge of fate had turned and a new chapter in our nation's history began on that awful day.

Any murder is a horrendous crime because it robs the victim of his future, but if the victim is a great leader it robs many people of the future that might have been theirs if the deceased had the chance to attempt to live out the realization of his vision. If the victim is the President, the assassination robs the entire nation of the future they hoped for when they cast their votes. We felt as though something we treasured had been stolen from us.

Looking backwards, the great unanswerable question is whether JFK would have involved America in Vietnam to anywhere near the extent that LBJ did. Could the great debacle have been avoided? Could the defining event of our generation have been something other than that bloody quagmire? It is true that under Kennedy we had about 15,000 "advisors" in Vietnam, but it was Johnson who made the fateful decision to commit American combat troops. That was not until March 1965, so it could only loosely be termed a continuation of what JFK had begun, and yet LBJ had retained most of Kennedy's foreign policy advisors, "the best and the brightest" who supported this escalation.

My own gut feeling has always been that JFK had been burned too badly by following his advisors' guidance in the Bay of Pigs affair to be drawn into a large-scale land war in Asia, and that incident also demonstrated that he could admit when he had made a mistake. My generation will always be haunted by the knowledge that we will never have the answer to that question. I believe that a major reason for the endless conspiracy theories about the assassination is that many people are simply unable to come to terms with the possibility that a single vicious act of senseless violence by a pathetic deranged nobody such as Oswald could have started a chain of events that led to the deaths of tens of thousands of Americans and hundreds of thousands of Vietnamese. Our hunger for reassurance that we inhabit a universe governed by at least a modicum of order and justice leads us to rebel at such a thought.

The unmistakable sense that somehow things had changed and that important events were rapidly heralding our transition into adulthood was soon reinforced on a more personal note with the death of my Dad's mother, Mary Agnes McGraw Atkinson, in January 1964. Perhaps because both of my grandfathers had died well before I was born, I was always especially close to my grandmothers. My mom's mother, Catherine Ambrose Ackerlind, or Granny, always lived with us, so Mary Agnes was known to us as "Other Granny," a term of deep endearment.

I have fond memories of spending days and nights with her in her mother-in-law apartment on the second floor of my Aunt Irene and Uncle Jim's house on the north side. Sometimes we would go downtown on the bus for lunch and a movie. Her cozy home was without a TV so we would listen to radio programs and I could look at my Dad's adventure books from his childhood, mostly cowboy stories. She worked in the kitchen in Bremer School just a few blocks from where she lived. Later on she took a job as housekeeper at the rectory of Incarnation in South Minneapolis, a big old house with lots of heavy woodwork and character. The position included her room and board, and she had a pleasant bedroom on the second floor. The German cook, who also worked there, Hedwig Kuehn, was always so jolly and friendly. Eventually Other Granny's health began to decline and she had to move to a nursing home on Central Avenue, which is where she passed away at the age of seventy-nine. I believe that the effort to come to terms with our President's recent death had enhanced my emotional maturity to the point where I could accept the passing of our grandmother with a large measure of both faith and stoicism, but it was a loss that we all felt deeply.

The same month, the buzz around school was that there was a new rock band that had turned the world upside down in England and was now coming to the American airwaves. It may seem odd but for Boomers the question "When did you first hear the Beatles?" is usually second in importance only to "Where were you when you heard Kennedy had been shot?" One January night I was listening to my little turquoise transistor radio in bed, holding it next to my ear at low volume as I enjoyed doing while drifting off to sleep. The song was "I Want to Hold Your Hand" and it was unlike anything I had heard before. Could this be that new English group? Sure enough, at the end the DJ said that's the Beatles, a crazy name to go with the unique sound. The guitar work was confident and intriguing if not particularly accomplished, but it was the vocals that made their new sound so distinctive. Their Liverpool accents did not come across in most of the singing but the harmonies were unusual, outrageous, and yet utterly charming.

When we saw their pictures, here were four young guys with wide grins who looked like they were having the time of their lives, three of them good-looking and one endearingly homely. But what in the world was the story with the hair, those pudding-bowl haircuts with the bangs? Of course, as soon as we heard our parents and teachers make fun of them, longer hair became the height of fashion for most adolescent males in America, driving another wedge between the generations as our parents registered their displeasure with the look as well as the sound.

The Beatles began the British Invasion and the resulting rejuvenation of rock music produced a body of work from both sides of the Atlantic that became the soundtrack of our generation. The music was always entertaining and it often celebrated both the angst and joy of love, but it also reflected our aspirations, as well as our impatience or even anger over perceived oppression when we felt that our attempts to realize those hopes were being frustrated by those in authority. We would hear a new song by artists such as the Beatles, the Rolling Stones, or Bob Dylan and immediately realize that they were reflecting and clarifying the same thoughts and emotions with which we had been struggling.

This central role of music in our lives was a new thing for us, but like nearly all my classmates I had been digging rock since about 1957. I remember Elvis, especially "Hound Dog," as well as artists like the Diamonds and Chuck Berry. The crazy harmonies and vocalese of songs such as "Get A Job" by the Silhouettes, "Book of Love" by the Monotones, and "Yakety Yak" by the Coasters were irresistible ear candy, but I thought it was just a bunch of guys making a lot of noise and singing goofy. I had absolutely no idea that this music had roots and that those roots were primarily black. I certainly didn't realize that many of the singers were black. I had not heard of jazz, doo wop, or rhythm and blues. It never would have crossed my mind that the term "rock and roll" had originated as black slang for having sex. In fact, I had only the vaguest notion of what that sinful thing known as having sex even was.

My enduring love affair with the first golden age of American rock began one day in 1958. My folks had invited their friends the Dodges and their son Dougie over for a picnic. Since it was raining we had our picnic sitting at the ping pong table in our basement amusement room. Doug was my age and something of a cut-up, the kind of kid that might be termed "hyperactive" these days. Since things were getting a little boring he asked if we had a radio and he began turning the tuner dial listening for a specific station. He soon exclaimed, "that's it," and there was a song I had never heard, which turned out to be "I Wonder Why" by Dion and the Belmonts, a real American hot wax classic. This was news: There was a radio station that played only rock and roll. Forget about Frank Sinatra, Perry Como, Patti Page, and Dean Martin—here was a station just for us, the young people. Of course what really sold me on it was the eye rolling and snide comments of our parents. It was WDGY, AM 1130, our local member of the Storz network complete with all the jingles, contests, sound effects, and hyped-up DJs. But the main attraction was always the music, and especially the Top Forty Show.

As much as we enjoyed this music that seemed to annoy our parents and teachers so much, it was still the music of people older than us. We were only twelve years old. Even so, I soon received my own transistor radio as a gift from my parents and it was always tuned to either WDGY, nicknamed "wee-gee," or KDWB, AM 630, our two rock stations. As we moved through the late fifties and early sixties, the music seemed to lose much of its fun and spontaneity. When Elvis got out of the army, he was more a movie star and ballad singer than a rebellious rocker. Then there were the syrupy offerings of the Lettermen, Frankie Avalon, and all the Bobbys. I liked the country crossover work of Johnny Cash and Patsy Kline. Roy Orbison was a special favorite with his three-minute miniature symphonies usually ending in one of his signature high notes along with a crescendo of strings and choral voices. Things became a bit more interesting in 1962 when I first heard the Beach Boys' "409," and soon their songs of cars, surfing, and girls led me to imagine Southern California as the coolest place on earth to live. By this time the artists were only a few years senior to us.

***

To accompany our harsh transition into young adulthood heralded by the death of JFK near the end of 1963, the popular music of that year reflected the change that was in the air. The Village Stompers, the Rooftop Singers, and Peter, Paul, & Mary (PP&M) soon had me thinking that Greenwich Village might be even more hip than LA. When PP&M released "Blowin' in the Wind," a soulful meditation on the two great human tragedies of war and racism sung in beautiful harmony, it was my introduction to protest music and the urban folk scene. One of the pictures on the back of the album *In The Wind*, featuring that song, showed the trio singing before a sea of listeners at the March on Washington. Clearly these people aspired to be far more than just entertainers, and the concept that white people as well as black should be working to end racial injustice was new to me.

PP&M were relevant, and before long one of the most common ways of denigrating someone on the other side of the great divide that eventually came to be called "the generation gap" was to dismiss them as "irrelevant." It was especially intriguing to learn that the song had been written by someone from Minnesota named Bob Dylan. We could not have known that greatness had been walking the streets of Dinkytown before he left for New York City (NYC) in January 1961, but this enigmatic young man with the seemingly inexhaustible capacity to reinvent himself was soon to become the leading prophet of our generation.

The same month I first heard the Beatles, January 1964, Dylan released the album "The Times They Are A-Changin'." The title track said it all but, as with most truly prophetic utterances, we could not understand the full implications of what he was telling us until the subsequent fateful events began to unfold. The same album contained the scathing antiwar piece, "With God on Our Side," as well as the haunting indictment of racial injustice, "The Lonesome Death of Hattie Carroll." Then there were the beautiful love songs "One Too Many Mornings" and "Boots of Spanish Leather," pieces that were worlds away from the saccharin offerings of all the Bobbys and

Frankies. Dylan's love songs were complex meditations on his desperate need to achieve true communion with another person and the exquisite pain that enveloped him when he and his lover inevitably failed to achieve that elusive bond. He was way ahead of his time with these sophisticated compositions but the times were rapidly changing and once you heard that voice you could not forget it, whether you wanted to or not.

Later that year he released "Like a Rolling Stone," and the next year another new British group, the Rolling Stones, released "Satisfaction." It would not be difficult to argue that these are the two greatest rock songs ever recorded, and they are both very angry songs. As we left high school and started college, the vague sense of discontent we had been feeling since the death of JFK was not abating, but instead seemed to be growing stronger almost by the day.

Then there was the problem of President Johnson (LBJ). No one could have hoped to fill the gaping void left by the death of JFK, but LBJ appeared singularly unsuited to the role. Kennedy had been handsome, but Johnson was quite homely. Kennedy spoke with that wonderful urbane Boston accent, whereas Johnson spoke with a Texas drawl that soon began to grate on our Northern ears. And yet LBJ presented a vision for America he called the Great Society that, while not as exciting a title as the New Frontier, held out the promise of addressing some of our most pressing problems. Medicare, Medicaid, and food stamps must have made it seem to our parents as though LBJ was taking over where Franklin Roosevelt (FDR) had left off when World War II interrupted the full implementation of the New Deal. But the real shocker was that a president from south of the Mason-Dixie Line would take giant steps to end racial injustice in America with immigration reform, the Civil Rights Act of 1964, and the Voting Rights Act of 1965. His unexpected determination to do the right thing regardless of political cost was perfectly illustrated by his prophetic comment that with the Civil Rights Act the Democrats had "lost the South for a generation."

These were major accomplishments that made America a far better and more just nation, and yet it will always be LBJ's fate to be remembered most frequently as the president who led us into full-scale combat in Vietnam.

Chapter 2
FRESHMAN YEAR
UNIVERSITY OF MINNESOTA
1964-65

In the late spring of 1964, I graduated from De La Salle, got my first real job at a McDonald's knockoff called Robby's near the University of Minnesota (UM) campus, and began reading books for my fall classes at the university. These seemed like giant steps toward full adulthood and, even though I could not avoid some misgivings about the challenges ahead, the single thing I remember most is the feeling of freedom. Now I would have my own money, be responsible for keeping up with my studies, and be able to make many decisions about my future on my own. Registering for the draft when I turned eighteen was something I could have done without, but as a college student I would have an educational deferment and it clearly was another milestone on the road to full manhood. The military held little appeal to me but I enrolled in Army ROTC because I felt that if I ever did serve it made sense to do so as an officer. There was no risk involved because the cadets did not have to sign a contract to serve after graduation until the start of our junior year. The chances of actually fighting in a war seemed slim to nil.

The job at Robby's occupied much of my time in the summer of 1964, as well as weekends and after classes for the next couple of years. It was part of a small chain in Wisconsin and southern Minnesota, and our place was on the northwest corner of 25th and University Avenue SE. Our menu was virtually identical to McDonald's, featuring hamburgers for fifteen cents, cheeseburgers for twenty cents, fries for twelve cents, and shakes for twenty cents. Our advertising slogan was that we featured "reddi-quick service." The owners apparently felt that they could get by piggybacking on McDonald's success but we did have one item to set us apart: the Dandy Burger, a quarter-pound California-style hamburger. The place stayed open for about five years and then folded, but that was my first real job so it was important to me. I met guys from various backgrounds, learned many aspects of the business, including operating a large meat grinder and patty machine, and even served as one of the night managers after about six months.

For the first time I felt that I was now largely responsible for my own destiny, but what seemed like the most important decision of them all, the question of how to try to find the right girl to marry, left me utterly baffled. I liked situations where the guidelines were clear, like in the classes I was taking where we were told exactly what was expected of us in order to earn a good grade. But with the prospect of courtship and ultimately marriage the suggestions seemed to be few and frighteningly nebulous. You went out on dates, eventually you found a special girl, and finally the two of you got married. How would you know she really was the right girl? What if the girl you thought was the one for you did not think you were the right guy for her? Worst of all: What if you ended up getting married to a girl who turned out to be the wrong one in the end? I had another major problem right from the start as well because I was too shy and introverted to meet many girls, let alone ask them out. Looking back, I realize that I was experiencing at least some degree of depression, but the thought that I might benefit from some professional help never even occurred to me.

The pace of change also continued to increase on the local and national scenes as a large contingent of volunteers from the northern states attempted to begin making Dr. King's dream of nonviolent change a reality by bringing Freedom Summer to Mississippi, continuing the work that the Freedom Riders of the summer of 1961 had begun. Seventeen college students from Minnesota contributed to the effort by teaching in Freedom Schools and working for the Freedom Registration campaign. Their goal was to register as many black voters as possible and their efforts were met with violent acts of resistance, including arson, bombings, and four murders. That August Congress passed the Gulf of Tonkin Resolution, allowing the President to "take all necessary measures" to prevent further communist aggression, essentially ceding the legislative branch's constitutional power to declare war to the executive. A very nonscientific student poll conducted by the *Daily* showed that those questioned favored the measure seventy-four to eight. By the end of the year America had over twenty thousand advisors in Vietnam.

Then, in the fall of 1964, the Free Speech Movement began out at Berkeley. Local police, with the complicity of the university administration, refused to allow people to distribute material on campus denouncing racial injustice. The students reacted with a degree of vehemence that caught the authorities off guard and most likely surprised the protestors themselves as the crowd mentality fed off of itself. In the eyes of some, the police and the university administration were taking the side of those who murdered the Freedom Riders in Mississippi. A student named Mario Savio soon became the unofficial leader of the movement and on December 2 he delivered his "bodies upon the gears" speech, which could have easily served as a de facto credo for what would soon come to be known as "the resistance." The most famous lines: "There's a time when the operation of the machine becomes so odious—makes you so sick at heart—that you can't take part. You can't even passively take part. And you've got to put your bodies upon the gears and upon the wheels, upon the levers, upon all the apparatus and you've got to make it stop. And you've got to indicate to the people who run it, to the people who own it, that unless you're free, the machine will be prevented from working at all."

I certainly followed these events with interest, but Minnesota was never part of the advance movement of the resistance and we had a less earth-shaking problem to grapple with in our beloved Dinkytown, a small area of shops and eateries just off the East Bank Campus. Dinkytown might be called Minneapolis's version of Greenwich Village, which is what had led Dylan there three years before when he left Hibbing. As well as catering to students' needs for food and supplies, it was well known as a center of artistic expression and progressive thought. A bookseller named Melvin McCosh was being threatened with eviction from his 4th Street shop because Bridgeman's, the neighboring ice-cream parlor, wanted to expand their kitchen into the space he rented. Undoubtedly inspired by the sit-ins at segregated southern lunch-counters, a bunch of folks decided to stage "sip-ins" at Bridgeman's, buying one cup of coffee and then sipping it for hours, thereby preventing other potential paying customers from finding seats. They held their planning sessions a block north on 14th Avenue at The Scholar, the coffeehouse where Bob Dylan had first performed solo.

One day some Dinkytown moms and kids picketed outside, carrying signs with messages such as "man does not live by ice cream alone" and "mind over malted." The cleverest sign was "better read than red," which implied that those trying to kick out McCosh were unwittingly aiding the dreaded communist conspiracy by fostering ignorance. The relatively tame Minnesota version of bodies upon the gears could not prevail against The Man in this case, however, and in July Melvin moved his business over to the old firehouse on the west bank of the Mississippi River that now houses the Mixed Blood Theater in the neighborhood known as Cedar Riverside, a residential and business area adjacent to the West Bank Campus of the university.

A more troubling event occurred that same summer in late June when the House Un-American Activities Committee (HUAC) came to Minneapolis to hold hearings at the downtown Federal Building investigating "student peace activities." Eleven Minnesotans were subpoenaed to appear and the Minnesota VFW helped draft a list of questions, such as "Are teachings of individual professors required to meet any minimum standards of morality, decency, honesty, accuracy, and judgment?"

Denis Wadley, who was later to teach at De La Salle, was the press secretary of Citizens Against HUAC, a group that picketed the Federal Building during the hearings. One University student refused to answer almost ninety questions based on the First, Fifth, or Sixth Amendments. The most damaging evidence the bizarre witch hunt could unearth was from a witness who testified to the old news that there had been four communist cells at the University in the early 1950s. The *Minnesota Daily* conducted a poll asking if people thought communism on our campus was a serious problem, with the results being ninety "no," four "yes," and fifteen "don't know." We never were sure why HUAC had been so concerned about "peace activities" on our campus but the lack of tolerance for even the mildest form of dissent seemed like a throwback to the worst days of McCarthyism and the resistance to it was certainly a portent of things to come, although at that time we could never have imagined how volatile such clashes would soon become.

※ ★ ★

Near the end of September fall quarter started and I began my studies at the U with a schedule including Freshman English, early modern European history, physical anthropology, trigonometry, and a military science course entitled "firepower." I found the work challenging, but I was used to a fairly rigorous academic environment at De La Salle and never had a serious problem with keeping up. On the social side, the impossible seemed to be coming true when a girl named Glenda in freshman English class actually seemed to be interested in me. We met because of a mistake by a clerk in the registration office who gave me an IBM card for the section Glenda attended rather than the one on my registration slip. We did some studying together and even went out a few times, but then she decided she did not want to do that anymore. In retrospect I cannot blame her for that—I certainly was far from ideal boyfriend material back then since I was afflicted with guilt and shame because of old religious ideas and also quite withdrawn because of shyness and depression. We were only eighteen. She was a nice girl and, in my total lack of experience with affairs of the heart, I fell for her pretty hard. I became obsessed with the thought that a great girl had liked me and I totally messed things up. That kind of situation happens all the time among young people, of course, but it dealt a blow to my fragile self-confidence and I never did have a serious girlfriend until I met my future bride Bev four years later—a happy ending at last. Instead I concentrated on my studies and the jobs I found to pay for my expenses, spending my free time enjoying books, music, and movies, but nearly always on my own.

Like everyone who touches our lives in anything more than a passing way, however, Glenda from Pine Island left me with a gift. Now whenever I listened to a song or read a story involving lost love I had an experience of my own to relate to the exquisitely mixed emotions those tales of woe conjure up. Given the brief amount of time we had spent together she certainly had a major role to play in my fantasies for, like many introverts, I always had a very rich inner life.

In October, the *Daily* ran an editorial with the hopeful prediction that the draft would end soon due to consensus on both the far left and far right, as represented by William F. Buckley, Jr. If that had actually happened I would have said goodbye to Reserve Officers' Training Corps (ROTC) the same day. The next month the *Daily* ran a piece entitled "Let's Get Out of Vietnam" which noted that another 1,200 US "technicians" had been sent just that month, and that "our ostensible purpose there, to 'defend freedom,' has resulted in more and worse oppression than was the case under the

French." The editorial writer concluded with a remarkably prescient query: "One wonders how long it will take the US government to concede that the war in that country has been lost." In December the Young Democrats (YDFL) passed a resolution asking for the withdrawal of US personnel from Vietnam, and a sympathy rally for the students and faculty at Berkeley was held on campus. I took an interest in these things and read a book about the situation at Berkeley, but at that point I was still ambivalent about Vietnam. It was something most of us spent time pondering, of course, but the need to keep monolithic communism in check still seemed like a very valid concept, and besides, since the only US personnel involved were voluntary advisors, the issue had not yet become a personal one.

Popular music continued to hold our attention more closely all the time as the British Invasion introduced us to a host of new artists, but the biggest story continued to be the Beatles. "I Want to Hold Your Hand" had hit number one in February 1964, and two months later the Fab Four held the top five positions on the US singles charts, a feat not even Elvis had ever achieved. The legend is that Dylan introduced them to pot that summer. That might even be true, but they would certainly have soon explored hallucinogens on their own in any case because their art would require it.

In December the album *Beatles '65* was released. Perhaps the most notable thing about it is that only four of the songs were not by the Beatles themselves and this, rather than marijuana, may have been the most significant message Dylan left them, by example if not by direct advice: They must begin to compose their own work because, as with him, no one else could possibly express what they had to say. A year later in December 1965, they gave us *Rubber Soul*. They had written all the songs and most of them were music such as we had never heard before. Dylan himself demonstrated his refusal to be categorized when he cut loose at the 1965 Newport Folk Festival in July with a torrid electric set including "Maggie's Farm," with Mike Bloomfield's scorching blues guitar riffs and Al Kooper's keyboard work sending a sound system geared to acoustic nuance into paroxysms of screeching feedback, a sacrilege Theodore Bikel compared to whistling in church.

I continued my freshman year studies in 1965 with English, History, and Military Science, as well as Biology and Public Health. The biology class was considered difficult and my academic confidence was bolstered by receiving A's for both quarters of it. I had chosen the class out of interest sparked by studying it in high school, and because it was a lab science that did not involve math. Another advantage was that, since I have a poor sense of smell, the formaldehyde used to preserve our specimens to be dissected during labs did not bother me, although cutting up the fetal pig did leave me feeling a little sad. The public health class was required for education majors and had been taught for decades by a jovial older professor named Stuart Thompson. He was sort of a character and one of his favorite stories was recalling how a coed had misspelled the name of his course as "pubic health."

My freshman English instructor that quarter, Charlie Norman, introduced me to John Updike, who quickly became one of my favorite writers. His keen eye for the telling detail along with his masterful prose style made reading him a pleasure, but his finely crafted portraits of lost souls in contemporary America were what drew me most irresistibly into his books. I could always identify with their vague fear that somehow life was passing them by. I also enjoyed Updike's graphic descriptions of their compulsive sexual encounters, even though it was all too apparent that their frequent couplings were usually inspired less by lust than by a futile effort to fill the yawning spiritual void at the center of their lives.

On our campus, a controversy over dorm visiting policies that seems almost comic in retrospect began in January 1965. The Frontier Hall Council proposed that open houses be increased from four to eight hours per week, but the real sticking point was over a second part of the plan that liberalized the position of doors during these visiting hours. The current policy dictated that when guests of the opposite sex were in dorm rooms during these hours the room door must remain open at least 45 degrees, whereas the proposed change would allow the door to be closed. Dr. Donald Zander, Director of the Student Activities Bureau, solemnly warned that "we are quite a distance apart on this complicated matter." The position being advanced by the dorm council was not that consenting adults should be allowed to have private sexual relations on university property, a proposition that would have been dismissed as outrageous at that time. What they were arguing was that the students were mature enough to be trusted *not* to engage in such behavior while their doors were closed. The issue appeared to be resolved in a manner worthy of Solomon in February when the proposal was changed to state that "the doors of rooms where guests are registered shall be partway open at all times," but shortly after that Dean of Students Williamson issued an order to the dorm counselors that the doors were to continue to remain at least halfway open.

You might say that this question represented a warning shot in the coming sexual revolution, but it was also an early instance of exploring and testing the boundaries of the broader issue of the relationship between college students and the administrators of their schools. The doctrine of "in loco parentis" was the principle behind many of the policies governing this relationship—the belief that the administration, in the absence of the students' parents, was responsible for ensuring the proper conduct of their charges as well as for providing their educational environment.

A central tenet of the "student movement" that had begun out at Berkeley was that people, especially young people, should be free from all unreasonable demands by those in authority, a position at glaringly obvious variance with "in loco parentis." This belief was soon to be adopted by many groups within our society that saw themselves as oppressed by those with their hands firmly on the levers of power, especially racial minorities and women. These injustices were the great unfinished business left by our parents' generation for us to resolve, and the efforts to close the vast disparities between the promise and the reality of life in America for many of our citizens were soon to rend our society along numerous fault lines.

For many of us the most painful division was the "generation gap," which was soon to find us strangely alienated from the parents who had done so much for us during our childhoods and early adolescence. These conflicts were inevitable as more and more of us gradually became aware of the serious problems with the nation's status quo, but the war was a catalyst that brought them all to a head at almost the same time. The rhetoric and tactics of the antiwar movement were soon to be adopted by the other protest movements as well.

The vehement opposition by those in authority to "the resistance" made it all too clear that the changes being sought would not be forthcoming voluntarily—if we really wanted them we would have to fight for them. It soon became just as clear that it would be foolish to try to achieve these goals by playing by society's rules, because that was a game that only those with the most money and influence could win, a lesson that was never taught in our high school civics courses. Just as those fighting our troops over in Vietnam were smart enough not to meet our overwhelmingly superior military in pitched battles, the resistance on the home front had to "take it to the streets" rather than attempting to bring about change by following the acceptable methods of the society we were determined to change. Of course all of this is in hindsight, but it is endlessly intriguing to me how portents of events to come can be seen through the perspective of history in things as seemingly insignificant as the angle of a dormitory door.

The war was never far from our minds and the American bombing campaign against North Vietnam was the subject of a small and largely civil rally in front of Coffman Memorial Union in early February, drawing about one hundred people on each side of the issue. The same week, the Minnesota Student Association (MSA) Senate passed a resolution supporting a US withdrawal from South Vietnam. This was quickly followed by an effort by a number of MSA representatives to recall the senators who had supported the resolution. Then domestic violence struck again as Malcolm X was assassinated in Detroit by members of his own movement, the Nation of Islam, who felt he had moved too far towards advocating racial peace rather than conflict. The next month introduced us to the term "escalation" as Johnson and his advisors began the war in earnest. Rolling Thunder was a bombing program against North Vietnam running from March 1965, through November 1968, during which the US dropped about seventy percent more explosives on North Vietnam (NVN) than we had employed in the entire Pacific Theater during World War II. The reason it was eventually terminated was that the massive campaign failed to meet any of its objectives, largely because we were employing the World War II tactic of massive airpower in a very different type of conflict. That same March, LBJ made the fateful decision to commit US combat troops, rather than just "advisors," to the conflict. By the end of 1965 our troop level in-country would be approaching 200,000 and the national draft quota was increasing nearly every month.

In March, Professor Mulford Q. Sibley of our political science department gave a speech criticizing America's liberals for their "uncritical acceptance" of the American economic machine and their knee-jerk tendency to equate technological advances with true progress, tendencies that he felt all too often led to justifications for starting wars. Professor Sibley was the most well-known lefty on our faculty and was to remain involved with the anti-war movement for the duration. He had written a very well-received book approximately ten years before on conscientious objectors during World War II, and the good counsel he gave to draft resistors during Vietnam as well as his dignified and articulate criticisms of US foreign policy would earn him the unofficial title of "the conscience of the University."

He had begun his faculty career at the U as an associate professor of political science in 1948 at the age of thirty-six. As a Quaker, socialist, and pacifist he always believed strongly in social activism, as well as reflecting his beliefs in his classroom teaching. He wore a red tie "to remind himself and others of his solidarity with the working class and the socialist movement," and because to him the color signified "the common blood that flows through the veins of all people regardless of power, wealth, or station in life." In other words, he was what many back in that era would have regarded as a nut at best and an insidious red influence at the worst.

He was certainly sincere in his principled and faith-based opposition to war, conscription, and any unwarranted intrusion of the power of the state into the life of the individual, but he was also not above having a little fun at the expense of tightly wrapped right-wingers. On December 3, 1963, he had written a letter to the *Daily* in response to the latest flap over the possible presence of communists on campus, which concluded:

> Personally, I should like to see on campus one or two Communist professors, a chapter of the American Association for the Advancement of Atheism, a society for the promotion of free love, a League for the Overthrow of Government by Jeffersonian Violence (LOGJV), an anti-automation league, and perhaps a nudist club. If we don't sow seeds of doubt and implant subversive thoughts in college, when and where, in heaven's name (if there be a heaven), will they be implanted? And if they are never sown, moral and intellectual progress may be even more doubtful than many of us think.

Not surprisingly, the outrage on the right was swift and intense, and soon Milton Rosen, the St. Paul Public Works Commissioner, was demanding that the U fire Professor Sibley. Instead, the decision was made to hold a debate between the two on academic freedom in Coffman Union in January 1964. The Sibley-Rosen debate actually aroused such strong public interest that a crowd of 1,500 turned out for it. In addition, it was broadcast live on TV and radio state-wide to an estimated audience of about 280,000. This was not the type of public interest the powers that be at the U wanted to attract. Vice President Shepherd attempted to defuse the situation in fine bureaucratic fashion by issuing an assurance that "there was nothing wrong with what Sibley was saying... The public assumed he was advocating some of these things, when he really meant that they ought to be subjects you would discuss and examine on their merits." It would have been more concise and to the point to say that Rosen was a reactionary idiot, but that would also have been politically unwise because there was no doubt that much of the public joined the commissioner in his fears of a red under every rock.

Later that April, thirty-one UM students traveled by bus to DC to join an anti-war protest on the national mall, with counter-demonstrations by the American Nazi Party and the Delaware Valley Citizens for Victory Over Communism. Joan Baez, one of my favorite singers, and several other well-know folk artists performed before a crowd that grew to about thirty thousand, depending upon who was providing the estimate. The *Daily* published an op-ed piece objecting to ROTC on campus, as well as an editorial complaining that "it is becoming more and more difficult to find out what is going on in Vietnam" since the State Department was attempting to rewrite history to justify our intervention there. The national draft quotas continued to rise to support our increasing commitment in Vietnam, with 3,000 called up in February; 7,900 in March; 13,700 in April; and 15,000 in both May and June.

All this was troubling and impossible to ignore, although not a personal threat because I still had three years left on my student deferment. The Selective Service was also granting deferments for graduate school so it appeared that remaining a student in good standing would be a way to avoid the draft indefinitely, or at least until the war was over. As for my status in ROTC, I still had a year to decide on that. I admired the protestors' commitment to acting out in some way on their beliefs and I also found myself agreeing more and more with those beliefs as the weeks went by, but my support remained passive rather than active.

The anti-war movement was escalating right along with the war itself as the first Students for a Democratic Society (SDS) demonstration drew 25,000 to DC. Berkeley continued to be the nerve center of student activism as the first draft card burnings were held there in May 1965. Later that month 30,000 people attended a "teach-in" at Berkeley, a type of gathering that would soon become commonplace on campuses around the country.

Also in May a US State Department official named Marvin Cramer gave a speech at CMU reiterating the official government party line on the need to contain communism and our government's willingness to negotiate being ignored by the North Vietnamese, while a group of anti-war picketers marched outside the building. Cramer said that "to demonstrate merely to express an opinion on an issue which you cannot influence directly does not achieve anything that a letter to a congressman or the State Department wouldn't achieve." He failed to grasp that the activists did not accept his premise that they could not hope to influence the issue, and also seemed to be implying that the letters he was suggesting they write instead would just be ignored. Later that month the *Daily* ran an editorial objecting to a curtailment of student deferments by Lieutenant General Lewis B. Hershey, head of the Selective Service, because of the current world situation. General Hershey would soon become one of the primary symbols of everything the anti-war activists hated about the authoritarian response of the government to anything challenging the war and the draft. His firm belief in using the draft as a way to punish dissenters was especially repugnant, and of course it also gave the lie to the right-wing claim that wearing the uniform should be considered an honor.

On May 24 we had a Vietnam teach-in of our own at the University. The format was to present both speakers supporting the government's position and others opposed to it, with a welcome by President Wilson and many seminars and discussion sessions led mostly by University faculty members. One memorable moment was when Clark MacGregor, a supporter of the government's policies, asked that Socialist Norman Thomas, 81, be restrained for continually interrupting him. The event lasted until 4:00 a.m. The next day a *Daily* editorial noted how much more articulate the anti-war speakers were, but then reflected that "perhaps a good case just can't be made for American intervention." The event generated a good deal of coverage, including favorable comments about the large number of people attending such an event on a Monday night.

Later that week anti-war protestors picketed outside the Armory building, as well as counter-pickets including two female students with signs expressing their affinity for ROTC men. A rally followed across the street in front of the Bell Museum where the Reverend Vincent Hawkinson and Professor Sibley were among the speakers. Sibley asked the listeners to play the same role as the boy in the tale of the emperor's new clothes by pointing out all the lies and contradictions in what the government was asking us to believe, to which the counter-protestors responded with jeers. The relevance of these events to our own lives was starkly illustrated by an article in the *Daily* noting that Minnesota's draft quota had risen 500% in the last five months and that the average age of inductees had dropped from 24.5 years in early 1962 to less than twenty-one now.

We were briefly distracted by another issue in early June when President Wilson proposed raising our quarterly tuition and fees from $105 to $125. This sounds absurdly low today but in 1965 I was only making one dollar an hour at Robby's so the increase would mean having to work over sixty more hours in the course of a year. That really did not bother me much because it was apparent that the cost of attending the U would still be a relative bargain. I never had any trouble earning more than enough to cover my tuition, fees, and books, and Dad and Mom covered my room and board by allowing me to live at home the entire time.

Taking their cue from the anti-war protestors' tactics, however, some students planned rallies and a "Berkeley–style" sit-in at the main administration building, Morrill Hall, to protest the increase. This was to be a Minnesota version, however, so one of the rallies was to feature speakers giving equal time to arguments for and against the increase. The more radical Berkeley influence was reflected in one group's plans to present a list of demands to the Regents, to have students with "begging bowls" asking the Regents for money to pay the increase, and to stop traffic on Washington Avenue as a protest. The *Daily* responded with an editorial on "reasonable dissent," but also warned that the administration must take students' concerns seriously to avoid having "another Berkeley on their hands." The increase was passed by the Regents, and an all-night sit-in was held at Morrill with about three hundred people coming and going during the night.

Jack Mogelson, director of the U's chapter of the Summer Community Organization and Political Education (SCOPE) Project announced that some of our students would be working in the Deep South again that summer to assist with Negro voter registration in spite of the violence many such workers had endured the previous year. SCOPE was a part of Dr. King's Southern Christian Leadership Conference (SCLC), and was essentially an effort to continue the earlier work of the Freedom Riders on a more organized and wider scale.

As the academic year drew to a close the *Daily* editorial page made note of the "tremendous student participation in many forms of political and social action," but also pointed out that only a minority of undergraduates were actually participating and expressed hope that the number would increase next year.

Chapter 3
SOPHMORE YEAR
UNIVERSITY OF MINNESOTA
1965-66

In the summer of 1965 I worked full-time at Robby's. I never took summer classes during my undergraduate years because the jobs helped pay for my expenses at the U for the following school year, but I also welcomed the change of pace from my studies. I have always spent a great deal of time reading and that was especially true back then. I also enjoyed learning to play the guitar, and of course my goal was to be able to do it like Joan Baez. I took in many movies and fell in love with "art house" films. It was a revelation to me that film could be more than just entertainment, and the ones I enjoyed the most, especially the New Wave works, were a fine complement to the reading I favored because, like the superb short stories of John Updike, they dealt mainly with human emotions and relationships, especially what happens when they go sour. In the films I attended and the books I read they rarely failed to go sour in the end. All this reinforced my increasingly gloomy, self-absorbed attitude toward life in general that is so typical of undergraduate liberal arts students, and world events only buttressed my beliefs further. In other words, I was a college sophomore. I also liked the British film versions of books by Alan Sillitoe, as well as the ones staring Rita Tushingham. I had a crush on Rita because of her rather unconventional looks and those sad but mesmerizing puppy-dog eyes. You always knew her heart would be broken in the end but her characters never hesitated to follow where love was beckoning them. I wished I had the courage to do that, but I was so shy that my dates were few and far between and never resulted in anything even remotely serious.

Back on campus that summer an incident of apparent rental discrimination attracted attention when a landlady in Dinkytown refused to rent to a biracial couple. Some students responded with the by now familiar tactic of picketing the property.

One hopeful piece of news for students was a proposal for a glass-enclosed heated walkway on the upper pedestrian level of the new Washington Avenue Bridge that crossed the Mississippi to include bookstalls, information and ticket booths, and exhibits. The *Daily* cautioned readers that the plans were "still nebulous," and I cannot help smiling when I reflect on how things actually turned out. For some reason, once the long-anticipated walkway was finally completed, the glass panels soon proved to be an irresistible target for vandals, most likely folks returning from late nights at the watering holes across the river on the West Bank. As they were broken out, the U replaced them with Plexiglas, but when even that material began succumbing to drunken kicks the next step was to fill in the empty rectangles with plywood. So eventually the sides of the walkway were wood on the lower half and Plexiglas on the upper half. The stalls and booths never appeared and the heat was permanently shut off during the 1970s energy crisis. Those endowed with a more acute sense of smell than my own also complained that the passageway often smelled of urine, but at least it still provided shelter from the winter winds that whip down the river valley. Another item of good news, although too late to benefit me, was that the weekly lectures for freshman English in Northrop Auditorium were to be discontinued. There were several classes held in Northrop back in those days and, since it seated nearly five thousand students, that setup must have been a University financial officer's dream come true.

World events and the war were always on our minds, and in late July LBJ doubled the draft call, resulting in a tightening of the standards for student deferments. Now, in addition to being registered, a man would have to be making "normal progress" toward a degree. It was unclear how this determination would be made, but the possibility that the U would be called upon to assist in doing it was troubling. The new stipulation applied to graduate students as well. The *Daily* ran an editorial asking questions based upon LBJ's most recent speech on Vietnam. One of these was that, since we now had only 125,000 troops in country and the military estimated that it would take 500,000 to get the job done, were we prepared to send an additional 375,000 men? The implication was that we should end what the numbers indicated was an exercise in futility, but few of us would have guessed that by 1968 the government would actually bring our troop level over the half million mark, by far the largest commitment since World War II.

LBJ and his advisors elected to accomplish this deployment without calling up the National Guard or Reserves due to the well-grounded fear that such a major disruption in the lives of men already well established in employment and family responsibilities would be politically unpopular. Instead they would rely heavily upon the draft since conscription would fall more upon younger men with fewer commitments and less political clout than the part-time troops who had been trained and paid by the government for years with the expectation that they would be ready and willing to bear a significant part of the burden should the nation go to war. The problem here was that what made sense politically was not only patently unfair but also a militarily unsound decision: The level of technical expertise in the standing army was too sparse to support such a large call-up since that level had been set based upon the expectation that men who had already been trained in the National Guard (NG) and Reserves would be called up if such a large mobilization was ever required. The result throughout the course of the war was a chronic shortage of soldiers with many of the critical skills required for support positions in an army increasingly reliant upon complicated technology.

Even at the height of combat operations in 1968 only a small number of the available NG and Reserve units were called up and many such troops proved to be poorly prepared for duties in the war zone, a situation less than surprising since by that stage of the war many of the "weekend warriors" were men who had joined up primarily to avoid service in Vietnam. Since the government was forced to rely upon conscription for a significant number of our troops throughout the long course of the war, it was clear that all the pseudo-patriotic blather and dire warnings about the threat to our national security posed by the Vietnamese communists failed to inspire an equally enthusiastic response among young Americans eager to do their part to neutralize the red menace. There was a notable disparity between the number of voices on the right maligning the anti-war movement and the number of true patriots willing to prove the sincerity of their convictions by actually putting their lives on the line to back up all the bluster.

In August, the *Daily* published a disturbing two-part opinion piece by Zev Aelony, a well-known local activist and one of the "Minnesota Six" Freedom Riders from the summer of 1961, comparing methods used by US and South Vietnamese forces in Vietnam to those employed by the Nazis in World War II, especially torturing prisoners to attempt to extract information. He also argued that the US intervention violated the Nuremberg Charter of 1945 because it was an invasion to suppress an internal conflict, or civil war, between factions of Vietnamese. This was an argument that was becoming more and more common among anti-war activists. Of course, our government's position was that one communist was the same as another whether they were Vietnamese, Chinese, Soviet, or any other variety. The pro-war stance was based on the conviction that the forces of freedom were locked in a fight to the death with monolithic communism. This was an all-too-familiar concept to our parents since their generation had spent years enduring the grim struggle against the Axis, and we had been brought up to believe that just such an enemy was once again threatening the free world. This was what JFK had termed the "long twilight struggle," a cold war with occasional hot flare-ups in places like Korea and Vietnam, and the eloquent resolve of his great inauguration speech was still fresh in our memories. What were we to believe? We did not yet know, but two or three years before it would have been inconceivable to even hesitate at all before attempting to answer that question.

There were also reports on the activities of the Minnesota members of the SCOPE project. Jack Mogelson said that twenty-four people from the University had worked in Peach County, Georgia, that summer focusing on community organizing, education, and especially voter registration. He felt that they had accomplished a good deal but less than they could have done with more people and funding. The project had been supported by voluntary contributions, and he said that federal aid would be needed if it was to continue. He mentioned harassment by whites but not any overt violence.

That month brought us one of the most significant musical events in Twin Cities history as the Beatles played a concert at Metropolitan Stadium on Saturday, August 21. I'm sorry now that I missed it but at the time going to live performances was not something I ever thought about doing. Also I was quite cost-conscious in those days and I didn't see the point of paying for a ticket when I could get a couple of their albums for the same amount. The idea that I was passing up an historic opportunity never crossed my mind. The Fab Four were already famous, but we had no inkling of what they were to become. We loved popular music but it was not yet "important."

That same August the black Los Angeles neighborhood of Watts was rocked by race riots in what was to be the first of several summers of these frightening events in big-city ghettos around the country. The precipitating event was the familiar one of conflict between young blacks and white police officers, but the underlying causes were the rage, frustration, and hopelessness caused by living in these urban hellholes. Race riots had been around ever since the end of the Civil War made emancipation a reality, but now the fact that they were being instigated by blacks rather than by whites stoked the fears of many Americans that black demands for justice would somehow diminish the position of whites in our society and that blacks were attempting to "take over." It was only a matter of time before those harboring such fears and resentments would come to identify the people trying to improve the lot of blacks in America by actions such as the voter registration drives with the same ones who were opposing our government's actions in Vietnam, a conclusion that was often accurate. The early skirmishes of the Culture Wars were already upon us.

***

Fall quarter began with the last week of September and I approached my studies with more confidence than I had as a freshman. In addition to getting a grasp on the subject matter of my courses I was also learning how to learn, as our advisors and instructors often termed this process. Many of the exams were machine-graded multiple-choice tests and, much like learning the strategies for solving a particular type of puzzle, the ability to think through this type of challenge came with practice. Knowledge of concepts and mastery of facts were essential also, but I soon learned how to think like the people writing the exam. Short-answer tests were the next easiest. Essay tests and papers required the most thought, but I was an English major and frequent practice with this type of writing also brought slow but steady improvement.

I had a class in advanced expository prose with a very particular instructor, Ned Edgington, and that is where my ability and confidence as a writer really began to gel. He assigned each of us a writer to focus on during the quarter and mine was Thomas Wolfe. If a person wanted to nurture a passion for writing, could there be a more appropriate subject? His manic need to put every detail of his life on paper was my inspiration to fill pages writing about him, and that class was certainly a major stepping stone in my long and varied academic career. Even the setting and season contributed to making it seem like everything a college class should be. At that time the English Department was in Vincent Hall and our classroom was up on the second floor with a beautiful view of the Mall, an ideal place to enjoy the changing colors of the leaves as fall quarter 1965, moved along.

The quarter was only three days old when the *Daily* reported that the need for additional troops in Vietnam was causing draft boards to look more closely at the grades and academic progress of men with student deferments. The article led off with a lame attempt to soften the seriousness of the situation: "Men, if that D you got last spring has slipped your mind, better look again—it may stand for 'Draft' within the next few months." Colonel Robert P. Knight of the State Selective Service Office explained that a 111-A marriage deferment carried more weight that the 11-S student variety. My own classification was 1-D, the ROTC variety. He also gave us a helpful reminder that men who were drafted stood a good chance of being shipped off to Vietnam. During the next week the court of the Architecture Building was crowded with male students signing up for their deferments. The *Daily* reported that 3,500 such delays had been granted in 1960; 14,000 during the 1964-65 academic year; and that about 20,000 were expected for the school year just under way.

In October the *Daily* reported on the University Health Service's policy on dispensing birth control pills. The pills were given to coeds who were married, or to those who were engaged provided that they furnish the date of their planned nuptials and the name of their fiancé. If the doctor was satisfied with the information provided he would prescribe the pills far enough in advance of the date of the marriage so that they would be effective by that time. The article never even hinted at the possibility that healthcare professionals might wish to assist in preventing unwanted pregnancies in unmarried students, apparently because that could be construed as encouraging immoral behavior. In only a few short years such a policy would be dismissed as ridiculous, but obviously in 1965 "in loco parentis" overshadowed any hints of the looming sexual revolution.

That month marked the 25th anniversary of Coffman Memorial Union (CMU) and the campus landmark hosted several events and exhibits to commemorate the milestone. A highlight was a visit to campus by the humorist Max Shulman, who was very well-known at that time because of the popularity of the TV show *The Many Loves of Dobie Gillis*, which was still being broadcast in syndication. I always loved the show because of all the wacky characters, especially Bob Denver's masterfully understated portrayal of the beatnik Maynard G. Krebs. The primary focus was always young adult romantic angst reflected in Dobie's unending stream of crushes. The unrequited love of Dobie for Thalia Menninger and of Zelda Gilroy for Dobie led to countless problems and hilarious plot twists, and in my less morose moments I was able to contemplate the distinct possibility that my fixation on Glenda was equally ludicrous. Like Dobie, of course, what I was really in love with was the idea of being in love. The girl was secondary.

While Shulman and Tom Heggen, author of *Mr. Roberts*, were students at the U in the late 1930s and early 1940s they had written humor columns for the *Daily*, "Sauce for the Gander" and "Saturday's Child" respectively, and the paper reprinted a couple of them to mark the occasion of Max's visit. At a press conference he reflected that "college humor today is as dead as the dodo. It was a phenomenon of the '20s, kind of limped into the '30s, and died in the '40s, as it should have." He went on to say that humor itself was far from dead, but that now it was more "far-out" and "free-form" and not centered on campuses. He did not mention the term, but the "put-on" was rapidly becoming a dominant mode of humor. This was the comedic equivalent of enclosing a joke or an entire bit in "air quotes," which always left the performer with the perfect escape of claiming he was being ironic if his material failed to amuse, a tactic that shifted the onus back onto the listener for not getting the joke.

I had to admit that the old columns seemed dated and largely irrelevant, but was there ever really a time when college had been so much fun? I had a vague vision of nattily dressed pipe-smoking young men strolling down the mall with coeds on their arms, breezing through their classes with a gentleman's C, and living for football games and frat parties. Hip flasks would have been a mandatory accessory. That may indeed have been at least somewhat true in the 1920s when colleges were still largely bastions of privilege for the well-off, but the pieces the *Daily* ran were from early 1941 and by that time all the joking was probably mostly to provide a bit of distraction from the decade-old Depression and the looming crisis represented by the unending Axis conquests in Europe and the Pacific. Shulman's point that this writing was from the era when such humor was dying was well-taken, but when he reminisced about the "non-stop gag session" that he had going on with Heggen and his other buddies at the *Daily* and *Ski-U-Mah* I still could not resist at least a twinge of envy.

That October was also a milestone in Minnesota sports history as our Twins got into the World Series in only their fifth season. The games were shown on the big screen in Northrop Auditorium where we had our videotaped lectures for introductory psychology. I had been a Twins fan from day one so I followed their games closely against the LA Dodgers and their pitching ace Sandy Koufax. Like all the best Series' it went to seven games and when I heard they had lost the last one I still remember exactly where I was—in Cooke Hall on my way to a judo class. The same month, the new Washington Avenue Bridge spanning the Mississippi River finally opened. It was a big event in the history of the University because it made the increasingly important West Bank Campus more conveniently accessible by connecting the two areas of the Twin Cities Campus with a more modern span. The enclosed and heated pedestrian walkway on the second deck above the one for motorized traffic was a real boon to students accustomed to trudging across the boardwalks next to the traffic lanes of the old bridge while enduring exhaust fumes and the winter winds whistling down the river valley.

***

The rapidly expanding scope of our involvement in Vietnam, however, made the war the dominant subject on campus for most of us. Brian Coyle, then a member of Students for a Democratic Society (SDS), had a piece in the *Daily* decrying the tendency of the government and its supporters to accuse protestors of disloyalty and urging readers to become active in the anti-war movement. A few days later there was a piece by Professor Ed Coen, Economics, providing a point-by-point analysis of why he felt that our goals in Vietnam were not grounded in reality and were therefore doomed to fail. He debunked the viewpoint that all communists represented an equal threat to the US and compared our obsession with stopping Ho Chi Minh to a crusade in that it was based on strongly held beliefs that were completely divorced from military reality. Toward the end of the month two pro-war student organizations, the Young Americans for Freedom and the

UM Republican Association, pledged to gather at least 10,000 signatures on a petition supporting our government's position and then send it to LBJ and General Westmoreland. They also announced plans for a blood drive for the troops in Vietnam. A member of the Minnesota Committee to End the War in Vietnam said there was no doubt that the majority on campus supported the war but that the number opposed was increasing. An SDS representative, on the other hand, felt that those supporting negotiations far outnumbered those favoring continuing the war and went on to outline plans his group had for more anti-war activities.

That same month coordinated rallies against the war in the US and the rest of the world drew an estimated 100,000. It is sometimes easy to forget, especially in those early stages of the war, that public opinion was rarely in favor of the demonstrators and that the two sides often got into verbal and even physical confrontations. We were not yet able to comprehend what historical hindsight would make so painfully apparent: A war within America was slowly but inexorably escalating right along with our misadventure in Southeast Asia, and we would soon see the truth reaffirmed that no war is as bitter as a civil war.

In November Brian Coyle had another important piece in the *Daily* in which he compared the illegal but moral positions and activities of the anti-war activists and the civil rights workers. Although he did not mention Thoreau specifically, he also used the term "civil disobedience" in reference to the activities that would become necessary if our government continued its misguided policies. The allusion to Thoreau was significant because his conviction that it was not just the right but the duty of good citizens to follow the dictates of their consciences rather than those of their government was to become one of the primary tenets of the resistance. Coyle also did not mention the principle that came out of the Nurnberg trials that an individual could actually be held accountable for participating in an unjust war even if he had been following orders, but that corollary to Thoreau's position would also be cited frequently by those in the anti-war movement over the next eight years. The government's stance, of course, was that one could be designated a conscientious objector only if he opposed all war. With minor variations, this conundrum was to be the focus of endless arguments and discussions over the course of the war until the end of the draft in 1972, but the levels of passion and intolerance for the opposition would increase to levels we could never have imagined when we were studying the problems of democracy back in high school.

In early November the *Daily* ran an editorial urging readers to take some time on Veterans Day to think about what the troops in Vietnam were enduring. In the same issue, a representative of the Minnesota Committee to End the War in Vietnam announced that they would be sending about seventy-five students to Washington, DC, for a convention and march on the White House later in the month. They hoped for a turnout of around twenty thousand. He felt that such activities could be "very effective" in changing foreign policy decisions. The group headed out to DC on rented buses over the long Thanksgiving weekend and the attendance ended up somewhere between 25,000 and 50,000, with speeches by Dr. Benjamin Spock, Dr. King, Norman Thomas, and others. There were about 200 counter protestors as well and the confrontation began to get physical when a Viet Cong banner was displayed, but things were reported to be peaceful and disciplined for the most part.

November also brought us news of the first large-scale conflict of the war, the battle of the Ia Drang Valley, resulting in the death of 300 Americans and 2,000 Vietnamese. This was a shocking number of American troops to lose in a single engagement, but introducing a military frame of reference that would soon become all too familiar, General Westmoreland termed the battle a success because the "kill ratio" so decisively favored our forces. We had not gained territory that we intended to hold and the communists did not appear to be at all discouraged by their troop losses, so it was necessary for the government and the military to come up with some other measure that would demonstrate that the efforts of our own forces had resulted in victory. Kill ratio was it. By the end of 1965 over 1,800 US soldiers had died in Vietnam that year.

Among other items attracting attention in late November was an interview with General Hershey, head of the Selective Service since 1940, in which he expressed his "concern" that local draft boards might begin to cancel deferments because of student anti-war protest activities. I imagine most of us understood this statement as the thinly veiled threat it was intended to be. An item of good news was that Professor Arnold Rose, Sociology, finally won his three-week libel trial against an organization of ultra-right "Christians," yet another chapter in the crusade of harassment against alleged communists on campus. As if to emphasize the point that our beloved campus was not a hotbed of radicalism, the *Daily* ran an editorial supporting the concept of "in loco parentis" in the ongoing controversy over the extent of dorm visiting hours.

In December Rep. Don Fraser conducted two days of hearings on the war featuring six U faculty members, three on each side of the issue. One of those in favor of US policy in Vietnam was Rodney Loehr, who was to be my instructor for American military history the next quarter. The second day feated presentations from twenty organizations, with those against the war being in the majority. At the conclusion the congressman expressed satisfaction at having heard "a spectrum of views" from his constituents. Meanwhile, the blood drive for the troops sponsored by two conservative student organizations resulted in almost 200 pints being collected in what the *Daily* termed a scene of "mass transfusion." Max Shulman would have been proud. A dental hygiene student named Kay stated that she wanted to donate because "you feel like you're really over there if your blood is in someone else." The unfortunate thing about the otherwise admirable event was that it reinforced the tendency to equate supporting the troops with supporting the war. Most likely the anti-war activists also equated donating with supporting the war because they failed to appear, missing a golden opportunity to demonstrate that opposing the war and supporting the troops were completely compatible positions and that in fact opposing the war might well be the biggest favor we could perform for our men in uniform.

The Second Vatican Council's document *Gaudium et Spes*, published in the first week of the month, included a grim observation that, in retrospect, can only be regarded as eerily prophetic:

> The unique hazard of modern warfare consists in this:
> …through a certain inexorable chain of events, it can catapult men into the most atrocious decisions.

Also in early December, Professor Karlis Kaufmanis, astronomy, gave his annual talk on the Star of Bethlehem, a holiday tradition on campus. He explained that in 7 BC Jupiter, known to Jewish astrologers as the King Star, and Saturn, the star of the Messiah, were both in Pisces, the "House of the Hebrews." This would have been a rare and impressive thing to view but, even more significant, they believed this conjunction was the sign that the Messiah was about to appear. Professor Kaufmanis said he thought it likely that the "wise men" were actually Jewish astrologers in exile. He gave a detailed explanation of how the "star" could have appeared to be resting exactly over Bethlehem at the time they were approaching the town. This edifying combination of faith and science was always a welcome part of the holiday season right before the start of finals week.

As a coda to this year of increasing tension and uncertainty, December also brought us the first broadcast of *A Charlie Brown Christmas*, that quirky, touching, and ultimately irresistible little tale that immediately became an American holiday classic. I felt that Charlie was speaking for me when he lamented, "I don't feel the way I'm supposed to feel." In the years before home video, the annual rebroadcast of this understated masterpiece was a must-see for millions of us. Was it really possible that our hearts could come to see how beautiful life could be if we would only pause long enough to truly appreciate Linus's message of what Christmas was truly all about? Many events of the next few years would make it difficult to answer "yes" to that question, but for a half-hour each December the miraculous transformation of Charlie's little tree presented us with a symbol and an ideal that just might briefly cause us to view the violence and strife around us with more shame than anger.

★★★

As 1966 began I was pleased with the way my studies were going. I had gotten mostly A's in fall quarter and was finding the classes interesting. Psychology was fascinating to me, especially since I had never studied it before. American history was far more compelling than the European history I had studied during freshman year, and the American military history class we had in ROTC was a useful supplement. Education majors had to take three physical education classes, so I had taken golf during freshman year, and now studied judo and ballroom dance as a sophomore. Oddly, my judo instructor, Ed Dorey, was also one of the instructors for the dance class. I have rather pleasant memories of waltzing and fox trotting around Norris Gym with the girls in the class, but my technique must have been somewhat lacking because I pulled a C for the class, not all that easy to do for a Phy Ed offering. I don't think that many of us took these required one-credit courses very seriously.

My favorites that year were the English literature survey courses, a sequence of three classes held in the big room at the north end of the third floor of Vincent. In the fall I had Lonnie Durham during his first year with the department. He brought a jovial informality to his teaching style that helped with some of the rather dry material. We needed to read some lengthy passages from *The Faerie Queene* that were not in the Norton anthology, and I remember trying to pore through them in the old college library on the ground floor of Johnston Hall. We had David Haley, also in his first year, for the second and third quarters of the sequence. He was considerably more formal than Lonnie, but obviously passionate about his love for what he was teaching. This made me recall Jim Elsenpeter back at De La Salle and his excitement when delving into a classic work. I was also amazed by David's ability to recall names and authors of secondary sources faster than he could scrawl them out on the blackboard. This was real college-level instruction in the subject I enjoyed the most and those classes provided a solid foundation for many of the ones I took in the following years.

The rapidly escalating war continued to cast a shadow over everything else, however, and the January issue of the *Ivory Tower* contained this grim assessment of the previous year.

> For us, 1965 was a dreary, frightening year; the world seems older, but to no effect. It was a year in which every young man's most visceral thoughts were about a faraway war of indistinct purpose to which his government was committed irretrievably because it had decided too late that the price of maintaining a military dictatorship in Saigon against heavy odds was more than it would have wanted to pay.

The same month, the US Justice Department ruled that a Michigan draft board had acted illegally by revoking the deferments of antiwar protestors and dissenters based upon their political activities. This case was a welcome check to the power of the Selective Service, but it also provided further proof of the increasingly obvious fact that the draft was more and more often being used as punishment. How could this be denied when those convicted of a crime were sometimes given the option of going into the military or going to prison? In another news item relating to conscription, the SS announced in January that it would begin drafting men into the Marines rather than calling up men in the Reserves.

Two visiting speakers on campus offered discouraging views of

America's chances for success in Vietnam. One was an official of the W.E.B. DuBois Clubs—a youth organization sponsored by the Communist Party—who had recently visited North Vietnam, but since that organization had communist affiliations, his opinion was hardly unbiased. The second one, John Scott, commanded more credibility since he was a correspondent for *Time* magazine. The *Daily* reported his judgment was that our goals were not hopeless but that the lack of stability and strong national identity in South Vietnam, combined with their history of internal religious conflicts, made our efforts at nation-building a daunting task. He observed that recent history in other nations illustrated the difficulty of suppressing insurgent movements unless the anti-insurgency forces enjoyed an approximate ten-to-one advantage. In Vietnam, however, the numerical advantage of the South Vietnamese government forces and US troops combined over the Viet Cong was only about five-to-one. In other words, our chances of success seemed rather doubtful because the mightiest military force in the history of the world only outnumbered its opponents by five-to-one!

The story makes it appear that Mr. Scott was doing his very best to be objective about a highly charged subject, but the advantage of historical perspective makes it almost incomprehensible how our leaders and foreign policy experts could have been blind to such clear indications that our mission was doomed to failure. To help understand this widespread apparent failure to comprehend the true situation in Southeast Asia, it is important to remember the intensity of the anti-communist zeal in that era. The generation that sacrificed so much to defeat the Axis was now faced with the prospect of another unholy alliance bent on bringing down America and all it represented. The leaders of the USSR certainly did their best to stoke this fear with all their overblown rhetoric about burying us, not to mention the insufferable screeds from Castro, the man who had almost precipitated World War III. Memories of Hitler's notorious rants were sure to be awakened in our parents' generation by such overwrought verbal taunts. It is also well to keep in mind that most of the American people agreed with our government's foreign policy at this early stage of the war and that, even though lack of a critical mass of domestic support ultimately made continuing the conflict impossible, a sizable number continued to support our intervention right up to the bitter end.

Another essential ingredient in this recipe for disaster was the personality of LBJ. In addition to being a veteran of World War II, he was a stubborn man who could not tolerate the thought of losing a fight by backing down even once he started to realize that he had taken on an opponent who was far tougher than he had anticipated. The situation bore more than a slight resemblance to a Texas-style bragging contest where a man makes so many increasingly stronger public statements about his determination to never back down that in the end he has to keep on fighting even though he has come to know in his heart that his ultimate defeat is inevitable.

As LBJ said, he was not going to become the first US president to lose a war. The frequently used metaphor of a quagmire is most appropriate because with each forward step into the muck, with each increase in our troop strength, our president and his advisors always held out the hope that this time our feet would begin to find solid ground. The metaphor of the compulsive gambler, always convinced that the next bet will be the one where his losing streak begins to turn around, also comes to mind.

On our campus, Reverend Vince Hawkinson of the Grace University Lutheran Church continued to serve his indispensible role of social activist and prophet. In retrospect, he and Professor Sibley truly were the consciences of our campus community during those years, and would that those in authority had heeded the words of people such as them. Vince had recently returned from a trip to Mississippi as part of a race and religion course at Gustavus Adolphus and he admitted that he was shocked by the situation there. He agreed with many in the civil rights movement that the federal government must continue to enforce laws aimed at achieving racial equality because such an initiative would never come from the southern state governments. Indeed, the term "states' rights" was a euphemism for the right to maintain racial separation and hence inequality. Between legal devices such as the Jim Crow laws and murderous vigilante groups such as the KKK, blacks in the south had long been subjected to what can only be termed a deliberate and sustained campaign of domestic terrorism.

Vince's blunt assessment of life in the south was that "everything is under the umbrella of race." That is also an accurate description of America as a whole, both then and now, but back then the outrages in the southern states were so egregious that places like Minnesota looked good by comparison. It would not have occurred to us as we savored our feelings of smugness over our admirable tolerance compared to our backwards southern brethren that a major reason for our own lack of racial strife was that our "negro" population posed a negligible threat to the white majority because it was so small and isolated as to be nearly invisible.

The issue of freedom of expression is always a hot topic at a university, and it came up once again when Ronald Brodigan, director of the Lower Edge Gallery on Cedar Avenue, was charged with obscenity because a Catholic priest had complained about the display of a painting depicting nudity. In short order some University students formed a committee to assist Brodigan with his problems, claiming that obscenity ordinances should be a thing of the past because the free exchange of ideas was so important. A leader of the committee also noted that obscenity was virtually impossible to define anyway.

Near the end of January the Committee to End the War in Vietnam sponsored a panel discussion that included Professor Sibley. He warned that the war would soon begin to divert resources away from vital domestic needs, turning the US from a welfare state to a "warfare state." He also expressed his concern that the anti-war movement would begin to become irrational in the face of mounting escalation and government intransigence, truly a prophetic statement. Irrational actions often provoke an irrational response. A former Marine who had served behind the lines in the Republic of Vietnam (RVN) was also on the panel, and he told the audience that they were better informed about the situation than the average serviceman who had been brainwashed during his military training.

★★★

That same winter, I had my first serious encounter with alcohol. Mom and Dad were out for the evening on a weekend night and I was home to watch over things. After my younger siblings were asleep I went to get a snack from the fridge. There was a bottle of home-made dandelion wine in there that was a gift from my Mom's Aunt Tress, and my folks and Granny obviously did not care much for it because the bottle had been there in the back for months. I had never had a drink before and I decided to try a little. This was not something I had planned. The stuff was sweet and syrupy, certainly not something I would ever drink for the taste. The closest comparison is to some sort of cough medicine. One drink didn't seem to have much effect but I had heard all the usual stories from friends and the media about how pleasant drinking could be, so now that I had started I wanted to find out what that was all about. One drink led to another and I ended up putting away a good part of the bottle. Either Aunt Tress really knew how to brew up a mean bottle of wine or else (most likely) she had reinforced it with something stronger because the next thing I remember is waking up in bed about three in the morning with my head spinning and sick as a dog. I had thrown up the yellow stuff all over my pillow and nightstand. I felt that way for the better part of two days.

My folks never called me on it even though it was obvious what I had done. Mom just said she hoped I felt better soon. I was back on my feet by Monday or Tuesday but the wretched experience made my stomach turn at the smell of any alcohol for about six months. The peculiar thing is that I don't recall any pleasant aspect to my intoxication at all, but I realize now that that is most likely because I had drunk myself into an alcoholic blackout and hence had no memory of the last hour or two before I passed out in bed. Such was the most inauspicious beginning of my relationship with something that was to become both my best friend and worst enemy for about twenty years. Never be too quick to judge based on a first date.

***

In February the *Daily* reported that the Selective Service System (SSS) soon would begin using a test similar to one employed during the Korean War to determine if male students would be able to retain their II-S deferments. Colonel Robert Knight, Director of the Minnesota SSS office, informed us in his usual irritatingly patronizing style that this would be an aptitude test "to determine those that are capable of absorbing and benefiting from college work." He went on to say that some college students did not belong there and that "hopefully, the test will weed them out." He did not explain why he felt that the SSS was more qualified to make that judgment than the university itself. There was already a time-honored way of weeding out students making unsatisfactory progress toward a degree. Had he ever heard of flunking out?

Knight compounded this arrogant intrusion of the SSS into the academy by explaining that a deferment decision might also be based upon a young man's course of study, noting that a draft board might choose to defer a science major rather than an arts major. Of course, the reasoning here was that after graduation the scientist would have skills more valuable to the military, but this apparent devaluing of the arts and humanities was particularly galling to someone like me who was studying English. It would not be long before the Army was wishing the local draft boards had provided them with a few less men experienced in exercising critical thinking.

Students who were in "good scholastic standing" could choose to be deferred based on that status rather than taking the exam. This was defined as being in the top 75% of their class for a senior, the top 67% for a sophomore, and the top 50% for a freshman. This meant that the whole exam issue would not affect me personally because I met those academic standards and, in any case, my deferment was based on being enrolled in ROTC even though by this point I had all but decided to drop out of that at the end of the academic year. Nevertheless, this latest demonstration of the power of the SSS over our lives was both irritating and frightening. Especially disturbing was the fact that the U would be required to play a role in this process by providing the government with the class rankings of male students. The *Daily* published an editorial in the same issue lamenting this latest consequence of the war but the tone was one of sadness and regret rather than anger.

Meanwhile, Ronald Brodigan of the Lower Edge Gallery pled not guilty at the opening of his trial on obscenity charges. He was provided with legal support by the ACLU and with moral support by the Committee to Aid in the Defense of Ronald Brodigan, which also announced that they soon expected to obtain official status as a campus group with the purpose of opposing "irresponsible censorship of artistic works." They had already acquired a faculty advisor from General College. During the trial it was revealed that the citizen filing the complaint was a Catholic priest from St. Elizabeth's. At the end of February Brodigan was acquitted.

Four art experts had testified in his defense, including Anthony M. Clark, Director of the Minneapolis Institute of Arts, who testified that he failed to find the painting in question arousing. Indeed, he opined that the work was not erotic at all but that "the main theme of the painting is melancholy…The face of the man is unhappy and the profile of the woman looks like a bulldog. The painting to my mind would certainly turn me off." Apparently Judge Riley passed up the golden opportunity to ask the prosecution's witnesses if they were aroused by the work because the story reported no such exchange. This tempest in a teapot probably reinforced the impression among many members of the community that the U was a haven for left-wingers and degenerates, but many of us enjoyed seeing folks like that annoyed. I know I did.

At the beginning of February KTCA-TV, Channel 2, our public TV channel, announced an upcoming ten-part series entitled "Vietnam Briefing." The goal was to examine various aspects of our involvement, but the selection of presenters and the titles of the episodes seemed to heavily favor the official government position. What was especially troubling about this was that several of the participants were U faculty members, including Colonel William Beard, the commanding officer of my Army ROTC unit, and Professor Rodney Loehr, the instructor for the ROTC US military history class I was taking that winter. Actually, my personal impression of both these men was favorable, but there was no doubt that they were both strongly in favor of our intervention in Vietnam. The *Daily* ran a well-reasoned editorial expressing concern about the situation and asking KTCA to make the presentation more balanced.

On campus, the Committee to End the War in Vietnam (CEWVN) was also organizing events at least once every week by this time. That month they held a rally to show support for anti-war activists in the south, which was notable for once again making the connection between the civil rights and anti-war movements. The chairman stated that "Negroes in this country, because of their own experiences, are quicker to see through the lies of the government." Dr. King had already begun voicing strong doubts about the war in 1965, and in 1967 he was to begin to lend his prophetic voice to proclaiming that the two struggles were really just different fronts of the same war. Now, in early 1966, the first inklings of this insight were showing up more and more often in the speeches and writings of those involved in what would soon come to be known as "the resistance."

We received further clarification on the draft situation when the SSS announced that their new standards would require freshmen to have a GPA of at least 1.9 to be deferred, a sophomore 1.8, and a junior 2.1. Men meeting these standards would not have to take the upcoming test to be deferred. A university official said that freshmen would receive more information in next year's orientation sessions on their military obligations because of the steep increases in draft quotas, but he did not feel this would cause them to devote less time to university activities and more to studying because "most of our leaders and students who are active in organizations have good averages anyway." An assistant athletic director expressed relief that Big Ten and U academic standards had resulted in GPAs for athletes that would keep most of them safe from the draft, but he did express concern that eventually the loss of players to the military might make it necessary to use freshmen on varsity teams since this had happened during the Korean conflict. War truly is hell sometimes.

Toward the middle of February the CEWVN held another rally, this time in front of the Union. The crowd numbered about 500, which was large for this relatively early stage of activism in Minnesota. The speakers included some of the now-familiar participants such as Zev Aelony and Vince Hawkinson. Chi Psi fraternity had received official permission to picket the demonstration, and what made this event more memorable and controversial than usual was that things turned ugly with scuffling, burning of anti-war signs, harassing of speakers, and damaging of the sound equipment. The *Daily* ran an editorial decrying the actions of the pro-war faction, as well as a number of letters mainly critical of those disrupting the event.

The level of concern over this thuggish interference with free speech in an academic setting soon rose to the point where the U Senate determined that an investigation was in order because members of Chi Psi and others appeared to have violated the terms of their permit that required them to abide by a statement adopted by the senate in 1963 after harassment of speakers at a rally for Fair Play for Cuba. This reawakened unpleasant memories because Lee Harvey Oswald had belonged to that organization. The level of passion evident at the rally soon began to characterize the investigation itself, as Professor Cooperman termed the disruption "the most severe lack of moral behavior I have ever seen," and members of the frat expressed fears of a developing "witch hunt." Not surprisingly, there was even sharp disagreement over what had actually happened.

Yet another controversy involving the war developed in early 1966 when Staff Sergeant Barry Sadler's song "The Ballad of the Green Berets" became a national hit and held the *Billboard* number one spot for five weeks, a fact that clearly demonstrates the high level of public support for the war at this time. The song, certainly a pedestrian musical offering at best, praised the role of our special forces soldiers in Vietnam and, most disturbingly, ended with a dying soldier's wish that some day his own son would serve in the same outfit. Robin Moore, who co-wrote the piece with Sadler, had also written a popular book that I had read about the US Special Forces. The book was already dated because it described events during our advisory period in Vietnam before the introduction of large US ground units, but it certainly did not leave me with the impression that Vietnam was a place I would ever want to be. The *Daily* ran an op-ed piece that was highly critical of the song as a piece of propaganda that attempted not only to justify but to glorify our efforts in Southeast Asia. Some students wanted the U radio station to stop playing it.

An article in the February issue of *Ramparts* magazine by Donald Duncan, another Vietnam veteran, presented a starkly different perspective on our involvement there. He had been drafted back in the 1950s and served ten years in the army, including a tour of duty during the early phases of the war. Basically, Duncan's views were the exact opposite of those of Sadler and Moore. His experiences led him to conclude that most of our troops, far from seeing their role as one of assisting a people under attack in their noble fight for freedom, disliked and disrespected the Vietnamese, treating them in ways that resulted in mutual contempt or even hatred. He praised the anti-war protesters as people with the best interests of the troops at heart because any effort to shorten the war would reduce the number of soldiers being killed and maimed. The title of his article was a trenchant summary of his viewpoint "The Whole Thing Was A Lie!" Ironically, Duncan had been selected the previous year to brief Defense Secretary McNamara on Special Forces operations in Vietnam. Either he had softened his story out of deference to McNamara's high office or the secretary had turned a deaf ear to news he did care to hear, most likely the latter.

On February 28 Marine Lance Corporal Arthur C. Pederson, Jr., was killed by hostile fire in Thua Thien Province. This is the region that includes Hue, the old imperial capital, and these Northern provinces were always especially dangerous since their proximity to the demilitarized zone (DMZ) made them easy targets for infiltration by regular NVA units. In fact, more American deaths occurred in Thua Thien than in any other province. Arthur was the first of two men from my De La Salle class of 1964 to die in the war. I did not know him, but our yearbook relates that he was from St. Lawrence parish in Southeast Minneapolis and his ambition was "to be a good Catholic."

In March, the Angel Flight Air Force sorority, which had sponsored a Christmas gift program for GIs in December, continued their efforts to support the troops by starting a pen pal program. This resulted in some descriptions in the *Daily* of operations there that were far more graphic than usual for a college paper. One soldier sent a picture of a captured Viet Cong, writing that he was later killed because the orders were to take no prisoners on Search and Destroy missions. Another wrote a description of how his unit wiped out fifty-three of the enemy. Like so many GIs in the RVN, they were counting the days until their return to the states. One sister was puzzled about how to respond: "What do you say—hope you're enjoying the war?" Others said they wanted to do what they could to help improve morale because the guys always told them how much they relied on letters and news from home. One young lady gushed, "It's a lot of fun. Like an interminable blind date." Some GIs requested reading material, so the sorority went on to organize a book drive that resulted in literally a ton of books numbering over twelve thousand volumes and including items as diverse as bibles, *Playboys*, and a medical dictionary from 1906. The Minnesota Air National Guard arranged to fly them to Vietnam sometime later in the month.

In addition to the draft and the war, the papers reported some other more amusing things that were on our minds that winter. The ads for the frequent dances at the union always included the stern advisory: "Girls: No Slacks." One article lamented yet again the most recent changes in Dinkytown, noting that the closing of the Scholar coffeehouse and McCosh's bookstore had "taken away some of Dinkytown's reputation as an artistic center." The writer found consolation in the fact that "while the original, local paintings and folk music of the Scholar have moved elsewhere, reproductions of works by better known artists and performers are readily available in Dinkytown." The Scholar claimed the distinction of probably being the first place Bob Dylan had appeared solo on stage as a folkie, but a former owner said that he ended up banning him because he "drove away customers." Truly, a prophet is without honor in his own country.

The *Daily* ran a story on marijuana use around the U area that concluded it was around but not that big of a deal. One anonymous student offered his view that "a significant number of West Bank people—the CLA-type (College of Liberal Arts)—have tried pot." Garrison Keillor and Jonathan Sisson were the two most prominent student writers on campus back then, carrying on in their own very distinctive ways the proud tradition of Shulman and Heggen. I admired them both. In April, our campus radio station, KUOM, announced plans for a weekly show called "Saturday" hosted by Garrison that would feature "a highly experimental format of using public affairs, cultural misadventures, and avant-garde humor." Garrison had been announcing on KUOM since 1963, but he was to graduate in June and said that he had no plans to work in radio after that.

✦✦✦

Spring quarter, 1966, began with a continuation of events related to the draft and war. The April issue of the *Ivory Tower* included a lengthy piece by Francis Galt on his reasons for resisting the draft in which he explained that even applying for conscientious objector status was against his principles because he felt the government had no right to pass judgment on the sincerity of the voice of his conscience. Fran was soon to become one of the most prominent local draft resistors.

Two days later, the *Daily* announced that materials for the college draft qualification test were now available at local draft boards and the University. They printed two sample questions that were fairly easy, especially for students versed in the skills of taking multiple choice tests. That no books or notes would be allowed was to be expected, but the instructions also included the draconian warning that cheaters would be reported to their local draft boards. Cheating on exams is always a serious matter in college but this might have been the first time it carried a possible death sentence. We were also told that young men taking the test would be fingerprinted, although a U official offered the reassurance that this was "just for identification." The same issue of the paper contained an ad from a company in Brooklyn, New York, for a mail-order book for $3.95 on how to pass the exam. Maybe the first tip was not to bring this book to the test site. The paper also carried a story about Army Basic Training by John Moon, a former *Daily* sports editor now serving in the Army at Fort Leonard Wood, Missouri, who was halfway through his basic. He seemed satisfied with the knowledge he was acquiring and the treatment he was receiving, and also assured us that the process was not all that difficult because the training had to be geared to the men of lowest intelligence. A fellow trainee from Minneapolis observed that "it's just a place where every Army man has to go whether he is a pea-brain or a genius."

The uneasy relationship between "in loco parentis" and the reality of life in the dorms arose again in April when the Student Activities Bureau proposed liberalizing the hours policies for students under the age of twenty-one living in Comstock Hall, one of our women's dorms. The current policy was that they could stay out until midnight, except for Friday and Saturday night when the young women did not have to be home until 2:00 a.m. The possible change was to eliminate curfews for all seniors and some juniors. Dean Williamson made the surprisingly progressive comment that "if a girl is intelligent enough to be here, she should be trusted until she proves otherwise." The open-mindedness of his observation was mitigated, however, by his failure to explain why the U had considered these girls less trustworthy than males, or why the administration would continue to regard freshmen and sophomores with this low level of trust, for there were no restrictions on the hours of male dorm residents of any age. He offered his assurance that the proposal was "definitely not a quick and harebrained notion," illustrating his disinclination to rush into things by noting that he had supported such a change since he became dean in 1941.

A survey of Comstock residents found the majority being in favor of the change. This was the expected result, especially since over half the respondents noted that they had already stayed out all night at least once anyway. The top reason given for these unauthorized excursions was intriguing to say the least: "desire to continue activity." Conservatives could take at least some solace in the assurance of a U official that the privilege could be revoked if a young lady's parents objected.

The new policy was implemented later the same month, and the *Daily* ran a favorable op-ed piece by a male editor, who noted that this change reflected a national trend of colleges lessening restrictions on students' activities. He did point out that the change was not without some drawbacks, such as coeds no longer having the curfew to use as a way of avoiding "extended dates with creeps." The dean might have replied that he believed the girls were intelligent enough to be trusted to come up with more creative excuses. L.F. Snoxell, head of the Disciplinary Counseling Office, also offered his support of the new policy, even though the prospect of altering something that went "all the way back to the Puritans" appeared to leave him rather aghast: "We are living in times fraught with change."

As spring quarter moved along and the date of the draft deferment test drew near, the *Daily* began devoting increased coverage to both the test itself and the larger issues raised by what many regarded as an unwarranted intrusion by the Selective Service into the life of the campus. Colonel Knight was largely unsympathetic to these concerns, stating that "no one will be drafted who should be in school." Echoing the men interviewed for the recent article on boot camp, he also reminded us that "the Army needs intelligent men as well as the less intelligent." He reiterated the now-familiar refrain that to obtain conscientious objector status the applicant had to be opposed to all wars, not just the current one: "Where is the cutoff—Saigon, Paris, Seattle, St. Paul?" It was easy to recognize this as the same old caveat from the Red Scare days of the 1950s: If we did not stop communist aggression wherever it originated, before long they would be at our doorsteps. This was not such a far-fetched proposition for Knight's generation that had lost so many lives defeating two ruthless and fanatical enemies in World War II. For us Boomers, it was a far more dubious assumption. Did questioning the US role in a civil war in a tiny country on the other side of the world amount to appeasement? Were the Viet Cong really cut from the same cloth as the Soviets who had put the intercontintental ballistic missiles (ICBMs) in Cuba?

A university official from the Student Counseling Bureau responded to the question of whether the test was unfair to minorities by admitting that "the test is biased just as college is biased." Actually that response was hard to argue against, except perhaps to point out that two wrongs do not make a right. He said that when students questioned his staff about preparing for the test "we tell them there is nothing to do." He clearly meant in terms of studying for the exam, but this unintentional echo of *Godot* reinforced the growing perception that the whole affair was beginning to resemble a plot from the theater of the absurd.

The local chapter of Students for a Democratic Society announced plans to distribute a "counter test" on the war near the test site. A number of college and university officials and faculty, both here and at other institutions, expressed strong reservations about releasing the class standings of their male students to draft boards. Some also felt uncomfortable about assigning poor grades to their students, knowing that the result could be death in Vietnam. Professor Bayman, Physics, apparently did not accept the proposition that attempting to prepare for the test was futile because he conducted briefing sessions in math and the physical sciences every day for a week in early May. He had held similar classes for students preparing for the draft exam during the early days of the Korean War in 1950. Other U officials said that the only preparation needed was to be "relaxed and in good shape."

Meanwhile, the Selective Service demonstrated that it did not always turn a deaf ear to complaints when it announced in response to numerous nationwide objections that fingerprinting would be optional. U of M officials announced that there would be no fingerprinting at our institution, although students would be required to present positive identification. An official of the U's Selective Service Office (yes, there really was such a place) explained that one reason for the test was to allow students whose lower GPAs might be due to attending an institution with high standards to demonstrate by a high test score that they did indeed deserve to be deferred anyway. The ever-helpful Colonel Knight cautioned, however, that such students might be drafted because their low grades and high test score could be interpreted to mean that they were not working up to their potential.

In our eyes, this threat was yet another example of the draft as punishment, but punishment for what—having the misfortune to come of age during the presidency of a man too stubborn to admit he had made a terrible mistake? After the test was finally administered, one student reported that it had been a tedious and poorly organized affair, beginning with one of the monitors taking forty-five minutes to read the written instructions aloud.

The *Daily* devoted extensive coverage that spring to other issues relating to the draft and the war, such as a speech by Senator Walter Mondale in which he supported the war but expressed concern over the way in which it was distracting the US from other pressing issues, an editorial on Senator Ted Kennedy's proposal for a draft lottery, an antiwar "read-in" organized by poet Robert Bly, and a proposal by Secretary of Defense McNamara on mandatory national service as an alternative to an exclusively military draft. Two "girl reporters" spent a day on bivouac playing war games with some ROTC cadets up at Camp Ripley. Tom Brothen, a CLA junior, wrote an op-ed decrying the brutality of a joint US/ARVN operation code named "county fair" that he had seen described on TV. I did not know Tom then, but less than three years later we would be in basic training together.

I even got my own name in the paper as the recipient of the annual US Army Military History Award at the ROTC annual review. That was because I had received the highest grade the previous quarter in Professor Loehr's American Military History, one of our ROTC classes. The prize was a nice hefty book on US Army operations in the Pacific during World War II. I still have it. Long before the annual review, however, I had decided to drop out of ROTC after sophomore year. Colonel Beard, our commanding officer, was disappointed about this, of course, and asked how I would meet my military obligation. He appeared distressed when I replied that I would serve as an enlisted man if drafted, but I was still a civilian so all he could do was wish me well, shake hands, and say farewell. I always respected him.

Chapter 4
JUNIOR YEAR
UNIVERSITY OF MINNESOTA
1966-67

I continued with fast-food work in the summer of 1966, but switched to the Red Barn, a chain of restaurants much larger than Robby's. I worked at a brand new one up on 49th and Central in Columbia Heights. The building was actually shaped like a barn with a gambrel roof and, even though the chain went out of business over twenty-five years ago, a close observer of commercial architecture can still spot some of these distinctive buildings being used by other businesses, usually some other fast-food outlet. The one over at Oak and Washington is still there with a newer façade, but looking at the profile of the building from the rear, there's the gambrel roof of the barn. We did not have to grind our own hamburger there, but we did make our own fresh French fries and onion rings, starting from scratch with gunny sacks of potatoes and onions.

The food was clearly a step up from Robby's. Our specialty was "dignifried" chicken, and the biggest item on the menu was a Barn-Full of Chicken, which was twelve pieces along with a big scoop of fries in a bright red barn-shaped box. This was not the sumptuous family meal you might expect because, although they were real pieces of chicken rather than nuggets, those pieces were almost comically small. It was very tasty, but I remember being asked more than once where we got such tiny chickens.

We also had a special hamburger, the Big Barney, which was two patties with all the trimmings, including a special sauce that tasted like some sort of seasoned mayonnaise. That one was a special favorite of mine. The new surroundings and co-workers helped to relieve the inevitable tedium of this type of work, but eventually I went back to Robby's because the managers at the barn had a bad habit of scheduling big crews in case business was heavy and then telling some of us to punch out for the day if the volume was less than they had anticipated. We spent a good deal of time with little to do at Robby's, but at least there you could rely on getting in your scheduled number of hours.

I was enjoying movies, music, and especially reading, but I also continued to be bothered by the nagging feeling that my life was far less full than I felt it should be. Part of this was just the normal emotional state of late adolescence, but I really should have been living on campus because that would have forced me out of my shell. I saw the choice of living arrangements in strictly economic terms and thought there was no sense paying for room and board when our home was only four miles from campus. I was hardly alone in my choice; almost half of the undergraduates at the U did live at home, but the stunting effect that decision would have on my personal and social development escaped me at the time.

I was also continuing to nurture a deep resentment toward all things religious, which was remarkably intense considering how central our Catholic church and school had been to our upbringing. I rarely darkened the door of a church for about ten years. This painful decision was less than liberating, however, because Catholic guilt is not as readily discarded as the habit of regular attendance at Sunday mass. I recognize this indoctrination now as the emotional abuse that it was and, as with most instances of abuse, the adults damaging us in this way were doing it because they had the same thing done to them in their earlier years. They felt the lessons they were passing on must be normal and true, and were unable to break the cycle of one generation bequeathing this misery to the next. It fell upon our generation, aided somewhat by the more merciful and liberating teachings of Vatican II, to challenge this dismal view of the human condition, and this was but one area, albeit a major one, where conflicting worldviews would soon expand the normal gap between generations into a chasm.

Even shy young people usually find at least one good friend eventually and, as that summer went by, a soul mate came my way. The problem was that it was an inanimate object. I decided that my earlier misadventure with alcohol might have been just a bad first date and so made another foray into the pleasures of drinking. This time I was smitten, and it was far deeper than just a summer fling. I liked pint cans of Budweiser, and by the time I was about halfway through the second can I was arriving at a place I had visited only rarely for about the last ten years. It was a place where I felt warm, secure, happy, and at peace with the world. I was not shy anymore and enjoyed talking with people. It was a place where I liked myself. For many years, drinking held a very special place in my life and, even in these early days when I was far from being a daily drinker, it was often on my mind. This is not a healthy thing and my enjoyment of secretive drinking was also a danger sign. Mom and Dad never drank much, but Dad always had a pretty good supply in the basement, and I enjoyed sampling those bottles. I clearly remember choking down three or four quick shots of whiskey, reveling in the burn, and just loving the way the world began to seem a few minutes later. As I savor the journey of recovery now I realize that the mistake I made back then was to allow booze to take the place in my life that should have been occupied by people, but alcohol is such a fine temporary antidote for shyness and depression that many of us find it impossible to resist. By the time the remedy has become worse than the original malady, a person has crossed a line into the realm of pathology, but back then I never saw drinking as a problem. Quite the contrary, I saw it as a solution.

***

Interesting events around campus that summer included the reopening of the Scholar coffeehouse. The crumbling Dinkytown building that included its former storefront quarters had been gutted by a fire the previous December. The new location was on the corner of Cedar and Washington on the West Bank where the vacant lot is now next to the building housing Theater in the Round, which at that time was the home of Bimbo's Pizza Emporium and Dance Hall. The lot is vacant because that place burned down too, although, as with the one in Dinkytown, after the coffeehouse had already moved out. Between the Scholar and the Triangle, the West Bank was clearly the center of the increasingly vibrant off-campus music scene. John Koerner, Dave Ray, and Tony Glover, or some combination of those three, appeared regularly, along with the great Leo Kottke and folk artist and historian Maury Bernstein. Another item of note on the arts scene was the Minnesota Centennial Showboat production of *Fashion*, featuring Linda

Kelsey and Loni Anderson in leading roles. Both of these future TV stars were studying Theater Arts at the U.

The *Daily* ran a piece on the drug scene around campus, concluding from anonymous interviews that drug use was around but not widespread enough to be a serious issue. One interviewee gave a straightforward reply to the question of how one gets drugs: "Stand on Cedar Avenue until a friend comes by and ask him." It was indeed no secret that there were more drugs on the West Bank than the East. Another offered the observation that "the difference between the East and West Banks is that if a student sleeps with his girl on the East Bank he sneaks out the back door of the apartment in the morning. If a student sleeps with his girl on the West Bank he greets the milkman in the morning." Even back in 1966 home delivery of milk was pretty much a thing of the past, but as the 1960s moved along the Cedar/Riverside area continued to live up to its reputation as a hotbed of Bohemianism that some would consider notorious, at least when judged by tame Midwestern standards. The East Bank was on Denis Wadley's mind, however, as he wrote an op-ed in the *Daily* on the perennial worry that our beloved Dinkytown was in danger of losing its charm and unique identity to greedy developers and corporate takeovers. He compared the situation to what had been happening in Greenwich Village and the comparison was indeed apt because the architecture and culture of Dinkytown does call to mind a miniature version of the village. The West Bank, on the other hand, could have been called Minneapolis's answer to Haight-Ashbury out in San Francisco, although few of us had heard yet about that scene.

Meanwhile, the cycle of brutal violence that began with the assassination of JFK continued to escalate both at home and abroad, sometimes in strange and frightening ways. Civil rights activist James Meredith was shot and wounded in Mississippi in June. As despicable as this racially motivated assault was, it was hardly unusual for a black man to be attacked in the Deep South, home of the KKK and lynching. But then in July Richard Speck tortured and murdered eight student nurses in Chicago, and in August Charles Whitman killed sixteen and wounded thirty-two by firing sniper-style from a tower at the University of Texas at Austin.

These atrocities were especially disturbing because they happened in our midst, but the violence that was always on our minds was raging in Vietnam. That was the year of the steepest escalation in troop levels as LBJ more than doubled our forces to nearly 400,000 by the end of the year.

Casualties increased even more rapidly, with the total US dead in 1966 topping six thousand, over three times the total for 1965. It seemed that hardly a week went by without a photo of a young local soldier gazing at us from the pages of the Minneapolis paper. These were not the ones being sent over; that probably would have required an entire page each week. No, when you saw one of those photos you knew the young man was dead. Most wore the solemn expression that they had felt suited their new role as a soldier but others, and these were always the hardest to take, greeted the readers with a big, friendly, boyish smile. I could not help but feel regret about these young men, some younger than me, being cut off in their youth. But that sorrow was never without a tinge of dread as well for those of us of draft age, or anyone close to someone eligible for the draft.

The antiwar movement in the Twin Cities continued to gain visibility as seven people were arrested in July for breach of the peace at a small demonstration at 7th and Hennepin in downtown Minneapolis. Police Chief Hawkinson offered the novel explanation that the protestors were arrested because the crowd was beginning to get ugly. The *Daily* ran an editorial questioning why the "ugly" spectators were not the ones incarcerated. One of the protest leaders was charged with violating a city ordinance requiring that an American flag be displayed at all public meetings of more than ten people. It seemed apparent that the police were suppressing free speech by harassment because they disliked the demonstrators' cause, but the hecklers' angry reaction also showed that the officers' feelings were shared by many others.

Another antiwar group that included some University students attempted to gain support for their cause by setting up booths at county fairs around the state. They were also often met with angry reactions from the likes of local VFW posts and the John Birch Society. The same controversy arose on the national level when a Republican congressman from California accused the National Student Association of un-Americanism because of antiwar activities, including sending observers to South Vietnam. These charges were refuted immediately by James Johnson, a former president of MSA and now an NSA officer, as well as Representative Donald Fraser.

Fran Galt was arrested in August so that he could be tried in Iowa for draft evasion. Some of his supporters formed a defense committee chaired by Denis Wadley, who explained their purposes as raising funds for Fran's defense expenses and educating the public on the distinction between being a conscientious objector and claiming the right of non-cooperation. The latter was Galt's position since, as he had explained before, he believed that even applying for conscientious objector (CO) status violated his conscience since that required working with the Selective Service system. Denis, no doubt influenced by post-Vatican II Catholicism, added that the core issue was the right of every individual to follow the promptings of their conscience. The problem there was that the church insisted the conscience must be an "informed" one, which is equivalent to saying that you may indeed follow your conscience as long as it leads you to believe exactly what the church teaches to be true. The federal government's reaction to Fran's position would be essentially the same. I did not share his strict pacifism, but I admired his courage because the penalty for his principled stance would be a federal prison sentence. Issues of conscience aside, was that really worse that a year of combat in Vietnam? Every young man receiving his draft notice would have to answer that question for himself.

***

As junior year began with fall quarter 1966, I was looking forward to courses that would delve deeper into literature and history, my two favorite subjects. I was finished now with most courses that held more marginal interest for me such as military science, the required lab science, and three physical education classes. My courses that fall included the American Literature survey as well as Shakespeare and a year-long sequence covering English literature of the Romantic period. The Romantic lit class was certainly the most demanding literary study I had undertaken so far, but I enjoyed the subject matter greatly, as well as the challenge of being in a course for the first time that included graduate students. Those of us preparing to teach also had our first education courses that year. I found most of these over the next two years far less interesting than literature and history but the one that quarter included a brief introduction to philosophy, which intrigued me because that was my first exposure to the subject.

These courses all required a fair amount of research and writing, as well as a great deal of reading. Even so, I continued to work part-time, but it finally dawned on me that if I was to stay with food service it would be much more convenient to do it right on campus. The pay was the same as Robby's and the Red Barn, and in those days there was such a high demand for part-time workers on campus that just about the only requirements for being hired were having a pulse and being willing to fill out an application.

I was assigned to the main cafeteria in Coffman Union, where about six of us had the duties of bringing stainless steel trays of food from the kitchen to the steam tables on the food line, as well as serving the customers coming through the line. The offerings looked pretty good to me, even though the quality of union food was one of the perennial complaints around campus. Unlike Robby's, however, where we were free to eat as much as we could stand, at Coffman we were not allowed to sample the wares at all. If we wanted to eat, we had to punch out, go through the line, and pay full price. Despite that drawback, I did enjoy spending time with the other students working there. They were a friendly bunch and we often chatted and played the card game Hearts before our shift began.

I even went out on a few dates with a co-worker; a nice Irish girl from St. Paul named Bernie. Neither one of us had much experience at the dating game but we enjoyed each others' company, even though she was a very conservative Catholic. Before long it became clear that nothing serious was going to develop between us, but we stayed friends for as long as we worked together. There was no heartache this time as with Glenda, and I hope I did not cause any for Bernie. I don't believe I did because it just wasn't that kind of relationship.

During the second week of the quarter, Selective Service student deferment applications for undergrads were distributed in the court of the Architecture Building. This was a form I needed to complete now that I was no longer in ROTC, but before the process even began a controversy arose over a sentence on the IBM card application that read: "With the submission of this form I authorize the University of Minnesota to supply the draft board with any other information about my record that is deemed necessary." Howie Kaibel and the MSA leadership urged us not to apply until this statement was clarified. A U official said that signing the form was optional, but, of course, so was submitting the form in the first place. Could the lack of a signature lead to the same result as no application at all, namely a 1-A draft status? Again, the troublesome question of the extent to which academic institutions were expected to cooperate with the Selective Service was coming into play. A U official warned that a delay beyond the current week in submitting the application could result in an induction notice. SDS members passed out leaflets at the distribution site, adding to the anxiety and confusion. About 15% of the applicants ultimately refused to sign the release form, but I felt there was no point in doing anything that could result in the loss of student deferment status. The SSS already had such intimidating power over our lives that it seemed crazy to give them an opening for changing my status over such a petty thing.

The logical choices were to either go all the way like Fran Galt, which my conscience did not lead me to do, or go along with the system. The need to voice any objections to going to Vietnam before accepting induction was made clear by a report from the Committee to End the War in Vietnam of three soldiers at Fort Hood who were facing court martial for refusing to go. I was not surprised when Professor Sibley offered to assist them. He continued to maintain his hour-long weekly silent vigil outside the Armory, which by now had inspired the formation of a Weekly Silent Vigil Committee. The professor was now part of a group that often numbered about fifty.

The *Daily* ran a well-reasoned op-ed piece on the need for a "particular war" objection clause in the draft law, although we all knew the chances of that happening were slim to nil. The reasoning here was that this clause made sense for wars where the US had not actually been attacked. Men should not be compelled to fight in a "discretionary" war. The highlight of the anti-war activities that fall was a teach-in at Coffman on November 7 that included so many speakers and discussion groups that it used much of the space in the union for most of the day. There had been a forum like this on campus two years before and they were common now on campuses around the country because many of those who questioned or opposed the war felt that views contrary to those of the government and military leadership were not receiving sufficient attention. I did not go but the attendance was impressive, especially for a weeknight. Reports stated that the speakers blasted the war of course, but also racism, Ronald Reagan for his inflammatory right-wing rhetoric, and even liberals for insufficient zeal in their opposition to the war and treatment of minorities. Again, the linking of opposition to the war with the cause of opposing domestic racism was notable and a portent of things to come.

Among campus issues other than the war that fall were the plans to build a Burger King in Dinkytown. Lovers of the traditional Dinkytown were particularly upset that it would occupy the former site of Bob Dylan's early performances at the Scholar, even though the building was now a crumbling rat-infested ruin. An op-ed in the *Daily* used the intriguing term "mild crisis" to characterize the situation. The contrast between the tepid objections over this intrusion and the heated conflict over the proposed new Red Barn in Dinkytown in 1970 is a perfect illustration of how the times changed in three and one-half years, and the primary catalyst for that dramatic shift was the war. The *Daily* also ran a story on some male high school students in Texas who belonged to a rock group and grew their hair out Beatles-style to look the part. A judge ruled they had to get haircuts before they could attend school again, and a left-leaning *Daily* op-ed writer equated this mandate with the requirement that male students applying for a deferment sign a permission statement allowing release of their academic records to the Selective Service. The writer warned that "both are struggles against a Behemoth conditioning citizens for a totalitarian society."

It was certainly true that long hair on young males was one of the things that right-wingers found particularly galling about the counterculture, and it was also a sign of the times that a left-winger would equate any unwarranted intrusion on personal freedom with the biggest such intrusion of all, the draft. Despite the slow rise of the counterculture, however, it was apparent that many students still took care to be well-dressed and conform because the *Daily* ran a fashion issue each quarter featuring photos of young men and women who were clearly not on their way to any sort of demonstration. Jon Sisson started writing columns that fall under the pseudonym of Jeets Cohen, a zany dilettante, which I found particularly entertaining. It was a relief to have any sort of break from current events, and Jeets, a hilarious caricature of a common type around any college, was blissfully oblivious to anything outside the world of culture and the arts.

In mid-October, on the weekend before the first mid-quarter for our education course, I received a phone call from Glenda. It was certainly unexpected—she and her current boyfriend had told me not to call her anymore, but now she had a problem. She had not been keeping up with her studies and asked if I could help her prepare for the exam. I was uncertain how to do that because there was a good deal of material, but I brought her over to the house and did my best. That resulted in more frustration than anything else for both of us; she did not seem to be familiar with much of it at all. After an hour or so we gave up and talked a little about us instead. She made it clear again that there was no future together for us. She was serious about her guy and some things she said made me suspect that a fair amount of drinking was involved as well, although I was never positive about that. She did end up marrying John, although eventually it ended in divorce. In some ways it was good for me to have our relationship, or lack thereof, clarified, although it was hard at the time. I think even then I knew in my heart that the last thing I needed was a moody girl who liked to drink—that was too much like me. We would have encouraged the worst in each other rather than bringing out the best.

Like most young people, I was confused and uncertain about my future, but one thing I was sure of by now was that I had no interest at all in serving in Vietnam. Since I had finished with ROTC, the draft and how to avoid it had become one of my primary concerns. These feelings were common among male students, of course, so in November the MSA sponsored a Draft Information Week. The first speaker was a figure I had developed a strong distaste for, Colonel Robert Knight. He continued his practice of attempting to make light of a situation we saw as deadly serious by stating that men who tried to extend their student status beyond four years by frequent changes of major would "rather switch than fight," a reversal of the slogan for a current ad campaign for Taryeton cigarettes. Just by coincidence, that happened to be John Berryman's favorite brand. He also explained that anyone who had obtained a deferment was subject to the draft up to age thirty-five, although it was highly unlikely that a man older than twenty-five would be called up. He dismissed the proposal for a draft lottery as "a lot of hooey" and offered this laconic advice as the best way to retain your 2-S status: study.

In December, the *Daily* printed a piece on how the Scholar was faring since relocating to the West Bank. The owner-manager, Mike Justin, was pleased with the larger crowds, which he credited to more space and regular appearances by musicians such as twelve-string virtuoso Leo Kottke. As with Dinkytown, however, concerns that a beautiful and fragile bohemian culture was being threatened by the crass and unrelenting forces of commercialism and conformity were never far from the minds of those old enough to remember the halcyon days of four or five years ago. Carol, a former waitress, ruefully observed that the "Joe-college crowd" had taken over what used to be a gathering place for campus artists and intellectuals. These newcomers preferred commercialized offerings such as Peter, Paul, and Mary-type music rather than a performance by a classical flamenco guitarist. Linda, a current waitress, complained that these young interlopers knew nothing about music and usually only came to hear their friends play. Mike agreed that the "campus beats" now hung out at other West Bank establishments. But he probably did not much miss patrons who would spend hours nursing a cup of espresso and smoking pipes and cigarettes while they played chess and discussed art and literature. Carol had a more pessimistic assessment, lamenting that the "the days of the beatnik coffeehouse are over." But one generation must always make way for the next and the West Bank was soon to be known as the nexus of Minneapolis's hippie culture.

As 1966 drew to a close we enjoyed the eagerly anticipated second airing of *A Charlie Brown Christmas*. It was a treat just to see the beloved characters moving around and to hear them speaking, but after we grew accustomed to that it also began to dawn on us just how special this production really was. Schultz, in addition to vetoing the idiotic laugh-track that normally accompanied programs the networks classified as comedies, insisted on artistic control over the entire show and, as with the strip, his deft mastery of minimalism and the haunting poignancy of a message as simply stated as it was profound left us longing to see it again. In the days before home video, that wait would be a full year. But that holiday season also brought us another instant classic, *How the Grinch Stole Christmas*, combining the unique visual and verbal talents of our childhood friend, Dr. Suess, with the voice of the man who had scared our pants off in the old Universal horror films that we had seen rerun on TV while growing up—Boris Karloff. This unlikely combination of talents resulted in another holiday treat that was welcomed with love at first viewing and widely enjoyed every Christmas season since then.

I worked as a Christmas Assistant for a couple of weeks that year down at the main post office. These jobs paid much more than the food service wages I was accustomed to, and they were considered hard to get. You had to pass a short exam, but the postal service had a well-established tradition of cronyism and you usually also had to know someone. Fortunately for me, Dad had worked at the post office for decades and so I got the job. Many of my co-workers were University athletes. What I remember most about it was a huge room about the size of a city block that took up most of one of the levels of the building. The floor was covered with hundreds of workstations where clerks sorted letters and packages. Conveyer belts moved mail around all over the place and some were even sloped to carry packages back and forth between levels. The whole scene looked unreal, like something out of a movie or from the imagination of a fantasy artist. We did the best we could but two weeks is not even enough time to begin training a person for working in such a complicated place, let alone to make them useful employees. This experience was as brief as it was unique, and when the holidays come around each year I still think about it, especially when I see a scene of elves working on the massive amount of mail received by Santa.

★★★

As 1967 began, my classes were continuations of the same sequences but with the addition of a fifth course in American history, the perfect companion to the American literature sequence. The English Romantic Poetry continued to be my favorite, however, and most of winter quarter was devoted to Wordsworth. The beauty of his versification was enthralling and some of his major themes were issues I was trying to sort out in my own life. I shared his fascination with childhood, but not his belief in a preexistent state. A major reason for the emotional tumult of adolescence, even its late stages, is the need to work through the mourning process over the loss of childhood. Looking back, I realize that I had not yet completed that transition because my tendency toward introversion, greatly reinforced by being the subject of bullying in grade school, was preventing me from the level of peer interaction this process requires. I was spending too much time alone and looking backwards rather than toward the future, as well as becoming fonder of drinking than is healthy. I tried to emulate the great poet's love of communing with nature as a way of fulfilling the spiritual needs formerly met by religious beliefs, hoping this could help lighten "the burthen of the mystery" for me as well. I relished the happy irony in the fact that the work he saw as the prelude to his masterpiece turned into the masterpiece itself. I have had many favorite poets over the years, but he has always been near the top of the list.

By this time the war had escalated to a level we would never have imagined two years earlier, with over 400,000 troops in-country and more than 6,000 US dead in 1966. Although dwarfed by the massive numbers of World War II, it was now painfully clear that we were in our greatest conflict since "the big one." The Selective Service announced that the draft test would be given again on campus in Spring Quarter for those who had not taken it before. I still had no need to take it because my GPA alone was high enough to qualify me for a student deferment. In March, a congressman from South Carolina warned that student deferments could end when the current draft law expired at the end of June if students continued to demonstrate against the government's war and draft policies. Rather than dismiss this statement as the ham-handed threat that it was, the *Daily* recommended that any planned demonstrations be delayed until July. This seemed like a disappointingly timid position for a student newspaper to be taking, especially since our campus was hardly a hotbed of the antiwar movement, but it does demonstrate the level of fear that the threat of the draft could instill.

On February 22 the US military began the massive operation in the area northwest of Saigon known as Junction City. By the time it ended in mid-May our forces had demonstrated decisively that the Viet Cong had no chance against our troops when we drove through their traditional enclaves with large formations supported by massive artillery support and air power. The communists' persistence was always tempered with a healthy streak of realism and so, tacitly acknowledging that their supply caches and top administrative units were no longer safe in the RVN, they moved these vital elements of their forces across the border into Cambodia where US forces were strictly forbidden to follow. And so yet again we had won a hollow victory and David had managed to prevail over Goliath. But another increasingly familiar pattern also repeated itself as the US command and our political leaders portrayed Junction City as a huge American victory because of the kill ratio and the number of enemy weapons and supplies destroyed.

At the end of February Senator Eugene McCarthy presented an address at our campus Newman Center, offering his professorial assessment that the government's justification for its policies in Vietnam "doesn't stand the test of any objective inquiry." I always had a high regard for McCarthy, even though he certainly did tend to react to opinions differing from his own with Brahmin dismissiveness. That did not bother me because he was usually right, meaning I agreed with him. Unlike Professor Sibley or Fran Galt, McCarthy was clearly not a pacifist, stating that in previous wars the US had been "not only righteous, but right." We were also on common ground there. At this point, the US actions he suggested were a halt to the bombing of the north and a partial troop withdrawal. These may seem like remarkably mild suggestions coming from someone who was soon to become one of the most outspoken and articulate opponents of US policies in Vietnam, but it serves as a valuable reminder that antiwar sentiment developed only gradually as it became more and more apparent that our goals in the RVN were unobtainable. Also, of course, McCarthy was of the generation that lived and fought through World War II.

Tensions over the draft continued in March as LBJ's commission on reforming it issued proposals that managed to accomplish the seemingly impossible: uniting SSS and MSA officials in opposition to the report. The essence of the recommendations was to abolish all student deferments and switch to a lottery draft system. Colonel Knight criticized a proposal to drastically reduce the number of draft boards by about 90%, fearing that such a draconian change would do away with any "personal touch" between young men and their local boards. It was often difficult to tell whether he was being serious. The lottery system, of course, was to be adopted in less than three years, but the *Daily* was even more radical in its editorial proposal to change to an all-volunteer army, something that was also to come to pass in about six years.

✷✷✷

As spring quarter began it was clear that antiwar activities were escalating just as rapidly as the war itself. Early April brought Vietnam Week, featuring fewer programs than the teach-in of the previous fall, but more encouragement to activism. The highlight was an opportunity to become active immediately by participating in what was expected to be a massive antiwar rally that Friday at the United Nations in New York City (NYC). The send-off for those making the bus trip out to the east coast was to be at a rally in front of Coffman Union on Thursday. There was also a smaller rally in front of Bridgeman's in Dinkytown on Tuesday with a crowd of about two hundred. The *Daily* described it as quite a low-key affair with many in the crowd enjoying ice cream cones in the mild spring weather.

About one hundred people from the U rode in a three-bus caravan driving twenty-six hours straight through to NYC. There they became part of a crowd estimated at anywhere from 100,000 to 250,000. One notable feature of the event was that the speakers included Dr. King and Stokely Carmichael, who described both the draft and racism as symptoms of American totalitarianism. An increasingly common theme of those opposing the war was that, in addition to being immoral and a violation of international law, it was also a reflection of American racism since a common perception was that a disproportionate number of young men being drafted and sent into combat were black. This was seen as an especially egregious injustice since they did not enjoy de facto equality in the US because of persistent racism perpetuated by a society that had never fully accepted the outcome of the Civil War. Dr. King had now made this a central theme in his ongoing struggle, voicing it clearly in his "Beyond Vietnam" speech in NYC's Riverside Church earlier in the month.

In some respects this seemed unfair because LBJ had incurred substantial political risk by proposing and supporting the legislation that finally put the full power of the federal government behind the effort to secure voting and other civil rights for black citizens. But he was also the primary instigator of the conflict in Vietnam and that was how he was perceived then and is most often remembered now. The rapidly increasing shrillness of the resistance, of course, was met with equally recalcitrant opposition from those who saw them as communist sympathizers or dupes and promoters of domestic anarchy. Many of the pro-war crowd were the same people who seemed to go through life obsessed with the fear that blacks were trying to take over. There were always numerous American flags displayed at rallies supporting government policies and the implication was apparent that those not supporting those policies were disloyal. That a Viet Cong flag sometimes made an appearance at anti-war events only exacerbated the situation. The fog of war that had settled over Vietnam in the Ia Drang Valley in late 1965 had now enveloped the domestic conflict as well, and in war the enemy can do no right. America was at war in Vietnam, but she was also at war with herself. The violence and thirst for vengeance that soon overpowers the force of reason when the fateful decision is made to "let slip the dogs of war" would continue to play an expanding role on the domestic front as well and, on both fronts, the outcome was a question that could only be answered by the slow and painful passage of time.

On a lighter note, the fascination with hallucinogenic drugs and all things psychedelic was also reaching the heartland, as illustrated by a *Daily* story on the Mellow Yellow craze, something that today would be termed an "urban myth." The story was that if you scraped the inside of a banana peel, baked the resulting residue, and then smoked it you would experience a marijuana-like high. One popular pastime of the 1960s was to parse the lyrics of hit songs for drug references, and of course many people felt that getting high from smoking banana peels was the subject of "Mellow Yellow," the Donovan song from the previous year. To me, Donovan always sounded like he was on such a natural high that he would have no need for drugs, but the story was remarkably persistent and there were always folks around who would swear that it had worked for them. It probably had for some people because the placebo effect led them to believe that it would, but the fad faded away as soon as it became apparent that it was mostly just a waste of time. The reporter did some digging, however, interviewing a professor of pharmacology and some students, including "two hippies," who had microwaved some banana peel residue and smoked it in a campus lunchroom. The conclusion was that the effort was just not worth any mild buzz that might result, but the experimenters seemed to agree that at least it was fun trying.

The struggle for racial justice was also on our minds that spring as Dr. King delivered a speech on the St. Paul campus in which he reiterated his now-familiar theme linking the "three basic evils of racism, poverty, and war" that were plaguing America as well as the entire world. He regarded those dissenting against the war as the soldiers' best friends. The *Daily* ran an op-ed piece by Lucien "Scotty" Stone, an MSA senator who seemed to have assumed the role of the leading angry young black man on campus, in which he acknowledged some of Dr. King's accomplishments but also criticized him for being too close to the white liberal establishment. Stone said that to achieve credibility with Negroes (his term) in the ghettos Dr. King would have to recognize that the goals of the Black Power movement were legitimate. He did not discuss the fact that the methods and rhetoric of that movement were often at odds with Dr. King's unwavering commitment to nonviolent methods. Stone's piece was a reflection of a growing feeling among young blacks that centuries of slavery followed by another century of domestic terrorism against blacks, mainly in the South but with complicity from the North, was long enough. Like the people protesting the war, the activists for racial justice were coming to realize that working within the system to try to change it was not producing results, at least not at what they felt was an acceptable pace. The Black Panthers had been formed the previous October.

Some MSA officials found themselves in the middle of a drama with black militants three weeks later in May when several members of Students of Racial Progress (STRAP) along with Stokely Charmichael "stormed," to use the *Daily's* term, into the MSA offices in Coffman demanding immediate payment of Charmichael's fee for a speech he had given the previous evening before he left town. An MSA representative told them that no such arrangements had been made and that payment that day was impossible, which anyone at all familiar with the U's cumbersome process for issuing checks could verify was not just a subterfuge. The belligerent visitors, obviously looking for trouble and attempting to portray the situation as just one more example of racial oppression, began verbally abusing anyone who tried to explain things to them and announced their intention to tear up the MSA offices. A Mrs. Elam, the vice-president of STRAP, confronted Joe Kroll, another student official, and threatened to cut him up with a razor blade. Charmichael also needed a ride to the airport and refused an offer of that service from the director of the Student Activities Bureau because he was white. A black student activities official then agreed to drive the car. Another participant in the heated discussion was the president of STRAP, Scotty Stone. This incident was totally foreign to the culture of our campus, but in only a month it would be obvious that it had been an early warning that another front in the war was about to move from words to guns and fire.

My schedule required me to devote nearly all of my time to studies and working in the Coffman cafeteria, but it was impossible to ignore the increasing level of tension on campus that spring. Even so, a sociology class conducted a survey to try to determine why things were relatively peaceful here compared to Berkeley. Might it have been because everywhere was peaceful compared to Berkeley?

Meanwhile, antigovernment protestors found another target for their wrath when a CIA recruiter visited the campus to conduct job interviews in Johnston Hall. They held a noisy rally on the front steps, but the pro-CIA spectators were equally loud and numerous. The ACLU placed ads in the *Daily* offering advice on avoiding the draft, while the Army published ads with its own solution to that problem: enroll in Officer Candidate School. The SSS announced that the draft test was being cancelled, at least for the following fall, with Colonel Knight speculating that the reason was that "the darn thing wasn't serving a worthwhile purpose." A more troubling announcement was that most graduate school deferments probably would be cancelled in the near future. Our troop level in Vietnam was rapidly approaching the half-million mark and, with tours of duty limited to one year, the need for more soldiers was increasing just as fast.

As the academic year drew to a close at the beginning of June, the Six Day War began and ended in the Middle East. I remember sharing the common feeling of amazement at the rapid success of the Israeli forces, although at the time it was not apparent how significant the brief conflict would be for the future of Middle Eastern affairs. The *Daily* attempted to be even-handed in its coverage by running a number of highly opinionated pieces on each side of the issue. It was impossible to ignore the stark contrast between the brevity of that war and the seemingly endless one we were conducting in Vietnam. Since the birth of Israel was one result of the holocaust and World War II, I felt the tiny state had a right to exist and to defend its existence, but the truth was that most of us were so focused on Vietnam that a war lasting less than a week in a part of the world that we knew so little about seemed like a sideshow.

Our president, O. Meredith Wilson, had announced his retirement and the *Daily* conducted a final interview in which he attributed much of the current national unrest to the increased educational opportunities of the past twenty years, largely due to the GI Bill. He felt this had made groups that had been treated unfairly in our society more aware of this fact. This observation made sense to me, but he also supported the US policy in Vietnam. Even though this was the most common stance among the World War II generation, I found it disappointing that a scholar in his position would not be more enlightened. It lent credibility to the claims of the resistance that the heads of our colleges and universities were among the leaders who could not be trusted.

Chapter 5
SENIOR YEAR
UNIVERSITY OF MINNESOTA
1967-68

Once again, I welcomed a change of pace over the summer of 1967 from a heavy course load at the U. With Dad's help, I had been hired as a temporary worker at the Post Office for the summer, thus carrying on a family tradition. My grandfather, Jesse James Atkinson, had worked there until he passed away at the young age of forty-six in 1931. My dad and my uncle Jim both worked there for years, and my cousin Jim also had worked there for a short time. The main job divisions were carriers, clerks, and mail handlers. I was hoping to be a carrier, both for the exercise and because that is what all my relatives had been. I started the Monday after finals week with a couple weeks of training and orientation. They took us over to the Farmers' Market to practice driving a mail truck with the steering wheel on the right-hand side. One of the training days was at the Downtown Station, which was right in the Main PO, and this was especially interesting to me because that is where my dad and uncle had worked after they had acquired enough seniority to bid successfully on two of the coveted downtown routes. Uncle Jim was still there, in fact, and it was a real novelty to spend a day at work with my godfather.

After training, I was pleased with my assignment as a substitute carrier, and I was all over the place in Minneapolis and the surrounding suburbs that summer, wherever the absence of a regular carrier made a sub necessary. Some of the stations I remember were in the Camden area of North Minneapolis, Dinkytown, Plymouth, Edina, Bloomington, and Columbia Heights. The Central Avenue Branch was my favorite because it was close to home and Northeast was the area of the city I knew best. I mentioned that to the supervisors when I was at that branch but everything at the PO went by seniority, and a sub, having no seniority, went wherever he was sent. I know of no better way of getting to know a neighborhood than by carrying the mail there, and I explored a good deal of previously unknown territory that summer.

The first day on any given route was the most challenging, so it was always good to be assigned to the same one for a week or two while the regular carrier was on vacation. The only real problem I had was messing up some deliveries in an area of west Bloomington that had some very similar street names, which, of course, resulted in some complaints from residents. I remember being unhappy because Dad talked to me about it. It did not occur to me at the time that I was probably being given preferential treatment because of his connections at the PO, and that this informal reminder of the need for accuracy was a substitute for the normal complaint report being placed in my personnel file. Dad and I never did have any truly serious falling outs, however, and I took the correction seriously. It was better to be late returning to the station, if that was necessary, than to deliver mail incorrectly. Besides, taking more than the allotted time on a route once in a while helped to make the regular carrier look good. In addition to the outdoor work during summer and the interesting variety of duties, the most attractive feature of all was that this job paid about four times as much per hour as my food service work. It was the best summer job I ever had.

Events continued to unfold at a rapid pace, with popular music fully participating. The Beatles released the long-awaited *Sgt. Pepper's Lonely Hearts Club Band* in early June, and music would never be the same. *Rubber Soul* had introduced a type of music we had never heard before, and *Revolver* carried it further, but it was *Sgt. Pepper* that brought it into its full, strange, and glorious bloom. Every track was a unique thing of beauty, all leading up to "A Day in the Life," a devastating portrait of the angst and seeming futility of modern life concluding with an ominous, sustained reverberating chord that might well leave the listener wondering what the point was of trying to go on in such a bleak environment. But the song itself also provided that point in the form of a hallucinogenic escape when the narrator had a smoke, got high, and then invited the listener to join him. This was their variation on psychologist and writer Timothy Leary's famous three-step method for finding a better, inner space as an alternative to all the nonsense being foisted on the world by governments and other authority figures: "Turn on, tune in, drop out." Instead of fighting it, leave it for a place where it was impossible for the fools tormenting you to follow.

Drugs other than alcohol were not for me at that point, but digging the music was in itself enough to partake in a culture that was foreign and inaccessible to our parents' generation. Not only did most of them dislike it but they were also incapable of understanding it. Were we willing to put aside our adolescent smugness long enough to try to explain it to them? Of course not, but if such an explanation was possible there would be no need for the art, and they would not have listened anyway.

The four lads who had been leading us to new places ever since we first heard the opening riff of "I Want to Hold Your Hand" about four years earlier had finally reached nirvana and brought us along for the ride. They, along with Dylan, were the leading gurus of this new type of high art that rock music had become, and they would be joined over the next several years by a host of other artists who would produce a body of work that would have been inconceivable just a few years earlier in the largely fallow popular music environment of the early 1960s. Rock had reached its high-water mark.

Dylan characteristically ignored the psychedelic craze with an artistic shift just as dramatic as going electric at Newport two years earlier. Following his motorcycle accident in the summer of 1966 he had retreated into a long period of withdrawal dedicated to physical recovery and artistic reinvention. Along with his touring band, the five musicians and singers who would later dub themselves The Band, Dylan holed up in tranquil West Saugerties, New York, to write and record music. Many of these sessions were in a makeshift studio set up in the basement of the nondescript salmon-hued house they nicknamed Big Pink, and as they jammed and explored free of the pressure of deadlines or contracts to produce records it seems as though many of their pot-infused musical meanderings became almost séances conjuring up the spirits of farmers, pioneers, soldiers, sailors, rounders, hobos, and drunks from America's past. The presence of brass and organ lent a distinctive and highly atmospheric mournful air to many of the tracks in a haunting style somewhat reminiscent of a street-corner Salvation Army band. As they intended, these sessions were not publicized other than by word-of-mouth among fans, but Dylan took a break in the fall of 1967 to return to NYC and record *John Wesley Harding*, an album incorporating some of the music resulting from the wonderfully prolific collaboration at Big Pink. There is no more striking evidence of Dylan's unyielding dedication to the call of his own inner muse than the stark contrast between the beautifully spare instrumentation of this unexpected collection and the equally masterful and ornate psychedelic experiments of *Sgt. Pepper*.

That was the Summer of Love, when the emerging counterculture quickly coalesced into a way of life readily identified by a distinctive type of music, dress, slang, and lifestyle. But above all else it was a new way of viewing life itself, a way of welcoming openness to cultures and philosophies that were foreign to those we had come to know during our earlier adolescence in the Eisenhower and even the Kennedy years. "Do your own thing" was perhaps the most common mantra. Altered states of consciousness were a primary way, as Aldous Huxley had explained, of flinging open the doors of perception to all these new possibilities, but this was about far more than drugs. Of course, the draft and the war were the very antithesis of these values, and there can be no doubt that opposition to these despised government policies was a catalyst that caused normal youthful rebellion to explode into anger and resistance to nearly any directive or guidance from someone older than us. "Never trust anyone over thirty" was another popular catchphrase.

The Summer of Love was ushered in with considerable fanfare by the Monterey Pop festival in the middle of June, featuring an amazing list of top performers that remains second only to Woodstock two years later. Equally breathtaking was the attendance: somewhere between sixty and ninety thousand. More gradual, but also more significant, was the arrival of some 100,000 young people in San Francisco for that memorable summer, drawn there to both experience and help define this new way of life. Since communal sharing, including free love, was an integral part of the new ethos, they also came to experience each other. By the time most of them returned to their homes and colleges in late summer the counterculture was well-defined. To be able to say you were in Haight-Ashbury, or the "Hashberry," during the summer of '67 was a sign of status that was always claimed by far more people than actually made it out there. But, then again, the important thing was your state of mind, not your physical location, and perhaps even more tantalizing than the drugs and sexual abandon was the belief that anyone could be free if they chose to be. As Jimi Hendrix asked, "Are you experienced?" Whether or not they had experimented with drugs, after that summer, there were young people all over the country who did not want to have to answer that blunt query in the negative.

It was the best and the worst of times, for that was also the Long Hot Summer of riots in the black urban ghettos of most of America's major cities. The worst were in Detroit, but during June and July, 159 of these uprisings exploded in poor black neighborhoods from coast to coast. The ones in Minneapolis were in the second half of July, precipitated by an altercation between two young black women in the crowds downtown following the Aquatennial torchlight parade. One of them shared her account of the incident with me many years later when we were coworkers at the University. The intervention of white police officers quickly transformed the situation into a racial confrontation, providing the spark that ignited tensions that had been smoldering for years in the black community. There were three major incidents over a two-week period resulting in numerous injuries but no deaths.

Other than lingering fear and anger both on the North Side and in the city as a whole, the most visible legacy of the affrays was the empty burned-out shells of a number of small businesses along Plymouth Avenue, many of them owned by Jewish merchants. This accelerated the migration of Minneapolis's Jewish population to the suburbs, primarily St. Louis Park, leaving a bleak vista of boarded-up storefronts along the avenue for years to come.

The *Daily* interviewed a Negro (still the most common term then) University student who attributed much of the black anger to mistreatment by a police force that was almost exclusively white. He felt our force was just as racist as those in the south, but was better at disguising it. Actually, that was a fair characterization of many white Minnesotans, not just the urban police forces. As demonstrated by the virulent anti-Semitism Minneapolis had been known for only a couple of decades before, beneath the "Minnesota Nice" façade we were hardly a paragon of racial and ethnic tolerance.

Another result of the disturbances was the presence of heavily armed National Guard patrols in the ghettos across the country, providing a modicum of safety to the residents but also reinforcing a perception among the more militant that they were victims of oppression by a police state. The similarity in dress and weaponry between these soldiers and the ones we saw in the news reports from Vietnam made it seem more apparent than ever that, as Dr. King had been bearing witness to for several months now, the struggles at home and abroad truly were two fronts of the same war.

The most notable University event that summer was the appointment of Malcolm Moos as president. He was a political scientist whose background included the intriguing credential of serving as President Eisenhower's chief speech writer for the final two years of his tenure in the White House. He had written much of Ike's farewell address in which he warned of the dangers of the powerful influence of the "military-industrial complex" on national policy. Coming from the greatest American military commander of the twentieth century, these words had been difficult to ignore, but the fear of advancing communism was even greater, and in Kennedy's magnificent inaugural address less than one week later our new commander in chief pledged that "only when our arms are sufficient beyond doubt can we be certain beyond doubt that they will never be employed." This was the familiar doctrine of mutual-assured destruction as the best deterrent to nuclear war, but now, six years later in 1967, what about a limited conventional engagement with those limits still undefined and no end in sight? Many of us suspected that the military-industrial complex bore a large share of the blame for the mess in Vietnam, and the fact that Moos had given an early warning of the dangers inherent in its well-funded influence lent him a considerable amount of credibility. He also seemed a bit more approachable and self-effacing than the unapologetically old-school Wilson, who had lost stature in my eyes because of his support for the war.

The local anti-war effort continued as several groups and individuals opposed to the war organized a series of projects they termed Minnesota Vietnam Summer. This was part of a loose national coalition of similar efforts with a headquarters office in Cambridge, Massachusetts. They called these efforts a "teach-out" because the Minnesota groups' goal was to reach out to neighborhoods surrounding the campus to talk with the residents about how they regarded the war. In the middle of August the participants reported that a little more the half of the people they had surveyed voiced at least some level of disapproval for the current government policies in Southeast Asia. The *Daily* had periodically published letters from soldiers in Vietnam criticizing those working against the war, so it was heartening to see a brief one from a Specialist Freeman encouraging the protestors and assuring them that thousands of troops serving against their will were looking forward to joining their ranks soon as civilians.

Events of August included the assassination of George Lincoln Rockwell, leader of the American Nazi Party, by a former member of his own organization. It was difficult to muster any grief for such a shameless bigot, but the shooting still contributed to the steadily rising level of national tension, which was increasingly manifesting itself in acts of murderous violence. I think most of us breathed a deep sigh of relief when it was announced that the shooter was a white man with a grudge against his former leader.

The film *Bonnie and Clyde* was released that month, employing many of the same techniques as the art-house cinema I had been attending since starting at the U. It seemed like a giant step toward serious filmmaking for the American industry. The outlaws' early exploits were portrayed as an almost playful Robin Hood-like reaction to the desperation and ennui of their Depression-era poverty, with Earl Scruggs's banjo virtuosity featured on the soundtrack, inevitably bringing to mind the silliness of *The Beverly Hillbillies*. These high jinks ended abruptly as the second half of the film included graphic portrayals of violence, ending with a protracted scene of the bodies of the title characters being torn apart by a barrage of machine-gun fire. Director Arthur Penn employed the familiar New Wave technique of ending his story *in medias res* with no dénouement, and the final scene ended with no commentary other than a slow pan shot of the two bloodied corpses. The over-kill of the lawmen's barrage could be seen as an allusion to the massive amount of ordnance the US was employing in Vietnam, as well as the increasing frequency of resorting to guns to settle problems on the home front.

In early September Nguyen Van Thieu was elected president of South Vietnam, an office he held until the communist victory in 1975. He would prove to be just as corrupt and largely ineffective as Diem, retaining his position only because of US support.

By late summer I had become comfortable with my mail carrier duties. The daily routine began with punching in at 6:00 a.m., followed by three hours of sorting the mail for the route I would be carrying that day. That mail had been sorted into bundles by route by clerks in the main office downtown. The process of organizing it for delivery was called "casing" because each route in a station would have a case made up of pigeonholes, or slots, one for each delivery address on the route. These slots were ordered in the sequence that the carrier would walk the route while making his deliveries. You could first survey a case to understand the logic of how the route was ordered, making the sorting faster and easier. Once all the mail had been cased it was pulled and bound into bundles called "splits," usually between eight and fifteen per route. Back then the only routes provided with a post office (PO) vehicle were the parcel post ones and the "mounted" letter routes where the postal inspectors had determined that the distances between addresses were great enough to make motorized delivery the most efficient. That was why the jeeps had the steering wheel on the right-hand side. I only drove mounted routes a few times, but the first rule was to shift the vehicle into park before you leaned over to put the mail in the box.

A station would have walk-out routes surrounding it, but most routes were far enough from the station to make a vehicle necessary. We used our own cars for this, and received a generous mileage rate in exchange. There were usually two or three parcel post routes per station and these drivers would deliver the splits for the walk-out routes to the olive-drab drop-boxes around the neighborhoods before they began the days' deliveries of packages. The carriers using their own vehicles would just carry the splits for their routes in their cars. The time for punching out was 2:30 p.m. and it was expected that most carriers would be finished by then, but it sometimes took a bit longer, especially for subs, and that was acceptable within reason. A cardinal rule for all carriers, but especially for subs, was to never return to the station early as that would make it appear that the route was too short, which might eventually result in a longer route for the regular carrier. After a day of deliveries, subs were often assigned the additional duty of using one of the stations' parcel post vehicles to pick up mail from boxes around the neighborhood, deliver it to the main post office, fill the vehicle's gas tank at the adjoining garage, and then return it to the station ready for use by the parcel post carriers the following day. I was usually able to get in forty hours per week, with some occasional overtime at time and one-half. The money was most helpful, because I would have less time for working on campus during senior year because of student teaching, so I worked right up until the start of fall classes.

Since I was a secondary education major, the most important part of senior year was to be student teaching, scheduled for the following winter and spring. My classes that fall included required ones in speech and education, both quite dry. There were two English courses, one on the history of the language and another on twentieth century American writers. This latter one covered Faulkner and Fitzgerald, but rather than completing the triumvirate of the greatest American authors of fiction of the first half of the century with Hemingway, the instructor chose Norman Mailer. This proved to be a timely choice as events unfolded that year.

My most engaging course that quarter was Arthur Ballet's *Introduction to the Theater*, one of the most popular on campus. You had to have an early registration date to get in, and so many people wanted to sit in just to enjoy his performances that they had to use a seating chart for the Scott Hall auditorium to ensure that all the enrolled students would have seats, a most unusual situation for a large lecture class. The first thing Arthur did when he walked out on stage was to place this chart on his podium, and he would not hesitate to call students by name if he saw them chatting or dozing. Often he would just choose a name at random and ask the student a question about the required reading for the day, lending an air of suspense to the proceedings and discouraging any lack of preparation. He was a gifted actor who performed his lectures in a way that often appeared to be extempore so, in addition to learning a great deal about the art and craft of theater, we were also treated to the best stand-up performance on campus. I regret never having taken a class from John Berryman, but I have always been grateful that my life was enriched by taking one from Arthur Ballet.

***

As the school year began the level of discontent over the draft and the war was rising almost by the day to a higher level of intensity than ever before. The solidifying of the values of the counterculture and resistance, the rapidly escalating troop levels and deaths, the almost inconceivable volume of explosives being dropped onto North Vietnam, and the increasing intransigence of LBJ and his team all combined to inspire a volatile mixture of frustration and anger that was often met with an equally strong emotional overreaction from those supporting the governments' policies. Just as many of the advocates of black power had concluded that peaceful resistance was accomplishing little or nothing toward achieving racial justice so, ironically, did many of the advocates for an end to the war begin adopting the same attitude.

Concern over the draft came to the forefront immediately, and it was announced that this year the deferment applications would be distributed by clerks at the east end of the Washington Avenue Bridge walkway. Congress had responded to widespread complaints of the draft laws favoring college students by tightening up the requirements for an educational deferment, resulting in a more complicated application process. I would have no problem demonstrating satisfactory progress toward a degree, but since I was a senior I was more concerned about the changes making it much more difficult for graduate students to obtain deferments. I had not planned on post-baccalaureate work, but given the way the war was going, it was starting to look more inviting all the time. That, of course, was just the kind of thinking that our old friend Colonel Knight wanted to discourage as he assured us that men who thought they could avoid serving by staying in college until the war ended were just kidding themselves.

The *Daily* continued to run numerous editorials and op-ed pieces on the war and the draft, although it seemed that by this point few of them broke much new ground. One notable essay by Democratic Senator J. William Fulbright of Arkansas lamented the fact that the level of domestic tension and mistrust, along with the huge commitment of resources to the war, had eroded LBJ's earlier efforts to continue the progress toward a more just society begun by the New Deal. He pointed out that the recent wave of racial unrest was a vivid demonstration of the need for greater attention to domestic needs rather than pouring young lives and money into a faraway war. The injustices sparking this discontent also undermined the image of the US in the international community: With such obvious problems in our own society, what right did we have to attempt to impose order and a new form of government on other nations? "The Great Society has become a sick society" said the senator.

In October, Gene McCarthy and the actor and U alumnus Robert Vaughn spoke on campus at separate events on the same day, both focusing on their opposition to the government's conduct of the war and both also stating that if that did not change soon they felt that LBJ should not be the Democratic candidate in 1968. Vaughn stated unequivocally that he would not vote for Johnson and instead favored Bobby Kennedy. McCarthy, as usual, was vaguer, but stated that change within the party was needed and if that change was not forthcoming from the current administration, he had not yet decided how he would respond if asked to run himself.

Racial issues continued to attract attention as well, as STRAP held a black power forum in the union, with Scotty Stone making a number of demands and accusing the U of racism. Another speaker advised young blacks to "get a piece of education." Milt Williams of The Way in North Minneapolis explained that even the most common term for referring to blacks at the time, "Negro," was a racially charged word invented by whites. As a side note, The Way is long gone but it is an important element in the history of the black community in North Minneapolis. It was founded in 1966 by some leaders of that community with the support of several city officials. Like everything involving race in America, it was always controversial. Supporters viewed it as a community center to provide black youth with opportunities for constructive activities and recreation, as well as a place to learn more about their history and identity. Others viewed it as a local headquarters of the Black Power movement, a hotly debated subject during that era of racial strife, urban riots, and burning neighborhoods. On the positive side, two academic fraternities accepted their first black members, although the fact that this was happening well into the U's second century was also a stark illustration of how pervasive discrimination had been both at the U and in the state as a whole.

The biggest anti-war rally yet was scheduled for October 21: the March on the Pentagon. The most common estimate of the crowd seems to be around 100,000, although other claims vary wildly from 35,000 to 500,000. The gathering place was the west end of the National Mall with speakers addressing the crowd from the Lincoln Memorial, an echo of the March on Washington four years earlier. After the rally on the mall, participants were encouraged to walk across the Arlington Memorial Bridge over to the Pentagon, surround it, and gradually move in as close as the security forces allowed. Several hundred chose to commit civil disobedience by crossing the lines and being arrested. In a publicity-generating display of street theater, Abbie Hoffman had organized a boisterous group of followers to sing and chant in an attempt to end the war by levitating the Pentagon. Another sight that was to become common at future rallies was protestors, especially young women, inserting flowers into the barrels of the rifles of the MPs and National Guard members performing security duty. Giving the lie to the admonition to never trust anyone over thirty, there was also an impressive showing of intellectuals and public figures from our parents' generation, including Dr. Spock, William Sloane Coffin, Noam Chomsky, Robert Lowell, Dwight McDonald, and Norman Mailer. Mailer, among those arrested, commemorated the event with a lengthy account published in *Harper's* the following March, which he then expanded into his book *The Armies of the Night*. Rallies were held at the same time in Europe and Japan.

To show solidarity with the DC event, local opponents of the war held a rally in front of Coffman attended by about 300 and featuring speakers such as Fran Shor. One goal, to encourage people to discuss Vietnam, was clearly met as the usual shouting matches developed between those supporting opposite sides of the issue, as well as a number of heated but more civil conversations. Racial issues were a subject as well, thanks to a member of STRAP who gave a speech on the goals of the Black Power movement. Protests continued the following week as recruiters from Dow Chemical, the maker of napalm, were met by a sit-in outside the placement office in Johnston Hall as well as pickets at the main entrance. That night, some protestors spent the night in the Regents' Room in Morrill Hall, vowing to stay until the president met with them. The next day Moos met with them for five minutes but only to read them a prepared statement, after which they left feeling that their point had been made. The protests here had been nonviolent and largely orderly, but that was not the case any longer at centers of the resistance such as Berkeley, Madison, and Columbia. The *Daily* ran an editorial expressing concern over this trend, but it was increasingly clear that many in both the anti-war and Black Power movements had already reached a level of frustration that caused them to lose faith in achieving their goals through nonviolent means.

With the usual exception of homecoming, even the newsworthy events on campus that fall that did not relate directly to the war and draft still mostly reflected discontent with things as they were, often paired with demands for immediate change. The week before the Dow protestors took over President Moos's office, he found twenty-five students sitting around the hall outside his suite conducting a "stone-in" to protest a recent rash of drug-related arrests on the West Bank. This time the demands were that the U not take any disciplinary actions against the students who were arrested and that Moos "say something on the issue." As the president left his office and walked by the group, he said he would meet with anyone who cared to make an appointment with him.

The *Daily* editorialized that pot laws were too harsh and that the U police should not continue to join forces with Minneapolis law enforcement authorities in such operations. By this time marijuana use had become one of the primary issues dividing the mainstream culture from the counterculture.

Since smoking pot was illegal, doing so was a way of thumbing your nose at The Man, but it was also a portal to a realm that establishment folks could never even dream existed, let alone enter. Despite my fondness for drinking, I never seriously considered trying pot during my undergraduate days, but I passed a major milestone in my long affair with alcohol that fall when I turned twenty-one and could suddenly walk into the liquor store and pick out whatever I could afford. The most fitting description might be the common cliché of a kid in a candy store.

"Student power" also continued to be a hot-button issue, as the president of MSA issued a statement asking that students be given the right "to make the rules they live under," including "full and equal participation… in the decision-making processes of the academic community." The U was scheduled to host a National Student Association (NSA) conference on student power the following month that was expected to attract about 400 student representatives from eighty institutions. This was far from a new controversy, but the immediate motivation for the statement may well have been an interview the previous week with Dean of Students Williamson in which he stated that, while students' opinions were considered, it was essential that the U administration continue to have the final say on all issues of student life on campus. Regent Andersen also gave an interview, saying he was not frightened by the current unrest among young people. He regarded it as a healthy sign that students were not content to accept conditions they felt were unjust, but also pointed out that increased power required assuming increased responsibility. A wise man known for seeing things in their broad historical context, Elmer L. Andersen even found positive things to say about the recent controversial and stinging departing words of Dean of the Institute of Technology, Athelstan Spilhaus, who had termed our venerable institution a "great gray mediocrity."

As the end of the quarter approached, national news on the war included a Gallup poll reporting that the American people supported the war 59% to 34%, sometimes an easy thing to forget on a campus where the reverse seemed to be true. It was reported that between six and ten thousand "draft dodgers" had fled to Canada, which refused to extradite them because Canadian law did not consider their actions an offense. ROTC enrollment had decreased, a disappointment for the Department of Defense, which had been expecting it to rise. Clearly, the statistics on the causality rates for junior officers were making an impression. At the end of November, LBJ's inner circle sustained a major loss as Secretary of Defense Robert McNamara, one of JFK's "The Best and the Brightest," resigned when the president turned down his recommendations to freeze troop levels, stop bombing the north, and turn over ground fighting to South Vietnamese forces. The following day, Senator McCarthy announced his candidacy for the presidency. In the first week of December, Dr. Spock and Allen Ginsberg were among those arrested in New York for attempting to close an induction center. The same week, the NSA filed suit against General Hershey for recommending that local boards draft anti-war protestors. Like many protest activities, this one was meant mainly to generate publicity and make a point, but that point was a very valid one: The "privilege" of serving was being used as punishment for exercising the constitutional right to free speech.

"Stop the Draft Week" was scheduled for the last week of classes in December, and the most dramatic event was a march from Northrop Plaza to the downtown federal building that concluded with the burning of several draft cards. The timing was poor since that is the time of the quarter when students devote the most time to study, and the event only attracted fifty marchers. The *Daily* carried an ad for caffeine tablets showing a newly drafted sad sack-type character in ill-fitting fatigues holding a rifle and steel pot with the caption, "I laughed when my roommate took NoDoz." That sounded like the type of humor Colonel Knight would appreciate.

On the less serious side, one subject of continuing interest since the Summer of Love was this creature dubbed "the hippie." A professor had opined that, despite their predilection for drugs and free love, the hippies were much like the puritans in that they saw themselves as a righteous remnant breaking off from the larger society to explore a purer way of life. A discussion session was held between a roomful of straights and self-professed hippies that resulted in a good deal of spirited conversation both between the two groups and between the hippies themselves. One thing the counterculture folks could agree upon was that they sought freedom to "do their own thing," and that a good way of doing just that was to attend a concert and "happening," such as those being held regularly at the two Fillmores in San Francisco and the East Village. Our own West Bank now had its version of such a venue as the old Dania Hall on Cedar Avenue soon became the best known place to dig live rock with a light show.

The dilemma faced by a confused young man trying to find his way in today's American society was explored in *The Graduate*, the second of the two most significant films of the year. The book had been written before Vietnam flared up and the film did not deal with the war and the draft at all. Benjamin's dominant emotion was confusion rather than anger, but his consternation over trying to figure out how he fit into a world he found so difficult to understand was something every young person could recognize. It seemed that the best advice his parents' generation could offer him was the cryptic admonition "plastics," which quickly became a one-word indictment of straight society. The film was accompanied by the beautiful music of Simon and Garfunkel, who had immediately become two of the most important American musical artists when "Sounds of Silence" was released in late 1965.

***

With graduate student deferments in a state of uncertainty as 1968 began, seniors like me were facing the prospect of being eligible for the draft in six months. That was a constant concern, but my immediate focus was on student teaching, which was scheduled to occupy nearly my entire schedule for the next two quarters. That winter my only additional class was one on nineteenth century European history, which I think I chose mostly because it fit into a gap in my schedule. Education majors were also required to perform some community service work, so I signed up to be a library monitor at the Boys Club in South Minneapolis. This was rewarding when there were kids there who were interested in reading and asked for help finding certain types of books, but on some days the duties amounted to little more than trying to keep them from damaging books and using the place for an indoor playground.

My first student teaching assignment was at Olson Junior High on 51st and Irving in North Minneapolis. I got off to a somewhat shaky start by reading them a piece of my favorite literature, a short story by Hemingway with some questionable words in it, but I soon learned to adjust my material to the age of the students. I developed and taught two units that quarter, one on the short story and one on the role of the newspaper in our daily lives. Kids that age are certainly a restless bunch and they will often try to see how much they can get away with when a student teacher is in charge, but I did my best to assume a stern demeanor when needed. I was less than satisfied with how things went but, whether or not the kids learned much, I had learned that I did not want to try teaching those grade levels as a profession. I have a high regard for people who are able to do that effectively.

After the tumult of the previous year the level of national tension was almost palpable, and 1968 proved to be the year that brought many of these festering issues to a head. It was not the end of anything but rather a turning point, what Churchill termed in reference to the mid-point of World War II "the hinge of fate." One unexpected meeting of the minds took place in the middle of January when Eartha Kitt, attending a meeting at the White House on juvenile delinquency, seized the opportunity to tell Lady Bird Johnson how much she despised the war in Vietnam. It was certainly unprecedented for a black woman, or anyone for that matter, to be this forward with the first lady. Three days later on January 21, the battle of Khe Sanh began near the Demilitarized Zone, eventually settling into a seventy-seven-day siege of the remote base defended by a battalion of US Marines. B-52s dropped more bomb tonnage on enemy positions than had ever been expended on any one target in all previous wars. In the end the number of enemy deaths exceeded ours by a ratio of twenty to one. The journalist Michael Herr was holed up with the Marines and his account of the battle is included in *Dispatches*, one of the finest books on the war. The most significant news medium providing coverage, however, was television. A protracted World War II type of battle such as this was unusual for Vietnam and as it ground on the American public received a jarring education on just what our soldiers were forced to endure. And then the base was abandoned by our forces soon after the end of the ordeal, further ratcheting up the level of anger and confusion over the conduct of the war among both the American public and our troops in the field.

As gruesome and disturbing as the news from Khe Sanh was, it was soon overshadowed by even more shocking events as the Tet Offensive began on January 31. Taking advantage of the lunar new-year holiday, a traditional time for a cease-fire, both "main force" Viet Cong (VC) and NVA regular forces waged fierce attacks on bases and strategic sites all over South Vietnam. This time the media had far greater immediate access to the fighting than at isolated Khe Sanh and, especially in Saigon and Hue, both the fighting and the coverage could only be described as devastating. Suddenly US troops were caught up in pitched battles in numerous areas that we had been led to believe were fairly well "pacified." The TV reports of urban warfare looked like something out of Stalingrad. The perimeter of the US embassy in Saigon was breached. The beautiful old imperial capital of Hue was blown to pieces as our soldiers fought from house to house in grim battles with a well-equipped and highly motivated enemy. Ammo dumps, including the massive one at Bien Hoa, were ignited by sappers. One of the iconic photos of the war captured South Vietnam's police chief executing a Viet Cong suspect in the middle of Saigon with a pistol shot to the side of the head, an event recorded by both still and video cameras.

Although we could not have known it at the time, we had just witnessed the turning point of the war. The hinge of fate had indeed turned. After all our efforts at pacification and the many solemn reassurances from our leaders that the war was progressing well, the enemy had demonstrated that we were still shockingly vulnerable. And yet that enemy had thrown everything they had at us and failed to achieve any significant lasting military results. Only later would we learn, in fact, that the VC had been so devastated by the vicious pitched battles with both US and ARVN defenders that the "main force" Viet Cong would no longer be capable of playing a significant role in the fighting for the entire balance of the war.

The final outcome on the battlefields was a stalemate, and that is also the best term to describe the last five and one-half years of our involvement there. In the end, the fact that enemy dead in the Tet battles outnumbered our own by about twenty-five to one meant nothing, and the acceleration of the erosion of the American public's confidence in our ability to prevail in Vietnam meant everything. Walter Cronkite, often considered "the most trusted man in America," broadcast a special report at the end of the offensive in which he predicted that "the bloody experience of Vietnam will end in a stalemate" and that the only rational and honorable course of action for our leaders was to begin to negotiate a settlement. His reports from the midst of the devastation wrecked by the urban battles while protected by a steel pot and flak jacket were especially striking, evoking the heroic legacy of Edward R. Murrow in London during the blitz. Johnson was said to have remarked in reaction to the great journalist's grim assessment: "That's it. If I've lost Cronkite, I've lost middle America." True to the twisted logic of a war where villages were destroyed in order to save them, an outcome that statistically was a crushing defeat for the communist forces was in reality the most crucial step toward their ultimate victory.

***

On our campus in January, the principled decisions of two men regarding the war provided much food for thought. As expected, Fran Shor refused induction in Minneapolis, saying he was fully prepared to accept the consequences. Not so expected, at least to those of us who did not know him, was the decision of forty-five-year-old Political Science Professor Harold Chase, a World War II Marine combat veteran, to volunteer for service in Vietnam as a civil affairs officer. The *Daily* ran a piece by Walter Mondale explaining the problems that the SSS's change in policy on drafting grad students would cause colleges and universities. Enrollments were at an all-time high and grad students were needed to teach and assist with many of the lower division classes. He once again endorsed a lottery as both the fairest method as well as the one that would cause the least uncertainty for those of draft age. The *Daily* supported this position as well, noting that the military itself was not all that pleased at the prospect of many of its enlisted men being college graduates used to thinking for themselves.

Local issues other than the war included a complaint by Phillip Richter, owner of the building on 5th and Cedar that included Dania Hall, that he was being harassed by Minneapolis building inspectors. He felt he was being singled out because of the "hippie dances" in Dania, but also noted that a wealthy developer wanted to force him to sell his property. He felt it was apparent that the neighborhood's conservative alderman and the developer were in cahoots. The same building housed Richter's Pharmacy, and it was rumored that the alley behind the drugstore was a prime spot for obtaining drugs that required no prescription. The friction between traditional folks, including some very well-heeled developers, and those embracing the counterculture lifestyle was to continue in the neighborhood until well into the 1970s.

In mid-January, we were treated to the debut of *Rowan and Martin's Laugh-In*, which continued on the air for the rest of the war years. The style and content served as a sort of bridge between *That Was the Week That Was* and *Saturday Night Live*, featuring a rapid-fire sequence of both topical and silly humor reflecting the inspiration of Ernie Kovacs, some music, plenty of very thinly veiled allusions to drugs, and sexual innuendo. *Laugh-In* seemed like the perfect show for the times because it could help us forget about all the problems for an hour, or at least help us to laugh at them, all the while maintaining a knowing attitude of irony without straying over into cynicism. That was not an easy balance to maintain in those days. It was a happening. It was a put-on. It was hilarious. Many of its recurring catch-phrases quickly made their way into the popular lingo, such as "Sock it to me," "Very interesting," "You bet your sweet bippy," "Here comes the judge," and Dick Martin's bemused "I didn't know that." There are few better ways of immersing yourself in the weirdly conflicted milieu of the home front during Vietnam than watching a few episodes of this iconic show.

As winter quarter 1968 drew to a close I was focusing on finishing up my first student teaching assignment and preparing for the second, but local and national events continued to unfold at such a rapid and intense pace that it was difficult to avoid becoming a news junkie as well. America was changing and we had no way of knowing where we were headed or how things would turn out. The daily news could only offer vague clues as to what our destination might be because we were in uncharted waters, and yet it was impossible to resist the temptation to read and listen to as much information as possible for fear we might overlook the one vital sign pointing the way toward the answer. The mood was always tense and often angry.

There had been hopes that the Kerner Commission Report would point toward possible solutions to the increasingly violent racial unrest. The Black Power advocates had at least been accurate in their belief that only force would compel America to look at the problem seriously, because the urban riots were LBJ's primary motivation for appointing the commission. The report's most memorable sentence was: "Our nation is moving toward two societies, one black, one white—separate and unequal." Dr. King described the document as a "physician's warning of approaching death, with a prescription for life." Unfortunately, the prescription called for medicine too bitter for many white Americans to swallow because the primary recommendation was to eliminate pockets of black poverty, the urban ghettos, through increased integration. An additional suggested solution that would certainly be distasteful to many people regardless of their race was to beef up law enforcement, mainly by improved intelligence gathered through the use of undercover cops and snitches.

Student activism reached a new level of intensity on the east coast as Howard University was rocked for five days in mid-March by sit-ins and protests over ROTC, the war, and the draft. As would be expected at a traditionally black institution, the demands also included some of those advocated by the Black Power movement, especially a more Afrocentric curriculum. General Hershey was unable to deliver a scheduled address as he was drowned out by the shouts of protestors, some proclaiming that, rather than Vietnam, "America is the black man's battleground." Toward the end of April, student protestors shut down Columbia University for a week. The immediate issues here were plans to build a university gym on park land that was used mainly by residents of Harlem and the administrations' refusal to stop engaging in classified weapons research, but problems that might have prompted negotiations and compromise in the past were now the occasion for disrupting business as usual by any means possible until the administration conceded or the protestors were forcibly removed. Anger and frustration over the war and racial tension outweighed any inclination to negotiate. Bodies were being placed on the gears, but it was clear that a growing number of activists had come to believe that the machine must be halted by any means necessary, peaceful or not.

As usual, events on our campus seemed tame by comparison, although student power continued to be a hot topic at MSA meetings and in *Daily* editorials and op-ed pieces. In early March, Minneapolis officials discovered the pitfalls of attempting to press trumped-up charges against a professor of philosophy when Burnham Terrell was briefly arrested for "unauthorized regulation of traffic." He had been directing drivers headed to a Gene McCarthy rally at the Pick Nicollet Hotel away from the Nicollet Mall where automobile traffic is prohibited and police were issuing tickets to those dropping off folks headed to the rally. It was apparent that right-leaning members of the police force were trying to create as many problems as possible for the McCarthy supporters. Burnham explained to the *Daily* that he would enter "a philosopher's plea…It is conceptually impossible that I could regulate traffic that has already been regulated by law. I didn't impose my own unauthorized regulations upon the traffic involved but signaled drivers to obey regulations lawfully in effect." The same issue carried a powerful op-ed piece from Professor Terrell in which he termed the war not just a political issue, but "the gravest moral threat that faces the American people today," and urged readers to attend precinct caucuses with that fact in mind. The same week, two members of the Twin City Draft Information Center were arrested for refusing induction. On the lighter side, Crane's Gifts in Dinkytown ran an ad describing their wide selection of counterculture gear, terming the store a "hippie haven."

Also in the first week of March, Norman Mailer visited the campus to deliver speeches and give readings from his upcoming book describing the march on the Pentagon the previous October, *The Armies of the Night*. I attended his presentation in Northrop, and it was quite a thrill to hear a writer I had just studied the previous quarter. I had already read most of the book because it had been published in *Harper's*, and it was a fascinating example of the New Journalism. This genre was a combination of fiction and news reporting in which the writer took an active role in the events related and, at least in Mailer's case, stirred up trouble to make the situation, and hence his story, more interesting. The reader expected him to be one of those arrested and of course he did not disappoint. The audience was friendly and he really was an engaging speaker, often funny but also fascinated by what he termed "a growing sense of apocalypse in American life." He was clearly enjoying living in such interesting times. Perhaps the most memorable line from the feisty World War II veteran was "I'm not against war. I'm just against bullshit."

***

As spring quarter began with the last week of March, the SSS announced that pre-induction physicals for seniors would begin in April rather than after graduation. Colonel Knight said there should be no concern about students being drafted before their scheduled graduation. Rather, the reason for the change was so that we would know our status as soon as possible in order to plan for the future, especially since between 20% and 25% of men fail their physical. This seemed reasonable, but we had learned to take anything Knight or the SSS told us with a healthy dose of skepticism. Later that week, an organization named Students Against Selective Service gave a presentation on how to beat the draft, but their only advice was to refuse to sign the security and personal history forms in the hope of being classified 1-Y, morally or administratively undesirable. Another speaker suggested just going to prison rather than accepting enlistment. That was what he had decided to do and he was currently awaiting sentencing. These were far less creative solutions than much of the advice that circulated by word-of mouth or even printed material, which ranged anywhere from deliberately injuring yourself, taking various drugs or medicines to throw off your blood pressure or urine tests, or virtually starving yourself for several weeks or months to come in under the minimum required weight. The goal of these tactics was to be classified 4-F: physically, mentally, or morally unfit.

My schedule for the quarter focused mainly on student teaching, but I also continued with the nineteenth century European history sequence. The real bright spot on the schedule was a Chaucer class that I took out of love for the literature, but also with a view toward grad school in the future since this was one of the requirements for an MA in English. My student teaching, unlike the previous term, was a choice assignment. University High School, located right on campus, was for the children of U faculty and staff—kids who were known to be smart and highly motivated. I was paired with an English teacher named Sally Legrande, whom I always found to be approachable and supportive. This time I was again assigned the task of developing two units, one on *Winesburg, Ohio*, and another on a subject of my own choice. I chose a topic popular with liberal arts types—existentialism. Things went well that quarter, and I found the students bright, enthusiastic, and genuinely interesting. Enforcing order was not an issue. Sally would remind me that this was hardly a typical high school teaching experience because these students came from privileged homes, at least in the intellectual sense, and were nearly all planning on going to college. Actually it was much the same as teaching college freshmen or sophomores.

The result of my two terms of student teaching was an obvious conclusion: What I would really like to do is teach college. That required continuing on beyond a bachelor's degree, so I applied and was accepted to study English in the Grad School at the U. I would not be a good candidate for a high school teaching position anyway with a 1-A draft status, which I expected to have as soon as I passed my physical and graduated. The other alternative was to go to work full-time for the post office until I was called up. I did hope to work there again during the upcoming summer, but the prospect of doing it for longer than that, and especially over the winter if I was still in Minneapolis then, was unappealing. Also, I was two courses short of the required credits for my bachelor's degree so I planned on taking those in the fall along with my first graduate-level classes. The unknown factor in these plans was the draft, but I decided to go ahead with what I wanted to do and proceed one day at a time until I was called up. I felt a greater clarity and sense of purpose about my future now that I had decided what sort of teaching seemed right for me, and I had also discovered that keeping busy was quite an effective antidote to depression.

National events continued to unfold at a rapid pace as Gene McCarthy came within seven percentage points of LBJ in the New Hampshire primary on March 12, signaling an alarmingly tepid level of support within his own party for an incumbent president. I remember a good deal of excitement on campus the next day over this unexpected good news. Four days later, the My Lai massacre took place, although it would not be made public until November of the following year. On the same day, Bobby Kennedy announced his candidacy for the democratic nomination and two days later he delivered a scathing castigation of LBJ's conduct of the war to a crowd of 14,500 students at Kansas State University. He questioned whether we had begun to fall far short of the noble ideals of the Founders: "From the beginning our proudest boast has been the promise of Jefferson, that we, here in this country would be the best hope of mankind. And now, as we look at the war in Vietnam, we wonder if we still hold a decent respect for the opinions of mankind and whether they maintain a decent respect for us or whether like Athens of old, we will forfeit sympathy and support, and ultimately our very security, in the single-minded pursuit of our own goals and our own objectives." He used another classical allusion to reflect his disgust at the notorious Orwellian comment of an American officer after the destruction of Ben Tre the previous month—that it had been necessary to destroy the village in order to save it. "I am concerned—as I believe most Americans are concerned—that our present course will not bring victory; will not bring peace; will not stop the bloodshed; and will not advance the interests of the United States or the cause of peace in the world. I am concerned that, at the end of it all, there will only be more Americans killed; more of our treasure spilled out; and because of the bitterness and hatred on every side of this war, more hundreds of thousands of [civilians] slaughtered; so they may say, as Tacitus said of Rome: 'They made a desert, and called it peace.'"

Then on the 22nd, the president announced suddenly that General Westmoreland was coming home from Vietnam to serve as Army Chief of Staff. What was a promotion on the face of it was in reality a well-deserved rebuke for the failure of the general's strategy in the RVN that the Tet Offensive had exposed so vividly.

On the last day of the month LBJ delivered a long televised speech from the Oval Office reiterating his fervent desire for peace in Vietnam, recounting the most recent efforts he had made to move toward that goal, recalling how all of them had been rebuffed by the North Vietnamese, and outlining further plans for achieving that elusive goal. Given the course of recent events, none of it inspired much hope, in me at least. Then he went on to say that he felt the need to devote all of his time to the duties of his office rather than to the distractions of a grueling reelection campaign, leading up to a sentence I can still remember clearly: "Accordingly, I shall not seek, and I will not accept, the nomination of my party for another term as your President." Dad and I watched the broadcast together and I recall that we both had to ask ourselves if we really had just heard LBJ correctly. Dad remarked that it was history in the making. So Gene and Bobby had achieved their goal of unseating the man who had led us into our great national debacle. What lay ahead we could only guess, but any hope that the tide was about to turn was quickly diminished eleven days later when the US troop ceiling in Vietnam was raised to 549,500, the highest of the war.

On April 4 the nation was rocked by tragedy when Dr. King was assassinated in Memphis. It now seemed as though the violence of war had truly come to define the domestic battle for racial justice as well. The immediate reaction was grief, but also fears that urban race riots would erupt once again. These fears proved to be justified as disturbances broke out in over 100 cities, although the extent and duration were less than those of the previous summer. The major exception was Washington, DC, where 1,200 buildings were burned in five days and the violence threatened to spiral out of control as LBJ assigned 14,000 federal troops to supplement the overwhelmed district police force.

Dr. King's last speech delivered the night before his death, as well as being magnificent oratory now also seemed eerily prophetic as he spoke of his likely death by violence, recommitted himself to doing God's will as he understood it, and compared himself to Moses, viewing the promised land but not entering it himself. "And so I'm happy tonight. I'm not worried about anything. I'm not fearing any man. Mine eyes have seen the glory of the coming of the Lord!" After he was cut down the next morning, it was impossible to ignore the comparison to Our Lord, as well as Moses, clearly foreseeing his own death and yet facing it unafraid because of his sure knowledge that he was doing his Father's will. One week after Dr. King's death, LBJ signed the Civil Rights Act of 1968, a much-needed beacon of hope during a period of grief and soul-searching, and also a poignant reminder of how different LBJ's legacy could have been without the war.

The *Daily* devoted extensive coverage to Dr. King's death and the resulting events and tributes. This included printing his 1963 "Letter from Birmingham Jail," which included a sentence to trouble the conscience of many of us: "Shallow understanding from people of good will is more frustrating than absolute misunderstanding from people of ill will." Yet another issue certain to exacerbate racial tensions surfaced when it was publicized that many urban police forces, including those of both Minneapolis and St. Paul, had purchased M-16 rifles for riot control. This was an obvious response to the disturbances of the previous summer, but many felt that it was an absurd and racially tone-deaf overreaction. The specter of police officers spraying bullets around the ghettos with the same lethal automatic weapons our troops were using against the Viet Cong filled many of us with dread over what the coming summer might bring, but it also aroused deep anger. There were other citizens in favor of these deadly armaments, of course, but the mayors of both Twin Cities found themselves under heavy pressure from activists to return the automatic weapons. Mayor Naftalin of Minneapolis made the decision to do so, but Mayor Byrne of St. Paul elected to keep them. Just by coincidence, Tom Byrne was an uncle of my friend Bernie.

Local events on the anti-war front included another march in early April from campus to the downtown Federal Building during which thirteen men turned in their draft cards. The *Daily* printed an interview with a former soldier from Fort Hood who had received an undesirable discharge for distributing anti-war materials to other soldiers. He said that anti-war sentiment among the troops was widespread and getting stronger all the time. Later in the month, the *Daily* published a special draft issue. This included an interview with Fran Galt, now out on parole, who said he found prison boring, dehumanizing, and a worse crime than any committed by the inmates. The entire issue was well-researched and informative, including descriptions of the induction process and basic training, types of deferments, and the option of moving to Canada. One article dealt with an aspect of the situation that was often overlooked: the feelings of women who knew and loved young men eligible for the draft or already in the military. They were just as conflicted as their husbands, boyfriends, and brothers, but for the most part seemed resigned and sad rather than angry. Toward the end of the month, several anti-war organizations tried to organize local participants for an international one-day strike on campus to protest the war, draft, and racism. An organizer from Colorado observed that "there is an air of defeatism on this campus." The outcome of the event was less dramatic than the organizers had hoped for, but some classes were cancelled and about 1,500 did turn out for a rally and speeches on Northrop Plaza, attracting the usual counterprotestors as well.

Academic matters were also a concern, as illustrated by an April *Daily* article on our English Department. Most of us majoring in the subject were at least somewhat aware of these problems but the story in the paper was particularly disheartening because, along with the usual budgetary problems common to all units at the U, the reporter observed that the department was torn by internal divisions and widespread discontent with the leadership of the chair, John Clark. It was quite a falling off from the glory days of Robert Penn Warren and Saul Bellow, and now Allen Tate would be retiring at the end of the quarter. At least we still had John Berryman in Humanities. The same month Dean of Students Williamson gave a rather confusing interview in which he seemed to be taking a page out of the counterculture's book when he observed that much of the current student discontent was due to the irrelevance of many college courses to their actual lives. His solution to the problem, however, was simply the old chestnut of suggesting that the faculty consider revising the curriculum. Having said that, he went on to dismiss the student power movement as something that was not a vital issue. Then he concluded with an unexpected expression of praise for black power.

The scene at Dania Hall continued to draw attention, and the *Daily* interviewed the most frequent performers there, The Paisleys, toward the end of May. They sounded like real products of the Summer of Love ethos, noting that the band, their wives and girlfriends, and the light show were like a family living a communal lifestyle. They attributed their musical style to the "love vibration" resulting from this close-knit way of life. A group of about 150 devoted followers attended most of their shows, and they loved the uninhibited audiences at Dania where "everyone does what he wants." Unfortunately for their local fans, however, the entire band planned to move to Vancouver soon. None of them were eligible for the draft, but they were "looking for a less violent society."

Less than two months later, Dania lost its dance license, largely because an undercover narcotics officer termed it the center of the illegal drug trade in Minneapolis. Phil Richter blamed it on the "personal vendetta" that the right-leaning alderman, Jens Christensen, had been conducting against him, but the old saw about not being able to fight city hall seemed to hold true in this case. The first week in July about 200 people protested the closing of the popular venue by planning a street dance on Cedar Avenue, but, when warned by police that blocking traffic would result in arrests, they danced in the parking lot next to the Electric Fetus Music Store instead. One policeman lent credence to the embattled Richter's suspicions of a frame-up when he noted that the officer who made the drug allegations had never worked at the Dania dances, but the decision had been rendered and the brief but colorful era of the hippie dances in the historic building was now a thing of the past.

Regardless of what may or may not have happened at Dania, it was no secret that drug use was an integral part of the culture of the West Bank and in May the *Daily* interviewed some folks who claimed to be in the know. For those not in the know, the reporter began by explaining some of the many drug references in recent popular music, including "A Day in the Life." The article focused mainly on pot, and one resident noted disdainfully that marijuana use had recently become popular with young people of middle class backgrounds. He felt that only folks who had smoked it more than four years ago "can consider themselves as being very cool." Other users appeared less concerned with their image and more with getting high, describing the pleasures and harmlessness of smoking. The head of the Minneapolis Narcotics Division warned darkly, however, that "the steady user is a nut. If you legalize marijuana, you'll just let the nuts make more nuts." It appeared that the main danger from smoking was getting caught, as the reporter noted that drug arrests in the area were up sharply since the police began conducting organized busts the previous fall.

There were two pop culture events that April that I remember well. The credit union Dad managed was one of the sponsors of the Cooper Theater, so he usually got a pair of tickets for each new show. The Cooper had the distinction of being one of only three theaters in the US built specifically for presenting films in the dramatic but short-lived and technically unwieldy triple-projector Cinerama format on a screen with a huge 146-degree arc. This time Dad gave the tickets to me and my brother Dave and they were for a film we knew nothing about: *2001: A Space Odyssey*. It was amazing and mysterious, and of course the time-travel light-show sequence near the end was utterly unlike anything we had ever seen before. I still enjoy watching this intriguing exploration of what might happen if we finally discovered positive proof that there was other intelligent life in the Universe, but that first time on the huge curved screen was unforgettable.

The second event was the Broadway opening of *Hair*. Even though I was not able to see a live performance until several years later, the soundtrack album came out soon after the opening and it has always been one of my favorites, especially the great concluding number. "Let the Sun Shine In" has been covered countless times, usually as a feel-good hippie-era ditty along the same lines as "Feelin' Groovy," but its true meaning only becomes clear when it is preceded by the much less frequently heard first part of the piece "The Flesh Failures," a devastating indictment of mainstream America during the war years leading to the same conclusion as Timothy Leary and the Beatles: Once you truly understand how violent and materialistic your society has become, the only rational response to this nightmare is to abandon it and begin anew with like-minded companions. Maybe the Paisleys had it right.

As the end of the quarter approached, issues related to the war continued to dominate the news on campus. Bishop Shannon gave a presentation at the Newman Center in late April advocating changing the draft law to allow for selective conscientious objection, supporting his position by citing the teachings of Vatican II requiring people to follow the dictates of their own conscience even when those promptings were in conflict with the law.

There was yet another teach-in on the draft at Coffman the following week. Near the end of May a coalition of anti-war groups held a six-hour series of events they termed "Vietnam Commencement" which, like many of the protest activities of the period, was organized as part of a nation-wide series of similar affairs. An expected highlight was to be a speech marking the return of Professor Sibley, who had been on leave at another institution for the year. We had been missing his inspiring presence. He delivered a strongly worded address in which he termed Vietnam "the most absurd war in history," criticized American higher education as "distorted and perverted," and praised the resistance as "carrying on a great American tradition of resisting illegitimate authority." One of his most memorable observations was: "Every act of resistance helps to transform society by pointing out the enormous hypocrisy of a society that praises freedom and burns children."

World and national events continued to offer little reason for optimism. In May the long-awaited Paris peace talks began and then promptly stalled for five months over the North Vietnamese insistence that the bombing of the north be halted before negotiations began. While it was clear that both sides were intent on digging in their heels, the stalemate greatly increased the level of our frustration over the ineffective efforts of our national leaders during a year when over 1,000 of our troops were dying every month. The following week, in one of the first and most dramatic of many such incidents, Catholic anti-war activists entered SSS offices in Catonsville, Maryland, removed 378 draft records, and then burned them with homemade napalm. Dubbed "The Catonsville Nine," they immediately became heroes of the resistance. In early June, Dr. Spock and four others were convicted by LBJ's Justice Department of aiding young men in resisting the draft, a flimsily supported conviction that was set aside upon appeal the following year. The authority our mothers had relied upon for advice when raising us through infancy and childhood was continuing to support us boomers through the most difficult phase yet of our young lives. I always had a very high regard for these anti-war activists who were members of our parents' generation.

***

As the academic year drew to a close, the war was rapidly becoming a stark personal reality for me as I reported for my SSS physical at the downtown Federal Building on Monday of finals week, June 3. I found that our group of potential future recruits included two of my classmates from St. Charles and De La Salle, Mike Debelak and Jim Mirocha. The three of us decided to protest the situation by refusing to sign one of several forms presented to us, a loyalty oath. We were told that action would have no effect on our eligibility for the military and I did not doubt that, but it still gave us a modicum of satisfaction to be bucking the system in at least some minor way. I received a letter several weeks later informing me that I had been found fit to serve.

Two days later on June 5, the wave of murderous violence that had begun with the assassination of JFK claimed another irreplaceable victim when Bobby Kennedy was shot while on the campaign trail in Los Angeles. It was a horrible loss for the nation and the Kennedy family, but the murder also had significant political consequences because Bobby had been the leading Democratic candidate advocating a rapid US withdrawal from Vietnam. It was impossible to say what the summer would bring, but it was difficult to imagine that it would be good.

Chapter 6
GRADUATE SCHOOL
UNIVERSITY OF MINNESOTA
1968-69

The summer of 1968 certainly brought no respite from that year's unrelenting deluge of shocking events, but at least my summer job carrying mail once again provided a welcome break from the academic schedule. I started two days after my finals were over, and my second summer at the post office was even better than the first because I ended up being assigned almost exclusively to the Central Avenue Branch, which served my home territory of Northeast Minneapolis. The carriers there were mostly a bunch of pleasant laid-back guys, and I got to know some of them fairly well because of being there all summer. The culture of the post office at that time included a good deal of kidding around and good-natured verbal sparring, although there did not seem to be a custom of hazing the new guys. There were a number of veterans there, including one Vietnam guy, and I think the habit of razzing and baiting your fellow workers reflected the military way of life where such behavior is common.

I had heard Dad and Uncle Jim mention this from time to time over the years and sometimes they talked about a number of the guys liking to drink as well, which also would be consistent with the behavior of many veterans. Considering the amount of time the two of them worked there, they were certainly in a position to know, but I did not see anyone's job performance affected by tippling during the brief time I carried mail. If there were heavy drinkers there they definitely had it under control, at least during working hours. Some of the guys liked to swap stories about women on their routes who flirted with them, but that was probably mostly wishful thinking. All I can say is that it never happened to this carrier, or if it did I was too dense to pick up on it.

The service area for our branch was St. Anthony Village and all of Northeast except a few routes down around the East Hennepin and Central Avenue area that were carried out of the Downtown Branch. I was assigned to many different routes over the summer and so got to know my own part of the city better than ever before. You see the least of a neighborhood by driving through it, more by biking, and even more by walking, but you take in the most by carrying mail because then you walk through the yards and right up to the front doors of the houses. I enjoyed observing the variety of architectural styles and way the houses became newer and newer as I moved north from downtown and east from the river. There was a range of ages from homes around a century old in the closer-in neighborhoods to those erected during the post-war construction boom near the city limits and in St. Anthony. I remembered some of those places being built because the forbidden fruit of a house under construction is an irresistible lure for boys.

Another thing that left an impression on me was the wide range in the length of the routes. Most of them seemed like a reasonable volume for casing and carrying in an eight-hour day, but there were a few where the length made doing that quite a challenge, at least for a newer guy like me. Then there were a few others that were so short they seemed almost like an auxiliary route rather than a full-length one. Since a postal inspector walked with the carrier once every three years to evaluate whether the route was the proper length, it was never clear to me how such a wide variance could occur, but that was not my problem.

What I enjoyed was the fact that I could finish most routes with an hour or two to spare. Since returning early was a serious faux pas I always had a book with me to pass the time until it was acceptable to return. The regulars filled me in on what to do: Sit around, usually in your car unless you were on a walk-out route, and move every half hour. That way if the proverbial "little old lady with nothing better to do" called the office to complain about a carrier loafing your reply would be that you were only there for a half hour on your lunch break. I appreciated the friendliness of the regular carriers, and I tried to return the favor by never commenting on the length of the short routes. The best way to stay on their good side, however, was to clean up any backlog of low-priority mail in their case on the days I had their route. This included product samples and bulk mail, which were to be delivered as time permitted after all first and second class items were gone. I always got rid of some of it for them, and often there was time to deliver the entire batch of it. An item that they especially disliked was toothpaste samples.

* * *

Much of the national and local news continued to be a series of disturbing events. In late June, protestors out in Berkeley supporting the unlikely cause of solidarity with anti-DeGaulle radicals in France clashed with police in confrontations that rapidly escalated into what the media termed a three-day "street war," complete with blocked traffic, burning barricades, curfews, mass arrests, and pitched battles between protestors throwing whatever they could get their hands on and police returning fire with tear-gas canisters. The disturbances at Columbia two months earlier had mushroomed into a new level of anger and violence, and the Berkeley riots increased the degree of militancy by a giant step. These were clashes of a type we had only read about in history books or heard described on the news in other nations, and on one of the sides were members of our own generation, our peers. Were they just hooligans or were their actions justified by the outrageous injustices of the war, the draft, and the shameless oppression of black Americans?

We knew that the war was the root cause of most of the domestic disturbances, but we had to ask ourselves if such radical actions could be justified. Over 1,000 American troops were dying every month, along with an unknown but much higher number of Vietnamese, including many civilians. Men who were drafted were being asked to put their lives on the line when many of us were unable to see any credible threat to our national security from the "enemy" in Vietnam. The government refused to modify its misguided policies in any significant way, but instead continued to drop more bombs and commit more troops. Here at home, people who tried to help black Americans in the south exercise their rights were beaten and murdered. If bodies on the gears did not stop the machine, then it would have to be smashed with whatever tools were at hand. The mindset of war was beginning to define the domestic front and one defining feature of that way of thinking was that those on the opposing side can do no right, giving rise to the common phrase from the time: "If you are not part of the solution, you are part of the problem."

But every war has two sides, and many Americans leaning toward a conservative philosophy were rapidly moving further to the right in response to what they perceived as a frightening breakdown of "law and order." The post office went so far as to issue a "Law and Order" stamp and, even though the engraving depicted a police officer leading a young schoolboy across the street, I always saw it as a timely right-wing political statement.

Reagan was establishing his reputation as a champion of the cause by his highly-charged speeches and strong actions as governor of California against protests and disturbances. His appeals to his political base were often laced with code words that were nothing more than thinly veiled pandering to the racial prejudices of many in his audiences, because even at this early stage of the rise of "movement conservatism" its proponents were well aware of the political advantages to be gained by exploiting those feelings.

The perception among many "traditional" whites that blacks were trying to take over was strengthened by the recently passed voting and civil rights acts, but most of all by the well-publicized spectacles of the urban riots and the disturbing rhetoric of black power radicals. Overt bigots such as Lester Maddox and George Wallace were less circumspect in their appeals to all the worst instincts of their followers, never hesitating to link the anti-war and black power movements for their own political gain. Those of us on the left made a similar connection, noting that many of the same voices on the right supporting domestic order by any means necessary were also strong supporters of the war. This perception was powerfully reinforced when General Hershey endorsed Wallace for president. Now the man who encouraged local draft boards to suppress our right to free speech by drafting protestors was joining forces with a shameless bigot who had devoted his life to denying black Americans their lawful rights. It was becoming clearer every day who our true enemy was, and it was not the people fighting for their homeland in Southeast Asia.

Other noteworthy events that summer included the July publication by Paul VI of the papal encyclical *Humanae Vitae* forbidding birth control. This teaching has never been accepted by the vast majority of Catholics, and since it disregarded the recommendation of the papal commission appointed by John XXIII to study this issue it also displayed a blatant disregard for the collegial spirit of Vatican II. None of this really bothered me at the time, though, since I considered myself a Catholic in name only.

That same month the film *The Green Berets* premiered, an uninspiring pro-war propaganda piece staring an aging John Wayne, now a darling of the ultra-patriotic law and order crowd, making a fool of himself portraying a Special Forces colonel in Vietnam. The US base at Khe Sanh was abandoned that July ending one of the crucial battles of the war, but also leaving many Americans puzzled over the purpose of the epic siege that had resulted in the deaths of 205 Americans. We had been told ad nauseam by now that this war was different from those of the past, but could anyone from the World War II generation ever have imagined abandoning the hard-won turf of Bastogne or Iwo Jima shortly after those legendary battles had been won?

In September, protests at the annual Miss America Pageant in Atlantic City brought the Women's Liberation Movement into the national spotlight. The highly creative activities included drawing a comparison between the pageant and livestock competitions by crowning a live sheep, and one lasting legacy of the affair was the often pejorative conflating of "women's lib" and bra burning, even though to this day there is uncertainty over whether any bras actually were burned.

The Black Panthers made headlines again the same month when Huey Newton was convicted of manslaughter for the shooting of an Oakland police officer during an affray the previous year in which Newton himself was seriously wounded. The verdict was overturned in 1970 and after two subsequent mistrials the district attorney declined to try him a fourth time and dismissed the charges.

Near the end of September, the Milwaukee 14—a group of fourteen antiwar activists—used homemade napalm to burn approximately ten-thousand draft records in that city, declaring that "the service of life no longer provides any option other than positive concrete action against what can only be called the American Way of Death." This was one of many such events instigated primarily by Catholic anti-war activists but it especially interested me because one of the participants was Al Janicke, a priest who had been one of my counselors at the Ascension Club summer program during his days as a seminarian. He ended up serving about a year in federal prison.

The upcoming political conventions that summer were highly anticipated events, especially since LBJ had announced his decision not to run again.

The Republicans met in early August in Miami Beach, nominating Richard Nixon and Spiro Agnew of Maryland. Agnew was largely unknown outside of the northeast but it seemed almost inconceivable that a discredited has-been like Nixon could make such a dramatic comeback. He had learned to exploit the fear and anger felt by many Americans over the rising tide of social unrest, although it was not until late in the following year that he began to describe these citizens as the "silent majority."

Two weeks later the Democratic convention convened in Chicago. Activists had planned massive demonstrations and Mayor Daley and his staff had refused to issue them permits, instead arranging for an astonishing 23,000 police officers and National Guard soldiers to provide security. It was clear that the situation would be volatile, but one of the first signs of things turning sour was a particularly ugly incident on the convention floor itself when Dan Rather was assaulted and knocked to the floor by security guards, all the while reporting the shocking occurrence to Walter Cronkite in the CBS booth high above the action. The most trusted man in America exclaimed, "I think we've got a bunch of thugs here, Dan."

On the 28th the notorious "police riot" broke out in and around Grant Park when 10,000 protestors and 1,000 police officers clashed in a series of pitched battles that left hundreds injured and thousands overcome by tear gas. Much of the battle was broadcast live to the huge TV audiences watching the convention, and the most memorable chant from the protestors was "the whole world is watching!" As expected, the Humphrey-Muskie ticket received their party's nomination, a setback for the anti-war cause because Humphrey had not yet distanced himself significantly from any of LBJ's policies. An unanticipated additional disappointment, however, was that opinion polls showed the majority of Americans supporting the tactics of Mayor Daley's security forces. Because of these outcomes, the result of the convention riots was somewhat comparable to that of the Tet Offensive in Vietnam. The activists had proven they could rally a massive number of protestors, bait the authorities into a violent over-reaction, and attract more media attention than they had dreamed possible. But at the same time, they found that all this dramatic activity accomplished little or nothing in terms of converting the public to the anti-war side. Indeed, it seemed to have had the opposite effect, driving more of the "silent majority" into the "law and order" and "America—love it or leave it" camps.

Mailer wrote another long article on the conventions for the November issue of *Harper's* that was published soon after that as the book *Miami and the Siege of Chicago*, another defining work of New Journalism, although, characteristically, Mailer himself balked at the term. He felt that the choice between Humphrey and Nixon was no choice at all. I agreed with him and that was a painful thing to admit since I had admired Hubert H. Humphrey (HHH) for years. I remembered him giving a rousing speech, undoubtedly on working people and the union movement, while standing on a picnic table at the annual Mailmen's Picnic at Ryan's Resort on Bass Lake in Crystal in the mid-1950s. He had also been a leader in getting civil rights legislation passed. Yet I could not be for anyone who was not against the war.

A local event of national significance occurred in the last week of July with the founding of the American Indian Movement in Minneapolis, an appropriate setting since our city boasts the largest urban population of Native Americans in the country. Here was another manifestation of the growing unwillingness of groups who had been treated unfairly, often for centuries, to tolerate the status quo any longer. Despite the resistance of much of mainstream America to this trend, it seemed like a healthy thing to many of us that long-standing injustices we had not even been aware of during our Eisenhower-era childhoods were finally being brought to light. If that made straight society uncomfortable, so be it.

***

In mid-August plans for the annual campus orientation program for foreign students at the UM were announced, and these included the usual panels and discussion groups on various aspects of American life as well as home-stays with host families. The student power movement would be discussed by a panel of two U administrators and two self-described "radical students," but what attracted the most notice was the text for this presentation: An essay published the previous year by Jerry Farber, an educator from California, entitled "The Student as Nigger." This piece took the rhetoric of the student power movement to new heights by comparing the relationship of college students and administrators to that between slaves and masters. This analogy, as well as the use of such a highly charged term in the title, certainly must have been offensive to many black Americans, but the author's style and content were a reflection of the militant and confrontational approach that had now come to define student activism and much of the counterculture on both coasts. Even so, orientation sessions for foreign students were hardly newsworthy affairs, especially since they were held at a time of year when most students were not on campus. What we did not know yet was that Farber's essay was also being distributed to the instructors for freshman English at their orientation meetings, a decision that would soon garner the attention of the entire campus community.

I was reading a good deal of literature and criticism and looking forward to the life of a grad student, but also enjoying my last few weeks at the PO during the pleasant September weather. By this time I was friends with some of the carriers and I loved it when they kidded me in a big brother sort of way, a sure sign that I had been accepted into the group. I had started growing a mustache in August and it was coming in slowly, so they said maybe I should use some shoe polish on it—stuff like that.

Our apple tree in the backyard was dying so I cut it down, burned some of the wood, and gave the rest to the Lundeen family across the alley because they could use it for smoking fish.

The first elections since I turned twenty-one were coming up, so I voted in the city primary. That was a good feeling, but the presidential race was the one that really counted, and how could I vote for either one of those guys?

One day I had a long talk with Ben, one of the carriers about my age, and he was complaining about the alimony he had to pay and how he hardly ever got to see his kids. That got me thinking again about what a scary thing the commitment of marriage was, and how messed up things could get if the couple decided they were not right for each other. Of course, I had no prospects there, although I considered asking Bernie if she would be interested in going out again, because she really was a good sort and we always had fun together. One of our last dates had been to a screening of some crazy underground movies at the Cedar on the West Bank. If I felt depressed I thought about Glenda, and if I was not depressed thoughts of her would make me that way, always a good reason for having a few drinks. I was hoping for better luck among the female grad students.

Things were in a state of transition and Dave Giel, another sub who was also a student at the U, had his last day at the PO on the 14th. We intended to keep in touch on campus. Dave was married and had been in the Army, so I enjoyed hearing his views on these unexplored areas that might very well be a part of my future. He liked being married but he had hated being in the Army.

Early in September, I had a check up with Russ Engstrom, who had been my dentist since I was a young child. He was very intelligent, read voraciously on a wide variety of subjects, and loved to converse, so appointments with him were always interesting. He could easily carry on a monologue when my mouth was full of equipment, but he was also genuinely interested in the views of others and usually asked questions when the patient could talk. I knew he really listened, too, because he often related something that another patient had told him. Since I was studying English, he asked if doing research in the humanities was similar to the social or hard sciences in that there was always the problem of limiting the subject matter. I was flattered that he would ask my opinion on something like that so I answered as best I could.

Although I did not mention it to Russ, it seemed to me that an even more formidable challenge would be finding a subject that had not already been covered, usually many times over. The endless shelves of literary criticism in the library presented a rather intimidating sight, not to mention all the unpublished black-bound masters and doctoral theses. He also mentioned that he had been over in Dinkytown the previous evening and was struck by how many young men were sporting some sort of facial hair. My own attempt at a mustache probably reminded him of that. I found that observation intriguing because, since I spent so much time on campus, I had not paid much attention to the gradual arrival of that trend. I imagine Russ was also struck by the contrast in dress and appearance between the campus and our home territory of St. Anthony Village and Northeast Minneapolis.

***

On the 17th I went over to the U for grad student orientation and registration. That was Welcome Week and the campus was a busy place. A small army of library workers was in the process of moving well over a million volumes from Walter Library to the new Wilson Library on the West Bank. Also on the West Bank, there was a new underground bookstore between Anderson and Blegen Halls. It was much plusher than the older campus bookstores, with wide aisles, bright lighting, and wall-to-wall carpeting. Unfortunately, despite the pleasant appearance it was soon to be plagued with chronic moisture and mold problems, and the U would eventually be forced by OSHA regulations to vacate the space after nearly forty years of smelly frustration.

Professor Bob Moore conducted our orientation session. He was kind and approachable, but did want to make sure we understood that these studies would be more demanding than those of our undergraduate days. I was pleased that he recommended taking only three courses the first quarter because that had been my plan. I was going to take a history class on the French Revolution and Napoleon and the first course in the eighteenth century English Literature sequence for undergrad credit to finish my bachelor's degree, and Old English as my first graduate-level course. Bob Moore was my advisor also, so after I filled out my registration materials I went over to Vincent Hall that afternoon to get his approval. He was intrigued by my dual status for one quarter, but did not see it as a problem. He said to take Samuel Holt Monk's section of the eighteenth century class, and this pleased me greatly since Professor Monk had edited the eighteenth century section of *The Norton Anthology of English Literature*. It seemed as though I was about to experience the best the U had to offer in my field of study.

The rest of the afternoon was an extremely frustrating sequence of long, slow lines and registration clerks confused by my status and sending me back and forth across the plaza between Morrill and Johnston. I was concerned about problems because with classes starting the following week there would be little time to work them out, but I finally got all three of the IBM reservation cards I needed. One benefit of taking only three courses was that I ended up with no classes on Tuesdays, which would allow more time for the uninterrupted study and research that Professor Moore had reminded us was necessary for success in graduate studies.

Among the local events of interest was Walter Mondale's call for an unconditional halt to the bombing of North Vietnam. This was especially noteworthy because Fritz was a co-chair of Humphrey's campaign and HHH had not called for such a halt. The ever-loyal Mondale said he still supported Humphrey and two weeks later Hubert changed his position, stating that he would halt the bombing if elected. Nixon disagreed with this stance.

The University of Southern California (USC) defeated the U in football at Memorial Stadium, with O.J. Simpson scoring four touchdowns, gaining 236 rushing yards, 50 yards by passing, and 72 on kickoff returns. With the Twins in seventh place and having nothing to lose, Cesar Tovar played all nine positions in one game and the team defeated Oakland 2-1. Nicollet Field in South Minneapolis was renamed MLK Park.

★★★

My last couple of weeks at the PO were uneventful, and I had Sunday the 22nd off before the first day of fall quarter. I took the bus to campus on Monday as I usually did and spent a little time exploring the new additions to the West Bank campus. Wilson Library was open now, although not fully functional yet. Like the entire West Bank campus, it struck me as sterile and corporate, but undeniably functional and comfortably furnished. My history class was in Anderson Hall, and the professor was Paul Bamford, a thin, highly strung man with the pale yellow hair of a red head going gray. I thought I was going to like him, and his first fast-moving lecture held my interest. I was taking the class for undergrad credit and no paper was required, which would free up more time for the two English courses. Professor Monk was close to retirement, but with a stocky build that seemed anything but fragile. He was another engaging instructor who obviously enjoyed what he was doing. I had been a bit concerned about taking a class from such an eminent scholar because Allan Tate had a reputation as an intimidating slave driver, but Sam Monk did not give me that impression and I felt fortunate to be in his class. The professor for Old English was Cal Kendall, the same instructor who had taught my Chaucer class the previous spring. He was so good-natured that I always felt comfortable around him, and I was impressed by his knowledge of such esoteric subjects as Old and Middle English. I was not looking forward to all the rote learning in the class, but it was a requirement for grad students so we were all in it together and Cal tried to assure us that the first few chapters of the text were the worst.

For a couple of weeks at the beginning of the term, concern over the war and draft were relegated to second place as the controversy over the possible use of "The Student as Nigger" ("SAN") in freshman English held the attention of the campus. The much-maligned Chair of the department, John Clark, had responded to the possible use of the piece by issuing an imperious directive banning the essay from departmental reading lists. He added the unfortunate observation that requiring freshmen to read such material was "imprudent" in a year when the state legislature would be setting the U's biennial allocation. This was a double assault on academic freedom because of the chair's unilateral ban and the implication that the faculty's choice of classroom material should be influenced by fear of offending state office-holders, many of whom made no secret of their strongly conservative leanings.

On Monday the 30th I had lunch with my friend Dave from the PO and his brother Jim, a freshman, on the steps on the east side of Coffman. As we were walking back up the mall there was a raucous rally being held on the front steps of Vincent protesting the banning of "SAN." A couple of speakers were shouting into a megaphone in an attempt to whip the relatively sedate crowd of about 200 into a state of at least mild excitement—a frenzy equal to that of the speakers seemed to be out of the question. They were employing the militant confrontational style of activism we had seen on newscasts of events at Columbia and Berkeley, and heard in speeches by black power activists. Some of the onlookers were picking up on it by shouting back both in support and opposition. The centerpiece of the crowds' attention was a large picket sign with the blunt message "Fuck Puritans" in big black letters. One of the speakers was reviling "the system" in equally graphic terms and when some onlookers began to take exception to her obscenity-laced tirade, she shouted "fuck society!" The noise level was rising rapidly, and one female freshman climbed the stairs and complained about an event such as this marring her first week at the U. There seemed to be no shortage of shouting and emotionally charged exchanges, but apparently it was not enough to satisfy the organizers because later that afternoon one of them complained during an interview about the small number of students willing to hold signs at the rally, concluding "they really are niggers!"

The level of concern raised by the chair's censorship memo was vividly illustrated by the fact that the next day a special English departmental meeting on the subject actually attracted 150 people. One of them was a *Daily* reporter and so the paper carried a firsthand front-page account of proceedings rarely observed by outsiders. As expected, John Clark came in for a hail of blunt criticism, although he was not without some supporters. He admitted he may have made a mistake and said he was perfectly willing to abide by the results of a vote on a motion to rescind the ban on the essay. The motion passed with only one hand raised against it, and I assume the reporter would have informed his readers if that vote had been cast by Clark. Meanwhile, the *Daily* itself was coming under fire from folks outside the U for printing obscenities, especially a large front-page picture that included the offending sign, which was almost certainly the first time the word "fuck" had appeared in our college newspaper. I remember laughing out loud at the sight. The editors replied as expected: They did not create the news but merely reported it, and they normally did not print obscene language but in this case felt it was essential to the story. Just to add to the excitement, on the same day some black power advocates held a "Free Huey Newton" rally on Northrop Plaza featuring boisterous speakers and a few indifferent onlookers.

I had read "SAN" to see what all the fuss was about, and the crux of Farber's argument was the same point that student power advocates had been voicing for the last several years: College administrators, including the faculty, treated students as inferiors by exercising unwarranted power over both our studies and our lives outside of the classroom. Farber focused much of his attention on the rigid caste system of the academic community, which is where he used the master/slave analogy, but he further illustrated his points with a number of graphic sexual metaphors, leading to the piece being branded as pornographic as well as insulting to blacks.

The editorial staff of the *Daily* now felt that the essay should be available to the campus community and they began printing the entire piece in a series of issues beginning on October 3. The Board of Publications, moving remarkably fast for a U committee, upheld the editors' decision to print the photo of the notorious sign, as well as the graphic language of some of the speakers at the rally. The *Daily* editor, Paul Gruchow, expressed surprise that, given the volume of angry mail and phone calls he had received, not a single person appeared at the board meeting to complain in person. The paper had printed a sampling of letters on both sides of the issue. Many of us found more humor than anything else surrounding the whole controversy, and the *Daily* reported that "perhaps the healthiest reaction was a professor's incredulous comment on the sign's inscription: 'Who would want to?'"

In early October, I received my Graduate Student Certificate to send on to my draft board, which was Local Board Number 40 in the Federal Building at Washington and 3rd Ave, the same building where I had my physical. It did not appear this would help keep me out of the military since the SSS was no longer issuing grad student deferments for most fields of study not deemed "essential," including English, but I mailed it to the board anyway just so they would know I was doing something constructive. The same week, the U dropped its policy of notifying draft boards when a student quit school or graduated. It was unclear why our administrators had adopted such a policy in the first place since the U apparently was the only college that did this, and even Colonel Knight had to admit that such notifications had never been a requirement. He did go on to warn us that students who took advantage of the change by registering and then dropping out would be caught eventually. It went without saying that the penalty could be a possible death sentence: being sent to fight in Vietnam. But, then again, the same thing would happen if you did notify them—Catch-22?

The link between racism and support for the war was strengthened the same week when Wallace named General Curtis LeMay as his running mate. The general was a prime example of a World War II commander whose obsession with communist aggression now seemed to have crossed the line into the realm of total irrationality. Back in 1965 he had written that the way to deal with North Vietnam was to bomb them "back into the stone age," and it was clear that he would not limit such an assault to conventional weapons since he also scoffed at many civilian leaders' phobia over nuclear weapons, explaining that "military men generally consider them just another weapon in the arsenal." Alpha Smaby, a candidate for the state legislature, reacted to the dismal choice offered by the three presidential tickets in language that reflected my own sentiments: "Politically, this year is the year of the turd."

* * *

My classes continued to provide a welcome relief from all the worry and turmoil of current events. Kendall's amiability helped to temper the tedium of Old English and, because he conducted a less formal classroom than Monk, that class was also the best opportunity to try to get to know some of my fellow English grad students. I wished that I was a teaching assistant like many of them because that would have been an even better way to become acquainted. Professor Monk had told us on the first day of class that he had been living in the eighteenth century for the last forty years, and the depth of his knowledge combined with his obvious love of the subject matter made that class a pleasure. He would give learned lectures on such charmingly esoteric subjects as true and false wit, grace, and sentimentalism. I often felt just barely able to grasp his meaning, but he never patronized his students and I loved the feeling of being challenged to rise to a higher level of scholarship. He insisted that the only way to understand the literature of any given era was to become familiar with the history and other arts of the period as well, and this made sense to me because that had been my experience when I studied American history and literature at the same time during junior year. Any great work of art will stand on its own, but the perception of the observer or reader will be greatly enriched by understanding its context. One thing he never said, although I would wager that he believed it, was that we could never achieve a truly solid grasp of these writers without knowing Greek and Latin.

Meanwhile, Bamford began his course with a series of lectures designed to help us understand the background of the French Revolution, beginning with descriptions of the three, and possibly four, estates comprising late eighteenth century French society. Anger over injustices that had festered for centuries reached a critical mass in a relatively short period of time, and then the third estate, the *sans-culottes*, exploded in a paroxysm of violence that would have been inconceivable only a few years earlier. To me, this situation bore an unmistakable resemblance to what was happening in contemporary America. Just as Farber had indulged in hyperbolic absurdity by comparing us to slaves, it would have been equally ridiculous to equate us boomers who had come of age amid such unprecedented prosperity to the starving French peasantry, and yet it appeared to me that there was enough similarity in the political and social environments to make a study of them relevant to our own current national unrest.

We found ourselves in the middle of a situation that none of us could have anticipated before the death of JFK, and now a government that many of us had lost respect for was compelling us, at the best, to give up two years of our lives fighting a war we had come to despise. The sudden unwillingness among racial minorities and women to tolerate injustices that had prevailed for centuries also bore a strong resemblance to the reaction of the oppressed French common people. Exactly what was happening and how would it turn out? Was our America in the early stages of a revolution? I hoped this course would help shed some light on these vexing questions for me, and I loved the fact that Paul leaned far to the left politically. He was more liberal than I, in fact, displaying an obvious affinity for the Marxist worldview.

On Friday the 4th I had lunch again with Dave and Jim. As we were going into Coffman there was a rally starting out in front organized by the Peace and Freedom Party to protest the fact that only two out of 600 workers on U construction projects were black. That was not surprising, and many of the hard-hats were among the counter-protestors at anti-war rallies as well. We went down and ate in the North Star Room which, along with the Ski-U-Mah Room, was one of the two large bag lunch and vending machine facilities in the union. In those days when so many students commuted, these places were always crowded, noisy, and messy, but that was just part of life on the campus. The situation in the basement vending area of Walter Library had gotten so bad that it was dubbed "The Bay of Pigs," and the U had removed all the food machines the previous year.

I had taken to eating and studying frequently in the vending room of the Science Classroom Building at Pleasant and Washington, an equally unprepossessing environment, out of force of habit and the lack of anything better. While we were down in the North Star Room, I saw another Dave that I had worked with in the dishwashing room the previous year, and he had grown a thick mustache that put mine to shame. As we left Coffman, the rally was ending and, like many such events in those days, it had more than one purpose: They were also protesting the fact that the U was not boycotting California grapes—in solidarity with a labor strike against the grape growers of California—and the students' next step was to march up the Mall to Morrill Hall and deliver a list of demands to the President's Office.

Mid-October brought a spell of warm and humid days. On Sunday the 13th I helped Dad shampoo the living room carpet and rearrange some of the furniture. I know now he was also feeling a high level of stress in those days, but the two of us still got along well and I enjoyed doing projects around the house with him now and then. The timing of our carpet cleaning was unfortunate given the weather and I think it took at least a week for it to dry out completely, but it was a job well done.

I had been riding my bicycle to campus most days, but I gave that up for the car or the bus to avoid arriving as a sweaty mess. Professor Monk was out ill for several days, but I always had plenty of reading to do so I usually spent the extra time in the library's reserve reading room.

One day in Bamford's class a student asked him the question I had been mulling over: Did he see any similarity between the French Revolution and the student revolt of today? As we had come to expect, Paul gave a long, convoluted answer that only a die-hard academic could love, but his conclusion was that today's students were too middle class to start anything close to a true revolt. The next day the guy who had raised the question asked me what I thought of the answer, because he did not like it. I said I did not care for it either, but that it was probably true. I had studied enough about Marxism to know that Paul would feel a true revolt must originate with the proletariat, not the spoiled children of the bourgeoisie. Even so, I felt he had addressed the issue too narrowly in his answer and that there was indeed much to be learned from the comparison.

Just when it seemed that every possible variation on the theme of draft resistance had been played out, something new came up. Sydney Walter, artistic director of the Firehouse Theatre—the former home of Melvin

McCosh's bookstore on the West Bank—had been classified III-A, exempt, because he was thirty-three years old and the father of three children. Despite the fact that he had no chance of being drafted, his principled opposition to conscription and the war was so strong that he returned his draft card to his local board. Following the now-familiar pattern of using the draft to punish resistors, his board called him up. On October 15, accompanied by about 200 supporters, he showed up at the Federal Building to refuse induction. There is an element of street theater to all demonstrations, but since many of his companions were actors this one was more flamboyant than most. The feature performance was "The First Miss Resist Contest," with a young lady named Carol Swardson taking the lead role in a fetching little black dress. Her apparel was soon abandoned, however, as she discarded every stitch of her clothing and proceeded to chop up a melon with a large knife on the front steps. She was not arrested because no police officers admitted to witnessing the display and none of the spectators would sign a complaint. The rally ended shortly after Walter left the building. The *Minneapolis Star* labeled the incident the "What Our Boys Are Fighting for Item of the Week."

As the month moved along, the heat was succeeded by a number of days of heavy rain that knocked most of the autumn leaves off of the trees. Professor Monk returned but his lectures were frequently interrupted by coughing spells. We were on Pope now, a favorite of mine, and I always looked forward to Monk's insightful analysis. We thought Bamford had concluded his discussion of the French peasantry since even he admitted that he had beaten the subject to death, but then he continued with it. This time, though, he gave us graphic descriptions of the abject misery of their existence that made his presentation far more compelling. The comparison with the privileged lives of the nobility and clergy revealed such a striking and gross injustice that now it became more clear to us how a class of people who had been treated as little better than beasts of burden could suddenly explode into an orgy of murderous violence. I had read *A Tale of Two Cities* at De La Salle, but I read it again for an additional perspective on the mad and unpredictable world that was revolutionary France. Dickens's famous opening sentence also described our own times for me because, along with all the depressing news and fear of the draft, there was also a level of intensity that I found both exciting and even addictive.

Paul never made a secret of his political views and they were all based on economics, but he limited his comments to the era of the revolution, making only some infrequent, covert, and vague comparisons to our contemporary world. I wondered if he had been criticized at some point during the red scare for being so left-wing. Sam Monk made far fewer political observations, but that made us all the more appreciative when they popped up in his lectures. He changed the date of our mid-quarter exam because he realized it was scheduled for the Wednesday after Election Day, observing that it would be bad enough waking up and realizing Nixon was president without having to worry about taking a test as well. Most of the class applauded. When he talked about Bernard Mandeville's *The Fable of the Bees*, he observed how the poem applied to our own civilization in that, just as the hive thrived on evil and vice, our own nation seemed to require a wartime economy to remain prosperous. World War II pulled us out of the depression and, despite Ike's eloquent warning of the dangers of the powerful influence of the military-industrial complex, our defense budget had been bloated ever since. That had been one of the lessons I took from studying twentieth century American history, but, coming from a wise old man like Monk who had lived through the entire century to date, the depressing observation had an even sharper poignancy. Cal Kendall, on the other hand, never talked about anything that happened after the middle of the twelfth century.

★★★

There was time for fun as well. Over the summer I had picked up the habit of watching a bit too much TV, and shortly before Halloween we were treated to the third annual broadcast of *It's the Great Pumpkin, Charlie Brown*, which had immediately become a ritual cherished almost as dearly as the Christmas show. The three younger kids and I had carved the pumpkin the night before Halloween. Mary dressed as a man, wearing an old hat and coat of Dad's along with a black cardboard mustache—it was hilarious. Jane was a gypsy. John went as Dracula, then came back in later and changed into a hippie—such creativity, or was this a scheme to hit the same houses twice? We had about sixty kids show up at the door, which was much fewer than when Dave and I used to make the rounds.

On Saturday, November 2, I went over to campus in the evening to see the film *Will the Real Norman Mailer Please Stand Up?* in the Nicholson auditorium. The sound was terrible, but we had been warned about that. Having read his account of the march on the Pentagon, it was especially exciting to see Mailer and Robert Lowell in action in those scenes. I knew he was a master of self-promotion, but I liked what he was selling so I did not mind. What would you expect from the man who wrote a book entitled *Advertisements for Myself*? I even saw a couple of people I knew from classes there, so it was a good time.

My brother Dave was starting his second year at the Minneapolis College of Art and Design with an emphasis on photography, and one of his projects was to take some shots of the hanging scene from the Ambrose Bierce short story "An Incident at Owl Creek Bridge." I had agreed to play the role of the condemned man, so on Sunday, November 3, the two of us set out to find an appropriate setting with no contemporary buildings visible in the background. We drove through Wirth Park and then south, finally finding a railroad bridge between Cedar Lake and Lake of the Isles that Dave said looked good. The next Sunday we returned, but even though the site had the required rural feel it was hardly deserted. First a parade of trains came by, and then we noticed some kids watching us from another bridge. I'm sure we did present a curious sight. I finally got out on one of the supports with the noose around my neck, but another train appeared before Dave could take a picture so we ducked down below. It was snowing and our feet were freezing, especially Dave's because to get the angle he wanted for his photographs he had to wade out into a pond wearing Dad's hip boots. We also noticed a railroad shack further down the track with men going in and out, so we were waiting for a chance when none of them were outside.

Finally, we were getting so cold that we decided to just go ahead, so there I was looking like I was about to be hanged when another train came by, but I just stood there like a fool until it passed and then Dave finally had his chance. But then two railroad workers snuck up behind me and starting untying the end of the rope from the bridge railing. I was glad they had not startled me because I might have fallen, although it was a short drop and we had made sure the rope was much longer than the distance to the ground. So then I told them we were taking pictures for a story and asked if we could use the bridge. They said that they were keeping watch because a woman had jumped off one of their bridges the previous week, but that we could just go ahead with what we were doing. The unfortunate dénouement to this little drama was that Dave developed the pictures that night and, because the camera was new to him, only two came out.

Tuesday, November 5, was Election Day and I had made my final decision only the previous day to write in for McCarthy. Mom and I drove over to the polling place in the early afternoon and there were no lines. I know she was disappointed in my choice of McCarthy, but that was my decision at the time. HHH took Minnesota, of course, despite the McCarthy write-in effort, but I learned from that election not to use your vote to try to register a protest or make a point. The only thing that makes sense is to support the candidate closest to your views who has a realistic chance of winning, because nothing can be accomplished by someone who is not elected. That seems like common sense now, but I was young and during wartime common sense is often in short supply. Wallace took several southern states, raising the possibility that neither of the two major-party candidates would receive a majority of the electoral votes, and I went to bed at 2:30 a.m. with the outcome uncertain but Nixon favored to win.

The next morning Nixon still had the edge and everyone was awaiting the final outcome from Illinois. I bet Mayor Daley was doing all he could to pump up the totals from Chicago and suppress those from the more conservative southern part of the state. I took the bus to campus and there was certainly no air of excitement among the other passengers about the close contest. There had been an all-night election "party" in the new lounge in Anderson Hall so I went over there to check things out. There was one black-and-white TV, a big coffee percolator, and a chattering teletype machine over in the corner. The drapes were open but it was heavily overcast outside with the look of approaching snow, so all the stark florescent lights were still burning. Some people must have pulled an all-nighter because they really looked beat, but most of us had arrived in the morning. No one seemed excited, and I kept thinking what a lousy way this was for most of us to begin our lives as voters.

The day continued to be a downer as Bamford gave his most boring lecture of the term so far with only about half of the class attending. Before Monk's class began, I heard a guy say that Humphrey had made his concession speech, and I felt no reaction.

Professor Monk gave a lecture on Pope's nature poetry that was easily the highlight of the day. He had mentioned before that he felt Pope and Tennyson were the two finest craftsmen in English poetry, and what a curious thing that is when you consider the vast difference in their styles. It speaks volumes about the versatility of the language. Cal had lost his voice so we had no Old English class. I went over to the Co-op Jr on Washington Avenue and bought four Modern Library books and the issue of *Harper's* with Mailer's long report on the political conventions and then went home to read the magazine. I wanted to read about the mess that was the current state of affairs in America as seen by someone I respected. It was so depressing to think that we had four years of Nixon coming up. Considering his rabid anti-communist views back during the Red Scare, it was frightening to speculate on how he might conduct the war.

The election was the most important event of that fall but there were other things going on as well and, as is always true, the lasting significance of some of them was not clear at the time. On September 30, the first episode of the comic strip by Gary Trudeau that was to become *Doonesbury* was published in the Yale newspaper, with the curious title of *Bull Tales*. The next day the first *Whole Earth Catalog* was published. Subtitled "Access to Tools," this work quickly became a staple of the counterculture. We still have our copy of the last one. On October 11, Apollo 7 was launched as the first manned mission of that series, and a highlight was the first live telecast from an American spacecraft. The successful completion of the mission was especially celebrated because it was the first attempt at a manned space flight since a fire had killed the three crew members and destroyed the command module during a launch pad test of Apollo 1 the previous year.

The next week at the Olympics in Mexico City, two US athletes raised their gloved fists in the black power salute during the worldwide broadcast of the 200-meter medal presentation, an act that resulted in the loss of their gold and bronze medals. Near the end of October, there was a week with 100 American deaths in Vietnam, the lowest weekly total in fourteen months. On Halloween LBJ halted all bombing of North Vietnam, a move widely seen as a half-hearted last-ditch effort to boost Humphrey's chances in the election the following week. In the middle of November, a five-alarm fire destroyed the S.S. Kresge store at 7th and Nicollet. The same week, Calvin Griffith, owner of the Twins responded to complaints from season ticket holders by declaring that players would no longer be allowed to sport "bushy" sideburns.

Treatment of racial minorities continued to attract attention as the Minnesota Human Rights Board declared that the state seal, which features a settler plowing his field with a musket at the ready nearby while an Indian rides his horse toward the west, should be redesigned because it depicted warfare and was derogatory to Indians. Nothing came of the proposal.

Scotty Stone was hired by black students at St. Cloud State to help them achieve their demands of a cultural center and more black teachers, and their efforts proved successful as the president agreed to most of their proposals. At that time there were twenty-four black students on the campus out of a total enrollment of 9,000. At Oshkosh State University, a group of predominantly black students seemed to be taking a cue from their classmates in Madison as they went on a destructive rampage through the administration building after the president there refused their demands. The campus was closed for a week and there were more than 100 arrests. Shortly before the presidential election, Whitney Young, Executive Director of the National Urban League, made the pointed statement that "black people who don't know which of the two to vote for deserve slavery." The next day, a rare and unexpected note of humor briefly lightened the tense atmosphere when aides for both Humphrey and Nixon called Young to thank him for his support.

It was time for mid-quarter exams and on Friday the 8th we had the one Professor Monk had postponed because of the election, plus another quiz in Old English. Before Cal's class got started I talked with some of the women in the class and they were nice enough to invite me to a lasagna dinner one of them was preparing that night. This was one of those rare and mysterious experiences that lead to an irrevocable alteration in the course of our lives even though, like most of the random events in our ongoing journey through time and space, they appear utterly trivial when they occur. One of the women who extended the dinner invitation was my future wife, Bev, and this was the first time we had spoken to each other. Unfortunately, I already had a ticket for *A Flea in Her Ear* at Scott Hall so I declined. I went to the play alone and found it amusing and clever. One of the actors was Pete Foy, a member of the DLS class of 1963 that I knew from the Dramatics Club, and that made the production particularly interesting to me.

As the term moved into its final weeks, the students and faculty began to feel the usual stress of deadlines for completing our work. Professor Monk said he had realized over the Veterans' Day weekend that the quarter was almost over and we had hardly started on Pope. I needed to write a paper on *Moll Flanders* for him, but was experiencing a serious attack of procrastination that could only be cured by the pressure of a deadline. I preferred to spend time in the beautiful high-ceilinged reading room on the north side of the second floor of Walter Library reading such things as Johnson's *Lives of the English Poets*, which were, after all, also part of the requirements for the class. Dr. Johnson related how Abraham Cowley held the degree of Master of Arts, and that seemed to me like a very fine thing indeed.

Paul Bamford said that many students had been complaining about their score on his last quiz, and then went on to reassure us that one quiz was only a small part of the entire course. He used a bizarre metaphor comparing taking a class to frying bacon, with the flash in the pan of one quiz being necessary if you wanted a nice crisp piece, or a successful conclusion to the course, at the end. Apparently, figurative language was not one of his fortes. I thought his quizzes were quite easy, especially since he told us virtually everything that would be covered, but at least he paid attention to his students' concerns, justified or not. We were making our way through *Apollonius of Tyre* in Cal's class, and he gave an amusing lecture on how the Old English scribes had toned down some of the love scenes. I finally wrote and typed my paper for Professor Monk, and in the end I found that I wished we would have been allowed more words.

On Thursday the 21st I drove to the U and walked through Dinkytown and the campus to Ford Hall for Old English class. I arrived early and there was Bev sitting on one of the benches in the hall. This was the first time we had a one-on-one conversation, so we started by introducing ourselves because, even though we were both in Monk's and Kendall's classes, we did not know each others' first names. In those days of greater classroom formality, our professors always addressed us as "Miss Minear" and "Mr. Atkinson." I had been hoping for a chance like this since the dinner invitation on the 8th. The only ring she was wearing was a college one, so that was good. I noticed she was reading *The Quiet American*, and a novel about Vietnam was certainly a very timely thing. She was from Florida, and as a lifelong Minnesotan I found that rather exotic. We had a good chat and I thought she was really something special, but socializing, and especially the stress of a first date, seemed out of the question at that crazy time of the quarter, not to mention the problem of my uncertain situation with the military. My hope was to spend more time with her after the holiday break and see what developed.

There was one mildly encouraging piece of news on the draft when General Hershey announced near the end of November that grad students who were called up would be allowed to finish their current quarter or semester. Since I had not received a draft notice yet and fall was almost over, that almost certainly meant that I would not be called up until the end of winter quarter at the earliest. Less hopeful was the news that Minnesota's draft quota for January was to be 633, which was 200 higher than December and the highest since the previous May.

On the night of November 7 arson fires had been set in the off-campus offices of both the Twin Cities Draft Information Center and Students Against Selective Service. On the 14th a number of anti-war activists from the U participated in the fourth National Resistance Day. The events included a secular "service" at a packed First Unitarian Church that included a call for those attending to turn in their draft cards, resulting in a total of 38 being collected. The biggest event was a rally on Northrop Plaza followed by a parade to downtown Minneapolis. The goal was to emphasize the liberating aspects of resisting the injustice of conscription and so the atmosphere was one of celebration, featuring costumes, music, balloons, candy, and plenty of leaflets. After greeting people on the Nicollet Mall, the group marched back to campus and ended up at the Armory where they decorated Iron Mike, the Spanish-American War memorial statue, with a red "Milwaukee 14" armband.

In the middle of November, problems with our English department attracted attention yet again when Chairman Clark issued a memo to the freshman English instructors informing them that they were required to use *Student Writing for Study*, a book written and published by the department, and going on to term any refusal to employ this text "a disregard for human and orderly procedure." Continuing his now-familiar propensity for unfortunate directives, Clark went on to say that the primary reason for this mandate was that the book sale income from the large number of students enrolled in the required introductory course was necessary to retire the departmental debt and to purchase instructional equipment. He made no mention of the text's academic merit, or lack thereof, and many instructors objected to both the tone and contents of the memo. The *Daily* ran an editorial terming the chair "Poor Old King Lear" but, after a healthy dose of the criticism he justly deserved, the editors also pointed out that the reason the unfortunate situation arose in the first place was the chronic University-wide shortage of funds caused primarily by shrinking state appropriations. Clark's memo had listed some of the recently purchased items, which even included chairs, and none of them were extravagant by any definition of the word. Whatever the eventual outcome might be, I am sure most of us associated with the department were hoping for at least some respite from unfavorable publicity.

In late November, Phil Richer accepted the inevitable and sold Dania Hall to Keith Heller and Gloria Segal, the developers who already owned about 80% of the property in the Cedar-Riverside neighborhood on the West Bank. He would be allowed to continue to operate his pharmacy as a tenant, and had also made a healthy profit on the sale.

The U Housing Office, in response to a petition signed by over 800 residents, announced that dorm cafeterias would stop serving grapes at least until winter quarter when all residents would have the chance to vote on the question. Two weeks later, some "pro-grape" students on the St. Paul campus held a demonstration protesting the ban. On the 24th an unoccupied U police car parked next to the station was destroyed by a bomb, an act that President Moos termed "terrorism."

The arson in the anti-war organizations' offices and the police car bombing were especially troubling because they represented a dramatic escalation in the level of violence on the domestic front, at least in Minnesota. On the overseas front, the inevitable rage and frustration of combat, and especially of a guerilla war, had already led to actions that could only mean the Geneva Conventions no longer applied. Civilians were being killed routinely in both North and South Vietnam right along with NVA and VC fighters, bodies of slain soldiers on both sides were being mutilated, and weapons such as napalm and white phosphorous that had not been intended for anti-personnel use because they literally burned their victims alive were being used against the Vietnamese.

Here at home, the level of anger and frustration on both sides of the controversy was rising by the day, and the impulse to resort to force and violence was also becoming more difficult for each to resist. I understood the anger that led to such acts, but personally could not condone tactics that might easily result in the death of innocent people. A police officer could have been in that car. To some of the radicals in the resistance, that risk was acceptable because the police, especially after the "police riot" at the convention in Chicago, were the enemy, forces of the establishment that were oppressing minorities and conscripting us to risk our lives in an unjust war. Once the fateful decision is made to "let slip the dogs of war," the conflict assumes a life of its own beyond the control of either side and the will to prevail outweighs any other more civilized considerations. Things were already out of control in Vietnam, and now we were slipping into the same nightmare scenario on the home front.

***

The Beatles retained their position as the most important rock artists by releasing the *White Album* in late November. The two-disc length of the work was impressive, but the pervading dark tone was what struck me immediately. The abrupt shifts between sweetness and anger in the movement through the thirty tracks was certainly a reflection of the personal and creative conflicts among the four members, but it was also a mirror displaying with uncanny accuracy the discord that had come to define our society. The Lennon and McCartney partnership had always been a subtle balancing of sweet (Paul) and sour (John), a fact that became readily apparent later after they had gone their separate ways and begun to record their own individual compositions. Paul's influence seemed to dominate in love songs such as "Michelle" and wise but humorous ditties like "When I'm Sixty-Four." John's forte was harder and angrier pieces, reflecting on how he used to beat up his girlfriend in "Getting Better" and even threatening to kill her in "Run for Your Life." Their best work was when the two influences were balanced and, even though such well-blended compositions were rarer by the time of the *White Album*, the resulting unnerving mood swings made the work an ideal soundtrack for the late 1960s. Confusion and anger, with frequent interludes of love and hope that all the turmoil would produce change for the better, were the defining moods of those times for me.

When the U was on the quarter system, the four-day Thanksgiving weekend was always a time to catch up on work, review material, and start cramming for finals. Monk had really picked up the pace in his determination to complete all the scheduled material. Bamford tried to do the same, but his predilection for going off on long tangents in his lectures kept him hopelessly behind schedule. If someone asked a question, his answer would sometimes consume ten or fifteen minutes of the allotted hour. Cal was the best of the three at sticking to the required pace, which was an absolute necessity for a language course.

On the 26th, the Tuesday before the holiday, I went out to the War Memorial Blood Bank on Park Avenue to donate a pint for the first time. Dad was a regular donor to the Post Office Blood Bank but he had some sort of health issue that made him ineligible that time, so I went instead to donate to the credit of his "account." The system was that current donors received blood free of charge if they ever required a transfusion. That was a new experience for me, but things went well and Mom fixed me a steak for lunch when I got home.

On Thanksgiving we had the big dinner at home and in the evening went to the wrestling matches. Our local promotion, Verne Gagne's American Wrestling Association, had established a tradition of a big card on the holiday, with kids admitted free with paid adults. Dad, and Mom to a lesser extent, had been fans for years and that sort of rubbed off on most of us kids. I think Granny was the biggest fan of all of us, but she preferred to watch it on TV. The main event featured everyone's favorite, The Crusher, against the arch-villain Dr. X, with the old pro Stan "Crusher" Kowalski acting as referee. The three of them put on a great show and the crowd was going crazy, but then X rubbed a mysterious "foreign object" in Crush's eyes and, to add to the outage, Pampero Firpo interfered by roughing up the temporarily blinded Crusher. Somehow Stan missed all these shenanigans and awarded the match to X when he pinned the helpless Crusher. There was little doubt in anyone's mind that in the near future there would be a tag-team match featuring the two miscreants and a partner of the Crusher's choice to exact revenge for this outrageous miscarriage of justice. We came home and pretty well finished off the turkey, ending a fun family holiday. The next evening, I saw *A Man for All Seasons* at Scott Hall, which certainly made clear that the issue of the conflict between the law and individual conscience was not a new one.

Monday, December 2, began the last week of classes, and the commencement ceremony was scheduled for the end of the following week. I went down to Coffman to pick up my commencement packet, but my name was not on the list of graduates so they sent me up to Morrill Hall to find out why. After waiting in two lines, the clerks finally determined that the problem was they did not have the paid fee statement for my graduation fee. I did not have my copy with me, but they said if I brought it in by 8:00 a.m. the next morning they could still get my name in the program. I suspected the foul-up had something to do with my dual-registration for fall, but I really did not care what caused the problem as long as I knew the solution. I did know that it would be a relief to no longer have this odd status. After Cal's class it was my time slot for registering for winter quarter, so I went up to Johnston and found that the classes I wanted were still open, except for the American short story course. I signed up for the second part of Professor Monk's course, a seventeenth century English Literature class taught by

David Haley, and the second part of Bamford's course. I was not planning on taking the third quarter of Paul's course because I did not expect Napoleon to be as interesting as the revolution, so I decided to take a second history class to complete my related field requirement: the second quarter of Harold Deutsch's course on World War II.

The next day, I got up early, drove in, and got to Morrill before the clerks. When they came in I showed them my grad fee receipt and that took care of it. Then I went to Coffman for my graduation packet, down to the bookstore to rent a cap and gown, and up to Morrill to turn in my registration cards. At that time of day there were none of the usual lines for any of these tasks. We had a grad student meeting that afternoon where Bob Moore went over some of the changes designed to speed up the process of earning an advanced degree at Minnesota. The new MA exam was a focus of attention since the outcome of that would determine both the final decision to award the MA and admission to the doctoral program. For one test to be so important was certainly a stressful thought, but that was in the future and the biggest uncertainty in my life now was the draft.

After the meeting, I waited for Bev to leave and we had a nice little chat. I was looking for chances to spend even small amounts of time with her. Then I went over to the Co-op and got a copy of Donne's poetry, one of the readings on the list we had just been given to prepare for the MA exam.

Wednesday the 4th was the last lecture for Paul's class. He finished with nothing special to wrap things up and received no applause. He would be covering the revolution itself next quarter, so I hoped that would be better. Professor Monk used his last lecture of the term to finish discussing *The Dunciad*, concluding with some grim observations on how Pope's predictions were coming true. He received a hearty and well-deserved round of applause, which made me feel sort of bad about Paul not receiving any acknowledgment at all from us.

Bev and I chatted before Cal's class. She had spent Thanksgiving down in Maryville, Tennessee, where she had done her undergraduate work. She also mentioned that she lived in a dorm. I unobtrusively checked to make sure her only ring was still the one from college. The next day was Cal's last class, and then began the week of final cramming and taking exams. Despite the stress, I always got some perverse enjoyment out of running on caffeine and adrenaline, and taking one exam after another until finally another quarter was complete.

The weekend was devoted to studying, except for going to mass, helping Dad move some furniture, and going with Mom and the kids to get a Christmas tree. We went to our usual tree lot over on Marshall and St. Anthony Boulevard, and it was so cold that we did not spend as much time as usual browsing. The annual choice of a tree was an important event so we hated to be rushed, but they had a good selection and in the end the decision was unanimous.

Bamford's test on Monday the 9th was as he had described it, and I was quite confident of an "A" in that class. The next day was Monk's exam and I took the bus in and studied a bit more on the way. By the time we got to campus I felt that I had taken in all of the material I could retain, so I went to Coffman and bought a couple of graduation announcements for souvenirs. Bev and I sat next to each other for the test and I felt I did well. I was expecting a "B" in that class, but I was concerned about Professor Monk's teaching assistant (TA), a woman who had worked for him for years, because she had a reputation as a tough grader. After the test, Bev and I chatted again. She was so easy to share things with and, in addition to her obvious attractiveness, was also gracious and kind. I was starting to wonder what she thought of me.

Cal's test was the next morning, Thursday the 12th. I drove to campus and the weather was strange: a dense cloud cover had brought record warm temperatures. I saw Bev and she said she was going home to Miami for Christmas. The test was challenging but not as hard as Cal could have made it. I figured I had a chance for an "A" in that class but that a "B" was more likely. It was so gloomy that the streetlights were still on when I left at 9:40 a.m., and that afternoon after I got home there was heavy rain with thunder and lightning.

One of my classmates, Phyllis, had invited a bunch of us to a party that night at her apartment over near University and 8th Avenue. She was of Swedish ancestry and was preparing a menu of traditional Scandinavian holiday fare, with glug—a mixture of brandy and wine flavored with almonds, raisins, and cinnamon—being the star attraction. This was actually my first social event with some of my fellow grad students and I was to learn in the future that alcohol usually played a rather prominent role at such gatherings, which suited me just fine. Even though most of us enjoyed a few drinks, however, this one was a quiet affair with pleasant conversation. Cal showed up and I thought that was a very cordial thing for him to do. Phyllis had gone to a great deal of effort in her preparations and she had deviled eggs, Swedish meatballs, glorified rice, fancy cookies, and several cordials. The hot glug was in a pan on the stove.

Bob Weinstein, a grad student from New York, brought his wife and seventeen-month-old daughter, a really high-energy kid who helped keep things lively. Most of the conversation was about school, travel, and the life of a TA. I wished Bev had been there, but she had already told me she could not make it. I think her flight to Florida was that afternoon or early the next morning. There were about a dozen of us there, and half of us left around 10:00 p.m. I had hoped that more would show up, especially after I saw how much Phyllis had prepared, but it was a nice get-together and a pleasant way to end the quarter.

The next day, Friday the 13th, was commencement rehearsal, so I went back to campus for that in the afternoon. Our guide, a paternal type with a gray crew-cut who reminded me of a high school teacher or coach, spelled it all out for us and it seemed simple enough. The situation had a feeling for me of coming full circle because it took me back to Welcome Week in the late summer of 1964 when our guides showed us around campus and helped us with our first encounters with all of the U's bureaucratic procedures. The next night, Mom and my sister Mary went with me to the ceremony. Dad and my sister Jane both had the flu, and we were hoping it was not the Hong Kong variety that was making the rounds that winter.

Since I was not leaving the U, the event did not seem as important a transition as such affairs usually are, but things went as planned, and walking across the stage past President Moos was memorable. Afterwards, there was a crush of people as hundreds of us were funneled into one of the basement corridors of Northrop where some wanted to turn in the academic garb and others just wanted to exit. It was one last experience of being part of the herd at the big state U. I talked with Tom Audette, one of my classmates from DLS, down in the garage, and he gave me updates on a few of the guys we both knew. Tom himself was already married, but he had stayed in ROTC and was scheduled to report for duty at Fort Gordon in January. I was glad I had dropped that program.

***

With my undergraduate career now finally behind me, I settled into a Christmas break routine at home. As always in those days, I read voraciously: books for the next quarter, for the MA exam, and for pleasure.

But the holiday preparations were also in full swing, and on Sunday the 15th we set up the tree. I had to laugh when the three younger kids argued about decorating it, because it seemed like a replay of the way Dave and I used to be. The next day I went downtown with Mom and Mary for some shopping, and I found a book for John. Mom asked me to pick out some presents for myself so I found a pair of brown Levis, *The Portrait of A Lady*, and the *Kama Sutra*. That last one seems like an odd thing for a mother to give her son, but it was something I wanted to read.

Later in the week, I finished my Christmas shopping up at Apache Plaza. On the 19th, things finally started to look like Christmas as we received almost half a foot of snow. Our neighbor, Ray, cleared the front walks with his snowblower and I shoveled most of the driveway. I received my 1-A draft notice in the mail on the same day, which was no surprise. A day or two later, I came down with the flu myself, and it hung on for about a week. That put a damper on some of my holiday activities, but as an adult the disappointment was minimal. I just wanted to rest and recover before winter quarter started. Christmas Day was pleasant, and in the evening the family went over to my Uncle Jim and Aunt Irene's place in Crystal while Granny and I relaxed at home.

Winter really settled in during the last week of the month and we ended the year with about eighteen inches of snow on the ground and some bitter cold temperatures. John thought he was getting too big to share a room with his sisters, so he and Dave moved their beds down to the basement amusement room, leaving me with a room of my own for the first time—the back bedroom on the main floor. I spent a quiet New Year's Eve at home watching a special live broadcast of *The Tonight Show*, one of my favorites.

With no classes and largely housebound by the weather, I had plenty of time to think about the draft and the Army. I disliked the idea intensely, but the alternatives were even worse. Going to prison or moving to Canada were both out of the question, and it was just not in my nature to deliberately injure myself. I knew I did not qualify for CO status because my objections were political, not religious. That is, I believed in the "just war" doctrine, but I did not believe the one in Vietnam fit that definition. The policy of drafting grad students was new, so we were uncertain how it would be implemented. I was in limbo, which is a difficult thing for someone who likes to imagine he is in control of his own life. My decision was to carry on with my studies and wait to see what developed. I was thinking about Bev down in warm sunny

Florida, too, and wondering what, if anything, fate had in store for the two of us. Things were in a state of flux and it was impossible to know if 1969 would bring some resolution to any of the unforgettable events of 1968.

The news in December certainly brought no respite from such events, including stories of racial unrest and demands for change at educational institutions. There were continuing disturbances at several campuses around the country, and Oshkosh State U ended up expelling ninety black students. There were less-serious versions of these confrontations at a couple of Twin Cities inner-city high schools. The Vikings concluded their eighth season by qualifying for the first time for post-season play, but then lost the Western Conference Championship Game in Baltimore to the Colts. North Korea released the crew of the USS *Pueblo* after eleven months of captivity. On December 20, two high school students were shot to death in Benicia, CA, the first victims of a serial murderer who would later come to be known as the Zodiac Killer.

The year ended on a memorable and hopeful note with the successful Apollo 8 mission. It was the first manned spaceflight to leave Earth's gravitational field and enter that of another celestial body, the Moon. After a three-day flight, the crew of three orbited the Moon ten times over twenty hours, thus becoming the first humans to see the far side of the Moon. The live broadcast attracted the largest TV audience so far, and the view of the "Earthrise" was truly unforgettable. On the ninth orbit, the crew read aloud the creation story in the first ten verses of Genesis, and concluded by wishing everyone back on Earth a Merry Christmas. It was a beautiful moment, combining an amazing scientific achievement with profound spiritual depth during the season of peace and love, although the wars at home and abroad illustrated all too vividly the magnitude of our nation's and mankind's failure to live up to the ideals of the holy season. What did that sort of unsustainable dissonance portend, and where were we headed now with the 1950s retread Nixon at the helm? Those questions were to be answered on both a personal and national level during a year like no other.

***

Winter quarter, 1969, began on January 6. I had classes only three days per week this time, but one was at 8:00 a.m. The drawback with that time was the traffic because congestion on the city streets during the two rush hours was very heavy in those years, and even worse when the streets were narrowed by snow. It took me about an hour and a half to get to campus on the bus, making me late for Professor Deutsch's class. That did not really matter because his lecture was presented in Burton Hall on black-and-white TV, adding to the ennui of a dull presentation to a room full of half-awake students. Mom had told me that Deutsch was quite eminent and I knew he had held an important civilian intelligence position during the war, so I had high hopes that things would improve and that I might even get to see him in person from time to time. I asked a classmate if I had missed anything important during the first fifteen minutes and he assured me I had not, adding the helpful advice that it was "pretty easy" to fake the list of readings we were required to submit. Bamford was as energetic as always and a bit more amusing, which I took as a hopeful sign for the new term. Professor Monk was the same, and our first major writer for the term was Swift. David Haley was as I remembered him from three years earlier: scholarly, serious, and yet approachable. He was beginning the quarter with George Herbert.

Coming home on the bus took almost two hours. As long as I got a seat I could read, but waiting outside in the freezing weather was a problem. I adjusted my schedule by switching to an earlier bus in the morning and a later one in the evening, deciding that I would rather wait out the traffic by studying in the library instead of sitting on the bus.

The quarter got off to a low-key start, which may have been at least partly due to my reduced energy level as a result of the flu combined with what seemed like one cold after another. I met Professor Deutsch when I went to his office for approval of Chuikov's *The Battle for Stalingrad* as the text for my primary source report. I was disappointed to find that one of my favorite study spots, the West Bank Library in Blegen Hall, had been closed, but that only made sense with the Wilson Library open right next door. One evening I ran into Joe Hagan, a friend from my Robby's days who had graduated from DLS one year after me. He was working as the first-floor night janitor in Blegen, so he took his supper break and we went over to Anderson to talk and get caught up. When I last saw him almost two years before, his life was in a state of uncertainty because his girlfriend thought she might be pregnant, but the first thing he told me was that it had been a false alarm. Joe had always been quite a raconteur, and he was at his best that evening as he filled me in on his exploits traveling, teaching high school in Chicago, and trying to evade the draft, all the while smoking pot and enjoying multiple girlfriends. I had no doubt he was exaggerating, especially about the women, but it was an entertaining tale of a lifestyle that was not uncommon in those years.

I saw Bev on Monday the 13th. We were outside and she was wearing gloves, so I just had to hope she had not gotten engaged over the holidays. She had an even heavier schedule than I did, because in addition to also taking twelve credits, she was working as a TA. That made the possibility of dating seem rather remote, but I was still trying to decide whether to invite her to go see *Henry IV, Part 1*, at Scott Hall in February. Transportation suddenly had become an issue, because my parents had sold our Pontiac right before Dave had an accident that disabled the Ford. In any case, it was great to see her again.

In early January, the *Daily* printed a letter from Specialist Fourth Class Ernie Eisenberg, who was an aircraft mechanic at the Phu Heip Army Base. Most of the reports I had read from the troops focused on combat, but this one was especially interesting because it offered a glimpse of what life was like behind the lines in the war zone. He said he had direct contact with very few Vietnamese other than the "Mama Sans" who worked on the base as maids, and the "Papa Sans" who burned the waste from the latrines and cleaned the showers. He talked about the language barrier and the slang that made up the few words and phrases the GIs had in common with the Vietnamese employees. Being stationed behind the lines afforded the luxury of having a full day off most weeks, which they often spent at nearby Tuy Hoa Air Force Base enjoying the superior facilities there such as movies, a library, a snack bar, and latrines with running water. He said the most common emotion was boredom as the days slowly passed, and that any GI there could tell you exactly how many days he had left in country.

During late 1968 and early 1969, the racial unrest at educational institutions was often more intense than the antiwar activity. The now-familiar tactics were militant words and actions combined with the presentation of a list of demands that usually included the establishment of an ethnic studies department. In addition to the disturbances at nearby Oshkosh, Wisconsin, there were confrontations at Washington U in St. Louis, NYU, Brandeis, Swarthmore, and Queens College. The worst violence, however, was in California at San Francisco State College and there the acting president, S. I. Hayakawa, with the full support of Governor Reagan, was determined to meet force with even greater force, offering a dramatic demonstration of his resolve by personally yanking the wires out of some loudspeakers at a strike rally. He termed the strike and attempted campus shutdown by minority students a "reign of terror" by "anarchists," and on December 5 ordered the police to clear the entire campus, warning any who chose to remain that "there are no innocent bystanders anymore." The very next day, however, Hayakawa announced that he was authorizing the creation of a College of Ethnic Studies, a decision that was sure to be greeted with triumphant joy by some and with disappointment by others who had hoped for an even longer and more intense confrontation as a way of radicalizing more young people.

On Tuesday, January 14, a group of about 70 people representing the Afro-American Action Committee (AAAC) met with President Moos and other U officials in the Regents' Room on the second floor of Morrill Hall to present a list of demands that included the establishment of a department of Afro-American Studies. Unsatisfied with the administrators' responses, the AAAC members went downstairs to the Office of Admissions and Records, the large room on the main floor resembling a bank lobby where we paid our tuition and conducted the various bureaucratic chores required for our journey through the academic labyrinth. There they closed the big double doors and declared that anyone who chose to could leave but that nobody would be allowed to enter, thus beginning the affair that would be remembered as the "Morrill Hall takeover." It was clear that one battle in the war on the home front was now taking place right in the middle of our campus as the occupation soon spread to include the entire building. One AAAC leader echoed the sentiment that had by now become familiar in the black power movement when he stated that "as black students, we feel this University and America have a debt to pay and we're not willing to wait another 300 years."

Moos and his staff, mindful of the recent blowups on other campuses, took a cautious approach. The occupied offices were essential to the functioning of the U but, to their credit, the administrators did not call in the police to have them cleared. Instead, they termed the occupation a "demonstration" disrupting the administrative workings of the U rather than the educational mission, and set about the delicate task of attempting to end it by negotiation.

The occupation lasted two days, and when the U workers returned after the protestors had left surreptitiously through the tunnel to the Physics building they found damaged equipment and scattered files, but far less destruction than many had feared. The U's official repair estimate was

$11,000, whereas a local TV station had stoked the public's ire by estimating it could run as high as $150,000. The president appointed a commission to investigate the affair, including determining whether disciplinary actions were warranted. Moos took considerable heat for his conciliatory approach, and Governor LeVander warned that such activities would not be tolerated in the future.

The reaction of the Legislature was also a concern, because even before the takeover they had recommended a huge cut in the U's capital request. As expected, the feelings on campus were mixed, but there was little doubt that the prevailing attitude in the larger Twin Cities community was highly unfavorable and that the local "law and order" politicians would be using the incident for their political advantage.

The takeover is still remembered as a significant incident in the history of the U largely because it set processes in motion that ultimately resulted in the formation of the Department of Afro-American Studies as well as the MLK Program for providing special academic assistance to minority students. A dramatic measure of the progress made since 1969 is that at that time there were only eighty-seven black students at the U out of a student population of over 40,000.

I still had the nagging feeling that my flu might be returning, but at least my classes were proving enjoyable. Deutsch would show up himself about once every other week, which was better than some of the televised classes I had taken as an underclassman where I never saw the professor in person even once. He was anything but a dynamic lecturer, but I felt that his insider knowledge of many of the events of the war made him an invaluable instructor. Even so, there were many early winter mornings when I wished the day was beginning with anything other than yet another dry lecture by Harold. Paul was now finally getting to the events immediately preceding the storming of the Bastille, such as the Reveillon Riots, the founding of the National Assembly, and the Oath of the Tennis Court. The exciting material seemed to inspire him to deliver more interesting lectures, although he was already behind schedule by the second week of class. Professor Monk was continuing with Swift, and his learned lectures were helping me to develop a more nuanced appreciation for this greatest of satirists.

Meanwhile, David had moved on to Sir Thomas Browne, whom I remembered fondly from three years earlier in the survey course. The rise and fall of the stately rhythms of his sonorous yet elegant prose reminded me of Milton's verse and, despite the depth of his Christian faith, he had such a profound air of melancholy about him that savoring that bittersweet emotion was irresistible when I entered his world of 300 years ago. He shared the common belief of that time that, as Dr. Johnson expressed it, "the world was in a state of decay." Life on Earth was losing its vitality, the end was near for "we whose generations are ordained in this setting part of time," and the most fitting attitude was not any sort of aspiration to greatness but rather pious resignation. David's solemn style of delivery was utterly appropriate to this material, and the setting of the class itself on late afternoons when the Sun indeed "makes but winter arches" through the windows of Vincent Hall seemed to lend an air of spirituality to the proceedings.

Nixon was inaugurated on the 20th. I watched very little of it on TV, but was pleased that there were protests during the parade. LBJ seemed like a changed man the last couple of weeks before the transfer of power: warm, benevolent, and relaxed. Indeed, he appeared almost likeable, but after the mess he had gotten us into, that was not in the cards for me.

On Wednesday the 22nd, I stayed on campus after classes as usual, this time with the goal of catching up on some of Deutsch's lectures I had missed because of sleeping later when I had been feeling under par. I went over to Dinkytown and had a mediocre supper at the pasty shop on the corner of 4th Street and 13th Avenue, then headed over to Burton. The room where the lectures were being shown was filled to overflowing so I went over to the West Bank to see Hagan. This time he talked about all the debts he had run up, including one at the U. He had to pay that before he could register again, and he also hoped to get married in March. It was the same story involving a girlfriend who might be expecting. I knew the girl was for real because I had met her, but I had surmised by now that Joe had a tendency to confabulate and that this might well be a symptom of some sort of emotional disturbance. That actually made talking with him all the more interesting because there was always the puzzle there of what was real and what was the very coinage of his brain. There were no empty classrooms with TVs available in Blegen, so I walked back to the East Bank and found a room in Burton that had plenty of seats available. I watched one complete lecture and part of a second one, then took the bus home.

There was some challenging winter weather toward the end of the month with both heavy snow and cold. One night it took three hours to get home on the bus, but at least I had a seat and, as always, books to read. It was clear now that four grad courses was a heavy load, but I just kept plugging along. There were weeks when all four professors seemed uninspiring, but that may have been a reflection of my own mood. Bev and I had looked at each other's schedules so I knew which classes she was taking and on Monday the 27th I went to Vincent to meet her before her Chaucer class. I asked her to *Henry IV*, but she said she was going out of town for one weekend so I said I would call her to see if there was a performance date that would work. That evening I studied for a couple hours in Wilson then went over to Blegen to check up on Joe. He said he had an EKG recently and the results made the doctor request a second one. Joe thought he was in poor physical condition, and he was hoping his draft physical on February 10th would verify that. He said he was cleared now to register for next quarter, and that the marriage plans were still the same.

***

I called Bev on Tuesday evening and was delighted to find that there was indeed a date that would work for the play. She was so easy to talk with and we had many common interests because of studying in the same field. I suggested that we study together the next evening.

The next day Professor Monk said he was having his usual mid-quarter worries about how much material needed to be covered in the time remaining, and I had to chuckle because I knew from his performance in the fall that he had no problems adjusting his speed according to the deadlines. After all, he had been teaching the same subjects for decades. I ate supper at Sandy's, on University next to the Co-op, then went over to Wilson to study and meet Bev, who came about 6:30. She was doing research for a paper she was writing for Toni McNaron's class on how Milton's poetry was better when describing Satan than when he was trying to depict God. We studied until about 9:30 and then I suggested that we go over to Caesar's. I saw Joe on the phone as we walked through Blegen.

It was a beautiful night for a winter walk with lots of fresh snow and a moderate temperature. I had not been to the bar before and when we got inside it looked sort of like a dive, but you could also term it "West Bank Bohemian," and it was a good place to chat. Bev had a 7-Up and I had a beer. A few other English grad students came in as we were leaving, so it was fun to see them as well. We walked through Blegen on the way back and Joe was on the phone again, which made me recall the issue with his long personal phone calls at Robby's. Bev was living in Comstock Hall and I had never visited there. Unlike Sanford, where Glenda had lived her first year, this dorm had plenty of nice lounge space. We talked more about writers and ideas and I left about 10:45 to take the bus home. I could not help thinking that this might be the beginning of something very special, and yet that made the draft an even bigger worry than ever.

On Friday the 31st, I was studying in Walter Library after classes and starting to feel discouraged because it seemed as though there was not enough time to give all four classes the attention needed for a thorough grasp of the material. I wondered how Bev did it while working as a TA at the same time. The ennui made it hard to concentrate so I left and ran into Bob Weinstein on the way out. We went over to the TA office in Vincent to compare notes, and he was worse off than I was. Bob, Maggie, and the two kids all hated the cold weather, and they felt it was bad for the kids' health as well. He was fed up with the stress of being a full-time grad student, a TA, and a father all at the same time. That was distressing because their plan when they moved to Minneapolis was for Bob to complete a doctorate, but now they felt there was no way they could live here for three more years. They were from New York City, but were obviously looking for a place warmer than there as well because he had applied for positions in Florida, teaching high school if necessary. He said they might even move on from there to the Bahamas. Phyllis came in, too, and we talked about the good and bad points of college teaching versus high school. I loved studying literature, but a person could not ignore the question of what came after college. Bob and Maggie's situation made it clear that starting a family while in grad school was asking for a lot of stress.

On Saturday, I wrote my review of the Chuikov book on Stalingrad for Deutsch's class, and then called Bev. She was working hard on Milton, and I was not surprised, because I had heard that Toni set a high standard for her students. David's mid-quarter was on Monday so I spent Sunday studying for that. The next day, Paul started going over material we had already covered in the fall, which was a concern given the amount of material we had for the current quarter. He often expressed the same anxiety about time pressure as Professor Monk but, unlike Sam, seemed powerless to adjust his presentations accordingly. The saving grace was that he was an easy grader. I knew that because I had received the highest point total in the class for fall quarter. I had worked hard, but I had not expected results like that.

In the afternoon, I went over to Vincent and asked Bev if I could come over that evening. Then I met with Bob Moore about the ongoing problem of finalizing my bachelor's degree. He was very apologetic and said it was yet another U bureaucratic snafu. I needed to get a signature from Education on my petition and then turn it in again, so I did that the same day. Bob was so good at his trying job and talking with him always boosted my morale. I thought David's test went well, and hoped he would feel the same. After studying in the library, I went down to Comstock to meet Bev, and this time instead of studying we just talked. She told me about a trip that she and some of her friends took out west the previous summer where they slept in a tent six nights every week. The next summer, she was going to be a counselor at a Girl Scout camp, and then go to Germany where one of her sisters and her brother-in-law lived. I liked Bev more every time we talked and left feeling happy, with the mid-winter blahs temporarily banished.

Classes on Wednesday, February 5, were routine but what I was looking forward to all day was studying with Bev, so after a quick supper at McDonald's I headed down to Comstock. She was wearing a white sweater and mustard-colored ski pants, and looked beautiful. After studying, we went over to the North Star Room to talk and I told her what had been troubling me: everything was colored by the fact that I could be drafted at any time. I was sharing that with her because of what that meant in terms of what might be starting to happen between us, and I knew she understood it in that way as well. I was afraid of losing something wonderful before we even had it in our grasp, because I was so happy when we were together, but mostly the whole situation just made me depressed, exactly the opposite of the previous evening. It was the worst I had felt in almost three years, and I could feel our conversation dying. I was hoping she understood that I would have felt even worse if she had not been there. We said goodnight.

When I got home Mom and Granny were waiting for me because I had received a letter from Local Board Number 40. We all knew what it was: I had been drafted and was to report for induction on the morning of March 17th. It was already pretty late so I went to bed but could not sleep. I got up and drank a bunch of wine, and then I slept.

I spent all day Thursday at home thinking and unable to do much studying. One thing I realized was that I needed a little more free time and less pressure before I left, so I decided to drop one of my courses. David's seventeenth century class was the logical choice, because that would mean one less paper to write and it was the course I had devoted the least time to so far. I could tell I felt more detached in my classes on Friday, but I was determined to finish the remaining three courses. I also found out that the college office had returned my petition yet again, so I was going to have to see if Bob Moore had some way to cut through the red tape and get it resolved. I needed to see him anyway to tell him I would be gone after the current quarter.

Friday night was when Bev and I were going to *Henry IV* in Scott Hall. We both enjoyed it, but that was a play I had studied in such detail freshman year that I had a mental picture of how each scene should be played, and if the interpretation was not the same as the one in my mind it was distracting, although a highlight was Peter Michael Goetz's portrayal of Falstaff. All in all, it was a perfect first date for a couple of English scholars. We went over to Dinkytown afterwards and had a pizza at Vescio's.

I had thought about bringing Bev home so she could see the place and we could have more privacy for conversation, especially if the time seemed opportune for telling her I would be leaving for the Army, but it was almost midnight by the time we left the restaurant, so we drove back to Comstock and talked in the car in the parking lot for awhile.

We were both pretty shy and inexperienced, but then she said "let's go inside." We talked more on one of the couches in the basement lounge, which was pretty much deserted that time of night, and then just started kissing. It was something I had been yearning for, but not something I had planned out. Something just told both of us that the time was right, the time was now. She whispered "be good to me," and I knew that meant that she was starting to care. I could not bear to tell her about the military then, so after we finally parted I drove home in an emotional tumult. Since I received the draft notice two days before, I had known I was at a major turning point in my life, but now the situation had been complicated in a way I would never have anticipated only two weeks before. Did I dare to even dream that the unknown path ahead would be one that Bev and I would walk together?

She was going to an Allen Ginsberg talk on Saturday, but I felt a little tired for that, plus I had two mid-quarters coming up on Monday and I needed to start outlining my paper on *Joseph Andrews* for Monk's class. I was already feeling less academic pressure because of dropping David's class so that decision, although made reluctantly, was proving to be a good one. If I had known Saturday was Bev's twenty-third birthday, I would have gone with her to the talk and given her a little remembrance, but we had not begun to share details like that yet.

The tests on Monday for the two history classes were just as the professors had described them. After that, I studied at Walter and then went over to Vincent and saw Bev. She said she had goofed off over the weekend and now had to spend most of this week writing a paper, just like me. I hoped that I was the reason she had trouble concentrating.

We were now past the mid-point of the quarter and still had tons of reading ahead of us before the craziness of finals, so I could not help but wonder how much time we could afford to spend together. I saw Bob Moore and he called Johnston Hall to resolve my problem while I was sitting there, which I appreciated more than he could have known. I also told him I was being drafted and he said "Oh, I'm *so* sorry." He said that, contrary to what one might expect, there was no form required for withdrawing from grad school, so all that remained was for him to sign my withdrawal slip for Haley's class. I took that to be recorded in now-unoccupied Morrill Hall, and then I was free for the rest of the day. It was tempting to study with Bev, but I knew we both had a lot of work to do, especially her, so I decided not to for that evening at least. I just went home and relaxed.

The high level of tension over the war and racial issues continued to result in angry confrontations. In late January Marine Corps recruiters in Coffman were challenged by boisterous protestors from Students Against Selective Service (SASS), Students for a Democratic Society (SDS), the Minnesota Committee to End the War in Vietnam, and another group calling themselves simply The Resistance. The Marines refused to talk with the anti-war people but there were spirited discussions between protestors and those supporting the recruiters. The *Daily* continued to take progressive positions by running an editorial calling for ROTC to be banned from campus. The same week, a scheduled debate in the West Bank commons room on the Morrill Hall takeover ended in a shouting match. A switchboard malfunction resulted in a bizarre incident related to the takeover during an appearance by President Moos on WCCO-TV. Some calls by the public into the show were intercepted by an unknown man identifying himself as Moos who asked the callers if they wanted to talk about "the University niggers." The station received about twenty complaints and the phantom Moos was never identified. In early February John Clark announced that he would resign as chair of English effective at the end of June, one year before the end of his current term. The only reason he gave was that he felt eleven years as department head was long enough.

The local cultural scene offered some relief from anger and controversy as the group that had handled the light shows at Dania Hall announced that the Labor Temple at 4th St. and Central Ave., now the home of the Aveda Institute, would be the new top Twin Cities rock club. They opened the venue in style on the night of February 2 with a packed house of 2,000 enjoying a concert by the Grateful Dead, and promised future appearances by big-name acts such as Jethro Tull; Procol Harum; the Who; and Blood, Sweat, and Tears. In late January a troupe of local players presented *Dionysus 69* in Coffman with some much-anticipated nude scenes deleted, but two members of the audience were so inspired by the production that they stripped instead. The company announced that the production would move to the Firehouse, offering assurances that it would be presented there as the author intended. The same month, *Minneapolis Star* staff writer Suzanne Hovik conducted an experiment to determine the acceptability of females wearing slacks when, accompanied by her husband, she wore a conservative pantsuit to several restaurants. The results were that they were refused seating at the Rosewood Room in the Northstar Inn and Camelot, and allowed to dine at Charlie's, Murray's, Jax, Harry's, the Edgewater Inn, and the Flame Room at the Radisson Hotel. Schiek's staked out a middle ground in the struggle for equality of the sexes by seating the couple, but at an undesirable table next to the waitstaffs' serving area. In early February the St. Paul parks commissioner chose nutrition over political correctness by ruling that the animals at Como Zoo would be allowed to eat grapes. Near the end of the month the last dorm hours were eliminated at the U, including those for girls under 18.

On Tuesday, February 11, with mid-quarters completed, I worked on my *Joseph Andrews* paper and it was falling into place well. Bev called me, which pleased and encouraged me greatly but also got me thinking once again about the best way and time of telling her about my upcoming departure for the military. On Wednesday Deutsch started on the war at sea which, for me at least, proved to be a refreshing change from the first half of the quarter. Bamford began covering the drastic changes in the status and role of the Roman Catholic Church in France caused by the revolution. Monk continued with *Gulliver's Travels*.

After studying in the library, I went down to Coffman to hear Bob

Moore's talk on *The Beggars' Opera*, the upcoming production at Scott Hall that Bev and I would be attending on the 28th. Bev was already there and she told me about a book of medieval romances she was reading that John McNally had lent her for a paper she was writing on the *Physician's Tale*. She was not thrilled with the Chaucer class, which made me glad I had taken it as an undergrad and so had not had to write a paper. I was intrigued by Bob's accent, and Bev said it was eastern Tennessee. Some members of the cast were there to sing *Over the Hills and Far Away* and *Youth's the Season Made for Joy*, both delightful. It was inspiring to hear these songs of young love and its power with Bev sitting right next to me. We talked for a minute before she went over to Comstock for supper and I was taken with how beautiful she looked with the light of the setting sun on her face. I went to Sandy's to eat, to Walter to study, and then down to Comstock. I gave her a red heart-shaped box of chocolates from Fanny Farmer for Valentine's Day, but we both had a lot of work to do before the end of the quarter, so we really did study.

On Thursday at home I wrote my paper for Professor Monk and called Bev about the hockey game we planned to go to the next night. I was deliberately cheerful because I thought I had been a bit too morose the previous night. I just did not want her to think that my occasional moodiness was any reflection on how I felt about her, which was all the more reason to tell her soon about the Army.

The next day in Vincent Hall I ran into my old elementary and high school classmate Mike Debelak who had joined me the previous June in refusing to sign the loyalty oath at our draft physical. Mike had always been heavy and now it had finally paid off: his draft classification was 1-Y, overweight. He said he knew two guys who had already finished with the service and were going to college now on the GI Bill. That was one of the few things that seemed attractive about the military. Monk was not there for the first time that quarter, and I hoped that he was not sick again. The upper respiratory things really got him down.

The hockey game had been Bev's idea. I had never been to one before and there was plenty of action with a goalie stunned by a puck to the facemask, some fights, and one guy kicked out of the game. I brought her to the house for the first time afterwards for a drink and some music. I just loved spending time with her because it was so relaxing just to talk and be together. She may not have known at the time just how much her companionship and affection meant to me, but without it I could easily have gone into a depressive state.

I called Bev the next day, Saturday the 15th, and she was working on her Chaucer paper and then babysitting that night for Mark and Kay Davis's son Geoffrey, a perfect child to care for while working on a Chaucer theme. On Sunday my godparents, Uncle Jim and Aunt Irene, came over in the late afternoon, along with my cousin Rick. He had just turned seventeen the day before and was already taller than me. They did not say much about me going into the service and I did not want to talk about it, so that worked out fine.

***

Mid-February brought a welcome break from the harsh winter weather. On Monday the 17th Professor Monk talked about Gulliver's third voyage. The good news was that he did not have another cold, but missed class on Friday because he had thrown his back out while bending over to wash his face. I ate lunch and then went over to Crane's in Dinkytown and got Mom some stationary for a slightly late birthday gift. I walked down to Walter and finished the reserve room reading for the quarter for Monk's class, and then ate supper at McDonald's. As always, the food smelled and tasted exactly like what we had served at Robby's, and that memory caused me to start reflecting on my last four and one-half years at the U. Since receiving my draft notice, I had been lingering a bit more than usual during my walks around campus to reflect on all the memories that the familiar sights brought to mind. It would seem strange not to be here.

Lost in these thoughts, I walked through Dinkytown and across the campus over to the West Bank where I found Joe sweeping out a classroom in Blegen. He said that his follow-up EKG was normal. That was good to hear, except that some sort of minor heart irregularity would have been a nice way to avoid the draft. His girlfriend was not expecting after all, so the wedding plans were postponed. He was still planning to register for spring, but was not sure what classes he would take. I told him I would soon be going into the Army and he was sorry to hear that. Other than those updates, it seemed as though we did not have much more to say to each other, so two typical guys with problems expressing emotions just said "so long." I walked back across the bridge, sat around Coffman for a while, and then went over to Comstock. Bev had a mild cold and I had already studied enough for one day so we went down to the lounge in the basement and watched TV for four hours while enjoying each others' company, especially after we realized we were alone. Whatever the uncertain future might bring, I wanted to face it with her, and I kept hoping that she felt the same.

I called Bev Tuesday night but did not go over because we both had work to do. She was working on her Chaucer paper, and I used the evening to finish a book on Napoleon for Paul's class, which completed my reading for the course.

On Wednesday the 19th, Deutsch finished with the war at sea and started with Africa and the Near East. Paul, who had picked up the pace noticeably, finished with the Legislative Assembly and moved on to the Convention. Professor Monk talked about Gulliver's fourth voyage, which ended with the protagonist so thoroughly disillusioned with humanity after his voyage to the country of the Houyhnhnms that he could barely tolerate being around people, instead spending hours every day in his stables speaking to the horses. The first time I read this part the previous summer it struck me as humorous and even absurd, but now this scene struck me as so dark, misanthropic, and nihilistic that I found it reminiscent of some of the late work of Mark Twain. The deeply pessimistic tone struck a personal chord, given my present situation of being sent against my will to a war I had come to despise. I was thankful I would be with Bev that evening.

I went home, ate, slept for about two hours, and then drove back to campus. We drove over to Wilson to study, and I was thinking that it was almost inconceivable that the first time we had done that was exactly three weeks before. So much had happened since then. She read Robert Frost and I read some Churchill on World War II. We drove back to Comstock and talked in the parking lot. I had intended to tell her about the Army, but somehow it just did not seem like the right time. But we were going to see *The Graduate* on Saturday, and we were also resolved to tell each other about ourselves then.

Bev had a very heavy schedule the last few weeks of that term between taking four classes, working on her paper, and grading exams, so we did not see each other again until our movie date. I had difficulty with motivation on Thursday and did not get much done. On Friday, I realized that Professor Monk was finished with Swift because he started discussing the role of mountains in eighteenth century aesthetics. I called Bev that night just to check in, but she was grading exams and neither of us had much news.

On Saturday the 22nd, I slept late and then went out and pulled some snow off of the roof. I finished Churchill's *The Grand Alliance*, then picked Bev up about six and drove up to the Chief movie theater. I was really glad to see her after two days. It was natural that we enjoyed *The Graduate* because any young person can easily identify with Benjamin and Elaine's struggles to find their way along the tortured path toward full adulthood. In the end, the future is as uncertain as ever but they are elated by their decision to face it together. Could any film have been more perfect for the two of us? We came home and Bev met Mom, Dave, Mary, and Jane. I was pleased with that because she was coming for dinner the next day so she now had fewer new people to meet. We had some little pizzas and wine, then talked and enjoyed each other's company.

Finally, the time seemed as right as it would ever be, so I told her about being drafted. She was sad, of course, but took it well, and I was both touched and impressed by how strong she was. Now I knew that I would soon ask her if we could have an agreement about our future together before I left. That might seem like a great deal to ask of a woman that I had only been seeing for less than a month, but I had to know. I could not leave without knowing her answer. After returning Bev to Comstock, I got to sleep sometime after 3:00 a.m.

On Sunday I went to noon mass, and then brought Bev back to the house in the late afternoon. The dinner, as always at our place, was very informal, and Bev got to meet Dad, John, and Granny. It seemed as though everyone enjoyed themselves, and I could tell Bev was a big hit. How could it be otherwise? We did need to study, so after dinner we went downstairs to the amusement room. She was reading *The Monk's Tale* and I had moved on to *The Hinge of Fate*. I was struck by how thoroughly she read Chaucer, stopping to read all the notes and glossary references. We drove back to Comstock and talked in the parking lot again. She said that she loved me, and I said I felt the same about her. My heart was beating like crazy—with joy. This was unexplored territory. As Hawthorne had written so succinctly in *The Scarlet Letter*: "Then, all was spoken!"

On Monday the 24th, Deutsch talked about Rommel and the war in North Africa. Paul gave a rather dry lecture on the various constitutions of the revolutionary period. Professor Monk continued discussing the growing enthusiasm for wild natural scenes as the eighteenth century progressed, which eventually matured into the full-blown obsession with nature so characteristic of the Romantic Period.

Bev and I both had colds so we just rested that night. I did call her, of course, and she had chosen a poem by Frost for her last paper of the quarter. On Tuesday I still had a sore throat, so I rested and read some more Churchill. I called Bev that evening and we decided to get together after all, so I picked her up and we went to Mr. Hobo's, the former Winn's Drive-In, in the village and got some root beer and fries. We drove up to the favorite parking place on Ridgeway Road east of Honeywell known as "the plantation," but it had not been plowed, so we drove over to another spot by Columbia Park at St. Anthony Blvd. and 5th Street where we ate, talked, and enjoyed each other's company. She said she would wait for me, which was by far the most treasured keepsake she could have offered. That promise, which I assured her was mutual, would sustain us over the difficult days ahead. There was still the question of whether we should announce a formal engagement, but as long as we knew how we felt the rest of the world did not seem all that important.

On Wednesday the 26th, Deutsch made one of his in-person appearances, telling us about his recent trip to Germany where he interviewed three men who had known Rommel. He finished with North Africa and began discussing the war in the Pacific. That made me wish I could be around for the next quarter, but I knew I could read about it on my own as well sometime, especially with the help of the reading lists he had provided. Bamford took a great leap forward by talking about the Directory, one of a series of governments established during the era of the French Revolution, and starting on Napoleon, skipping over a host of crucial events such as the Flight to Varennes, the execution of Louis XVI, the Committee on Public Safety, the declaration of the Year I, the assassination of Marat, the Reign of Terror, the rise and fall of Robespierre, and all the foreign wars. Given his rambling style of lecturing, it was the only way to get through all the material, and he had told us that the readings would be our guide to the events he did not cover in class. Professor Monk prepared to bring the term to a close by beginning a series of lectures on some minor writers of the mid-eighteenth century. I called Bev that evening just to hear her voice, and she was plugging away on her Frost paper.

On Friday the 28th, all three professors continued their rapid late-term pace, moving on again to new subjects. Deutsch talked about MacArthur, Bamford about Napoleon's Italian and Egyptian campaigns, and Monk about James Thomson. I came home, ate supper, then drove back to the U and parked in my favorite lot on 15th Avenue and 5th St., now the site of the Bierman parking lot. It was warm for late February, and I enjoyed the walk through the campus down to Comstock even though now I was coming down with laryngitis.

Bev and I both enjoyed *The Beggar's Opera* at Scott Hall and then walked over to Sammy D's in Dinkytown. It was crowded, there was music we liked on the jukebox, and the food was as good as always. We came back to the house and had a couple of glasses of wine.

Mom and Dad came home from a credit union dinner, but it was late and I could only whisper, so they soon went to bed. Despite my voice, Bev and I had a long conversation, exchanging ideas about people and religion. At that time I considered myself an agnostic, although I respected the beliefs of others as long as they reciprocated. Bev had been raised Presbyterian and, like most people raised Catholic in that era, I knew next to nothing about the various Protestant denominations. She explained her views and, even though she was more of a believer than I was, they were liberal and it was nothing that could ever come between us. As kind and intelligent as she was, I never had any qualms about that, but it was still vital for us to understand each other's thoughts on such an important subject. After that night, we were together. I took her home and got to bed about 4:00 a.m.

✶✶✶

Our attention was all on our suddenly blooming romance and our studies that month, but local and national events continued to reflect the rancorous disagreements over what America was all about. Since the unyielding mentality of warfare had settled in, it had become routine for each side to demonize the other. A troubling situation arising from the Morrill takeover occurred on February 11 when President Moos and nine of the regents were called before a legislative committee to answer questions on the takeover in particular, but also on more general issues of U policies and the political activities of administrators. The situation bore a disturbing similarity to events during the Red Scare, but was unprecedented because, since the U was founded seven years before Minnesota became a state, it had always claimed a type of autonomy in its relationship with the Legislature, a degree of independence balanced by the fact that the elected body held the purse strings. To their credit, the regents stood behind the president and also made it clear that U faculty and administrators owed the Legislature no explanations regarding their political activities and beliefs. Their principled stand made me proud of them.

Meanwhile, events at Berkeley and UW-Madison served as a stark example of what could have happened if President Moos had taken a more forceful approach to the Morrill Hall takeover. Students in Madison reacted to the administration's refusal to consider demands made by black students with angry demonstrations, occupation of buildings, and a call for a strike to shut down the campus. Governor Knowles and Chancellor Young, noting that the police were vastly outnumbered but also expressing a determination that the campus would not be forced to close, activated the National Guard. Most of the campus remained open and Chancellor Young, perhaps mindful of the riots the previous summer at the convention in Chicago as well as the recent events at Berkeley, pulled the 2,100 Guard members off campus before they had any serious confrontations with approximately 12,000 protestors. He also elected to take a more conciliatory position on the demands, angering many on the other side of the issue both on and off the campus. The *Daily* ran an editorial comparing the situation there with that on our campus the previous month, concluding that Moos's decision not to employ force was a wise one.

In similar incidents on other campuses, administrators had found that requesting the assistance of outsiders, such as the police or National Guard, in an attempt to restore order often had the effect of arousing support for the protestors among previously apathetic students. An issue the writer did not address was that Madison was well-known as a center of militancy, whereas even the most raucous confrontations on our campus had been mild by comparison.

On campuses all over the country, young people were challenging authority figures they no longer viewed as legitimate, and this confrontational attitude was sometimes even cropping up in lower-level schools as well. A "racial transfer program" in the Minneapolis schools resulted in a most unfortunate incident when some black students bussed to Sheridan Junior High in Northeast Minneapolis were beaten and some students from the North side then broke into Sheridan to retaliate. At Robbinsdale High School, over 100 students were suspended for wearing blue jeans to school, and the principal explained that the punishment was more severe than usual for such an infraction because "this was an organized demonstration to defy authority."

In early March, the government released grim statistics showing that serious crime in the US had risen 17% in 1968, mostly in the cities and suburbs. A few weeks earlier, a presidential commission had found that young people commit most of the violence in the country and that "legitimate" violence, such as war, was providing an excuse for "illegitimate" violence such as demonstrations and urban riots. This was nothing more than typical "establishment" rhetoric from a government that no longer commanded the respect of many of our generation because of the war and a failure to fully acknowledge the just grievances of racial minorities. For many of us, the determination of what authority and what violence was legitimate had become a decision we would make for ourselves.

In Vietnam, the war continued to grind on in a deadly stalemate as the communists launched a major post-Tet offensive in late February. While nowhere near the scale or significance of the events of Tet 1968, the fighting was again brutal and 789 US troops were killed in a two-week period. Nixon responded in March by ordering the bombing program in Cambodia known as Operation Breakfast, although the American public was not informed of the secret offensive. How Nixon would approach the war was a great unknown, but none of the parties at the Paris Peace Talks, which had begun the previous May, seemed in any hurry even to begin serious negotiations let alone attempt to bring things to an end.

***

There were a few welcome distractions in the local news from all the disturbing events. In early March, the Twins signed the volatile and hard-drinking Billy Martin as their new manager. They also re-signed their star pitchers Jim Kaat and Dean Chance, lowering both of their salaries from $60,000 down to $55,000, while keeping the popular and versatile Cesar Tovar on board for a more modest $30,000. Judy Jarosak, an employee of the Red Baron, decided to advance the cause of feminism by tending bar in defiance of a Minneapolis ordinance prohibiting women from engaging in the profession. She warned city authorities that she had the support of the Minnesota Civil Liberties Union (MCLU). Our own tortured bard, John Berryman, won the National Book Award for *His Toy, His Dream, His Rest*, a continuation and conclusion to *77 Dream Songs*, for which he had been awarded the Pulitzer Prize in 1964. On February 23, the promoters at the Labor Temple offered another big-name concert with the appearance of Procol Harum. Even though they never again matched the success of their

1967 debut hit, "A Whiter Shade of Pale," that haunting and cryptic offering became such a musical staple for our generation that it earned them a lasting place of honor in the boomer musical pantheon.

On Sunday, March 2, I was still overjoyed from the previous Friday evening with Bev after *The Beggars' Opera*, but also tired, and I knew she would be too. In the afternoon I brought her to the house to study: She read Chaucer and Wallace Stevens, and I finished with Churchill. We ate, listened to records, and just had a good time. I realized that my unofficial fiancé was now my best friend as well. How lucky could one man get?

On Monday, the beginning of the last week of class, the three professors continued to wrap things up. In fact, that was the last class for Professor Monk because he was at a stopping point after finishing with Thomson, and decided to cancel the last session to give us a bit more time to study for finals. I was finishing with things as well: completing my reading list for Deutsch and turning in my book review for Bamford.

On Tuesday evening, Bev and I studied at the house again, had a drink, listened to some music, and talked. It seemed as though we never tired of talking because we were so eager to know as much as we could about each other. We also knew we would be separated in less than two weeks now.

On Wednesday, Deutsch concluded his last class with the Battle of Midway, a good breaking point. Bamford received a round of applause after his lecture, which I thought he deserved because he really was more focused and organized than in the fall. I got home, went downstairs, had a couple drinks, and reminisced with my old friends, the Beatles. Later I called Bev and she was in an upbeat mood as she began her studying for finals.

Also on that day, the second of my two high school classmates to die in the war, Phillip E. Taylor, was killed during the fourth month of his tour of duty while riding in a truck that ran over a mine. He was a first lieutenant assigned to the 11th Infantry Brigade, a unit of the ill-fated 23rd Infantry, or Americal Division. I knew Phil from the Dramatics Club where he had played lead roles in a number of productions, including Henry Antrobus in *The Skin of Our Teeth* and Henry Higgins in *My Fair Lady*. He was a smart and multi-talented guy, the kind who appeared to be headed for great things in life. He was from St. Thomas the Apostle Parish in South Minneapolis and his stated ambition in our yearbook was "to be happy and to have peace of mind."

On Thursday, Mom and I took Uncle Dell to the hospital and back. That was Fidelis Ambrose, one of Granny's brothers, who was being treated for prostate cancer. He was as cranky as ever, which I chose to take as a positive sign. I studied for Paul's final the rest of the day, but I was caught up enough with my work so that I did not feel much pressure. Also, with Bev and the Army on my mind, my studies had dropped from first to third place in my mental priority list. I called Bev during a break from studying, and she suggested we get together the next day. I eagerly agreed, although I was also pleasantly surprised because we had both felt that we should just concentrate on our studies over the weekend. She said she had talked with her close friend Joyce Coulam, and it was apparent that her attitude had changed. She was more relaxed and less stressed about her upcoming tests. Joyce was very quiet and contemplative, a wise and deep thinker who would only offer advice after careful consideration. I would have loved to have heard that conversation, especially since it had such positive results.

On Friday, I studied the French Revolution again, then went and got Bev in the evening. She brought me up to see her room for the first time and it was a homey little place with books, pictures, and posters all over the place. Back at the house later, two professional students celebrated their love by taking a break from studying on Study Day. We played games, listened to music, talked, and enjoyed each other's company.

On Saturday, I studied for Professor Monk's test, and then in the evening Bev and I went to the Gopher-Michigan basketball game, another first for both of us, with Joyce and her friend Ed Curle, a grad student in Economics. The four of us went over to Vescio's later and had a pizza, then back to Comstock and up to Bev's room to play Yahtzee. I had won three games in a row the night before with Bev, but that night Joyce and Ed won both of the games we played. Guests had to be out of the dorm by midnight, so Ed and I took our leave and I got to bed at a good time.

On Sunday, I was looking for an excuse to skip church, and my lingering cough served that purpose quite legitimately. Bev and I talked on the phone, but we both really did study that day.

***

Finals Week was also my last week as a civilian, so it was something of a blur. I was satisfied with my tests, even though that was no longer my main concern. I bought Bev a pearl ring at Dedrick Jewelry in Stadium Village to wear as a token of our love and promise to each other—for us it was the same as a diamond. We were both finished with our finals on Thursday afternoon, the 13th. Bev still had exams to grade, but she did that during the days so that we had the evenings and nights alone together, except for joining Mark and Kay Davis for dinner at their place on Friday evening.

We said our goodbyes on Sunday night after I brought her back to Comstock, and it was one of the most difficult things I can remember. I know we both shed tears after we parted, but we knew we had to be brave for each other. In the words of perhaps the most poignant of all the popular songs of the World War II era, "'Till Then," we both hoped with all our hearts that our only loss would be time.

On the early morning of Monday, March 17, Dad gave me a ride downtown to the Federal Building. Our farewells marked the passing of the torch of a male American's military obligation from one generation to the next, but any pride I might have felt was drastically muted by the knowledge of the vast difference between our two wars. As always, we refrained from expressing our emotions in words.

Our family's new house at 3022 Stinson Blvd. in 1950, the year after my parents had it built. The future home of the Luniewski family, our neighbors for many years, is under construction on the lot to the north.

Rear view of 3022 Stinson a year or two later. The home of the Gamache family, our neighbors to the south for decades, is on the right.

1951: Steve, my father's mother Mary Agnes McGraw Atkinson ("Other Granny"), and my cousin Jimmy

My brother Dave, left, and I in 1952, with our mother Margaret C. Atkinson, her mother Catherine Ackerlind, and our father Robert V. Atkinson.

Boomers! Steve & Dave behind Mary, Jane, and John in 1958. We are in the knotty pine basement room that Dad finished himself, an iconic 1950s home improvement project.

The five of us two years later in 1960 upstairs in the living room.

SELECTIVE SERVICE SYSTEM
ORDER TO REPORT FOR INDUCTION

Approval Not Required.

The President of the United States,

To   Stephen B. Atkinson
     3022 Stinson Blvd.
     Mpls. Minn. 55418

LOCAL BOARD NO. 40
HENNEPIN COUNTY
215 SOUTH 11th STREET
MINNEAPOLIS, MINN. 55403
(Local Board Stamp)

Feb. 4, 1969
(Date of mailing)

SELECTIVE SERVICE NO.

GREETING:

You are hereby ordered for induction into the Armed Forces of the United States, and to report at 2nd Floor Lobby; Federal Office Bldg. 3rd Ave. So. & Washington; Mpls. Minn.
(Place of reporting)

on 17 March 1969 at 6:30 A.M.
   (Date)   (Hour)

for forwarding to an Armed Forces Induction Station.

[signature]
(Member or clerk of Local Board)

IMPORTANT NOTICE
(Read Each Paragraph Carefully)

IF YOU HAVE HAD PREVIOUS MILITARY SERVICE, OR ARE NOW A MEMBER OF THE NATIONAL GUARD OR A RESERVE COMPONENT OF THE ARMED FORCES, BRING EVIDENCE WITH YOU. IF YOU WEAR GLASSES, BRING THEM. IF MARRIED, BRING PROOF OF YOUR MARRIAGE. IF YOU HAVE ANY PHYSICAL OR MENTAL CONDITION WHICH, IN YOUR OPINION, MAY DISQUALIFY YOU FOR SERVICE IN THE ARMED FORCES, BRING A PHYSICIAN'S CERTIFICATE DESCRIBING THAT CONDITION, IF NOT ALREADY FURNISHED TO YOUR LOCAL BOARD.

Valid documents are required to substantiate dependency claims in order to receive basic allowance for quarters. Be sure to take the following with you when reporting to the induction station. The documents will be returned to you. (a) FOR LAWFUL WIFE OR LEGITIMATE CHILD UNDER 21 YEARS OF AGE—original, certified copy or photostat of a certified copy of marriage certificate, child's birth certificate, or a public or church record of marriage issued over the signature and seal of the custodian of the church or public records; (b) FOR LEGALLY ADOPTED CHILD—certified court order of adoption; (c) FOR CHILD OF DIVORCED SERVICE MEMBER (Child in custody of person other than claimant)—(1) Certified or photostatic copies of receipts from custodian of child evidencing serviceman's contributions for support, and (2) Divorce decree, court support order or separation order; (d) FOR DEPENDENT PARENT—affidavits establishing that dependency.

Bring your Social Security Account Number Card. If you do not have one, apply at nearest Social Security Administration Office. If you have life insurance, bring a record of the insurance company's address and your policy number. Bring enough clean clothes for 3 days. Bring enough money to last 1 month for personal purchases.

This Local Board will furnish transportation, and meals and lodging when necessary, from the place of reporting to the induction station where you will be examined. If found qualified, you will be inducted into the Armed Forces. If found not qualified, return transportation and meals and lodging when necessary, will be furnished to the place of reporting.

You may be found not qualified for induction. Keep this in mind in arranging your affairs, to prevent any undue hardship if you are not inducted. If employed, inform your employer of this possibility. Your employer can then be prepared to continue your employment if you are not inducted. To protect your right to return to your job if you are not inducted, you must report for work as soon as possible after the completion of your induction examination. You may jeopardize your reemployment rights if you do not report for work at the beginning of your next regularly scheduled working period after you have returned to your place of employment.

Willful failure to report at the place and hour of the day named in this Order subjects the violator to fine and imprisonment. Bring this Order with you when you report.

If you are so far from your own local board that reporting in compliance with this Order will be a serious hardship, go immediately to any local board and make written request for transfer of your delivery for induction, taking this Order with you.

SSS Form 252 (Revised 4-28-65)   (Previous printings may be used until exhausted.)

My draft notice from early February 1969.

With Bev during my last days as a civilian in early 1969 at 3022 Stinson shortly before I left for Basic Training.

With Ed Curle in Bev's dorm room in Constock Hall on March 8, 1969.

One of the Army's very few attempts to add a touch of humor to the Basic Combat Training (BCT) experience.

Staff Sergeant Robert Johann Seufert, drill sergeant for Company D.

A postcard I sent home showing a typical view of the rifle range.

Map of Basic Training area at Fort Campbell, Kentucky, that I drew on April 13, 1969.

My Basic Training picture. These were the portraits the Army provided to hometown newspapers.

Left: Looking very serious here.

Below: Looking more relaxed the next day, but with the sun in my eyes.

```
      May 3. 1969
   Pvt. Steve Atkinson
 Battalion Field Day, D-4-1
  Fort Campbell, Kentucky
```

5/4/69

To Bev, with love - Steve

A card I sent to Bev on April 4, 1969.

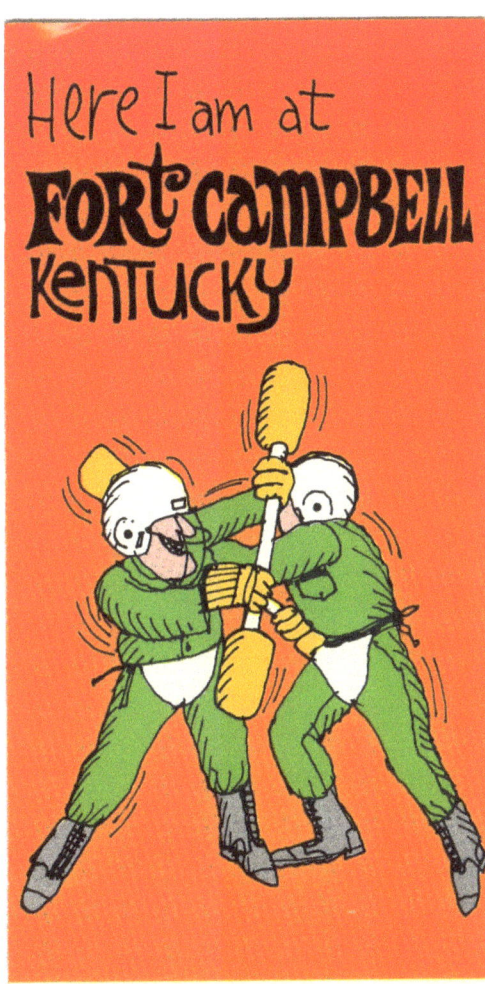

Another one that I sent on May 4.

And one that Bev sent to me on the same day.

I am the third soldier from the left in the top row.

A postcard I sent home on July 31, 1969,
showing a fire crew with an 81 mm mortar.

Joyce Coulam and Bev having fun in a photo booth.

A vintage view of my favorite haunt at "Fort Mac," other than the beer joints.

Another old view of Fort McClellan, although barracks of this vintage were the ones we called home in 1969. The tall pines and Southern Appalachian foothills on the horizon are also very familiar.

HANDBOOK

FOR US FORCES

IN VIETNAM

PUBLISHED BY MILITARY ASSISTANCE COMMAND, VIETNAM
DEC 68

HAYSTACK USED FOR HIDING PLACE AND MEETING PLACE

Outside appearance

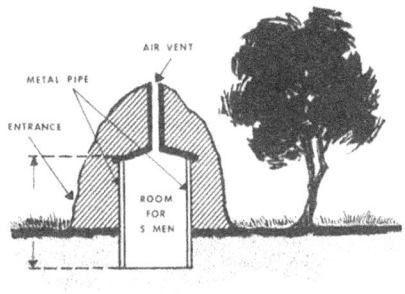

HIDING PLACES UNDER LOCAL HOMES

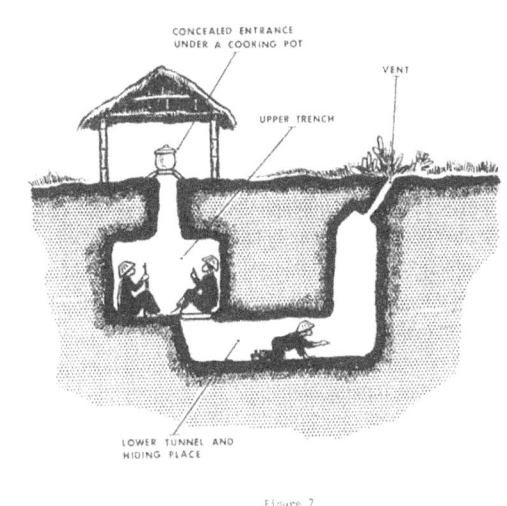

Figure 7

US troops were trained to understand that any village could also harbor Viet Cong insurgents, and this knowledge contributed to the brutality of a war in which many of the casualties were civilians.

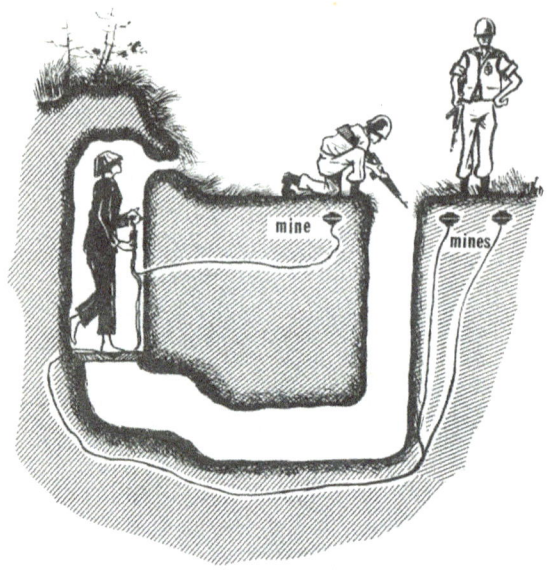

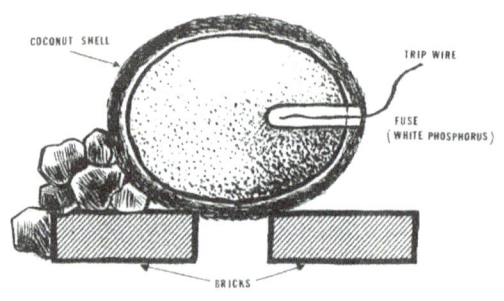

Sample pages from the handbook.

STANDARD DESIGN ANTIPERSONNEL MINE POMZ-2

STANDARD DESIGN ANTIPERSONNEL MINE POMZ-2 (CHICOM COPY) OF THE SOVIET POMZ-2N ANTIPERSONNEL MINE IS A COMMONLY USED MINE.

Figure 47

Standard design antitank mines TM-46 (on left) and the TM-41 (on the right) are frequently used against vehicles, armored personnel carriers and tanks.

Figure 48

A couple more typical pages.

A rather strange attempt to present vital information on the M16 assault rifle in a format designed to attract and hold the troops' interest, by the well-known graphic artist Will Eisner.

NINE RULES

FOR PERSONNEL OF US MILITARY ASSISTANCE COMMAND, VIETNAM

The Vietnamese have paid a heavy price in suffering for their long fight against the communists. We military men are in Vietnam now because their government has asked us to help its soldiers and people in winning their struggle. The Viet Cong will attempt to turn the Vietnamese people against you. You can defeat them at every turn by the strength, understanding, and generosity you display with the people. Here are nine simple rules:

DISTRIBUTION — 1 to each member of the United States Armed Forces in Vietnam

USARV GTA NO. 21-2 (SEPTEMBER 1967)

NINE RULES

1. Remember we are guests here: We make no demands and seek no special treatment.

2. Join with the people! Understand their life, use phrases from their language and honor their customs and laws.

3. Treat women with politeness and respect.

4. Make personal friends among the soldiers and common people.

5. Always give the Vietnamese the right of way.

6. Be alert to security and ready to react with your military skill.

7. Don't attract attention by loud, rude or unusual behavior.

8. Avoid separating yourself from the people by a display of wealth or privilege.

9. Above all else you are members of the US Military Forces on a difficult mission, responsible for all your official and personal actions. Reflect honor upon yourself and the United States of America.

PPC-Japan

US Army propaganda at its most blatant. If, as Rule 1 proclaims, we were "guests," that was the longest and strangest party I ever attended.

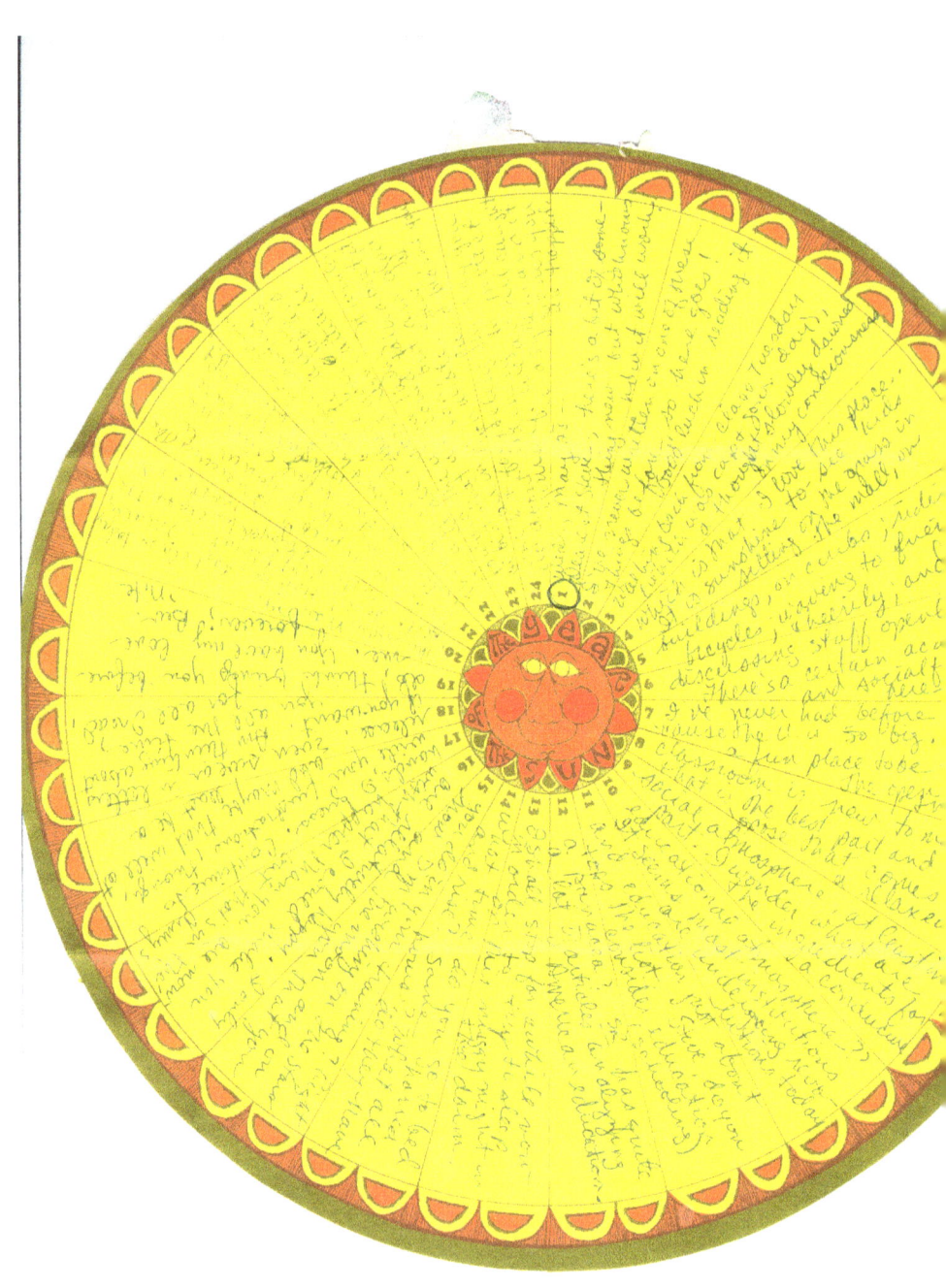

Bev's round sunburst letter of May 28, 1969.

SEPT. 9

dear STEVE,

H👁! No, 👁 am not crAzy — yet. The ☀ was not out much today because of ☁ and BRR weather. Please bring the ☀ with you when you come on the ✈, OK? Just happened to think — aren't ✦ faces interesting?

Another example of Bev's creativity, from September 9.

Home on leave in September, and more clowning in the photo booth.

In the backyard at 3022 Stinson shortly before I shipped out for the RVN. When I returned in late 1970, I bought the 1969 Pontiac Tempest (in the background) from Dad.

Bev's mother Marcia Minear, Granny, Mary, Steve, Jane, Mom, and John.

Mary & Bev.

The happy couple, enjoying a few days together before being far apart for over a year.

Mom and Bev

Bev and her mother, Marcia Minear

One last shot from my pre-deployment leave:
Bev & me outside 409 University Ave. Southeast

III.
TRAINEES

These are the times that try men's souls.
— *Thomas Paine*
The Crisis

Chapter 7
BASIC TRAINING
MARCH-MAY 1969

Entering and leaving the military are no doubt among the most dramatic lifestyle changes a person can experience. I was used to the discipline required for success in college and grad school, but it was a self-imposed regimen and I was accustomed to setting up my schedule and allocating my time to complete my work by the end of each quarter. Now I was abruptly entering an environment where all decisions would be made for me, and where the level of instruction would, out of necessity, be geared toward the slowest learners.

Other than sharing a bedroom with my brother Dave, I had never lived communally before, and now I would be sharing Spartan quarters with about fifty other guys. I had never had much interaction with people from other parts of the country, especially the south, and now I would be living and working with them full-time. That was one thing that would prove to be interesting, although the stressful environment and full schedule of training prevented developing any friendships beyond the superficial. I had functioned for years in an academic environment where respectful dialogue and decorum, at least in the classroom, were the norm, and now my peers and I would often be treated like idiots or cattle by men who had the power to mete out punishment designed to be as much humiliating as corrective. Perhaps the most succinct way of describing it is being sent to prison without having committed a crime. The fact that local boards sometimes used the draft as punishment and judges offered some offenders the option of the military rather than prison provided powerful reinforcement to this perception. An added irritation was that many of our taskmasters had Southern accents, evoking mental images of scenes from *Cool Hand Luke*. Our only offense, however, was being males who came into maturity during a great national debacle, and now we were being required to put our lives on the line because a second president could not admit that our leaders had made a horrible mistake.

How I was to think and act in such a strange and hostile environment was a question I had been pondering for at least two years. I had considered every possibility many times, but my reluctant conclusion was that I would serve if called but do everything possible to remain my own man whenever that was at all possible. The love Bev and I shared was what sustained me more than anything else through my time in the service, but there were also two thoughts that served as talismans for me. The first was from Professor Otto Pflanze, one of my history instructors. When discussing Bismarck's belief that a military draft would help instill a devotion to the German state in the young men who served, Otto observed that "the truth is, of course, that what the military really teaches involuntary recruits are the arts of evasion and subterfuge, and how to survive under a totalitarian system without bowing to it." That was as good a definition as any of my own goals for the next two years.

The second was from "Revolution" on the Beatles' *White Album*: When asked for a contribution to some sort of cause by a true believer, the speaker only replies that he will do whatever his present circumstances allow. In war, it is up to each person to do what they can for the cause but, like the speaker in the song, the cause of LBJ, Nixon, and the Army was not my cause. My cause was to remain as free of oppression as possible and, when the chance came up to throw a little sand in the gears without putting someone's life in danger, I might not pass that up. It would depend on how fairly I felt I had been treated. Clearly I was angry and not above trying to prove it had been a mistake to draft me, but I was also not dumb enough to challenge The Man directly on his own turf. Evasion and subterfuge sounded good to me, but everything would depend on how events unfolded. As with dogs in a kennel, a good part of the life of a soldier in training is spent waiting around to see what will happen.

After Dad dropped me off on the morning of March 17 and I reported at the Federal Building, the men in charge there began the very first steps in the long process of trying to make soldiers out of a random selection of often-reluctant civilians. Much of the day was an appropriate introduction to the Army way of life because we spent it just standing or sitting around. Before we took our enlistment oath and the traditional one step forward, the man administering it advised us to take our last breath of civilian air because it was going to have to last two years. And so with that fateful step we fell into the State. The demand for troops was so high then that even the Marines required some draftees, and one poor guy in our group got picked for that. He was trying to talk his way out of it and I hoped he would succeed. We walked over to a nearby restaurant as a group for lunch and supper, and we were soon to learn that "chow" was one of the main things for a soldier to anticipate as a source of at least some enjoyment and a break in the routine, another similarity to dogs in a kennel.

In the afternoon they asked if any of us had been to college, and several of us raised our hands, perhaps hoping this would mean a chance at an assignment to some sort of responsible position. All they wanted, though, was some help with filing, which I found irritating because it seemed like a way of mocking us and, of course, I was already mad at my draft board anyway. I responded by dutifully going about the task, except that I deliberately misfiled all the folders I had been given. This reminded me of the protestors who had destroyed draft board files, because I knew that, with the massive amount of records they had there, misfiled was as good as lost. I was doing what I could for the cause. Talk about a bad first date: It seemed that my relationship with the Army had hit a snag only two hours after I took the oath. But in my military career I never approached things with the idea that I intended to cause problems. I performed my duties as assigned if those giving me the orders were at least halfway decent in their behavior to us lower-ranking guys. My definition of acceptable treatment, however, was quite particular and if I felt it had been violated I would try to find a way to at least partially even the score. That was not always possible, of course, but I had spent enough time at the U to be a strong believer in the enduring tradition of the old college try.

After all the paperwork and "hurry up and wait" procedures were finally completed, they bused us out to the airport. We had each been given a copy of our first special order, a type of document that was required for any important change in a soldier's status, which indicated we were assigned to Fort Campbell, Kentucky, so we knew where we were headed. We took off about 9:30 p.m. on a fan jet that seemed to be a commercial passenger plane that had been purchased by the military. I had never flown before so that was a thrill, although one that was considerably muted by the circumstances. We stopped in the Quad Cities, Peoria, and St. Louis, remaining aboard at all of them, and arrived at Fort Campbell about 12:30 a.m. The pilot wished us well over the intercom, closing with "Gentlemen, keep your tails down." Then there was more paperwork until we finally got to bed about 3:00 a.m. Reveille, a recording of the traditional bugle call, broadcast through loudspeakers around the base, woke me up at 4:30 but they let us sleep in until 8:45 a.m. since we had gotten to bed so late.

★★★

The next three days began what was often called "zero week," since it was not actually a part of the eight-week period of Basic Combat Training (BCT). As with our first day in Minneapolis, most of the time was spent sitting or standing around, but we also went through a number of procedures. The most dramatic in terms of changing our appearance was the haircut. I opted for the shortest one, the "trainee traditional," which cost 75 cents, took about half a minute, and left me with a layer of fuzz that felt about like a three-day growth of beard. We got our blood tests, and they got my type wrong, so I asked them to check it again and that time it was correct: O+. I knew what it was from the time I donated at the War Memorial Blood Center. They embossed our dog tags for us, and I said to put "none" for religion, but the official designation for that was "no pref." We received a number of vaccinations during Basic, many of them this first week: smallpox, yellow fever, polio, tetanus, flu, and typhoid fever. Most of these were administered by an air gun that felt about like someone punching you in the shoulder. It was a real production line, and some guys came down with Hepatitis C later in life from being infected by that method of administering the shots. Next was the eye test, and we were told that men like me who wore glasses would soon be receiving a durable Army-issue pair.

Then there was a security check, which was a set of questions dealing mainly with any sort of criminal background. We had a set of written tests that seemed about like the level of ones used for high school placement to gauge intelligence and aptitude for various types of Military Operating Specialties (MOS). There was even a job preference interview, and the guy

I talked with said that they put most college grads in Personnel. The main factor determining our assignments, of course, would be what the Army needed and we all knew they needed a lot of riflemen, or "grunts." There was also a pep talk on Officer Candidate School and I took the test, but that would never really be a choice for me because, understandably, they would not guarantee you would not be in the infantry, and it also meant a commitment of three years rather than two. The commander was absent from the commander's reception, so a lieutenant filled in for him, and the program was mostly boring training films. The food was all right if you were hungry and the beds were all right if you were tired enough. Our version of guard duty was fire watch, spending an hour awake to alert the other men in case of fire. That seemed like a real possibility because our two-story barracks were old wooden structures from the World War II era where smoking was allowed when we were off duty. There were many old coffee cans around painted red and half-filled with sand that served as "butt cans." I had the watch one night from 2:00 to 3:00 a.m.

On the 19th we received our uniforms and other apparel, which was a pile of stuff big enough to nearly fill the duffel bags that we also received. The gear included a field jacket, one dress uniform, three khaki uniforms, three sets of fatigues, a winter coat, a raincoat, six pairs each of summer and winter underwear, and a few small additional items. Then we had to wait around outside for two hours for alterations. We chose the shady side of the building, of course, but then a sergeant made us come around and sit on the sunny side. After a couple of hours of that I was as thirsty as I had ever been before as the clear weather gave us our first taste of the early southern spring.

Sitting there gave me time to contemplate the singularly unattractive setting, with row after row of box-like buildings and a landscape of sand, gravel, and brown grass. Another sergeant at the reception center reassured us that the drill sergeants were not allowed to lay hands on us. I had to wonder how strenuous the training could be because some of the recruits looked like kids who belonged in the eighth grade whereas a number of others were quite heavy. The guy who bunked above me was pretty hefty and every time he turned over at night it felt as though the bed was going to collapse. It seemed like many of them could have avoided the draft if they had just eaten a little more for a few weeks before their physicals. I only weighed about 145 pounds, but if I had been as close to the weight cut-off as some of those guys I would have seen to it that I went over the weight limit like Mike Debelak.

We were encouraged to write home often, which I did to both Bev and my family, but one sign confirming that we were now soldiers was that we also needed to mail home our civilian clothes. I sent my folks the details about the life insurance policy the government provided, as well as how to arrange for emergency leave through the Red Cross if that ever became necessary. The Salvation Army provided us with some toilet articles to go along with the ones we brought from home.

One complication for us was that the power outlets in most of the barracks' latrines were dead, which made shaving with a blade necessary. That was a quick learning process for me because I had rarely done that before, and the first results were not without blood, but it was a needed skill for Army life. Many of us showered and shaved in the evening before lights out to save time in the morning when the showers and latrines were packed. It was also apparent that traveling as lightly as possible was the best way to go because whenever we moved to different quarters we had to carry all our gear in our duffel bags, but I kept all the books I had brought along because reading something worthwhile was the fastest temporary escape from our disagreeable surroundings. One guy ruptured an old hernia carrying his duffel, resulting in a thirty-day convalescent leave after less than one week in the service. I hoped he and his doctor at home could work out a way to get him discharged. I was pleased that I had everything I needed already because the Trainee PX was always packed, although I did go over there one night and have a beer. We really were not supposed to drink at the reception center, but we were already learning which rules could be ignored as long as you kept a low profile.

On Friday the 21st, we finished at the reception center and moved to some different barracks in a unit where we would perform kitchen patrol (KP) duty for a few days until it was time to start Basic. That duty was easy enough, and washing dishes reminded me of my old job doing the same down in the Coffman bakery. Later on KP would have the advantage of excusing you from a day of training, but the immediate advantage it had for us that week was that we got to eat first and could usually eat as much as we wanted. That was a rarity in training because the portions were relatively small since so many of the guys needed to lose weight, and I took immediate advantage of the situation by eating three portions of the fish entree. The rule in the mess hall was silence, and guys who forgot that and talked got kicked out whether or not they were finished with their meal. The next day I had KP all day accompanied by three big meals. We also helped ourselves to some chocolate cake in the kitchen storage area. An assistant cook griped about that to us when he noticed it was gone, but who pays attention to an assistant cook? Those of us who pulled a full day of KP got the 23rd off, and that was a welcome opportunity to rest up because our new quarters had much thicker mattresses than those at the reception center.

Spare time was not really a good thing for me, however, because I went into a depressive state almost immediately when I had the opportunity to contemplate our surroundings and what lay ahead both in training and later. Talking with the other guys offered little relief because instead of bolstering ourselves with some soldierly camaraderie, we usually ended up just venting an unhealthy combination of fear, anger, and cynicism that seemed to leave most of us feeling even worse than before our bull sessions. Most everyone had heard rumors of what it was like in Vietnam and they did not hesitate to share the worst of the stories. Many of us felt we would welcome the start of training so that we would have more to do and less time to think. I wanted to be as honest as possible with Bev and my family, but I also knew that one of my duties was to try not to add to their worries by writing them about how miserable I felt. After all, I had been in the Army less than a week. I was aware that the situation would certainly reawaken feelings in Mom and Granny going back to when Uncle Joe left home in 1942 to serve in the Merchant Marine. I regret that I sometimes failed them by writing letters that were bound to increase their anxiety. Most of my gloomiest epistles were to Bev and those must have been hard to read.

In all of the many letters the two of us exchanged, however, we pledged our love and often dreamed about our life together in the future less than two years away. Bev was an especially good letter writer, because she would share whatever was on her mind or what was happening. That was the kind of thing I longed for since it made me feel as though I was sharing in her life vicariously at least.

She attended Rev. Vince Hawkinson's church, Grace University Lutheran, on Sunday the 23rd and heard him preach on "The Real Jesus and Our Inherited Ideas." She said his main point was that many young people in their relentless quest for "relevance" were returning to the essence of the Christian message while rejecting many of the meaningless rituals and outmoded ideas that had come to encumber and distort it over the centuries. He went on to say that we create our own heaven and hell within us, a thought with a decidedly Eastern caste, and yet Luke 17:21 is good authority for that as well. Bev said she had thought about the spiritual dimension of her life a great deal, partially prompted by questions raised during her studies of literature, and she responded at length to my feelings of anger and hopelessness. She had gone through a time of doubt herself after taking a logic course at Maryville, but was now more optimistic about God and the ultimate prospects for humanity. I could not share in her hopeful attitude, but it meant a great deal to me that someone as thoughtful and intelligent as she was had arrived at a more encouraging philosophical position than my own. I had never discussed my thoughts on these issues in such depth with anyone before. We often reminded each other that our love was proof there was still beauty and reason for hope in the absurd world where we found ourselves now.

She had a restful week over spring break, spending a few days at the Davis's place shopping, sewing, reading, and playing with Geoffrey. She had talked with Mom several times and that pleased me; I knew they would soon be close friends. She also said that her mother, Marcia, had written the longest letter she had ever received from her, and that Marcia and Bev's dad, Bob, both sent their greetings and best wishes to the two of us. That made her happy, but also reminded her how much she missed her folks. Classes started on Monday the 24th: She was taking the American novel course with Marty Roth, and over break had already read *Tom Sawyer*, and *The Red Badge of Courage*. She said she needed to keep busy or else she would think too much, and I knew I needed to take that to heart myself. She had also found time to see a couple of movies, *Then Came Bronson* and *The Misfits*.

I used my day off to read some D. H. Lawrence and to write home, sending postcards to my three younger siblings, a belated eighty-fifth birthday card to Granny, and letters to Bev and my folks. We had been told that we could make no phone calls for the first two weeks, so writing was especially important.

It was a stormy day and a good one to be able to stay indoors other than three trips to the mess hall for chow. Misery loves company and we could never resist shooting the bull during our rare leisure time. The old rumor mill was usually in full swing. Someone said that a guy intentionally shot himself in the foot on the rifle range the day before hoping that would get him out of the Army, and he was now in the hospital. Malingering was a punishable offense, of course, but would the punishment be worse than being sent to fight in Vietnam? And if he had succeeded in rendering himself permanently unfit to serve, would the Army really go to all the trouble of a court martial and imprisonment rather than the alternative of an undesirable discharge? We did not know the answers to these questions. Actually, we did not know if the incident had really occurred at all. Someone else said that another guy got discharged because he claimed he was queer. Obviously, guys who managed to dream up new and creative ways of getting kicked out of the Army were always a favorite topic of conversation. One guy had heard that a sergeant in our company was getting busted for mistreating recruits at the reception station, and that is another type of story that soldiers always enjoy.

On Monday the 24th, we moved to our barracks for Basic Training, exact clones of our quarters for the previous week, where we were assigned to the 1st Platoon of Company D. We found out later that we were using the quarters of the 101st Airborne Division, The Screaming Eagles, who were deployed in-country at the time. Then came an event most of us had been anticipating with some anxiety: meeting our drill sergeant. The fear, of course, was that he would turn out to be a big prick, but Staff Sergeant Robert Johann Seufert was anything but. He was a good-looking guy of twenty-nine with a cocky military bearing and a higher-pitched voice than you might expect. He had been seriously wounded in Vietnam, and there was no doubt that he commanded respect, but right from the start he impressed me as someone who would be fair with men who did their best and took things seriously.

These first impressions proved to be accurate and as the weeks went by I came to appreciate our good fortune in being assigned to his unit, especially when I considered the senior drill instructor (DI) for Company D, Sergeant First Class Quick, who was pretty much an old-school Army jerk. One of the first things a recruit learns is not to address a drill instructor as "sir," a designation reserved for commissioned officers. A DI's response to that frequent error was to reply "don't call me 'sir,' I work for a living," followed by ordering the offending soldier to "give me ten" or more, meaning to perform ten push-ups. One of the first things Sergeant Seufert told us was that we were not required to spit shine our boots, shattering one of the Hollywood stereotypes of boot camp. It soon became apparent that the reason some of these traditional trainee disciplines were being ignored was that the Army had us on a fast track to finish training and get over to the war zone. With over half a million troops in-country and one-twelfth of them coming home each month because their tours of duty were over, well over 40,000 new men had to be sent to Vietnam every month.

Physical training, or PT, is the bane of most trainees' existence, and we got our first taste of that with two one-mile runs. Those did not bother me much because I was light and in fairly good condition from riding my bike, but I knew I could afford to be in better shape. On the 25th we began a more rigorous training regimen. The "alligator crawl" was considered the most difficult exercise and the first time I stood up after forty yards of that I felt like I was going to pass out. Another hard one was the fireman's carry, running with a buddy on your back, but they teamed us up with guys of equal size and so I ended up with Larry Anderson of Beloit, Wisconsin, who weighed in at 135 pounds. We went hand-over-hand on the monkey bars, and some of the heavier guys really had blisters after that. Push-ups, sit-ups, and jumping-jacks were nearly always part of the routine, either on gravel or in the red southern dirt. The strenuous activity helped take my mind off my troubles for a bit, and after a few weeks it would become obvious that we really were turning into better physical specimens. Even so, PT was always near the top of our gripe list.

Mail call, on the other hand, was one of the things that made a new soldier's life worthwhile. Bev wrote that she had received a wonderful letter from her dad expressing his pleasure at our happiness and the fact that we had found we "can enjoy together on the same high principles the varied ways of life." Naturally I took that to mean he hoped we were not having sex, which was probably true, although his context made it clear that he was also referring to much more than that because she went on to quote further from his letter: "Certainly Steve's decision to measure the value of citizenship, rather than to seek escape from its responsibilities, has not been easy, but his decision is one that is better faced than run from. The progress of our country and our freedom has been won by men and women *who know why they don't like what they see*, and who work with vigor nonetheless to build a better life for ourselves and for others." In the all-too-short time that I had the blessing of knowing him, Bob was to become a major influence in my life, but of course I had not yet met him and, while I appreciated his support, I was not then in a place where I could find any inspiration in his encouraging words.

Bev also related that Malcolm Boyd had spoken at a convocation at

Augsburg College the day before and said that young people must work within the existing institutions in order to change them. I did not agree that that was always desirable or even possible given the intensity of the culture wars and the intransigence of those holding the reins of power, but I loved the fact that Bev was thinking so intently about these issues and also thereby causing me to reevaluate my own positions. Thinking was one thing the Army could not control.

She went on to describe a bunch of things going on in her life. Snow and cold had returned to Minneapolis. She had dreamed that we were in Florida together and that she was showing me all the sights around her home territory. As always, she was reading every day and enjoying recordings of classical music. She ushered at Northrop in exchange for hearing most of the performance of "The Bewitched Child" by Ravel. She and Joyce were spending some time with Kay and Mark, but there were two Joyces and sometimes I was uncertain which one she meant, although she usually made that clear by giving the hair color, dark or blonde. The one with dark hair, a Mormon, was Joyce Coulom, her closest friend at the U. The other was Joyce Rolla from Duluth. She mentioned how high-strung Marty Roth was, and how one day he nearly lit the filter end of his cigarette. I had to laugh because he did the same thing when I had him. She was also taking Joe Kwiat's Whitman/Twain course, and I really wished we were doing that together.

***

Among the many things we were issued during our first week at Fort Campbell was *Department of the Army Pamphlet 360-232; Troop Topics; May, 1968; Basic Training*, a comic-book-sized thirty-page publication heavily illustrated with humorous drawings. The cover featured a drill sergeant surveying a lineup of new recruits still in their civvies. They looked mostly like unlikely prospects that had been caught in the draft, including a guitar-toting hippie, a kid that looked like he belonged in high school, and a cowboy. Near the beginning was a brief section entitled, "Your Responsibilities as a Soldier," which included this statement: "When you serve as an American soldier, you are performing a duty for your country. This is a privilege; be proud that you have the necessary physical, mental, and moral qualifications." That seemed like such unadulterated BS that I pretty much ignored the rest of it, because if serving was such a privilege why were so many of us there against our wills? Why the draft? The booklet went on to advise us to have confidence in our instructors and follow instructions to the best of our ability. "Above all, do your best and retain your sense of humor." That advice seemed geared to the Beetle Bailey peacetime Army rather than to the humorless environment of a bunch of guys training for what could very well be brutal combat but, even so, I read at least far enough to understand the objectives of these eight weeks:

1) Adjust yourself to Army life and Army discipline.
2) Learn to live with, work with, and understand your fellow soldiers.
3) Understand why you are learning to fight.
4) Develop a sense of individual responsibility.
5) Understand the fundamental moral principles and basic obligations of a soldier—in other words, learn the rules.

On Thursday the 27th, the training became more serious when we were issued our M14 combat rifles. It was a large weapon, with a weight unloaded of over nine pounds and a length of 44 inches, but it felt familiar in my hands because of the almost-identical dimensions of the M1s we had trained with in ROTC. We had used the M1s for drill and ceremony training in college but had never fired them. We knew the troops in Vietnam were using the M16 for their basic combat weapon so some of us wondered why we were going to train with M14s and, of course, we were also hoping that might mean we were not destined to be sent to the war zone. Sergeant Seufert was a wounded combat veteran, but he was never given to bend our ears telling war stories. Even so, he was quite taken with the M14 and did talk about it at some length. He felt it was the best combat rifle ever made, and said that many of the old-timers were not sold on the M16, mainly because of its propensity for jamming. The new model had a chrome cylinder and the hope was that would solve the problem. A round from the M14 could go through at least seven men, but the M16 round was smaller and designed to begin tumbling upon impact in order to do maximum damage. The M14 was, in essence, a powerful hunting rifle, whereas the M16 was designed specifically as a combat assault weapon to give US troops a source of firepower as versatile as the Russian AK47 used by many of the communist fighters. A primary reason for the use of a smaller and less stable round was that a wounded soldier reduced the other side's fighting capabilities more than a dead one because they had to devote manpower and resources toward moving him to a medical facility and attempting to restore him to health.

Sarge went on to describe a host of other weapons for us as well, including the Claymore mine. He had been wounded in the head and shoulder by ball bearings from an exploding Claymore, and now had a steel plate in his head that prevented him from running for fear of jarring things loose. Recounting his own injuries seemed to get him started and he went on to explain to us why he hated the VC by describing some incidents of mistreatment of American troops in graphic detail. We already knew about such things since the war had been in the news for about four years now, and we also knew that the atrocities were a two-way street. Who started doing it first? No one knew that, and in war it does not matter anyway—the conflict assumes a monstrous identity of its own and all that matters is revenge. Seufert was by far the best drill instructor I encountered because of his propensity for bending the rules and his approachability, but all of them were pro-war fanatics who believed that America would be overrun by communists if it were not for the armed forces. That is the only thing I would have expected a professional soldier to believe after what they had experienced in Vietnam.

If doubt about the righteousness of our mission there had ever entered their minds, the resulting cognitive dissonance probably would have driven them mad. Most of them did not appear to be particularly deep thinkers but, then again, everyone believes whatever they need to in order to function. As the war went on over the next several years, more and more of these "lifers" would be unable to reconcile the contradiction between what the Army told them and the things they observed with their own eyes. There were some miserable days during the earlier portion of my military sojourn, but one thing I never suffered from was the knowledge that I had bought the lie. That comes at a terrible price. But what did it mean that I had accepted a situation where I might eventually have to kill for a cause I believed to be wrong? I was still working through that one, and grateful that we had scarce time for contemplation.

The weather was pleasant by the end of March, and the training seemed to be going well. We were running two or three miles on most days. I liked that best in the early morning when it was cool and the sun was just rising. Campbell was a dusty place because of all the exposed ground and whenever even a moderate wind came up everything, us included, was soon covered with a fine layer of soil. Sarge said we were lucky not to be there in the summer when it was much worse. The other PT exercises were more challenging for me, but I was making progress and I was far from the worst in the platoon. Sarge said he had observed that I was about the best in the platoon at rifle drill, so when he asked me where I had learned that I told him I had two years of ROTC. The operating rod handle on the M14 was different from that on our old M1s, so I had to be aware of that for the four-part movement of "inspection arms," but I was surprised at how rapidly the old training I had not used for almost three years came back to me: order arms, port arms, present arms, right shoulder arms, rifle salute, and inspection arms.

The Basic Training manual had mentioned that the drill sergeants also served the role of counselors and, although I had read that with a healthy dose of skepticism, I gradually realized that Seufert actually attempted to assume that role. He was about six years older than me, so it was sort of a big brother type of relationship. It must have been more obvious than I realized how unhappy I was about being there, because he told me that after Basic the Army was not so bad. I appreciated his concern, but with Vietnam staring us in the face that was hardly reassuring. Even so, I admired him for his efforts at bucking up our morale, especially since he could have made life pretty miserable for us if he had been so inclined.

Our official eight weeks of Basic were scheduled to begin on Monday the 31st, although they were already keeping us busy with PT, rifle drill, and learning to march as a unit. The rest of our duty hours were filled out with miscellaneous "details," the Army term for whatever odd jobs needed to be done such as painting, mopping floors, and "policing" the grounds. President Eisenhower died at age 78 on March 28 and was buried the following week in an $80 steel GI coffin in Abilene, Kansas. The base was subdued for several days as the nation mourned the loss of one of our great leaders, and the announcement that the Vietnam battle death total was rapidly approaching that of the total for the Korean War, about 33,000, further enhanced the somber mood at Fort Campbell. The hushed atmosphere may have turned my thoughts to spiritual matters because I attended mass on Palm Sunday in a theater on the base, but there was an ulterior motive as well because we had been told that guys who did not attend would be assigned to details. Seufert said that would not really happen, but why take chances? The priest did not deliver a sermon but instead read the long gospel of Our Lord's Passion.

Far more interesting than the mass was what had happened before the service when we were waiting outside. As soon as the DIs went inside the building a car pulled up, some southern belles for short-term hire got out, and one of them began sashaying up and down the ranks, giving us the eye. The graphic choice between the flesh and the spirit reminded me of a Bergman film and lent yet one more surreal touch to the rarely predictable and sometimes bizarre life of the new recruit. None of my comrades were stupid enough to try to take the girls up on their offer.

One day we marched down to the parade grounds to watch a Basic graduation. I think the purpose was to boost our morale by showing us the recognition that awaited us at the end of our training, but to most of us the primary thing finishing Basic meant was that we were one step closer to Vietnam. I wrote my folks that they would be receiving an invitation, but that the curt missive was merely a required formality.

Bev wrote while she was babysitting Geoffrey again. She appreciated getting a break from dorm life and enjoying the atmosphere of a friendly home. She and my mom were growing closer all the time and Bev was coming over for dinner on Palm Sunday. She mentioned how much Mom missed me and how much they enjoyed sharing time together and conversations on the phone. I could tell how good they were for each other and that made me so happy. I knew that by the time I returned Bev would already be like one of the family. She had finished reading five cantos of *The Faerie Queene* for the MA exam, and was working on some Henry James in Marty's course. For Kwiat's class, they were reading some Emerson as a background to Whitman, but what she was especially looking forward to was the Mark Twain portion of the quarter.

She had a pleasant surprise one night when four of the girls from her quad from the previous year at Maryville called to chat with their former counselor, although that also reminded her of how painful it had been to leave the close friends from her four years there. Even so, now she was making new friends in Minnesota, including her lucky fiancé. Bev, Joyce Coulam, and another grad student were planning to go to Rochester to spend Easter at Joyce's brother's place. He and his wife were both doctors and had a Scottish nanny from Edinburgh named Harriet for their two children. Bev had met Harriet before and said she was a bit crude and a real panic. She called Bev "Nellie" because of her middle name.

Snoopy was one of Bev's favorite characters, and so on Palm Sunday she sent me the first of many Snoopy cards. His hyperactive imagination and especially his sheer joy at just being alive always lifted our spirits. She had gone to Palm Sunday services at Vince Hawkinson's church, and included the program in the card. The closing hymn included the verse: "Cure Thy children's warring madness, Bend our pride to Thy control." Always true to his ideals, Vince included a notice in the program of the upcoming four days of Resistance and Renewal on April 3 through 6. Later she went up to the house for dinner. They showed her the pictures Dave took of me about to be hung, and some others in my cap and gown. She played Crazy Eights and Sorry with my sisters Mary and Jane, then thirteen and eleven years old, and declared them "characters." She was already putting together plans to ask them to spend a night in Comstock, which I knew would thrill them to death, and it struck me that she would soon be like a big sister to them. Hearing from her always lightened my burdens and, no matter how much I might sometimes complain in my letters, I always made it a point to tell her how much I needed her.

***

In addition to all the rifle drill movements, the "drill and ceremonies" training included many movements we had learned in ROTC, such as left face, right face, about face, and how to march in squads and platoons. These skills were needed so that when we were on the move we would look like disciplined soldiers instead of a big bunch of guys each walking along at our own pace. It was called doing things "in a military manner." When we were marching from one training area to another, a leader would usually start a cadence call, and hearing one of these is one of the surest ways of stirring up memories for men who have served. One I always remember is:

> I want to be an airborne Ranger.
> I want to live a life of danger.
> I want to go to Vietnam.
> I want to fight the Charlie Cong.

There were endless variations on the "Jodie" chants encouraging soldiers to forget about civilian life because another guy had already moved in on their territory, usually in a call-and-response format, such as:

> Ain't no use in looking back,
> Jodie's got your Cadillac.

Ain't no use in feeling blue,
Jodie's got your girlfriend too.

One version of Jodie made getting in step especially easy because the names of the two feet were incorporated right into the call:

You had a good home when you left – you're right!
But Jodie was there when you left – you're right!

Others were just reworked versions of old dirty camp songs, such as "The Prettiest Girl I Ever Saw" and "Old King Cole." Many of the chants were profane, but that was expected. What would be far more disturbing by today's standards was that a common theme was denigration of women, or even glorification of sexual violence. In fact, the worst insult a DI could hurl at a recruit was to call him a "pussy." Others insulted homosexuals, civilians, or even officers, as in a favorite couplet of mine:

Second lieutenants are at it again:
Fighting the war with a fountain pen.

We had our first locker inspection on Saturday the 29th, performed by none other than our company commander. Sarge had told us that he thought the captain was crazy and, after a class he had conducted the previous day, that seemed like a reasonable assessment to me as well. He was a very intense person with unblinking, gleaming eyes who always paced around as he talked, and his voice often rose to a shout for no apparent reason. Maybe he thought that was the proper bearing to assume for training guys to go to war or maybe Sarge was right and the guy was nuts, most likely due to service in Vietnam. But at least Captain Harris was all right during our inspection and, in any case, trainees like us would have very little contact with someone so much higher in rank.

At this early stage of our military careers, virtually every day brought new revelations about how life was conducted in this strange new environment. As in the contemporary civilian world, the length of hair was a hot-button issue and we had to get a haircut every week during Basic, although I took advantage of the option to let the top grow out a little longer. The skimpy meals continued to be an annoyance, and yet guys who needed to lose weight often found they were unable to finish. Maybe the Army really did know what it was up to sometimes. The Basic PX was not as crowded as the one at the reception center, but we were not allowed to buy food. I tried buying a bag of miniature candy bars, but an overweight sergeant took them away. Sarge said that next weekend we could each have two beers at the PX, and that he might close his eyes if we wanted more than that. In addition to all of our clothes and two pairs of combat boots, we each had quite an array of equipment: a gas mask, steel-pot helmet with liner, the folding shovel know as an entrenching tool, half of a tent known as a shelter-half, and some smaller things as well. We did not keep our rifles in the barracks, and had not yet seen any ammo.

During one lecture, we were informed that all four varieties of North American venomous snakes were found in this region and that if we should happen to encounter one we were to avoid it, but not try to shoot it. All firing was restricted to the firing range. Another rule was that, to help prevent the spread of germs, the barracks windows had to be wide open all night, which made for some chilly nights for the first few weeks. I always particularly enjoyed the feeling of getting away with something. One night I had detail in an area with a Coke machine, and I took advantage of that by enjoying a couple of Cokes, something forbidden to trainees. Seufert had not told us to always follow the rules. Instead, he advised us not to get caught when we broke them. One reason I liked him was that he impressed me as a troublemaker, and something he said made me think he had been busted at least once.

My fellow recruits were quite a diverse bunch of men. Some of them were southern country boys, and Seufert usually called them "ridge runners" instead of hillbillies. One of them was pretty scary, always yelling about how he was looking forward to killing Charlie. We never got enough sleep in the best of circumstances, but this wild man would also often scream and run around the barracks in the middle of the night in his sleep, usually taking a swing at the guy who finally got fed up and woke him up. The most disturbing part of it was that I do not think he was trying to get discharged as mentally unfit, but who really knew? At the opposite end of the spectrum, there were a bunch of college guys like me who had been drafted. Tom Brothen was just a bit older than I, and he had been doing grad work in psychology at the U. Bob Calandar, an accountant and also from Minnesota, had been married for only a few months. One of the guys was working for a brokerage firm and had a wife who was expecting. We sought out each other's company so we could commiserate about our unfortunate situation and, like all soldiers, gripe about anything and everything.

As we moved into our first week of Basic I started to get into the routine of things and to feel less angry and depressed. The full schedule helped but the biggest morale-booster was our first mail call. There was such a backlog of mail that it lasted for over an hour. Sarge said that someone must love us, but he didn't know who. I received the long letter Bev had written at the Davis's and two from Mom, and that did wonders to help relieve the feeling of isolation that had been troubling me. I wrote back right away to let them know how much I appreciated their letters. Several days later, the letters Bev had mailed to me at Company C in the reception center appeared as well, forwarded by the Army postal system.

As always, I could have eaten much more than we were served at chow but the shortage of sleep was becoming even more of a problem. I was able to sleep pretty well during the time allotted for rest because of the heavy schedule of physical training; but Reveille was at 4:00 a.m., many of the guys were noisy sleepers, and about every third night we had fire watch. The advantage of fire watch was the quiet time for reflection and writing letters home. Making the rounds of the barracks in the dead of night was strange because the peacefulness was such a stark contrast to the usual atmosphere of barely controlled chaos and shouting. I was more concerned about the crazy sleep-walking hillbilly than fire, so all was well if he was still in his bunk and the guy who snored like a foghorn was not on his back yet. A poor guy who had been sick for three days was moaning, and I wondered how long they would wait before sending him to the infirmary.

One day I was walking over to the orderly room to report for some sort of duty when I saw a sergeant who had been driving by in a car chewing out a trainee for being outside in his underwear. The combination of the non-commissioned officer's (NCO) apoplectic outburst and the hapless recruit's mute befuddlement suddenly struck me as hilarious, for this type of encounter is the basis for so much service humor, from Sad Sack to Beetle Bailey to Gomer Pyle. It was times like that when I was pleased to realize that I actually was following the advice of the training manual by retaining my sense of humor. I wrote to Bev that "actually, most of what goes on here is utterly absurd if you can step back far enough to appreciate it," and suggested that she read my copy of *Catch-22*, perhaps the most pitch-perfect depiction of military life ever written. Of course, Heller also wrote of the utter terror of combat, and I know that the guys who were becoming my buddies all hoped that we would never encounter that most extreme experience in the life of a soldier.

My skill at keeping a straight face was tested again the day Roscoe Crawley appeared. We were standing in formation on a rainy April 3 when I noticed there was a new black guy in the line. He was skinny and carried himself crookedly, like a scarecrow on a pole, and he had a blank look on his face combined with an unblinking stare. He must have received his gear at another unit because it was different from the identical garb the rest of us wore. He sported a long raincoat that almost touched the ground and a strange flat helmet that looked for all the world like the ones the doughboys wore in World War I. He was wearing that weird headgear tilted so far forward that you could just barely see his eyes. Sergeant Seufert was giving us some kind of instructions, but I noticed that he keep glancing over at Crawley's zombie-like visage until Sarge finally blurted out "you're giving me the fucking creeps, you know it?" I could hardly keep a straight face for the rest of the class. We found out later that Roscoe was one of the recruits who had been given the choice of the Army or prison, although he never talked about what crime he had committed. Actually, he never talked much about anything and when he did I found his ramblings nearly incomprehensible. His unexpressive face made it impossible to read his emotions and that, combined with the knowledge that he might very well be prone to violence, caused most of us to avoid talking with him.

Later the same day another sergeant was giving us a semi-literate lecture on subversion when his mike went out, making it necessary for him to step forward to the apron of the stage and speak loudly in order to be heard. Apparently his training had not prepared him for this unexpected development because, instead of carrying his notes with him, he left them on the podium, came forward to speak two or three sentences, returned to the podium to peruse his next point, and then walked back toward us to speak again. The whole remaining part of his lecture was the same back-and-forth routine, like a scene from a service comedy. Many of the training films were also funny despite their often-graphic content because the acting was so hopelessly wooden, and they seemed to date from around 1950 so the clothes, cars, and even many of the colloquial expressions already appeared antiquated. The ones about avoiding veneral disease (VD) always drew the most snickers.

One of the DIs told us "you may as well give us your heart and soul because your ass belongs to us." That meant nothing to me because of my determination to maintain my own emotional freedom but, of course, I also knew it was crazy to challenge The Man directly in his own neighborhood. One of the most vital skills a new recruit learns is how much he can get away with, and learning that skill takes time because you try to just gently nudge the rules to see what you can do without being punished, sort of like learning how much you can maneuver an unfamiliar pinball machine without tilting.

I knew Sarge could tell I was unhappy because one day he asked, "You don't like the Army, do you?" I told him the truth, but we had a relationship of mutual respect and, as the training manual had advised, we were learning to understand and live with each other. He was obviously much less gung-ho than most of his comrades and I sometimes wondered what he really thought about the war, although I also knew he would never share that with us. He claimed to love the Army, and he was smart enough to see what Vietnam was doing to that institution, but for many of the career men support for the war was based on more than just their geopolitical beliefs and hatred of a foe who had killed some of their comrades. It also meant more money and rapid career advancement for them, and I also believe that a significant number of them only felt truly fulfilled if they were doing what they had trained for years to do: fighting in a war. Sometimes one of them would remark "I know it's a lousy war, but it's the only one we've got right now."

✷✷✷

Bev wrote on April 1 while listening to Beethoven's Pastoral Symphony to help her relax. I admired her appreciation for classical music because I had never had much exposure to it other than in some movie soundtracks. She had been keeping in close contact with the Davis's and my mom. She said that they talked about me whenever they chatted, and that Mom always said how worried she was about me. She said that when she talked with Dad while he was driving her back and forth to the dorm on Palm Sunday he also mentioned Mom's worrying. I was always concerned myself that my being in the service would reawaken emotions that Mom and Granny most likely never worked through thoroughly when Uncle Joe died, so I appreciated Bev telling me this, because it made me realize I would have to sound as upbeat as possible in my letters to the family. With Bev, of course, I could be more honest, but I was beginning to learn that the uncertainty my buddies and I were facing was even worse for our loved ones back home since they had to rely on our periodic written updates for information. When one of those much-anticipated letters finally arrived it would really be depressing if it was a total downer.

Bev said she had a phone call the previous evening from Wanda, one of her best friends from Maryville, although the excitement of the call was tempered by the fact that Wanda's idealism had been "crushed" by her failure to make any visible difference while working in an inner-city church in Indianapolis. Joyce Coulam said to thank me for the card and letter I had sent her from the reception center, and Bev mentioned again how much her friendship with Joyce meant to her. I had asked Mom if my diploma had arrived yet, so Bev explained that there were still administrative snafus holding things up, one of which was that the U had once again failed to properly record my paid graduation fee. She went on to describe her visits to various campus offices as my advocate to get things straightened out, and I had no doubt that she would eventually.

Bev also went on to talk about Liberation Week, the series of events referred to in the church bulletin she had sent in her previous letter. The purpose was to educate the U populace and surrounding community about the indictments of three people involved in the Morrill Hall occupation, the purposes of the occupation, and the implications of the indictments in terms of further control of the U by the state and city governments. Indeed, the legislature was already considering two bills that would greatly increase the penalties for demonstrations that involved interfering with the use of public property. These proposals were similar to a pair of recent federal laws reflecting Nixon's "law and order" approach to dissent on campuses. The key word here appeared to be "disruption," for students convicted of a crime related to disrupting normal campus activities would lose their federal financial aid. Cases of students who participated in a protest without being arrested were to be judged by the campus authorities but, here again, if the administrators determined that the disruption was serious enough financial aid would be withheld.

Most college leaders who spoke to the press about these draconian measures came down squarely on the side of free speech, but it was still disturbing that financial aid had now been added to the threat of the draft as a tool to suppress the right to openly dissent. The U administration continued to take a lenient approach to the Morrill Hall situation by stating that it was impossible to determine which specific individuals had caused damage, although officials cautioned that some disciplinary actions might still be forthcoming. The Hennepin County Grand Jury had no such reservations and issued several indictments accusing the defendants of "mutilating, defacing, breaking, littering, scattering, piling, and barricading" U property during the two-day affair.

Bev said she had learned a lot in the last two days because classes had been opened to discussions led by students involved in the movement. Horace Huntley, one of the indicted U students, spoke in her Whitman/Twain class and she was very favorably impressed with his dedication to peace and concern for all of American society, not just blacks. She said she had never felt the value of demonstrations or marches, but had now made a decision to participate in a campus rally and march to the courthouse downtown to protest the indictments and demand that they be dropped. I was pleased and impressed that she was taking a more activist stance, especially since I knew that her faith and sound judgment would prevent her from going overboard. It was always good to receive news of the resistance because on an Army base it was easy to forget about that front of the war. As she often did, she closed by reflecting on her love for the beauty of nature, and reminded me to look for at least a few signs of beauty in my unfamiliar southern surroundings as well.

Some other items of interest back in Minneapolis included the city's first St. Patrick's Day parade. Humphrey began his duties at the U by appearing as a guest lecturer in political science and history classes. The ongoing intergenerational sore point of hair length and facial hair attracted attention once again when Mankato High School refused to allow a practice teacher in the classroom because he sported a mustache, and the Minnesota Civil Liberties Union (MCLU) announced that it planned to intervene.

Bev wrote on Wednesday, April 3, that the Minnesota spring weather had really turned beautiful. She was still working on solving the problems with my records at the U, including the fact that Deutsch had no record of receiving my paper on the Chuikov book. I knew that Bev and Mom would work through things eventually with the help of my files at home so I was not concerned, but I was also struck by how unimportant these U snafus seemed now that I had more pressing things on my mind. I had a subscription to the *Saturday Review* and Bev said she was sending me an issue she had enjoyed, especially an article about DNA and RNA (ribonucleic acid). She always loved e e cummings, and included a couple of his spring poems in her letter.

I could not help but find her optimism and love of life contagious. She said that Joyce Coulam had bought a wig that made her hair look much shorter, and they were just waiting to see Ed's reaction. Bob and Maggie Weinstein were continuing to experience various problems, but he was hopeful about a possible teaching job in New York state. Bev was reading some Dreiser and Whitman for her classes. John McNally had been in a zany mood on Monday, calling her into his office, teasing her, and pretty much treating her to a comedy routine. Apparently she had not been around the previous week when he expected her, so he asked her if she had been out drinking. I loved hearing about what was going on in her life and I felt as though no detail was too small to include.

∗∗∗

Holy Week was also our first week of Basic. Some of us had KP again because the policy was that each man was to have it at least once each on a weekday and weekend during the course of Basic. Both lists were alphabetical, so that is how the A's and B's had two assignments so close to each other near the beginning. It was tiring work but you also got out of some PT and boring lectures. The PT was tough, but I found that I was in better shape than I expected. It helped to be light because we ran nearly every day, always wearing combat boots and often carrying some gear as well. The alligator crawl continued to be the hardest exercise, but that was true for everyone. The only difficult thing about the classroom work was staying awake, and guys who dozed off in class got put on detail. This was due to inadequate sleep, but also because most of the material was deadly boring. We were told to avoid drugs and snakes. There were lectures on types of warfare, the roles of the Army, military awards, the benefits of physical conditioning, the most common types of injuries, and the appropriate first aid for each. There was a class on map reading which, other than military history, had been my favorite subject in ROTC. There were even presentations on safe driving and fire prevention. There were several lectures on the M14 since we would be starting to use that rifle on the firing range the following week.

The early spring weather was very changeable. Some days were cool and rainy but others were hot and muggy, giving us a taste of what was to come. Easter was the official Army date for switching to summer fatigues that year, which was a big help. I noticed that there were a few blossoms on the apple tree by the mess hall, but our location was not a good one for observing signs of spring. Outside the front of the barracks, facing south, there was a big dirt field where we marched and had PT. That turned into a real dust bowl if a few days passed without rain. The back of the building faced north and across 50th Street there was a huge weed field dotted with the foundations of old barracks that had been demolished. On the other side of the field was a wind-break of evergreens, and past that the airport where we had landed three weeks before. Every morning before dawn I could see a yellow and green flashing signal light over at the airport, reminding me of the green light at the end of Daisy's dock in *The Great Gatsby*. Like Gatsby, to me the light meant hope and optimism, because I thought the airport might be where I would return to Minneapolis after Basic. But one of the many uncertainties we lived with was whether or not there would even be leaves after Basic.

My first Easter in the Army was a strange one. Since I had gone to mass on Palm Sunday, I was planning to go to the Protestant services for Easter, but when the buses came I was in the middle of writing a letter to my family so I decided not to go, especially since Seufert had told us that the story about getting detail if we did not attend church was untrue. Then Sergeant Quick, the senior DI, came in wearing his dress uniform and all his decorations, and announced that he was mad at all of us who did not go to church. He had us go out and shovel gravel until the buses returned with the church-goers. That was just more petty harassment, but I preferred the manual labor to going to church under duress.

After that I saw Quick as one of the enemy, and yet we needed to pay attention to fools like him to learn survival skills for Vietnam, just one more paradox in the strange life of a new recruit. It was also apparent that Quick's Easter morning devotions included starting his drinking for the day. Seufert had told us that our platoon was the best in the company, and I noticed that we also had the fewest men going to church. After dinner there was a movie, but I was planning to skip it because I wanted to write letters. Then another sergeant came in and said that if we did not go we would have to work, so I went after all. I was surprised by the choice of film, *Cool Hand Luke*—the story of life on a southern prison farm was hardly one to take our minds off of our unpleasant surroundings for a bit. The sound was bad, the picture was distorted, and the tin building was hot. I dozed through much of it. After supper we had to clean the barracks and pack our gear for the next day, which was to include a ten-mile hike.

★★★

Bev wrote on April 4, Good Friday, that the three of them had arrived in Rochester that morning and that they had already had a tour of the Mayo Clinic, the museum, and the medical sciences building. She said the Coulam house with the two doctors-in-training, two very lively kids, Harriet the nanny, and the three guests was quite chaotic compared to her quiet dorm room at Comstock. The march to protest the indictments had been the day before, and she was still analyzing her feelings about it. She was glad she had participated but was unsure if she ever would again. Some of the speeches given at the "teach-in" on the Mall before the march were far too emotional for her. That evening she had supper at Centennial Hall with Joyce, Ed, and someone named Linda; then went to the communion service at Grace Lutheran Church. Pastor Vince, of course, had also been in the march that afternoon.

After that she was planning to go home and collapse for a bit, but Jennifer and Sharon suggested going to a movie, so they went to see *The Heart is a Lonely Hunter*. She was impressed with Alan Arkin's portrayal of a deaf mute, but exhausted by the time they got home after ice cream at Bridgeman's. "Born Free," one of her favorite songs, was playing as she wrote but that, combined with the anniversary of Dr. King's death, only got her thinking about the lack of freedom for so many people in America. She was feeling down in the middle of all the activity around the house, and I was touched that she was sharing that with me.

As always, she wrote of our love for each other and hopes for the future, and also sent a little Hallmark book of poetry entitled *In Quiet Places*, which included brief selections by Byron and Wordsworth. The chaos continued throughout the weekend, and on Easter Bev sent a postcard she wrote while sitting in the dining room while Joyce was sewing, Harriet was knitting, and Linda was playing solitaire while The Mamas and Papas were singing in the background with everyone humming along or chewing gum in time. She had planned on reading Dreiser, but was unable to concentrate with all the surrounding activity. Like me, she was in need of being alone with her thoughts, but finding herself in a place where that was not possible. Joyce was hard of hearing, and thus had the advantage of being able to simply turn down her hearing aids whenever she needed to concentrate on a project or just to think.

★★★

The day after Easter, Monday the 7th, was our first of many out on the rifle range. There were several ranges two to five miles west of our barracks and part of our PT was marching or running out there and back while carrying about twenty pounds of equipment. I had fired BB guns, gas-powered pellet guns, and a shotgun before, but never a high-powered rifle like the M14. The recoil seemed about the same as a shotgun and, after firing a few tentative rounds, I felt comfortable operating the weapon. That is not to say I could hit much of anything at the start, but at that point we were shooting mainly just to get used to firing a military rifle. Sarge continued encouraging me, though, and after looking at my target he said he would not want me for an enemy. The noise when we were all on the line firing was incredible and reminded me of war movies, or perhaps the big showdown scene in a Western. The left-handed guys were at a disadvantage because the hot empty brass cartridge was ejected from the right side of the weapon, always threatening to graze the face of the shooter. I could see how that could make a guy gun-shy but there was no such thing as a left-handed M14.

Monday afternoon was hot and several men passed out on the return march, with some others coming near to it. Tuesday was overcast, a good day for marching and shooting. Wednesday brought a heavy all-day rain and we had to march, stand, and lie down in standing water. Our cumbersome rubber ponchos did little to prevent us from getting soaked. Some of the deep puddles were over the tops of our combat boots, so our feet were soaked as well. The boots were waterproof, so the water did not drain out and on the march back our feet felt like lead. The DI's only comment on the miserable situation was that it was nothing compared to the rainy season and rice paddies of Vietnam.

I wrote to Bev that I was glad she participated in the march to protest the indictments, and told her I believed such activities were important. At the end of any single event, it was natural to feel as she did that everything seemed the same, but I assured her that at the very least demonstrations put these issues before the public eye. This also had the effect of hardening the views of the pro-war folks, of course, but I believed that the anti-war activities had been a major factor in beginning to turn the tide of public opinion against the government's policies. I went on to mention that I was still required to go to meetings explaining the advantages of Officer Candidate School (OCS) but that, for at least three reasons, there was absolutely no chance I would be signing up for it. First, that required extending your term of enlistment to three years. Second, 2nd lieutenants in Vietnam had one of the highest causality rates, as even the gung-ho Sergeant Quick had pointed out. Third, and most important, was that I did not believe in the war and was not about to assume any type of leadership role in prosecuting it.

As mid-April approached, the weather was mostly pleasant and they also began to give us more food. I ate everything offered but could not really tell if I was gaining any weight. If I was, it was not around the waist. I decided to weigh myself on the next trip to the PX. We had been under quarantine for zero week and the first two weeks of Basic, but now we would be going to the PX periodically and be allowed to use the pay phones to call home. I was also feeling less depressed, although the regimentation and lack of personal time continued to present more annoyances than I had ever experienced in such a short period of time in civilian life. I lost my watch when the band apparently snapped while we were doing the alligator crawl in the pits by the mess hall, and I had to do without one until our next trip to the PX.

We had to have our laundry done frequently because of all the hard training and PT. This was done for us and it was returned in bundles with our names on them. The first time it came back there seemed to be none or not enough for some of the guys as we dug through the pile of bundles, so some of them began to take clothing from other bundles. This resulted in a chain reaction of guys trying to fill out the quota of what they had been issued by grabbing whatever clothing was not already in someone else's hands, even though we had written our name and serial number on each item. I think many items, especially underwear, made their way among several soldiers during the course of Basic.

***

As always, letters from home were the most potent antidote to all this nonsense, or bullshit, to use the military lingo. Bev wrote on Monday the 7th and included an e e cummings love poem, "the great advantage of being alive." She was glad to be back in her dorm room, but said the spring weather was so nice that some of them went outside to play Frisbee after supper for almost an hour. She said that the NW Bank weather ball indicated that cooler temperatures and rain were on the way, and I got a kick out of how she had learned to read that icon of Twin Cities popular culture. Mom, Mary, and Jane had stopped by to see her the previous evening, bringing a retyped copy of my paper for Deutsch and a basket from the Easter bunny. "People" was playing on her radio, and songs about love all had a new meaning for the two of us since we had met. She had taken advantage of being back in her own room by reading some Dreiser, Emerson, and Whitman.

The next day, Bev and Joyce went downtown after lunch and had a ball getting their pictures taken in the little machine in Grants department store. Then they went to Dayton's and she found a two-piece green, navy blue, and white bathing suit for summer Girl Scout camp. She described it as a little skimpy but comfortable. She had changed her mind and made a firm decision not to visit AnnaBelle, her sister in Germany, in August. Among her reasons was her reluctance to travel alone, a need she felt to stay in America during our prolonged national crisis, a desire for more time to study, and the possibility of the two of us having time together if I should happen to get leave sometime in the summer. She also said that going to Europe was the thing to do among students at the U and that she felt rebellious enough to not want to be part of that group. I loved that independent streak. After all, she was a redhead. Her sister Sandra and her husband Frank in Alaska were adopting a four-month old boy they were naming Greg. She also had an aunt and uncle who had three adopted children. Later I would learn that was Mary Alice and George.

On Wednesday the 9th Bev wrote that my most recent letter had raised her spirits.

> I read it while walking down East River Road to the Franklin Avenue Bridge. In spite of cloudy skies, I enjoyed watching life return to Minneapolis as I spotted several robins and a bright red cardinal which belted out his "pretty, pretty" song in defiance of the industrial society represented by the cars zooming by trying to drown his song. Then there is the grass which gets greener every day (the best thing about the rain) and the buds which are beginning to come out. And people smile and laugh and talk and look longingly at each other happily.

She said the sight of the happy young couples was what made her miss me the most, and this theme of the mystery of being so newly in love and yet so suddenly separated was one that resonated through many of our letters to each other. The only one more common was our dream for a future together. She also mentioned that the Minnesota River had reached flood stage at

Mankato and Marshall. Mary and Jane were going to be spending Friday night in the dorm and on Saturday the three of them and Joyce were going to see *Oliver* at the Cooper. On Sunday evening she was planning to have dinner with some friends from the Maryville faculty at the Davis's, including Dr. Young, a professor of chemistry who led a hiking group she belonged to in college. She said the best hike she ever had was the previous winter in Cade's Cove with all the snow and the frozen streams and waterfalls. She was missing the proximity to wilderness at Maryville, and was hoping to get out of the city for a bit to see spring in the country. "It really bugs me to try to see a beautiful sunset with the other half of the dorm in the way."

Granny also wrote on the 9th saying how glad they were to receive my last letter. She said that at least our busy training schedule would help to pass the time "and I know it hangs heavy." That was one of her old-fashioned expressions that I loved to hear. Patty Harris, along with her husband and their little boy had visited on Sunday. Patty was one of Aunt Margaret's granddaughters, and Margaret was Granny's sister out in Billings, Montana. After they left, Granny and the kids went out and raked up the yard, cleaned out the window wells, and cut the limb that was hanging down from the elm tree, "etc." She was glad they got the chores done, because it had been raining and sprinkling off and on ever since. Mom was hosting card club the next night "and as usual she is tearing the guts out of the place in preparation." I was sure it was good for Mom to keep busy as well. She closed "because there seems to be a dearth of news," but the little incidents of daily life at home that she had related were just what I looked forward to hearing. She enclosed an article from *The Billings Gazette* on the Connolly Saddlery and the current issue of the *DLS Alumni News*.

***

Down at Fort Campbell, we had our first PT test on Friday, April 11, with our company having the distinction of finishing last in the battalion. We had too many older guys like me, including eight college grads out of fifty-five men. This first test was only to set a benchmark for improvement. I scored 271 out of 500, but I knew I could pass in six weeks because that only required 300 points. The alligator crawl was still the toughest with its strength and coordination requirements. My partner in the fireman's carry dropped me twice, but since I was on his shoulders, I fell on top of him both times. When we returned we were sitting on the grass next to the barracks and one guy passed out. Sarge was unable to revive him and they took him

Basic Training: March-May 1969

away in an ambulance. In my thoughts I wished him luck with managing to finagle a discharge, but knew that we would probably see him again in a day or so.

Most of the classes continued to be deadly boring, covering such topics as Code of Conduct (COC), Marches and Bivouacs, Ambush Techniques, the Uniform Code of Military Justice, and Personal Hygiene. In the COC class, the sergeant told us how to behave if captured, but after the *Pueblo* incident everything he said seemed completely unreal. People only keep quiet when tortured in the movies but, of course, that is not to say that any of the information they provide is accurate. There was also a lecture on the Geneva Convention, which everyone in the room knew did not apply in Vietnam. On the more active side, we started bayonet drill, which was using dummies for practicing stabbing, slashing, and striking with the butt of the rifle, all reinforced with a loud "yup!" If we ever did get into combat I hoped we were never close enough to the "enemy" to need those skills. The highlight of that exercise for me was hearing Julio Burgos, a Puerto Rican from Ohio who looked like he belonged in junior high, mutter "When I get home, I'll give my girlfriend the Inverted Butt Thrust!"

On Sunday the 13th I called home for the first time from the bank of outdoor pay phones over near the PX. It was great to talk with my family, although I did not try calling Bev since I knew she was changing rooms and I did not have her new phone number. That was disappointing, but I knew we would connect before long. Mary and Jane both chattered about how much fun they had staying at Comstock and going to the movie. Mom said that Uncle Del's wife Tress had passed away. Like Del himself, she had been in poor health for some time.

I had called without asking permission, knowing that if that turned out to be against regulations all I had to do was plead ignorance. That may have been the only advantage of being so new. Some guys tested the limits much further than that and several of them had gone out and gotten drunk the previous evening. They ran between some barracks to avoid an MP and got caught in some barbed wire, probably the stuff strung over an alligator crawl pit to ensure that the soldiers stayed low enough. Despite their drunken state, they freed themselves eventually and the MP had not bothered to chase them, but that was more of a risk than I cared to take. You really could not plead ignorance on that one. Crawley came back talking more than ever before and told anyone who cared to listen how high he was and how he wished he could give some of his high to someone else. I thought he meant drugs, but despite his ebullient state I was not about to ask the mysterious Roscoe any questions.

We had most Sundays off and Basic was where I learned to really appreciate a day of rest. I spent the 13th writing home and reading Lawrence's *The Rainbow*, the *Saturday Review* Bev had sent, and the Memphis newspaper. The paper reported that the Mississippi was rising two feet a day in St. Paul. There were a number of letters to the editor, mostly anonymous, objecting to a picture of Ted Kennedy with his arm around a Negro politician. It seemed as though racists often craved anonymity, including the ones in the white sheets. Another privilege that had been added by "the powers that be" was occasional stops near our barracks by a bakery truck, so I enjoyed some rolls and donuts. Supper the previous evening had been a good one too. I drew a rough map for Bev of our immediate area. Nearly all of the buildings looked like huge shoeboxes with peaked roofs, painted white with green trim. They looked almost exactly like the World War II-era "temporary" buildings on our campus, except that they stood on cement pilings three or four feet off the ground. The ones at the U were from a base in Ottumwa, Iowa, that had been downsized or decommissioned after World War II, and I think ours were from the same era.

Sometimes I imagined the 101st Airborne soldiers who lived here preparing to go into battle in World War II. Their anxiety must have been at least as high as ours, but I wondered if it helped to be preparing for a war that nearly everyone considered a just cause that was necessary to protect our country. Most likely, their main concern was the same as ours: just to get through it alive. Some units of the current incarnation of the 101st were coming back from Vietnam and would be reoccupying these quarters in May when our training was over.

***

Bev wrote on Thursday April 10, still up at midnight and unable to sleep without "talking" with me first. She said that her plans for Mary and Jane's visit included going over to Mama Rosa's on Riverside Avenue for pizza. Mom had called earlier and told Bev about the card club and Aunt Tress. Mom would have to break this news to the ailing Uncle Del who was in very bad shape himself. Bev said the U had sent the three copies of my transcript they had requested and that she would take one over to the grad school to be recorded so that I would be cleared to register again when I returned. She also said she enjoyed helping in these ways because it eased the worries of my family and me. She had gone to the Minneapolis Symphony Orchestra concert at Northrop that evening, which included a piece by Ligeti that had been used in *2001*, but the highlight was one of her favorites: the *1812 Overture*. She enclosed a few pages of the program that included a description of the great battle from Chapter XXXIX of *War and Peace*:

> But though towards the end of the battle the men felt all the horror of their actions, though they would have been glad to cease, some unfathomable, mysterious force still led them on, and the artillerymen—the third of them left—soaked with sweat, grimed with powder and blood, and panting with weariness, still brought the charges, loaded, aimed, and lighted the match; and the cannon balls flew as swiftly and cruelly from each side and crushed human flesh, and kept up the fearful work, which was done not at the will of men, but at the will of Him who sways men and worlds.

I knew from studying history that all wars, once begun, assumed a life of their own and that, especially in modern "total war," the only goal quickly became victory at any price. But that perspective usually described the policies and decisions of national leaders, and here Tolstoy was describing how this attitude filtered all the way down to the common soldiers in the field. The war had assumed a monstrous, bloodthirsty identity of it own and now all the participants from the national and military leaders down to the "grunts" on the front lines had become its mindless minions. I had known this as well, of course, on an intellectual level but now I was in a position where I might soon be caught up in that madness myself. How would I react in a situation where wanton destruction of life was the norm, where such actions were necessary to try to help ensure your own survival as well as the lives of your comrades? These questions were often on my mind, and when Sarge interpreted my thoughtful demeanor as a reflection of my dislike of the Army he was only partially right.

Bev had also been enjoying physical activity, swimming at Cooke Hall and sharing the Frisbee fad with other women in the dorm. She wanted to build up her swimming strength to be able to take the lifesaving course at camp that summer. She was moving four doors down the hall to share a room with her friend Jennifer Hydeen whose roommate had not returned after spring break. She said the packing was actually good preparation for what she would need to do near the end of the quarter anyway.

The next day she went shopping in Dinkytown, buying a few books, a kite, and some doughnuts for breakfast the next morning with Mary and Jane. She said the weather was really "beautemous" now, with students all over the lawn on the Mall and tossing footballs and Frisbees around. She had seen a guy flying a kite from the Washington Avenue Bridge that had gone beyond Comstock Hall, which probably inspired her own kite purchase. She enclosed another poem by cummings: "I thank you God for most this amazing," a wonderful one for spring.

Bev wrote again on Saturday the 12th, but this time she was depressed, confused, and lonely because she had received a long letter from AnnaBelle in reaction to her decision not to visit Germany after all. The two sisters had not been communicating regularly and Bev had not realized how much her upcoming visit meant to AnnaBelle (AB) and Jack. Bev said the situation was rather involved, but that the main sources of stress were that their first baby was due soon and Jack was threatened with a second tour of duty in Vietnam since artillery officers were needed there. He was like me in the sense that the Army would not allow him to resign at that point. The long letter from overseas left her in tears and seemed to kick off all the emotions that had been building up since I had left. She said she was sure she would feel better the next day and, knowing her, I also thought that would be true, but I still longed to comfort her in person. On the positive side, AB and Jack were already "crazy" about me and joyful that Bev and I had found each other. I hoped to meet them someday, and I wondered if Jack and I would be in Vietnam at the same time. I liked the fact that he was reluctant to return because many of the NCOs and officers at our training center seemed to welcome it, or at least that was the attitude they displayed for the benefit of us trainees.

Bev went on to say that Mary and Jane seemed to have a good time, but it was hard to tell because they were so quiet. Were these the same sisters who had been chattering away when I called a couple of nights before? They had gone to Mama Rosa's for pizza and then had a pillow fight before going to sleep on Friday night. Mary got the bed in Bev's room while Jane and Bev had sleeping bags on the floor. After doughnuts and milk the next morning, they flew the new Cloud Buster kite from the roof of the parking garage on

East River Road behind the dorm, easily getting it as high as the length of their string allowed. After lunch at Burger King, the three of them and Joyce drove to St. Louis Park in Ed's VW to see *Oliver*. I loved picturing Bev in a big-sister role with Mary and Jane, and she enjoyed the opportunity to get to know my family better.

She continued on Sunday the 13th and things did indeed look better to her then. She had spent most of the day sorting and packing her junk, and then moving part of it down to her new room and preparing the rest for packing up for the summer. Staying active helped keep her mind off her troubles, but the best thing she did all day was to call her folks. It was comforting to share with them, and her dad agreed with her decision to stay in America. They wanted her to come home in mid-August when camp was finished, and she thought that she would. She was staying flexible because of the uncertainty over when I would be on leave, but I was glad that she was not structuring her summer based upon that.

Her day really had been a full one, because she also enjoyed another evening with Maryville folk at the Davis's. This time the visitor was Dave Young, a chemistry professor, and he even brought a bunch of Tennessee spring flowers: violets, daffodils, and dogwood. She especially enjoyed get-togethers like this because the other women in the dorm did not really understand her attachment to Tennessee, although Joyce came the closest to appreciating it, which is exactly what I would have expected. Dave had asked her how it felt to be in love, and she had replied "great!" She closed by describing her hopes for our future together, saying she was listening to Judy Collins's version of Leonard Cohen's "Hey, That's No Way to Say Goodbye," a song somewhat like our lives as we contemplated our love and long separation, beautiful and sad at the same time. I knew from the tone of her letter that the mood of the song matched the mixed emotions going through her mind, and as I sat there in the lonely barracks reading it I felt the same way.

She wrote again on the 15th saying that she received a letter from me the previous day that was postmarked the 2nd. Thank you, Army postal system. She was feeling down again and the cloudy, rainy weather was not helping. "Rod McKuen says that spring is 'the other side of fall,' but to me it's the same rainy stuff so far, at least right now." The spring thaw combined with the rain had resulted in flooding on West River Road, as well as parts of St. Paul, Mankato, and Marshall. A young man had drowned in the Mississippi near the Franklin Avenue Bridge about 3:00 a.m. on Sunday and one of her friends had heard his cry for help. Bev was reading *Babbitt* for Marty's class and finding it slow going. I remembered the book well. Babbitt's version of a mid-life crisis led him to a half-hearted attempt to break out of the ennui of his bourgeois existence in Zenith, but this attempted escape was doomed to failure, largely because he knew no other way of life to adopt. Lewis resisted the temptation to portray George Babbitt as a mere caricature of the smug, soul-dead upper-middle class and instead rendered the existence of his hapless protagonist with an attitude of bemused empathy, even hinting at the end that his return to the fold was a bit less than complete. I was pleased to hear that Bev was beginning to see some saving grace and movement in the book; I remembered that slogging through to the end had been worth the effort.

The day before had brought a "minor catastrophe" when she dropped her left contact lens in the sink drain, but Marvin, the dorm's handyman, saved the day. He said he had only failed to retrieve one lens during his tenure at Comstock. Later that day, they had a birthday party for two girls in the dorm, and since one turned twenty-one, Bev got out a small bottle of wine she had since Christmas vacation. It was fun but mixed emotions struck again—we liked to have a glass of wine together and the occasion reminded her yet again of our separation. Then Joyce and Bev experimented with the group of about ten women by reading a couple of mildly erotic cummings poems, which she enclosed: "may I feel said he" and "I like my body when it is with your body," which also made her long for us to be together.

She took a break to go to class and then continued with a brief description of the Academy Awards show the previous night: *Oliver* had taken a number of Oscars. She had found Deutsch's TA again and gave him the paper that Mom had re-typed. The folks at the Grad School had been helpful and understanding as well, and she would let me know as soon as my diploma arrived. Kwiat had given a lecture on Whitman's characteristic technique of unifying seeming opposites such as I and you; past, present, and future; body and soul; life and death; high and low; and beginning and end. He had also dealt with the poet's metaphoric techniques. It all sounded a bit heavy, but it also made me wish I was back listening to learned discourses instead of the drivel and mind rot that dominated most of our instruction at Fort Campbell. She thought she would write her paper for Joe on Twain's *Mysterious Stranger*.

Basic Training: March-May 1969

Mom and Bev had a good phone conversation on the 14th, and Mom was quite concerned about the arrangements for Tress's funeral and the dinner she might have to prepare. She always took her duties of handling the affairs of departed family members very seriously. Mom mentioned that I had called and sounded good, and I was relieved to hear that was how I had come across. Bev described changing rooms again and, even though she had not had a roommate in two years, the adjustment had been easy so far. The new room was larger and that helped. She closed by mentioning that Joyce, Ed, and some of her other friends had asked about me, something a soldier away from home always enjoys hearing.

✸✸✸

I started a letter to Bev on the 13th while on fire-guard yet again. Some of the guys in our company had gone down to the EM (Enlisted Men's) Club earlier in the day and had gotten caught. The NCOs employed the time-honored technique of shaming the miscreants by punishing the entire unit, and in this case the penalty was the cancellation of our movie. Only in the Army would being deprived of the chance to sit for two hours in a sweat-box enduring a mediocre film with virtually unintelligible sound be considered a punishment. They even called a formation to break this shattering news to us and that turned into a comedy routine when one guy showed up smashed. His inebriated state inspired him to exit the barracks by the fire escape ladder rather than the door, and he showed up with his shirt unbuttoned and shoeless. We got him back inside before the sergeant showed up and then I had a chance to put my military discipline to the test by refraining from laughter until we were dismissed. I used the welcome and unexpected free time to read more Lawrence.

Everyone was sick to at least some degree. I had the same type of mild but persistent cold that I had been unable to shake for my last few weeks of civilian life. The previous morning we had received shots for typhoid, smallpox, and yellow fever that left many of the guys feeling somewhat under the weather, including me. Upper respiratory infections (URIs) were rampant, and as I sat on the stairs writing that night there was so much coughing that it sounded like a TB ward. At one point eighteen of the fifty-seven men in our platoon had been in the hospital, several with pneumonia. I had not felt the need to go on sick-call yet and I hoped to avoid it, because you usually had to make up the training on the following Sunday. We had been having huge meals because so many of the men were not eating, so between that and the bakery truck I was not hungry anymore. We were scheduled to march or run out to the rifle range again the next day, and I know we were all hoping for a break in the heavy spring rains. We had been told that the URI rate the previous cycle had been a near disaster. Once our cotton fatigues got wet they stayed that way and we spent the rest of the day in soggy clothes. Whenever they double-timed us there were lots of guys dropping out, and they were so weak that no amount of yelling could inspire them to muster the strength to resume running. Actually, despite my own URI issue I was one of the healthiest ones in the unit. My appetite was good and I was eating about three Florida oranges a week at chow, which always reminded me of Bev. I hoped she was escaping the worst of the spring colds as well.

The next day was cloudy and misty, but those were pretty much the ideal conditions for our strenuous activities. They double-timed us out to the range, again carrying all our equipment, and guys were staggering and dropping out the entire way. Actually, so many of us were sick that only twenty-nine of the fifty-seven in our platoon had been able to go at all. The activity for the day was zeroing our rifles, which is the trial-and-error process of adjusting the sights until the rounds hit somewhere near where you are aiming. When we finally returned, mad Captain Harris was upset about the condition of the barracks and we had to alligator crawl across the field and back. The field was almost pure mud with all the rainy days, so the crawl was almost like a type of swim. That made it take longer to reach your goal but it also eliminated the painful friction of doing it on dry ground or gravel. Also, we had found that the soil had such a high clay content that once it dried you could brush most of it off of your clothes. By this time we were getting used to petty harassment like this, but I hoped our sick-call rate would be even higher as a result. That was followed by one of our more useful classes: first aid.

The afternoon's schedule concluded with a seemingly interminable class on the Uniform Code of Military Justice (UCMJ), the legal system for members of the armed forces. There were a number of rights, of course, but not as many as for civilians under the Criminal Justice System. The theme was to stay out of trouble, because in the military that was a bad place to be, but they failed to mention Seufert's more realistic admonition: If you do break the rules, don't get caught.

The next day, Tuesday the 15th, we finished zeroing in our rifles and had our first target shooting, using pop-up targets displaying the upper half of a man's silhouette 350 meters downrange. Twenty-three was a good score, and 30 was excellent. I got 27, which was just about where I wanted to be: good but not outstanding. Sarge continued with his encouraging ways by mentioning his approval of my shooting. We had never fired weapons in ROTC, but I think the hours I spent with my brother Dave playing with our BB gun when we were kids had resulted in my feeling comfortable with a rifle, as well as giving me an understanding of how to make adjustments for accuracy. In any case, we had been told that our Advanced Individual Training (AIT) assignments would be determined before the final marksmanship test so there did not seem to be any drawback to doing well.

On Wednesday we had a break from the rifle range for our CBR (chemical, biological, and radiological) Warfare Training. This included yet another long lecture on the varieties of biological weapons, means of delivery, portals of entry into the body, and protective equipment. Chemical agents included compounds affecting the nerves or blood; producing blisters, choking, or incapacitation; and tear agents, which were painful but also the least harmful of these weapons. We could not have known then that the US, totally ignorant of its devastating long-term effects, was employing the potent and deadly product known as Agent Orange against our own troops all over the RVN by using it as a defoliant. The widespread occurrence of the same disease over a period of time was an indication that the enemy had employed a biological weapon, but the countermeasure was hardly one to inspire much confidence: wash with warm soapy water.

The last section, radiological warfare, was the furthest divorced from reality as the instructor described the initial effects of a nuclear blast followed by the radiation composed of alpha, beta, and gamma particles. The protection was to dig a foxhole, cover up with a shelter-half, and don a gas mask. There was no first aid. In other words, the instruction was based on the antiquated 1950s concept of a limited nuclear war where small versions of such weapons were used for battlefield tactics rather than to destroy entire cities with a single blast. The Kafkaesque quality of this bizarre presentation during the era of mutually assured destruction, which was delivered in all seriousness, was mitigated by the fact that we knew neither side was employing radiological weapons in Vietnam.

We also knew that this grim lecture was the prelude to one of the best-known and most-dreaded rites of passage of Basic: exposure to tear gas. In the first exercise we were crawling under barbed wire when a sergeant threw a gas grenade at us. We had practiced donning our masks and put that skill to good use, although struggling for breath through the mask's filter while exerting ourselves doing the alligator crawl did produce a feeling of mild panic. The highlight was the gas chamber where you enter with your mask on, take it off when ordered to do so, and then remain there until given permission to leave. It was painful, but some guys seemed to get a much heavier dose than I. They were totally incapacitated for a time. The Army had kept abreast of the times by renaming this substance "riot control gas," and that is when I realized how the protestors felt when the police used gas on them, but our schedule did not allow me much time to contemplate the war in the streets and on the campuses that had been so much on my mind a mere month before.

At this mid-point of Basic we had fallen into a routine of three primary activities: shooting out on the range, physical training, and classes. The lectures were sometimes in stuffy classrooms and at other times in outdoor areas with bleacher seating. The instructors were junior officers or NCOs with a wide range of public speaking abilities. The personas they assumed usually ranged from normal to no-nonsense military, but some took a gung-ho approach that seemed to border on the pathological. Captain Harris was a prime example of the latter. It was impossible to tell if they were really nuts or if they felt that level of intensity was the appropriate one for training men for combat in a hellhole like Vietnam. Maybe Vietnam had made them that way. Fort Campbell was a pretty bleak place but the new leaves on the trees and blossoms on fruit trees were reminders that spring was upon us. These rare glimpses of beauty usually caught my eye when my mind was wandering during yet another soporific lecture, and then I often thought of Henry Reed's "Naming of Parts." Irony was unavoidable but, unfortunately, achieving detachment was always difficult and often impossible.

With so many of us sick, the captain ordered health measures. The standard remedy for a URI is to rest and drink plenty of fluids but, since our tight schedule did not allow for additional rest, his alternate approach was based on the supposed virtues of fresh air. The windows in the barracks were to remain wide open and the heat was to remain off. I woke up at 3:00 a.m. one night seeing my breath and, despite my exhausted state, was too cold to get back to sleep. Bev had a lingering cold as well, but she wrote that she disliked Formula 44. I told her that I loved it and encouraged her to give it another try as well as drinking lots of orange juice. The Vicks concoction helped a person sleep if nothing else, and anything with alcohol was fine by me.

The letters from home were the most welcome distraction from the training routine, with reading coming in a close second. Sarge was intrigued with my small collection of literature, especially T*ess of the d'Urbervilles*, but he was not sure what to make of it. The local newspapers were poor and we had no chance to watch news on TV, so I would read magazines like *Time* to try to keep up with the outside world. One issue had a review of Baker's biography of Hemingway, always one of my favorite writers. The cover article was about unrest on the campuses and I hoped that would increase in intensity if Nixon did not make a dramatic move soon towards winding down the war. I always saw the resistance as the true friends of the troops, whereas the mindless and superficial patriotism of the flag-wavers would only result in more casualties.

Another break in the routine for me was being excused from some training so that I could type in the supply room, which raised my hopes of getting a clerical assignment after Basic. It would be hard to say if riflemen or clerks were more important in the Army, because without enough men to process orders and requisitions things would quickly grind to a halt. You could not do anything important without the required piece of paper in your hand, and this was long before the era of desktop computers and high-speed printers. The only drawback was that once they found out I was a fast and accurate typist they sometimes called me in to do it on Sundays as well.

***

Bev wrote on Wednesday the 16th that she was absorbed in Twain's *Mysterious Stranger* and was planning on writing a paper about it for Kwiat's class. She was also continuing with Whitman and was approaching the end of *Babbitt*. After supper that night, Joyce had asked Bev if she "would go be alone together with her; that is, if I would go with her as she was alone in her thoughts and I in mine." They walked down the East River Road to a spot of grass just north of the I-94 bridge where Bev read *Babbitt* and Joyce just thought. Bev felt the need to take more time to just think "in order to regain a perspective I may have lost." They ended up spending about three hours together, and Bev wrote again about how much they valued each others' friendship. They certainly were good for each other, and I always had to laugh about the stoic Joyce having a crush on Cal Kendall.

In other news, noisy construction was still underway in Vincent Hall, making Marty Roth even jumpier than usual. I wished I had been there to see that. Bev received her Teaching Assistant renewal for the following year, a relief. She had received an A and two Bs the previous quarter, but she thought it strange that one of the Bs was in Milton, which she loved, and the A in 20th Century Writers, "a class I barely said boo for." By coincidence, my grades for winter quarter had been two Bs and an A as well. She also wanted to work on a paper on Wallace Stevens but was not finding the time because of all the reading, talking with friends, and socializing. But she was not seriously troubled by this since she believed that such discussions were a vital part of the educational experience.

Bev and Joyce were taking great interest in their first Minnesota spring, including the new leaves, returning birds, and green grass. It really raised her spirits, which I was pleased to hear. She was glad I was putting on a few pounds, and admitted that she hardly paid attention to the meals in the dorm because of all the distractions of her busy schedule. She closed with love, as always, but also said that Jennifer insisted that she inform me that she had an irritating cough, which Jennifer was doctoring by pouring "horrid" Vicks Formula 44 down her throat. I was sorry about the cough, but amused by the image of Jennifer making Bev drink the highly alcoholic concoction. Most likely that was a combination of friendly concern and Jennifer's need for some uninterrupted sleep herself. I had a nagging cough myself for a couple of weeks that was worse at night, but that was true of so many of the guys that yet one more hacking sufferer added little to the annoyance of trying to get some decent rest under such noisy conditions. That, plus the cold breeze through the wide-open windows, made for some restless nights in our barracks. I even heard the laconic Roscoe complain once during the wee small hours.

Bev was a faithful correspondent and she wrote again on the 18th about how the days had been going faster because she had been laughing so much she was almost rolling on the floor. Jennifer was obviously far more extroverted than Joyce, and since Bev moved in with her they had taken delight in teasing each other. When Bev wanted to get Jennifer's goat she would turn on a thick Southern accent that "drove her up a tree." The previous evening they had played Frisbee, untangled the kite string, ran around the roof of the parking garage behind the dorm, and then gone to Bridgeman's for sundaes. I wondered if more time to think was really what she needed, because it sounded like a little more time for play was doing her good. In any case, Joyce was always around as well and she was trying to find an interesting but educational topic for a persuasive speech. They came up with ideas such as the war, sex education, abortion, and a non-graded educational system. Bev finally finished *Babbitt* and started *The Sun Also Rises*.

She had also talked with Mom the previous night. Dave had sold one of his prints at the clothesline sale at his art school. Mom was much more relaxed now that Aunt Tress's funeral was over, and Bev was pleased about that because she knew that it had been bothering her. She enclosed an editorial from the April 17 *Daily* that had also run simultaneously in a number of other student newspapers calling for the abolition of ROTC. I especially appreciated hearing any news about the anti-war movement, because now that I had been sucked into the war machine it was more difficult to maintain a mindset of resistance.

On Sunday the 20th I finally got a chance to call Bev, the first time we had spoken by other than the written word in just over a month. That was a huge morale-booster for both of us. She wrote that evening and asked about another fellow at the adjoining phone who was talking with his wife. That was probably Tom Barrett from Ohio, a man much like me. Bev wondered how many of the guys were married because, of course, that offered no exemption from the draft. She said they had celebrated Mom and Dad's 28th anniversary by eating at Moy's Chinese Restaurant on Broadway over on the North Side, a family favorite. Dave, Jane, and John had the special; Mary had chicken Chow Mein; and Bev and my folks shared a variety dinner for three. She had not had much Chinese food before but enjoyed most of it. I remembered that one thing the kids always liked about Moy's was the little bottles of Coke, but the attraction was strictly the novelty factor, because you ended up with much less pop than with a full-size bottle. She liked being with my family because they joked around, and I believe that her presence tended to loosen them up as well. Her fortune cookie message was, "You will be called to fill a position of high honor and responsibility," and Dad said "Well, isn't that what you're after?" She liked being teased, and said she missed having me do it. That night she and Sister Paul Mary, another resident of Comstock, were going to an experimental ecumenical liturgy at Coffman. Bev liked Sister because she was always so joyful and enthusiastic about life in general and nature in particular. They also shared a love of poetry.

She wrote the next day that the liturgy had been exciting and much like the ones at the Newman Center. The priest there was like Sister in that he seemed to radiate happiness, and Bev suggested that we go to mass at Newman when I was home. That held little appeal for me at the time, but I was impressed by the role faith played in Bev's life. Her approach was a wonderful change from the "thou shalt not" mentality of traditional Catholicism that had so embittered me. She closed since her hand was "tuckered out" and her arm felt like lead because she had played tennis on Saturday for the first time in two years.

In a second letter of the 21st Bev wrote that she was going to write me one of her "happy-go-lucky, non-punctuated, stupid" typed letters, but Jennifer was using the typewriter. "Really, though, you don't know how nutty I can be." I was looking forward to finding out sometime, and also suspecting that some of Jennifer's zanily extroverted ways were contagious. After a day of strange and changeable weather, the night was clear and warm. She had stood out on the fifth floor sundeck enjoying the fresh air, the clear sky, the stars, and the moon, along with the city lights and the subdued city sounds. She had gazed to the south and thought of me, just as I often looked north with her on my mind, especially when I was on fire watch in the middle of the night. As reflected in the poignant song "I'll Be Seeing You," those emotions were at least one thing that World War II and Vietnam had in common.

She proposed a deal: we would each be certain to take good care of our colds. She enclosed an article from the *Daily* for that day that described a committee President Moos was setting up to examine the role of ROTC at the U. That issue also noted that this was the Week to Confront Campus Militarism, and that a committee that included George Crocker, another man who had been sentenced to prison for refusing induction, would follow in the footsteps of the Israelites under Joshua by encircling the Armory each day of the week, until finally it would crumble on Friday after they had marched around it seven times. In closing, she mentioned that they were going to a Glen Yarborough concert Wednesday night at the Hamline fieldhouse. She knew it would evoke mixed emotions; his music was a favorite of ours, especially "The Honey Wind."

***

As we proceeded with the second half of BCT the pace became so rapid that a rumor began to spread that we would be graduating a week earlier than our scheduled date of May 23. That date allowed for ten weeks at Fort Campbell, one for Zero Week, and nine for Basic. After a month in the Army I had already learned to disregard all rumors until we got the official word. Until then they were just fodder for bull sessions and there was always at least one guy absolutely convinced that he had the inside scoop. The two big unanswered questions were whether we would get leave after Basic and when we would get our AIT assignments. Since there was a leave between AIT and the first duty assignment, Vietnam or elsewhere, it seemed unlikely that there would also be one after BCT, but we still had not been told that for a certainty. As for AIT assignments, those orders could arrive any day.

Mary sent me a clipping from *Witness* about the Basic gas chamber and I wrote back telling the folks that we had already done that. The most dramatic event during the fifth week was grenade training on Tuesday the 22nd. The sergeant giving the demonstration said that, despite all the war movies we had seen, we were not to try to pull the pin with our teeth. As with many weapons, human ingenuity had made the fragmentation grenade even more lethal than the old "pineapple" World War II version where the outer body of the exploding grenade itself provided the shrapnel. The high explosive was improved, but the most noticeable difference was that the body of the grenade was smooth and roughly lemon-shaped. The shrapnel was from a serrated coiled spring inside the outer shell that shattered into about 1,000 pieces upon detonation, each travelling at a lethal velocity for about twenty meters. We were each to toss a grenade and there were concrete encasements to duck down into after the release. My natural impulse was to throw it baseball style, but we were required to use more of a pushing-type movement and the result was that my grenade landed a very short distance from our encasement. The sarge swore and put his arm around my shoulder to make sure we were both down and out of harm's way. The explosion seemed tremendous, especially compared to the modest size of the grenade, and drowned out any sound of the deadly bits of red-hot metal zipping by overhead. The instructors also demonstrated the various colors of smoke grenades for us, telling us that "popping smoke" was an important way of marking a location in Vietnam, especially for approaching choppers. Then there were the heat grenades that generated no audible explosion but burned at 5,000 degrees for about ten seconds. The sergeant put one on an old truck engine block to show us how it quickly fused the parts together.

Another highlight of the week was pugil stick practice and competition. These are large Q-tip-shaped sticks, and the purpose is to practice hand-to-hand rifle and bayonet combat. We had so much protective padding on that it would have been almost impossible to hurt someone, and because of that we could vent some of our frustrations by beating away on each other. Seufert put about thirteen guys on three of the men he did not like. That lowered my opinion of him because of both the unfair odds and his employment of the time-honored technique of turning trainees against each other. He had a purpose, however, because the three he picked to be beaten were among the most defiant in the platoon. They were the ones who seemed to have no self-discipline at all. They could not keep their mouths shut and followed orders only if it suited them. If they got tired during PT, they just quit doing the exercises. Sarge must have felt that a beating that would do no serious harm might pound some sense into them, or maybe he just wanted to see them humiliated. They certainly did not appear to be very intelligent and their attitudes made me wonder what they would be like in a combat situation, but, of course, none of us could know that until we were there.

Classroom presentations and physical training continued to be integral parts of our schedule as well. There was a seemingly interminable lecture on all the aspects of guard duty. Clearly this was an important topic, but how much information did they think a bunch of exhausted guys were going to retain? There was a shorter presentation on insurgency and counter-insurgency, but no explanation on why our efforts to prosecute this aspect of the war seemed to be a failure by any reasonable standard. It was not the military's place to ask questions like that. Our usual PT routine consisted of twelve basic exercises:

    High Jumper, or Jumping Jacks

    Bend and Reach

    Squat Thrust

    Rowing Exercise

    Squat Bender

    Push Ups, always the old reliable for both punishment and developing upper-body strength

    Side Bender

    Body Twist

    Knee Bender

Trunk Twister

Stationary Run

Eight-count Pull-up

We also worked in frequent sit-ups, with a partner holding our legs down. There was still the occasional alligator crawl, although by this point that was usually reserved for punishment. The most exhausting exercise was also one that had the most direct application to a combat situation: the man-carry. This was all supplemented by frequent running when moving from one training site to another.

We were still spending most of our time on the rifle range, and on the 24th and 25th we finally had our qualification firing. We fired at eighty-four targets and I hit fifty-three, which made me a Sharpshooter, the middle range between Marksman and Expert. That was actually the best I could do, but if I had thought I was getting close to Expert I would have missed a few on purpose. Once we were qualified with the rifle, the rest of our training was to consist of the quick-kill rifle technique often used in jungle warfare, a one-night bivouac, hand-to-hand combat, more bayonet training, and finally practice for the graduation ceremony.

The night of Saturday, April 26, marked another milestone in our training when we were permitted to spend as much time down at the EM Club as we desired. It was good to have a few beers, but the base was an uninspiring place to have a good time and the situation was mostly just a bunch of homesick guys listening to country music on the jukebox and trying to get drunk. Tom Barrett was there, and by now he was the man I felt closest to in the platoon. We had been up since 4:00 a.m. and after about eight Budweisers I started getting tired, so I stayed around the club a bit longer, then returned to the barracks and got to bed about 10:00 p.m. Most of the other guys were back by then too. One result of our outing was that in addition to standing out somewhat because of my skill with rifle drill, some of the younger guys were now also impressed with my drinking ability. The truth was that, as one of the older men, I had a few more years than them to build up my tolerance, but I also knew that not all of them were as drunk as they thought they were, or as they wished they were. It was apparent that many of them were amateur drinkers, which is actually a healthy thing to be.

We had Sunday off, and I took advantage of it to write letters home. This was a welcome respite from the more frequent routine of reading and writing letters in the latrine after lights out. Since the lights remained on all night in there, many of us made it our unofficial correspondence room. Only in the Army would men have to communicate with the people they cared about the most while sitting in a latrine. I told Bev that some of the guys were from Kentucky and Tennessee, and their families, wives, and girlfriends sometimes lived close enough to come visit them on Sunday, another privilege of the latter half of Basic. I envied them, and yet wondered if such a short visit would almost be worse than none at all. It seemed too much like a prison visitation. I was also curious if some of them managed to make it conjugal, but I never did get a straight answer on that one. I told Bev that my cold was slowly improving with fewer coughing spells, and that I hoped the same would soon be true of hers. I kidded her about the Formula 44 and told her I was surprised she was drinking Tang because I thought that was a mortal sin for someone from Florida. Perhaps it was allowed now that she was in Minnesota?

I took a break from writing and wandered over to the company day room. The base was homely but it was still nice to be able to stroll around while off duty. It was just a small taste of freedom. There was always a long wait to play pool so I did not bother with that. I had already read most of the old beat-up magazines so I listened to the radio and had an orange pop. There was also a TV room, but the Sunday morning shows seemed dull.

When I resumed writing I told Bev that one thing I missed besides her was watching some of my favorite shows like *Laugh-In* and *The Tonight Show*. I also told her that Basic had been much easier than I had anticipated. I had seen war movies depicting some really brutal training so that was a pleasant surprise, and what I really appreciated was the relatively low level of harassment. I attributed this mainly to the fact that, because of the unending need for troops in the war zone, those in charge were under so much pressure to move us through and on to our next assignments that they really did not have much time to waste bothering us.

Another rumor we had heard was that Delta Company had been real hell during the previous cycle, and after seeing Harris in action I could believe that one. That could have contributed to their high sick-call and hospitalization rate. The rumor mill went on to explain that Major Bear, the commanding officer of the 4th Battalion, had failed to live up to his name by telling Harris to hold it down this time. Last cycle the men of Delta did not even get post privileges until the seventh week, whereas we received this perk at the end of the fourth. We had also seen some pretty heavy-handed techniques over at Echo Company across the field from us and heard rumors of more, so you might say it could have been worse.

By this time we were at least somewhat familiar with all the drill sergeants in the company. They each had command of a platoon in the same way that a lieutenant would in an actual functioning unit, as opposed to a training unit. Sergeant Page, in charge of the Second Platoon, had a trace of the South in his voice but he really came off as the blond, blue-eyed all-American boy. He was slim with an extremely erect bearing, and was enthusiastic about the Army and America without being a fanatic about it. I considered him a good DI. Sergeant Harkins, Third Platoon, was on his first assignment out of DI school. He had gray hair and a boyish face, and wore Levis and jerseys when off duty. He really looked more like a college type than a DI and did not have a very forceful personality, but I figured he was intelligent and would improve with time. Sergeant Thomason, Fourth Platoon, was clearly the worst of the cadre. He was heavyset and sullen and drank too much. I had seen him drunk on charge-of-quarters duty more than once. His approach to managing his troops was to yell, scream, bluster, and basically just make a fool of himself.

Sergeant Seufert, in my eyes, was the best of the bunch. He had come from Germany about ten years before in his late teens, but by now had no discernable accent. He had black wavy hair and a movie-star handsome face. Sometimes he talked about how pretty or beautiful he was, and the other DIs liked to give him grief by leading a cadence call:

> Sergeant Seufert don't be blue.
> Frankenstein was ugly too.

He was married with three kids and had been stationed in Germany, the US, and Vietnam, where he received the head wound that nearly killed him. He was going back to the RVN in October. He had wanted to go sooner but the Army was so short on DIs that they would not let him. With all the NCOs coming back from the war zone, it seemed strange that DIs were in short supply, but I had no reason to doubt him. Maybe it was not considered a very choice assignment. He was something of a troublemaker, having been busted at least once and receiving three Article 15s, the UCMJ equivalent of a misdemeanor. I admired his candor for sharing this with us, and it was almost as though he considered it a badge of honor. He was planning on getting out in about two years, so it was clear he appreciated the fact that there was more to life than the Army. But the best thing about him was that he was approachable and understanding. I always felt that in another time and place we might have been friends. It was good fortune to end up in the First Platoon with him as our drill sergeant.

★★★

Other than mail from home, reading news about the outside world was the best way for me of breaking through the feelings of physical and cultural isolation that the Army often seemed to be encouraging as a way to help mold us into soldiers who would be unhampered in carrying out our mission by thoughts of our former incarnation as typical young civilians. My favorite sources for this information were issues of *Time* and *Newsweek* from the PX, and the stories I followed most closely, other than those of the war, were those of the resistance. One item of note from Vietnam was that our troop strength reached 543,000 that month, which would turn out to be the high-water mark. On April 9 several hundred students, many SDS members, took over University Hall at Harvard. The administration took a hard-nosed approach, calling in police who used gas and billy clubs to oust the protestors, a decision that sparked at least as much outrage in the campus community as the occupation itself.

Then on April 20 the People's Park episode began out in Berkeley when a group of students and street people took matters into their own hands by converting a plot of vacant land owned by the university into a pleasant place to have fun and relax. Governor Reagan, eager to burnish his future political fortunes by meeting all unauthorized progressive activities with overwhelming force, took a "law and order" approach to this display of initiative by sending in a small army of police, highway patrol, and construction workers to bulldoze the new sod, flowers, trees, and benches and erect a tall fence around the site. In the highly charged atmosphere of that campus, it was not long before nearly 2,000 students arrived to support the evicted amateur gardeners and a pitched battle with the police was soon underway as the officers used tear gas and shotguns in response to rocks thrown by the protestors. Reagan then upped the ante by sending in 2,700 National Guard troops and, yet again, the campus and city were in a virtual state of occupation for the next two weeks. On May 15, "Bloody Thursday," well over one hundred people were hospitalized with injuries from the clashes, at least twenty of them police officers. In one dramatic incident eerily similar to action in Vietnam, helicopters sprayed protestors with clouds of tear gas on Sproul Plaza in the heart of the campus.

By the time things had cooled down to an uneasy hiatus, the opposing sides in the war on the home front were even further apart and more entrenched in their positions than ever, and the little park had become a symbol for both of them. For progressives it represented the unreasoning brutality of an American establishment that would react to any activities not specifically sanctioned by law, even converting a vacant lot into a place of beauty and peace, with violence and gunfire. The absurd and militaristic overreaction had indeed been murderous since one man was killed and another blinded. But to conservatives, the governor's actions represented a long-overdue check on unruly and un-American young people with no respect for the values that built the nation that had provided them with so many freedoms and material benefits.

The conservatives had a new champion in Reagan. He may have been a mediocre movie actor but now he found himself cast in the role of a lifetime and he was certainly more than up to the task of assuming a persona that seemed to conjure up all the old-fashioned values that traditionalists longing for the good old days held dear. Of course, those were also days that were not so good for anyone who was not a white Protestant male, but in the warm nostalgic glow of the America evoked by Reagan's faux-folksy manner and speeches heavily laden with racist code words such problems had no place. The left was attempting to create a nebulous society of their dreams where all weapons and displays of force would be supplanted by peace and cooperation, while the right was trying to force a return to a society with clear-cut rules and unquestioned values that had been a nightmare for so many of its citizens. The culture wars were becoming more violent by the day and it appeared that any possibility of reconciling the opposing sides was every bit as elusive as peace in Vietnam.

***

Bev wrote her promised typed letter on Wednesday, April 23, but said it was not as crazy as she had hoped because she had just received the Round Robin from her friends and, with the exception of her and one other member of the group, they were all rather depressed and befuddled. With all the chaos surrounding us at home and overseas, it was easy to see why they felt that way, but she fell back on our shared belief that one should enjoy life as much as possible and not waste time worrying about things you could not change. She mentioned that Robert Frost said that all the time. The Minnesota weather was still "beautemous" and she was heavily into reading, as usual. She was finding *The Portrait of A Lady* fascinating, especially Isabel, who reminded her of herself in terms of her interests and fear of her emotions. Bev said she had always been the student among the three sisters and when AnnaBelle had told her that her new glasses made her look like a real scholar she was pleased with that. I think she was feeling that her academic achievements may have come at the expense of social and emotional development. I was glad she felt free to express these feelings, but to me, even though I was certainly impressed with her intelligence and scholarly accomplishments, she was also a well-rounded and emotionally mature woman. Our young ages, combined with the unexpected emotional intensity of our love for each other in the midst of such radically disruptive events, sometimes led us to the brink of self-doubt, but we always pulled each other back from sinking into total despair even though periods of depression were unavoidable. Maintaining this balance while we were apart was difficult, but motivation is always the key and love is perhaps the most powerful of all.

She went on to talk more about the novels they were reading for Marty's class as well as how erudite some of his insights were. He took extra time to discuss Hemingway, Faulkner, and Dos Passos, because he felt their portrayal of reality was important for our own times. He pointed out what he saw as an astounding similarity in the art of Hemingway and Eliot, which is something I had never considered because of the dramatic difference in their personalities and ways of life. He also discussed the importance of the worldview of the neurotic in understanding modern fiction, and indeed could any even moderately sensitive person escape at least a touch of neurosis in the twentieth century? I wished I had been there to hear the tightly wound Roth, no stranger to anxiety himself, rattling off these insights. She was also looking forward to Mailer's *Why Are We in Vietnam?* and perhaps *The Quiet American* as well. I guess she had never finished it the previous fall.

In other news, the river was almost back to normal and her cold was better. She asked what MOS meant, and mentioned that her friend Scrib had also used the term in a letter she received that day. He had been a close friend at Maryville and had enlisted in the Army Security Agency for four years. Now he was at a school in Arlington studying Thai and Asian history. I was gratified to hear that the Army was training scholars in an effort to actually understand a part of the world we were so intent on changing by brute force, but I also feared it was years too late. She enclosed a copy of the songs from the "para-liturgical" service at Coffman, which included songs of peace and friendship, as well as some beautiful love poetry. I wished I had been there with her and Sister, because it seemed like the diametrical opposite of our environment at Fort Campbell. She also included a newsletter from Comstock that was half jokes and thoughts from Joyce, but also included the admonition that, even though spring fever was rampant, shouting out of the dorm windows was a Judicial Board offense. Also: "The ice machine is now closed to residents due to the abuse of the privilege, like taking all the ice so there is none left for kitchen and dining room use." If it was a men's dorm I would suspect they were sneaking in kegs, but why would young women need so much ice? Here was yet another mystery to ponder.

Bev wrote again on Thursday the 24th during the quiet evening hours while listening to Glenn Yarborough singing Roc McKuen songs. She described the music as "melancholy," and I had to agree with that, but she liked it when she was missing me. Joe Kwiat's class was going well, and the following week they were scheduled to finish Whitman and move on to Twain. She said that she loved all the reading and was trying to get ahead of the game so that we could have more time together, but that made me worry that she was counting too much on me coming home on leave after Basic. I would have loved that but did not think it likely. She had another good lunch with Mark Davis and John Mitchell where they talked about the financial struggles of small colleges like Maryville, and exchanged opinions about the most effective degree of familiarity for instructors to establish with their classes. Mark felt it was best for a teacher not to stay at one college for too long to avoid becoming too attached. She was still contemplating the character of Isabel Archer as well as wondering what my next assignment would be.

Bev wrote on the 26th saying that she and Joyce Rolla, "the other Joyce," had played tennis that morning. She had used my ticket the previous evening to see *Camino Real* at the U Theatre, and from her description it was much more surreal than any of the Williams plays I had read. She wished we had been together to see and discuss it and, needless to say, so did I. She enclosed the program, which also noted that the U Theatre would be presenting *The Birds* and *The School for Scandal* on the Showboat beginning May 24. She thought she would get us tickets once I found out for sure that I would be home after Basic and, again, said how excited she was about the possibility that we would see each other in about a month. I just hoped it would not be too huge of a letdown if that did not happen. She also included a brief excerpt from *Daybreak*, the autobiography of Joan Baez, a great artist and also a great voice of the peace movement. Bev was still fascinated by Isabel, especially now that she had changed after her marriage to Gilbert. Her enthusiasm for the book made me think I should give it another try because I had found it pretty tough to get through.

She continued the next day after we had talked on the phone the previous evening. We always treasured these conversations because they were rare, and I could tell how happy it made her because of how much she talked. The reserved scholar was off duty that night. I felt the same way and did not want to spoil the mood by reminding Bev that I might very well not get a leave after Fort Campbell. I decided just to wait until we received the orders for our next assignments. She mentioned again her fascination with the research advances being made on DNA, and then closed because she needed to continue with James's meticulous and erudite exploration of the evolving character of the lady Isabel.

On Monday the 28th Bev wrote that she been in a crazy, hysterical mood and felt like crying because she missed me so much, and was also torn about whether to pay a brief visit to her friend Wanda in Indianapolis. She felt a little better now because she had made the decision to go, leaving on the bus on Wednesday and returning late Saturday night so that she would not miss our Sunday phone conversation. She thought the change of scene and seeing her close friend from Maryville days might help pull her out of a rut. She had finished with the James novel, "an amazing work of art," and was speculating on what might have happened to the characters in the future. Now she was already about halfway through *The 42nd Parallel*, which must have seemed like a breeze after James.

Then she went on describe a variety of her thoughts and activities, which I always found so enjoyable because it was the kind of random sharing we would do when together. It snowed the previous night and Duluth received nine inches, although nothing really stuck in Minneapolis. It amazed her, even though I had warned her that often happened in Minnesota, because it was such a different spring from those in eastern Tennessee. She said that DeGaulle had resigned and wondered what the effect on Europe and the rest of the world would be. After I called on Saturday, they went to see *The Lion in Winter* and Bev was impressed with the performance of both lead players but especially Katharine Hepburn. She had called home last night and had a wonderful conversation with her parents. Her mother was coming to a PEO, a women's philanthropic organization, convention in Des Moines in September and would then come up to Minneapolis to visit Bev. She was excited about showing her Mom where she lived and studied as well as introducing her to my family.

She reflected again on how much closer her relationship with her father had grown and how understanding he was when she described her perplexity over issues such as Vietnam and civil rights. From things Bev had said I knew her dad was quite conservative, so it was really good to hear that love and understanding could be more powerful than the generation gap. That had always been the case with my folks and me as well. She said they asked about me whenever she called, and I was looking forward to the day when I could meet them and see Bev's childhood home. AnnaBelle and Jack's baby was due any day and Bev sent them a book of pictures and short quotes called *The Mother*. She hoped I would get to meet them someday as well. She knew that it was uncertain whether there would be leaves after Basic, but said her hopes were "built up sky high," and she closed with a beautiful passage from *The Prophet* on love.

***

As Monday April 28 began another week of training, some things were looking up as the end of Basic was now less than a month away. The spring rains had abated so we were spending much less time in damp fatigues. Perhaps as a result, my cough and cold were on the wane. I had KP that day, which was usually a disagreeable experience at the training center because they bothered you all the time and made the job much harder than it really needed to be. It was bad enough taking guff from our instructors, but it rankled even more being ordered around by the often-overweight mess sergeants. The compensation, of course, was being excused from a day of training that usually included some PT. Tuesday was also free of training since it was Delta's day for detail. Five other guys and I got sent out to Range 26A to camouflage some targets and do a few other routine jobs. We spent about half the day just sitting around, which, other than being off duty, is always a trainee's favorite activity.

It was also good to have the rifle qualification process behind us, although now our weapons training switched over to the Quick Kill method on Wednesday the 30th. The military has never been known for its ability to change its ways very rapidly, but this was an adaptation of small arms training based on the realities of jungle warfare focusing on "close-in, fleeting targets at ranges of 50 meters or less." It seemed like a rifle variation on the countless quick-draw confrontations we had seen in Westerns as kids. For safety's sake we started with BB guns and this really did bear an uncanny resemblance to the way we usually played with these little rifles when we were growing up. In our group we had never shot at each other, but it was always more fun to try hitting your target, usually a cardboard box in those boyhood days, by shooting from the hip instead of taking careful aim in the traditional way with the stock against your shoulder, and that is exactly what the Army was training us to do.

We would walk slowly through a course with heavy brush and periodically a VC target would pop up briefly somewhere near us. The goal was to hit as many as possible with a BB before they again disappeared, and the hope was that this hand-eye coordination would become instinctive and carry over into using an M16 in this way in Vietnam. The next step was to repeat the process with our M14s and live ammo. One of the frequent admonitions out on the rifle range was "don't blow your buddy away," and that type of accident seemed like a distinct possibility on the quick-kill course, especially with some of the crazy trigger-happy characters in our platoon. The day's training program concluded with a section on night firing, first with BB guns and then with our service weapons. We finally got to bed about 11:00 p.m. for about five hours of sleep.

On Thursday we went out to Range 26A again, this time for a more realistic exercise in Quick Kill in a jungle warfare setting. This was the dangerous close combat course and the cadre hated it because of the very real risk of stray shots from green recruits like us. Instead of always firing straight downrange as on the standard range, on this one we advanced from point to point—shooting live rounds at random pop-up targets. The fast response time required increased the probability of poorly aimed rounds and the long lethal range of the M14 only added to the potential for trouble. The instructors' stations were well removed from the targets but, even so, one guy inadvertently pointed his rifle at the captain. The exercise ended with no more serious casualties than a bunch of perforated targets, the ones we had prepared during our company detail duties two days before. The last exercise of the day was putting the alligator crawl to good use by crawling under some barbed wire.

We had some hand-to-hand training as well, usually practicing on the same mounted dummies we beat and stabbed during bayonet drill. There is no such thing as fair play in combat, and the first thing we learned was the side kick to the groin. We continued with our bayonet training as well, and one day a lieutenant from another unit who happened to be passing by complained that our shout of "Yup" when we attacked the dummies was wrong. He wanted us to scream "Yaa" instead. Our DIs ignored him, reflecting their usual lack of regard for junior officers. All of our training sessions continued to be interspersed with frequent PT drills because we had to pass that test, as well as the comprehensive final exam known as the G3 test. Failing either one meant the likelihood of being recycled, which was being assigned to another Basic unit to repeat part of the instruction. Since that largely unpleasant prospect did have the one undeniable attraction of delaying being shipped to Vietnam, one purpose of what harassment we did have to endure was to reduce a recruit's desire to spend extra time in training. The other side of the coin was at least some praise for a job well done, and Seufert always preferred positive reinforcement.

On Saturday, May 3, we had battalion field day, a competition held on a big grassy field surrounded by bleachers that gave us the opportunity to show off some of the skills we had been learning. Since other trainees were required to attend, the stands held over one thousand people. The whole day reminded me of our old ROTC spring all-service reviews. Nearly everyone was in the platoon marching event and I was among the five out of about two hundred chosen for the Delta rifle drill team, thanks to being nominated by Seufert. The old ROTC training, refreshed by Basic, paid off and I did well while serving in the key role of stack man for Stack Arms, the most difficult movement to perform with anything like military precision. I made a minor gaffe with the operating rod handle during Inspection Arms and one guy's rifle slipped off his shoulder, but we put in a very respectable performance and finished second.

Our company tied for first in the marching event, but one of our guys had touched his helmet so we were rated second. Delta Company put in a rather poor overall showing, however, and we ended up coming in fourth out of the five units. Captain Harris was saved from his usual apoplectic fit over this dismal ranking when we regained the honor company banner for our high rifle qualification scores. We had lost it because of our low PT scores, so at least the old guys turned out to be pretty good shots. We also received two plaques, which the Army passes out like bowling trophies at events like this.

I had been the only guy from the First Platoon on the drill team and some of the guys, impressed with our performance, started to regard me as an experienced soldier. I was pleased to have helped make Sergeant Seufert look good, but mostly I just found it absurd that the Army attached such importance to these useless skills. During the previous cycle Sarge's platoon had finished first of the twenty in the battalion and, despite our performance that day, he felt we had a chance of duplicating that record. He was a good DI who did not hide behind his rank and his results proved that his methods were sound. He had also mentioned more than once that he had a fondness for Jack Daniels, so we planned to each chip in a dollar and buy him a case at the end of our cycle.

When we got back from the field day we still had an hour until chow, so Sergeant Quick took us to the picnic grounds to review for our G3 test. Quick was Delta's senior DI, and he came the closest of the men in the cadre to the stereotype of the movie drill sergeant. He was short and wiry with a gravel voice and a plug-ugly face. He liked to drink and it was obvious he had been hitting the bottle while we were going through the competitions out on the drill field. Like so many soldiers and vets, when he drank he liked to tell war stories, so he started telling us all kinds of horror stories about Vietnam and how most of us would be going infantry. I never cared much for him, but he had been there and knew what he was talking about. He made his keynote statement twice: "When you're over there, you're not fighting for freedom and all this bullshit. You're fighting for your buddies who have been killed and to stay alive." I looked around at the faces of the younger guys, little older than boys really, with their eyes glued on him and their mouths half open, and felt almost overwhelmed by a wave of fear and anger. We were cattle on the assembly line of the war machine and nobody, from the commander-in-chief on down, seemed to have the will or perhaps even the ability to stop it. These boys did not deserve to have this happening to them. But I knew Quick was telling the truth and not just trying to scare or impress us. Another truth was that if I was assigned to the infantry there was nothing I could do about it.

This brutal confrontation with the harsh reality of the jeopardy we were in left me in such a foul mood that I only ate about half of my supper. I received an overnight pass, probably for being on the drill team, but I had no desire to go into an unfamiliar southern town, so I went down to the EM Club and drank a six pack instead. That mellowed me out, and then I watched Lawrence Welk on TV because I knew that Mom and Granny would be watching it at home. I returned to the barracks and got a good night's sleep. The next morning I found out some of the guys had a beer party in the latrine while I was sound asleep. I was glad I had not known about it, because I would have drunk more with them, and after what I had at the club I did not need that. I walked down to the base shopping center after breakfast, but most of the stores were closed. The big snack bar was open though so I had a couple of éclairs, a big glass of pink lemonade, a cheeseburger, and a strawberry sundae, my first good ice cream since enjoying some back home with Bev at Bridgeman's. I returned to the barracks and wrote to Bev, thanking her for writing so much. "It means more to me now than you can know. Life has much evil in it, but I see more than my share here and you remind me of all the good. I can't say how much I need and want you."

***

Bev sent me some touching little gifts, including three pressed Tennessee violets from the flowers the visitor from Maryville had brought. A little book entitled *Springs of Humor* was a selection of bon mots and observations on human frailty and the need to maintain a healthy sense of humor in the face of life's many absurdities. I found one by Alexander Sacher-Masoch particularly intriguing: "Alcohol is a bridge but not a way." She sent a copy of Viktor Frankl's *Man's Search for Meaning*, a book that had influenced her view of the world, which I began as soon as I had the chance. I was particularly grateful for the loyalty and faithfulness of my betrothed, because a psychiatrist named Dr. Emanuel Taney had recently reported that the Vietnam War had resulted in more "Dear John" letters from wives and fiancés than any previous conflict due to the lack of popular support for the US war effort. He described the effect on the troops receiving such letters as "destructive," an understatement to say the least.

She started a letter on Wednesday the 30th while in the Greyhound Bus terminal in Minneapolis. She had a Dos Passos book and *Native American Humor* with her to keep abreast of her reading and pass the time. She was thinking that it would be good to be away from people she knew on the bus ride and to have some time to think. As fond as she was of Jennifer, she did miss having her own room and the chance to be alone with her thoughts. She asked if I knew what she meant, and I certainly did. On the bus she met a talkative lady with about six grandchildren, but eventually excused herself to take a nap because she did not want to listen to her all the way to Chicago. She finished *The 42nd Parallel*, finding it very relevant to contemporary America because of the perceived need for societal changes among the oppressed and the interaction of the people of Chicago with the police. She enjoyed the verdant spring landscape of southern Wisconsin, and the rolling hills reminded her somewhat of the foothills of the Smokies around Maryville. She hoped to show me that part of the country someday. She knew I loved San Francisco, so she asked me about that city. Kay and Mark might be spending part of the summer in Santa Barbara because Mark had been asked to teach a summer school course there. She mentioned how much she loved to travel, and closed as the bus was approaching Chicago.

On May 1 Bev wrote about how beautiful the spring weather and flowers were in Indianapolis. She and Wanda were enjoying talking together in person again so much that they had stayed up the previous night until 4:00 a.m. She had met a few more interesting people at the terminal in Chicago who were lonely and wanting to talk. The bus went through the city during rush hour and the traffic was terrible. Wanda showed her around the neighborhood on the south side of Indianapolis where she lived and worked. When they arrived at the church there were newly broken windows, which seemed to symbolize the frustration and discouragement Wanda felt because of the lack of any visible change due to her efforts in the run-down district. That night Wanda went to a concert at the university while Bev and a friend babysat the minister's two children in exchange for supper.

She and Wanda had been talking about faith and values, and Bev asked me to help her understand Catholicism. She said that faith and hope were an important part of her life, and she found these things reinforced most strongly by the people she knew. She mentioned again how meaningful she found the services at Pastor Hawkinson's church because he was a man of faith who was also actively involved in the world, and I shared this admiration for Vince because of his work in the peace movement, although I had never attended services at Grace University Lutheran. She was listening to some Rod McKuen again, and closed by hoping we could go on a picnic together when I got home on leave.

The next day Bev, Wanda, and a girl from Texas named LuAnn drove down to Brown County State Park near Nashville, Indiana, and she found the spring there almost as beautiful as East Tennessee. There was pink and white dogwood, redbud, violets, jonquils, wild periwinkles, and many other spring flowers. Bev and her freinds enjoyed riding six miles on horseback through the woods, although Bev was a bit sore because that was only the fourth time she had ridden.

Back in Minneapolis, she wrote on Sunday the 4th that her cold was "OK" but that she was going to the Health Service to see about her cough. She found that the brief break from her studies had helped, and now she was "raring to get work done." I loved that expression. She was going to start *Absalom, Absalom!* that afternoon, and hoped to do two papers during the next two weeks. She enclosed her letter in a Fran Mar "Moppets" card about couples separated by the service. I also wrote to her on the 4th explaining that we had our bivouac and Individual Tactical Training (ITT) coming up that week, followed by more review for the G3 the next weekend. That meant that time for writing would be scarcer than ever, but I did plan to call her later that day. I said I liked all of her ideas for things to do together, and also suggested Como Park. I wanted to show her all my favorite places in my hometown, just as she wanted to do the same for me in Miami and Coral Gables. I mentioned that it was unlikely we would get leave after Basic.

My romance with the California of my mind had now shifted north from LA to San Francisco, so I told her about the things I had enjoyed there on our family trip out West in 1963, such as Fisherman's Wharf, the Coit Tower, the cable cars, Chinatown, the Cliff House, and the colorful row houses on the steep hills. I also told her about how Mom and Dad had been stationed near there in Santa Rosa during the war. I wrote that, like her, I dreamed of the two of us traveling together, and doing everything else together as well. She had asked about religious services, so I told her I had not attended since Palm Sunday. But I also reassured her that I was pleased she found fulfillment in it and that I would become more serious about religion again if and when I felt the need. I sent her a Polaroid photo of me in my khakis that a black guy named Johnny Ivory had taken for fifty cents. The intersection of 50th and Kentucky was in the background, with our barracks just out of the picture to the right. I also sent my folks one taken the previous day at the field day of me in my fatigues, so I said maybe they could show them to each other.

On Monday the 5th we had classes on bivouac and night-fighting, including camouflage techniques. This class covered a variety of environments, even loam and white for a snowy environment. I imagine most of us hoped we would be sent to a location such as Germany where that would be appropriate. The bivouac portion was useful since we would set out on that the next day, although some of the tips, such as never pitching your tent in a dry stream bed, seemed almost comically obvious. The ability to keep a low profile in a combat zone is clearly a valuable skill, so we had yet another crawling exercise. This time it was under barbed wire strung very close to the ground, and the technique was to crawl on your back while keeping your rifle diagonally across your chest between you and the wire. If you did get snagged at least you were in a position to see the wire and get disentangled. The drawback was that it was difficult to avoid getting your pants caught on the barbs when you flexed your legs in preparation for pushing yourself forward. That was yet another skill we hoped we would never actually have to employ while the enemy was firing at us. I had some initial resistance to calling the VC "the enemy," but after hearing the term so many times in training it started to seem natural. You really cannot train for combat without having a term for the guys on the other side. Besides, it was more concise than "the guy who is trying to kill you before you do the same to him." The sentence in our BCT Handbook that provided the best description of our purpose was: "When facing the enemy, your job is to stay alive to fight and the best way to stay alive is to know how to effectively hit and stop the enemy." Quick could have written that, but it was hard to disagree with it.

The next day we set out on the Basic rite of passage known as bivouac, and the first step was to walk thirteen miles carrying about sixty pounds on our backs, well over one-third of my weight. We had prepared this equipment on Monday evening: a shelter-half, sleeping bag and cover, air mattress, field pack, poncho, C-Rations, shaving gear, pistol belt, entrenching tool, ammo pack, bayonet, canteen and cover, first aid pouch, M14 rifle, gas mask, and a few smaller items. We got buzzed by helicopters along the way, an unrealistic exercise since that was one thing the communists did not have, but they skipped the usual routine of dropping flour on us. We stopped in a grove to eat our lunch of C-Rations where we got hit with a gas attack, so we had to just sit there until the all-clear message allowed us to remove our masks. It was intriguing to sample C-Rations for the first time and I felt they were certainly adequate but not something I would choose if any more palatable alternatives were available. After that we abandoned the trail and made our way through thick woods. By that time of day it was hot and humid, a good simulation of what we had been told things were like in Vietnam. It seemed as though our regimen of physical conditioning had paid off, because we began staggering into the bivouac site about 2:00 p.m. and the entire unit made it eventually.

Tom Barrett and I tented together and, after a semi-comical period of trial and error, finally managed to transform our two shelter-halves into a decent two-man pup-tent. Just as we were beginning to feel somewhat secure in the knowledge that we were properly set up for a night in the woods, Sergeant Quick appeared about 6:00 p.m. bellowing that everyone was to pack up again because we were moving to another site. This was a part they had not mentioned in our class the previous day, and it turned out that we were going through an infiltration course. It was an extremely dark night until suddenly a flare burst, followed by a volley of machine-gun fire. The eerie and dimly lit scene inspired feelings of suspense and excitement rather than real danger because it was obvious they would be shooting blanks or aiming well above our heads. The exercise was relatively brief, probably because the cadre was out with us and eager to get settled in for the night.

When we finally reached our site you could not even see your hand in front of your face so we could not tell if it was the same place where we had briefly encamped earlier. The orders were the same as for a combat zone: no illumination of any kind. Tom and I went back and forth between laughter and frustration as we attempted to reassemble our little shelter in the inky blackness, and it was fortunate that we got along so well. Tom slept well, but I spent a restless night in the claustrophobic surroundings while the woodland quiet was interrupted at frequent intervals by yelling and shooting. First I was too hot in my sleeping bag because of the exertion of making our way to the site and getting set up again, but when I got out of the bag I was soon too cold. I think I finally settled into a deep sleep right before it was time to get up.

When we emerged from our tents at the crack of dawn on Wednesday our camp was anything but a model of military precision with tents leaning at crazy angles all over the place. Ours was so askew that when we saw it in broad daylight all we could do was laugh. The main exercise for that day was the land navigation course, and Tom and I were partners. Using our heavy-duty Army compass we followed the directions from point to point and ended up at the right spot. After that we had another march, but this time carrying only a portion of our equipment. We were ambushed again, but it seemed mild after the infiltration course. Tom and I had guard duty that night, but the man who woke up Tom did not make sure he got up and Tom promptly dozed off again. After my lack of sleep the previous night, I was exhausted and oblivious to all of this, so we both got a good night's sleep while inadvertently committing the cardinal military sin of sleeping on guard duty. No one was the wiser and the next morning we both enjoyed the feeling of having gotten away with something, albeit unintentionally.

For some reason, even though it was not Sunday, a chaplain appeared and led us in a nondenominational "Service of Worship for the Field." This included two prayers for peace, including that of St. Francis. The chaplain was obviously fairly progressive, or maybe just wished to appear "relevant," because next we sang Bob Dylan's "Blowin' in the Wind"—about the last thing I ever expected to hear as part of an Army service. The "unison scripture lesson" was the passage from *Ecclesiastes* about a season for everything that had inspired Pete Seeger's "Turn, Turn, Turn," a song released in a popular version by the Byrds several years before. Ironically, The Preacher's stoic view of life in this least-biblical book of the Bible was close to my own at that point, although that philosophy is not the primary theme of the chosen passage. I suspected the chaplain had chosen it because of the connection to popular music, as well as the fact that stating there was a proper time for everything was a suitably innocuous theme for a nondenominational service. This was followed by a prayer that included the following petitions:

> Lord God Almighty, hear our prayer during a time of great confusion and turmoil among men and nations of the world. May our presence wherever we go, be a source of pride to ourselves and our nation. May we bring not only physical benefits to people, but also by our compassion, patience, and understanding, be examples of the presence of God among men.

What was an Army chaplain to do during the nightmare known as Vietnam? It had to be pretty tough work and I always had a grudging admiration for the few that I encountered as long as they did not attempt to invoke religion to try to justify what we were doing in the war. This prayer did not go quite that far but, given the reality of what we were doing to the

Vietnamese, it was still more bullshit than anything else. I preferred Quick's frankness to this kind of stuff, because the things we were being taught were not designed to bring physical benefits to anyone unless their fondest desire was to be six feet under. Next we sang "Kum Ba-Yah," making our situation in the woodland clearing seem like a bizarre parody of summer camp. The concluding prayer offered thanks to God for a number of things, including the fact "that you are not ashamed to be called our God." All things considered, I had little confidence in that statement, but I saved the program and enclosed it in my next letter to Bev.

Tom and I got to know each other better on bivouac. His wife was expecting and he missed her so much that she was about all he ever talked about, and I told him about Bev and me. We felt a strong bond between us because of each knowing how the other felt about being separated from the woman he loved. We were both concerned about being assigned to the infantry so we talked about that as well. Tom had selected chaplain's assistant for his preferred MOS. Most of all, we enjoyed discussing our plans for after the Army. He was a good companion because of our common values and concerns, whereas the interests of many of our comrades seemed limited to cars and girls. "The powers that be" knew that news from home was good for morale, so we even had mail-call out in the field. I received two letters from Bev, always the most faithful of correspondents, and read then while sitting outside our tent. Something about that reminded me of a war movie, except there was no soft music in the background with a voice-over of the soldier's girl speaking the words of the letter. After we had our gear packed, the buses came out and took us back to our barracks.

On Thursday and Friday we got back into the familiar training routine, finishing up with hand-to-hand and bayonet, and reviewing our drill and ceremony. I was among the one-third of our platoon chosen to train with the M16 so we spent most of Saturday at a class on that. We were told that had nothing to do with our next assignment but that the Army was switching to this rifle for its standard combat weapon and wanted as many people trained on it as possible. During the next cycle all the trainees would be using the M16. We knew it was a deadly weapon but at first it seemed almost like a plaything compared to our M14s, reminding me of the toy guns we had played with as boys. It weighed about three pounds less than the M14 and had a number of plastic and polymer parts as well as a smaller round. The instructors told us it was an impressive automatic weapon capable of firing twenty rounds in 1.25 seconds. We had all heard the stories about jamming problems, but we were assured that those had been mostly solved. What else were they going to tell us? We were scheduled to use them on the range on Wednesday the 14th and the instructors said it was easier to qualify than with the M14 because there was much less recoil. Two other interesting facts they mentioned were that soldiers from Minnesota and Tennessee were known to be the most skilled riflemen and that Minnesota had the lowest draft rejection rate in the country.

Another thing the Army did to help boost morale was to provide a florist—Magnolia Flower and Gift Shop in Oak Grove, Kentucky—in our retail area so that we could wire flowers to mothers, wives, and sweethearts, so I sent Mom an arrangement for Mother's Day and one to Bev as well. Bev's mother sent me a postcard, which I thought was a very nice thing to do since we had not even met yet. I wrote Bev that I had starting reading the Frankl book and agreed with his description of the existential vacuum confronting people in our century. The point of the book was how he came to terms with that problem and ultimately rose above it while confined to a concentration camp during World War II, but I had not gotten to that yet.

I suggested to Bev that if she was interested in this philosophy she might want to look at some of the books on the shelves in my old room by Sartre and especially Camus. Existentialism was a popular fad among young people and its appeal to self-absorbed boomers was obvious, but this fascination with the philosophical worldview of disillusioned postwar French intellectuals also reflected our search for new values in a world where it appeared that those of our parents' generation had failed. What could be more appealing to young people in that situation than the proposition that existence precedes essence? We begin life with a clean slate and create ourselves by the choices we make and our responses to life's circumstances. I answered her question about Catholicism by saying I felt there was much beauty in all those centuries of tradition but that organized religion of any kind was not for me right then, even though I had a strong admiration for those who demonstrated their faith by caring for those in need. We were in total agreement on that.

Most of our weekend was scheduled for more preparation for our tests the following week, but we were given post privileges for three hours on Friday evening and most of the guys dedicated that time to heavy drinking. The need to cram as much alcohol consumption as possible into such a relatively short period of time produced unfortunate results. There was an 8:30 p.m. formation to make sure we were all back and it was notable for the number of guys swaying and puking. A few in the back row even turned around to pee. It was dark and all the DIs cared about was that we were there. Drunkenness was expected, if not encouraged. Actually drinking was considered good for morale, but the club was such an uninspiring place that I had only had two beers. We were given post privileges again for two hours on the evening of Saturday the 10th. I went back to the club for a couple beers and then walked over to the PX (post exchange) for some candy. I got on the scale while I was there and found that I now weighed 161 pounds with my shoes on and a bag of Boston Baked Beans in my hand. That meant I had gained twenty pounds since I had left home, and most of it was in the legs and shoulders. Even though that was the heaviest I had ever been, I felt that a little more would not hurt as long as it was muscle.

I talked with Tom Brothen, the psychology major from the U, and he said that the last time he called his fiancé she was peeved because all he seemed to talk and write about was the Army. I had seen that in myself as well. It was difficult to avoid having your perspective become incredibly myopic in the training environment. As much as I loved music, all I had been hearing was some morose country stuff on the jukebox at the EM Club. World events took a backseat to the question of whether or not we had PT that day. It was almost impossible to believe I had been there less than two months. I did not feel I had been brainwashed but, even so, I imagined our situation to be much like being in prison and I hoped that after Basic I would be able to regain a healthier perspective on all the important events going on outside of our tiny regimented world at Fort Campbell.

On Sunday we were given post privileges at noon. I went over to look at the base library and then joined Tom Barrett and a math major from Ohio State named John Cameron at the club. We ended up having a long conversation about morality and that turned out to be the inspiration I had been lacking for some serious drinking, because we also shared several pitchers of beer. Tom was a devout Catholic and John was an agnostic like me. Tom brought up one of the war stories Quick had shared about how American forces sometimes decapitated VC they had killed because Buddhists believed that this doomed the dead person's soul to wander for eternity, thus sending a warning to the comrades who came upon the mutilated corpses. We had no idea if this was true, and certainly Quick was no authority on Buddhism, but it served as fodder for an inebriated discussion.

Tom and John felt this was barbaric so I took the other side for the sake of having a debate, arguing that once a person had died the body was just an inanimate object so what difference did it make what was done to it? In fact, I said this practice would have the advantage of making the killer face up to the fact of what he had done in a far more graphic way than seeing a figure you had shot fall three hundred meters away. The morality of offending the deceased's comrades' religious sensibilities never came up, nor did the fact that the VC routinely mutilated the bodies of dead American troops. The only purpose of our long exchange was to spend some time talking about something other than cars and girls. After that, I called Bev and my family, hoping it was not too obvious I had been drinking.

✳✳✳

Bev wrote on Monday, May 5 that her feelings had soared and plunged many times since the previous evening. She was overjoyed with the flowers, and it made me feel so good to be able to do a small thing like that for her. She loved flowers so much that one day she had spent some time in Sheffield's flower shop just to look at some. The thought of flowers inspired her to share a few short prosaic poems from D. H. Lawrence's *Pansies* and *More Pansies*. Give credit where credit is due: the Army really did know what it was doing when it put a flower shop on base.

After supper that night she and Joyce C. walked down East River Road to I-94 and waved and smiled at all the people going by in cars. Most of the time they were rewarded with a return salutation and it made them feel they had spread a little bit of cheer. They ended up at Bridgeman's in Stadium Village for ice cream. The emotional low point came when Bev called a friend at Maryville and found that another young woman she knew there had been diagnosed with cancer. Sharing the sad news with Joyce, her closest confidant, helped to begin the journey of processing it.

Knowing how much I appreciated all sorts of reading material, Bev enclosed some pages from *Readers' Digest*. This included an article from the president of Notre Dame, Father Theodore M. Hesburgh, stating his view that the academic community itself was best qualified to deal with the widespread unrest on American campuses, and also expressing his fear that the strongly negative reaction to "campus chaos" among lawmakers, donors, parents, alumni, and the general public could lead to a "suppression of the liberty and autonomy that are the lifeblood of a university community." The observation that struck me most strongly: "the real crisis is not one of authority but a crisis of vision." He made it clear that this lack of vision and inability to see beyond the once-valid but now-myopic viewpoints of the past was a problem among civic and political leaders, not just those of the academy. It seemed especially intriguing that Nixon had asked Father Hesburgh to share and expand on these views with Spiro Agnew, because the good father would truly have to conjure up a miracle for his progressive views to have any impression on that authoritarian moron. I could not help but reflect on how much more important this issue had appeared to me less than two months before, but it was good to be reminded that the military milieu was but one front in a civil war that America was enduring, and that ultimately ideas were more potent than firepower on all fronts.

Bev was pleased with my role on the rifle drill team, and asked if I could call as soon as I got the orders for my next assignment. She also appreciated the reminder that it was unlikely we would get leave after Basic. That meant our next chance to see each other would be after AIT, most likely in late July or early August. She was planning on going home to Coral Gables after scout camp was over in August, but said that her plans were flexible because she knew that my schedule was dictated by the military. Until we knew more, she said to hold onto that magic word: hope.

Bev wrote again on Tuesday the 6th that she had finished *Absalom, Absalom!* and found its depiction of the decaying but dignified South depressing. How could it be otherwise? Slavery, as Faulkner always so readily acknowledged, was America's original sin and, even though the "peculiar institution" itself was a thing of the past, its bastard child of racism remained the most formidable barrier between America's potential greatness and our current reality of internal strife and suffering. Like anyone raised Catholic, I knew there was no absolution without true contrition and a determination to amend one's life, and our current racial discord demonstrated unequivocally that our nation was far from redemption. And yet we felt justified in attempting to impose our ways on others by force of arms. As for me, I was now in a prison-like environment in a former slave state and a part of the war machine. Clearly her depression was contagious. I was impressed that Bev had not even mentioned the effort of attempting to solve the Gordian Knot of Mr. William's labyrinthine narrative experiments, but I imagined Marty's erudite explication had been a big help.

The first of the spring panty raids had hit Comstock that night, but Bev and Jennifer stayed in their room studying. Then the two of them went for a walk before the sun set, ending up at Bridgeman's. "I've got this thing about ice cream!" Jennifer had made Bev go to the Health Service that morning, and Dr. Donovan prescribed a cherry-flavored cough syrup that she found much more palatable than Formula 44. She and Mom had a good conversation that night and Bev sort of invited herself over for Friday evening. I was pleased because I had been encouraging both Bev and my family, especially Mom, to spend more time together. I knew they were both more worried about my situation than they expressed in their letters and I felt they were the best ones to share and maybe assuage their mutual anxieties. I wanted Bev to start feeling like one of the family. She wrote:

> Often I think of not too long ago before we met and wonder what, if anything, I had to hold on to in dark moments. The many friends helped, but now our love is a hope, as you mentioned before; it is a hope unimaginable to me before.

Words like that meant everything to me because that hope is exactly what was sustaining me in the bleak, regimented, and death-haunted environment of BCT. Yes, friends helped, but love and hope were the anchors. She closed with a colorful crayon drawing and the assurance that "my thoughts are bursting with joy and energy for life in spite of everything else." That was my wonderful girl, and her optimism and zest for life were even more contagious than the inevitable occasional low points.

She wrote on Thursday the 8th that she enjoyed my letters describing the life of a trainee. She could not help but be worried about the things we were being trained to do, of course, but certainly wanted to hear the truth. I always believed that we owed that to each other, so I was more graphic in my letters to Bev than the ones to the family. I told them what we were doing as well, but tried to do it in a way that would worry them as little as possible. She was continuing to work on her Twain paper for Kwait, and Marty was still discussing Absalom. She went downtown with the two Joyces that night and had a grand time browsing through Powers' bookstore, Dayton's dress shops, and other places. She found some Girl Scout Bermudas for camp, some ribbons for her hair, which she was letting grow longer, and some stationary. Some big news was that the three of them had decided to find an apartment for the next year, and Jennifer would also be sharing it in the fall while she student-taught. It would be cheaper than Comstock and also more fun.

She mentioned again how the still-beautiful flowers reminded her of times we shared together, and how much she was longing for the time when we could do that again. She liked the idea of Como Park because she had not been there since the summer of 1965 when she had spent a few weeks in Minneapolis on a church-related project, and actually had never seen much of St. Paul at all. She liked my description of San Francisco and dreamed of when we could explore America together. She said that the differing role of religion in our two lives did not worry her. She had gone to church more that year than in her four at Maryville, most likely because of Pastor Hawkinson, a man of faith and peace who we both agreed was attuned to the genuine spiritual needs of his congregation and our troubled nation. She enclosed a mimeographed summary of the principal recent changes in the English graduate program, which I appreciated even though such concerns were far from my mind at the time. She also included a few cartoons from the newspaper of Stoo Hample's *Children's Letters to God*.

Bev wrote on Saturday the 10th about visiting and eating with my family the previous evening. She took the bus, but walked from Lowry when the bus turned west because she did not realize it would turn again to continue north. The walk was great, though, because of all the spring flowers and greenery. She played Jarts, a lawn dart game, with "the little kids" (Mary, John, and Jane). She and Mary lost 8-2 because John had such good aim. After a supper of salmon, potatoes, and Jell-O she did the dishes with Granny and Jane while Mom and Mary went to pick up Archie from Spokane, who was in town for a bowling tournament. He was the husband of Delores, one of Uncle Allie's children, and Uncle Allie was one of Granny's brothers. After they returned, the two girls and Bev looked at some Time/Life books in the *This Fabulous Century* series. At that time we only had the first two volumes covering the first twenty years. She had a good visit with Granny, too, and that pleased me greatly because I knew Granny was always concerned that my choice of a spouse be the right one. They showed her the Polaroid shot of me at the field day and she commented that she knew my glasses were Army-issue because they were just like Jack's.

She had slept until 9:00 that morning and then went to the Baltimore Lunch in Stadium Village for a good breakfast. On the way back she got caught in a minor hail storm, thinking at first that someone was throwing pebbles at her. She was continuing to work on her Twain paper, vowing "I will finish the rough draft this weekend, by gum." I loved those Southernisms, which I thought must have come from her years in Tennessee. She liked the radio for background music and said a weird song was on that sounded like water dripping to the tune of "Feelin' Groovy." She wrote out the lyrics because that is how she felt in spring and when we were together. She was also eating the graham cereal Clackers in an effort to keep her mind off the beautiful weather outside while she wrote and studied. The new cough syrup seemed to be helping at least somewhat. She included a statement from Reinhold Niebuhr that Wanda had sent on the roles of the virtues of hope, faith, love, and forgiveness. She also sent a quotation by Andre Gide:

> Look for your own. Do not do what someone else could do as well as you. Do not say, do not write what someone else could say, could write as well as you. Care for nothing in yourself but what you feel exists nowhere else – and out of yourself create impatiently or patiently – the most irreplaceable of beings.

She was so good at expressing thoughts and sharing those of others, and that strengthened my ability to avoid succumbing to the Army's none-too-subtle efforts at mind control.

Bev wrote on the 12th that her parents had sent a tape recorder along with two tapes they had already made. They were "a scream," especially one that was too fast, making them sound like chipmunks. They wanted to strengthen communication in the family and be able to hear voices, especially grandchildren, without the expense of telephone calls. With family scattered from Germany to Alaska to Minnesota that made sense in those days when long distance rates were quite steep. Without the long distance "meter" running they felt more free to just rattle on about their daily activities, such as Dad planting zinnias and Mom fixing supper. Her mom was leaving for Germany on Saturday.

Bev said it was delightful to hear me laugh so much on the phone the previous day, and was diplomatic enough not to mention the role that alcohol might have played in that. She said we were both lucky enough to be able to laugh away worries and take life as it comes and enjoy it. Speaking of laughter made her think about Jennifer and how the two of them almost had each other in hysterics the previous night. Bev claimed she could be crazy upon occasion, and when she was she sometimes did the Snoopy dance. I wanted to see that someday. She said the two of them were laughing so hard that Jennifer started getting a pain in her chest, so Bev left the room doubled over in hysterics. What a delightful contrast between the personalities of Jennifer and Joyce C.

She had finished *Roughing It* that morning, went to Marty's class for more discussion of *Absalom*, ran off some quizzes for McNally, and then sat in the classroom while the students took the quiz. Now she was sore because she had played tennis that afternoon. Her cough was much better, and the doctor had told her it was probably due to being in a climate that was new to her body. She wrote a few sentences in a type of hillbilly jargon inspired by the "Buck Fanshaw's Funeral" episode in *Roughing It*, and I could just hear her saying it, accompanied by Jennifer doubled over with helpless laughter. She was feeling great, and wrote out a favorite cummings poem, "maggie and milly and molly and may," that concludes:

> For whatever we lose (like a you or a me)
> It's always ourselves we find in the sea

She described her love of the sea and I understood because of my affinity for Lake Superior, although that did not include playing in the waves. Enjoying a Florida beach together was yet another of our dreams. She closed with a brief description of the quiet and peaceful evening on the banks of the Mississippi.

***

On May 10, in the A Shau Valley, a battle began for control of Dong Ap Bia or, in American military parlance, Hill 937, the elevation in meters. Over the course of eleven days, US commanders ordered repeated assaults by increasing numbers of troops against well-armed North Vietnamese defenders controlling the high ground at the summit. Finally, after the top of the mountain had been pulverized by massive airstrikes and artillery bombardments, it was taken by US and ARVN troops on May 20. Then, in an action that awoke still-raw memories of Khe Sanh the previous year, the lofty site now known as Hamburger Hill that had been won at the cost of eighty-four US killed-in-action (KIA) and 480 wounded-in-action (WIA) was abandoned less than a week later. US military commanders explained that the purpose had never been to hold the mountain but to disrupt the flow of NVA troops into the RVN from nearby Laos. They bolstered their claims of success with enemy casualty figures that seemed suspiciously high but were also, as always, impossible to verify.

I knew that many of my parents' generation supported the war because of their fear of communist world domination and an attitude of "my country, right or wrong," but how would they react to a brutal engagement that bore a strong resemblance, on a smaller scale, to one of the great battles of their own war, Iwo Jima? After the heroic 1945 assault finally succeeded with the photographically immortalized climactic tableau of the raising of the US flag on the summit of Mount Suribachi, what would the reaction have been if we abandoned the island once again to the Japanese? As the nation grew increasingly weary of the never-ending scourges of war and internal discord, even supporters of the conflict began to question our purposes in Vietnam. Hamburger Hill was significant on the home front not because it was an important military victory but because it served as yet another tipping point for many Americans from at least moderate support over to outright criticism of our civilian and military leadership. Some of the strongest questioning came from Ted Kennedy and other fellow Democrats on the floor of the US Senate, a very public forum that commanded coverage in all the major media. Then a Republican senator, Jacob Javits of New York, became the first from Nixon's own party to break with the president on his conduct of the war, accusing him of following the same "sterile" policies as LBJ.

★★★

Down at Fort Campbell, the week of May 11 was the BCT equivalent of finals week. Monday and Tuesday were review days for the G3 test and final practice for the big PT test on Wednesday. The most extensive review was on first aid because that subject would be a significant portion of the G3. Many of us in the First Platoon had been assigned extra workouts because of marginal performance on some of the PT events. The most difficult events for most of us, including me, continued to be the alligator crawl and the fireman's carry. The infiltration course was also scheduled for Wednesday. We expected that to be about the same as the one on bivouac, except that this time the rounds fired over our heads would definitely be live. That meant they would be far above us since the cadre was not about to risk mowing down a bunch of trainees. Wednesday would be a full day because it also included firing and attempting to qualify with the M16. I ended up qualifying as an Expert, one step up from my rating with the M14. On Thursday the 15th we took the G3 test, and that was pretty much the end of our training; the week of the 18th was for cleaning and turning in equipment and getting ready to leave for our next assignments. On the 16th we received booster shots for typhoid, tetanus, and polio.

Late in the week we finally got our next assignment and I was going to Fort McClellen, Alabama, for AIT. Nearly everyone in the platoon was going to Fort Polk, Louisiana, but the first five in the alphabetical listing were scheduled for Fort Mac instead. The surname that had nearly always landed me in the front row in school had determined my fate yet again, and this time it appeared to be for the better. That was because Polk was known to be one of the most miserable places to be stationed, in terms of both climate and facilities, but even worse than that was the well-known fact that everyone going there was to be in infantry AIT. Since we still did not know our MOS's, the fact that I was going to Fort Mac, a place I had never heard of, raised my hopes that I would not be assigned to the infantry.

Now that our formal training was completed, the usual custom was for the trainees to get a pass. Tom Barrett, John Cameron, and I had thought we would go into town together, but Captain Harris decided not to issue passes after all, a decision that seemed to be motivated by nothing other than meanness. This really sank morale and even Sergeant Seufert said he hoped we did not get the honor company award because that would reflect well on Harris as the CO. This disappointment, combined with the prospect of spending the next two summer months in the swamps of Louisiana, led to tension and anger in the ranks, and many of the guys reacted by getting stinking drunk when we got post privileges on the night of Saturday the 17th. There were some fights, too, which only further eroded the sense of unit cohesion among a group of men who knew that in a week they would no longer be a unit.

I called Bev and my family and told them about going to Alabama but not yet knowing my MOS, and also, let them know that there would definitely be no leaves in between BCT and AIT. After we got back to the barracks many of the guys immediately passed out in their bunks, and some men who were less impaired thought it would be funny to see how many they could lift out onto the floor without waking them up. By the time I turned in there were seven or eight guys sleeping on the floor in the center aisle. I wished I had been awake when the sergeant in charge of quarters (CQ) came in for bed-check—it must have been a riot. That's the kind of thing that passes for entertainment in the life of a trainee, but it seemed like a poor substitute for a night in town, even though we had only a vague idea of what we might have done there.

The next night, Sunday the 18th, I had CQ for an hour starting at midnight. I knew that our MOS's had been assigned by then, so I was determined to use the opportunity to find mine if at all possible. Alone in the Delta HQ office, I found the list on the First Sergeant's desk that gave our destinations and the number of our special orders. Mine was SO 110, Paragraph 37, but I could not find it among the stacks of paperwork. I decided to look one more time and was finally successful. I was down for the MOS of 11B10, Small-Arms Infantryman, also known as a rifleman, ground-pounder, or grunt. It was a terrible shock, probably worse than getting my draft notice back in February, because I had been hoping that I would be assigned to some sort of support function due to my educational background. I liked to think that I did not look upon myself as any better than the guys who had not gone to school as long, but we had been told that the Army placed men in positions based upon their abilities and that had been the basis for my expectations. But the Army also assigned men based on the Army's needs and, with over half a million troops on the ground in the RVN, the greatest need was for riflemen.

My mind was racing and I thought of the passage in *The Snows of Kilimanjaro* when Harry can feel death creeping up on him. I could feel death standing behind me: I knew the odds had greatly increased that I would be dead within a year. Over thirty thousand men had been killed in the RVN already. After the initial shock, what I felt was raw fear. Even at the best, it meant a year of physical misery and unbearable emotional tension that would make it unlikely that the man returning to Bev sometime in 1970 would be much like the one who bid her farewell. In religious terms it was a night of Gethsemane, or a dark night of the soul. I tried to take my mind off of it by perusing the only unofficial reading material in the office, a *Sad Sack* comic book.

When 1:00 a.m. arrived my relief man was still not there so I walked back across the field to the barracks and woke him up. He was going to Mac, too, so I told him that the five of us were to be eleven-bravos. He ran over to check for himself. I was unable to sleep and about a half-hour later the guy who slept next to me got up and stood there staring at me, adding to the eerie unreality of the terrible night. I knew he was asleep, so I woke him up and he said he had been having some sort of crazy dream. He was another of the five going to Mac so I told him the bad news about our MOS and he accepted it calmly. As I lay awake the words of Sergeant Quick about fighting in Nam to save your own ass came back to me, and I decided to get all I could out of AIT to make my odds of survival as high as possible. I hated the idea of killing but you do not go into a combat zone without clear goals and my top one was staying alive. The next ordeal would be breaking the news to Bev and my family.

***

Bev wrote on the morning of Thursday the 15th responding to my concern about becoming so immersed in the small and myopic world of the Army. She was interested in all my activities, and my reactions to them were a way for her to get to know me better. She understood about "back home" beginning to seem like another world because of the changes in her own life, such as leaving her home in Florida. She knew she could never live there again for any extended period of time. Leaving the security and friendships of Maryville the previous year had been painful as well, and her hesitance to visit Wanda had been due to the fear of crossing over into that world again and not knowing how to act or talk. That fear had proven groundless because Wanda had already entered another world herself. I felt that Bev's decision to come to an unfamiliar and distant place such as Minneapolis had been a brave one, and she said that now this was her home.

That made me feel good, because I knew my family and I were a big reason for it, but I also admired how she made friends and allowed people into her life. She was much better at that than I. She said many of the ideas I shared with her on subjects such as religion, piety, hypocrisy, and fanaticism were also things she had contemplated many times. She agreed that the description in *Portrait of the Artist* of Stephen discarding his habitual beliefs was good, as well as his learning ultimately to believe in himself as an individual mind and body, and she mentioned Hesse's *Siddharrtha* as well. She said that she feared the time when she might discontinue growing intellectually, and added that her desire to teach was a way to prevent such stagnation because a person does not dare allow that to happen when they know they will need to present and defend their ideas in front of a class.

As the end of the quarter approached, she was reading and writing like mad. She finished *Life on the Mississippi* and started *Black Boy*, but would not have time to reread *Huck Finn*. She was almost finished with her Twain essay and said that Kwait had given his approval for her to expand it into one of her "Plan B" papers. We needed to write three of these substantial essays as part of our MA program. She also had a paper due for Marty next week as well as about five more books to read, and in addition she needed to prepare the material for counselor training at camp that summer.

The night before, they had a birthday party at our house for Dad and my brother Dave. Uncle Jim, Aunt Irene, and their youngest son Rick were there, as well as my folk's close friends Dick and Mary Powers. Rick was very tall and had his own car now. He always loved cars and I knew having one of his own would be a dream come true for him. Bev enjoyed listening and had a good chat with Dick while they were out in the backyard watching the kids play their current favorite game, Jarts. Dave enjoyed his job sketching designs because it was related to his art studies. Doing the dishes with Mom, Granny, and Jane led to more conversation after the guests had left. Bev liked my godfather Jim's sense of humor just as I always did. It was dry and bordering on the cynical, much like his godson's. Mary had fun at her class outing at Excelsior Amusement Park, and even got sunburned. Going to that place was a huge treat in those days. She signed off because it was time to wake up Jennifer so the maid could clean their room, and then head off to class. That was a great letter for so early in the morning, or for any time.

She wrote again the next day, Friday the 16th, describing how she and five other girls from the dorm had gone over to Mama Rosa's for pizza and relieved some of the late-quarter tension by acting "stupid" the whole time, including singing camp songs such as *100 Bottles of Beer* on the way back. Back at Comstock, they got out a Ouiji board and one of its predictions was that the two of us would be married in a year. She had finished *Black Boy* and Wright's frank depiction of racism reduced her to tears. The cruelest irony was that his own race also rejected him because of his desire to be a writer. She wished we were together to talk about the universal human struggle to claim our rightful dignity and find our place in the world. Certainly contemplating the struggles of blacks in America shed a valuable perspective on our own troubles, because pervasive racism meant they were born with a burden we could never truly understand, let alone attempt to bear. I sometimes wondered if our lowly status as trainees who were expected to obey orders without question was giving me an inkling of their shameful plight, but that was another thing I could never know. She closed feeling lonely and listening to Judy Collins.

Bev wrote on the morning of Sunday the 18th about the beauty of the new day. I loved her innate optimism and joy in the beauty of nature. She reflected on how much she could get done on a Sunday morning without going to church. She and Mom had talked the previous night after I called, and Mom had already figured out the location of Fort McClellan. She said I might be able to visit Birmingham or Atlanta, and would probably learn more about Southern attitudes. Some of her reading for Marty's class had aroused her interest in that subject, so now she was reading *The Mind of the South* by W. J. Cash. Mark Davis was using it in his Southern literature course that summer. She and Mom had gotten onto the subject of movies, including Mary's current obsession, Zeffirelli's *Romeo and Juliet*. Mary got upset when people laughed at inappropriate times during the film. Mom mentioned her all-time favorite, *Gone with the Wind*; and they both agreed that Peter Sellers was a scream. She closed by including the lyrics to Rod McKuen's "In the Summertime of Days."

She wrote again the next night describing a circular discussion she had with Jennifer on the world's problems. I wished I could have heard that, but I would have preferred one of their silly sessions. She had grown frustrated with working on her paper and to try to clear her mind had taken an evening walk in the all-day drizzle, which reminded her of "sloppy-slurching" through puddles at camp. Jennifer was now dating a senior at Carleton named Steve DeLapp. The night before, Bev had eaten with the Davis family at the Lincoln Del. Kay and Mark had Ruebens but Bev opted for a corned beef sandwich because she and sauerkraut did not get along. She described again what a lively little character Geoffrey was. She went on to talk about the importance of our hope for our future together, and about all the people without hope in some of the novels she read that quarter, especially *The Day of the Locust*. That one was indeed a downer, but I had read all four of West's novels during a period when his prevailing tone reflected and reinforced my own perspective on life.

Bev wrote on Tuesday the 20th because I had called my family with the news about me going into the infantry, and Mom had shared the news with her. I had called Bev as well, but she had been out at the time and was now upset with herself about that. There was no reason for that, especially since it had not been a Sunday, the day I usually called, but that was just how she felt. Mom and Bev were both stunned even though I had tried to prepare them for that possibility. I knew that would be their reaction, and I was especially worried about Mom and Granny. I was ever so grateful that Mom had Bev for a friend, confidant, and future daughter. Bev could not help but be concerned about my mental state because she remembered how torn I had been about going into the military the night before I left and, as always, she reminded me that we must rely on our love and hopes for the future to see us through. She also reflected on how hard it had been to tell of her love because that had been the first time, as it had been for me as well, and closed with the hope that we could connect by phone soon. I was determined, whatever the next year brought, to do my best to be worthy of the gift of her love. That was what sustained me. About the only positive thing I could conjure up from the miserable situation was that at least the ordeal of telling them about it was behind me.

✱✱✱

Our last week at Fort Campbell, the week of May 18, was mostly uneventful and anticlimactic since BCT was now behind us. We cleaned and turned in equipment. There was some PT, but after the test that also seemed like just one more pointless routine. Our graduation rehearsals had not been promising but the actual event went well and we gave a passable imitation of real soldiers wearing our dress khakis and going through our drill and ceremony exercises in large units. Delta did end up losing Honor Company, but we somehow managed to win an even higher honor, the Commanding General's Award. Sergeant Seufert won the Outstanding DI award again, and that was the one that made me happy because he really had been a fine counselor and mentor. He said he ended up getting more attached to this platoon than he usually does, something he tried to avoid. I hoped that the conversations the two of us shared had contributed to those feelings and that he would think fondly of his former charges while he sipped his Black Jack.

Chapter 8
AIT AND LEAVE
May-July 1969

The old First Platoon was soon scattered all over the country, although mainly to Fort Polk. The five of us going to Fort Mac left on a Greyhound bus the afternoon of Friday, May 23. The guys going to Polk had left a few hours earlier. Some of them who lived nearby had relatives come to visit them before they left but those visits were limited to about a quarter-hour, which I thought would be worse than no visit at all. We went through Nashville and drove past the Grand Ole Opry, but what really struck me was how rundown and sleazy the city looked. We drove south through hilly country in Tennessee, reminding me of Sarge's term "ridge-runners" for the guys from this area. It was the most backward-looking country I had ever seen with many old, dilapidated houses that could never have stood up to a Minnesota winter, most of them with one or two wrecked cars in the yard or perhaps a piece of rusty and dilapidated farm machinery. Things got steadily worse as we motored south.

We stopped for supper about 5:00 p.m. in Huntsville, Alabama, at a cafeteria called The Piccadilly in a big shopping center. I had a delicious meal of barbecued chicken and it felt great to be eating in a civilian restaurant. After living with a wide variety of southern dialects at Fort Campbell for two months, the overheard accents of the civilian diners no longer seemed strange to me. We were just getting to the southern Appalachian foothills now and as we left Huntsville the highway climbed rapidly and we could look down and see the city in the valley below. For someone from a flat area such as central Minnesota such a rare sight was memorable. We drove through a charming little city called Guntersville—situated on a lake formed by a Tennessee Valley Authority (TVA) dam—that seemed liked the typical southern town as I visualized it from reading Faulkner. The obligatory Confederate war memorial statue was present and accounted for in the town square.

We arrived at Fort McClellan about 8:00 p.m., and the first thing that struck me was the topography, almost the direct opposite of flat and dusty Fort Campbell. Our training area was on top of a small mountain, or at least what a soldier from Minnesota would call a mountain, and was surrounded by many other such hills. The barracks were only one story high and laid out in an irregular pattern to follow the relatively scarce areas of level ground. Most of the ground was grass-covered and the smell of pines was in the air. Even in the relative cool of the evening, I could tell it was going to be hot there but it still seemed like a step up from Campbell. Most everything was painted with some sort of jungle motif and the name of the infantry training brigade was Tigerland. We arrived as night was falling and I could hear a returning platoon marching nearby and singing cadence to a song with the melody of the old Coasters' tune "Poison Ivy:"

> In Vietnam, Vietnam,
> Late at night while you're sleeping
> Charlie Cong comes a-creeping
> All around.

It had a mournful air to it in the southern twilight and, combined with the feeling of being in a strange and unfamiliar place and knowing that we were there to prepare to go fight in a brutal war, it evoked an overwhelming mood of sadness and dread in me.

The next day at our orientation session we were told that Fort Mac was a large base housing the Army Chemical School, the Military Police School, and the Women's Army Corps Center. Our unit was an AIT infantry brigade and we were assigned to Company E of the 1st Battalion. We were the first ones to go through a new ten-week training cycle for advanced jungle warfare and the environment was heavily focused on Vietnam. There were Vietnamese phrases along with the English translations on signs posted in sequences in the old Burma Shave style along paths in waiting areas such as the entrance to the mess hall. These were useful items such as "do you have trustworthy friends" and "thank you very much." Even the shaving mirrors in the latrines had bamboo frames around them. We were told this did not mean all of us were destined for duty in Vietnam, but I suspected that lame reassurance was mostly to try to discourage guys from going AWOL (absent without official leave) because we were also told the penalty for that was serving time in a military prison. The instructor went on to explain that such time behind bars was "bad time" that would not count against our term of enlistment. The whole thing was beginning to seem more like *Cool Hand Luke* all the time: We were technically not in prison but if we left and were apprehended we would end up behind bars. So our sorry situation was about as close to prison as you could get without actually committing a crime.

Despite this threatening and depressing introduction to life in Tigerland, things took a turn for the better the same day when the senior DI called all the college grads out of the formation and assigned us to the weapons platoon of Echo Company. This is the fifth platoon of the five in an infantry company, and at that time the primary weapon employed by such units was the 81 mm mortar. The DI went on to tell us that we were lucky because the training was a bit less physical due to all the required classroom time. The position had a higher status than rifleman and, best of all, it was less dangerous in a combat situation because the mortar men usually remained within the perimeter and fired rounds over the riflemen and onto the enemy positions as radioed back by the forward observers. It was impossible for us to know how much of this was really true, but it was a measure of the extent of our indoctrination in BCT that we took this as very good news. When you are at the lowest rung on the ladder the next step up seems like a big one. The DI for our platoon was Sergeant Doyle, a fairly easygoing guy packing a few extra pounds who appeared to be just a little older than I. Right from the start he tried to make us proud to be in the weapons platoon and he rarely passed up an opportunity to describe the advantages of the specialty.

We had all of the college guys in the company in our platoon, and when one of them was unpacking his gear I was taken aback because he had a copy of *The Gawain-Poet*. I asked him about it and he said that he had been going to the U of Alabama when he had to drop some courses, lost his deferment, and gotten drafted. There was Jim Anderson who had been doing grad work in marine biology at the U of Wisconsin at Oshkosh. A man from Virginia was still in something of a state of shock over being assigned to the infantry, and I knew he was not the only one. It seemed like an interesting bunch of guys and I anticipated some good conversations. I was sure we would be spending time commiserating with each other about our plight, hopefully aided by alcohol, because it also appeared to me that none of us belonged where we found ourselves. Would a bunch of smart guys used to thinking for themselves coalesce into an outstanding unit, or might we turn into one of the worst, by Army standards at least? Since men shipped over to the RVN as individuals rather than units at that time, did our unit cohesion or lack of it really matter at all anyway? Doyle started off on the right foot by giving us post privileges the second night we were there. I wanted to relax away from the din of an EM club so I just went to the PX and got a *Newsweek* and a bag of Peanut M&Ms, then came back to the barracks and caught up on the news.

I called Bev the afternoon of Sunday the 25th, and she told me how she was looking forward to Camp Bear Creek for a complete change of pace and scenery. We always talked about when we might see each other, and that was as uncertain as ever. We were scheduled to finish the first week of August, and Bev would be back in Florida by then. That presented the complication of deciding whether I would visit her there on my leave before going overseas, or if she would come up to Minneapolis. The camp was near Paducah, Kentucky, so if I got a weekend pass it did not seem likely there would be enough time for the round trip up and back for a visit. Ironically, she would be only about fifty miles from Fort Campbell. As we had been doing for the last two months, we knew we just had to wait and see what my Army schedule would allow, but at least we knew that every day meant the time of being together again was just a little closer.

✸✸✸

Bev wrote later the same day that she hoped I was feeling a bit better because I had sounded down on the phone. I was always sorry when our relatively infrequent long-distance conversations left her feeling worse because of me being in a down period, but we had made a pact to be honest and share our feelings as much as possible. She was working on her paper for Marty contrasting the concept of suffering in *The Day of the Locust* with that in *Black Boy*. Wright used his own suffering as a vehicle for empathizing with that of others, and the resulting feeling of communion with his fellow men allowed him to avoid falling into despair and to work through to a feeling of optimism about the future. This served as a reminder of another key part of our pact: never losing hope.

She went on to say once again how she could not understand why humanity so often found itself at war because her worldview was geared to trust. She mentioned my account of the conversation I had with Tom and John about mutilating enemy corpses. She had talked about this with Jennifer, as well as the fact that some of the guys in BCT had been so gung ho about war and killing. She said Jennifer was flabbergasted and that neither one of them could come up with any sort of reasonable explanation for how a man could have such a warped attitude. I knew, but I was pleased they did not, because there is a place in the world for a certain innocence and sense of innate goodness that is unable to comprehend the darker side of man's nature. It is no accident that man's redemption comes so often through the grace and sensitivity of women who are usually so much further advanced in emotional maturity and the ability to empathize. That was a major reason why the Army tried to distance us from our former lives with the women we loved. It was also why the feminine viewpoint was ignored or derided in our training through cadence songs that denigrated women as fools and sluts. And, of course, the worst insult in any DI's well-stocked arsenal was to call an inadequate recruit by a vulgar female term.

The highlight of the news from home was Mary's graduation from St. Charles. After the ceremony, Bev and my family went to Bridgeman's to celebrate while a big thunderstorm poured down outside. Then they went downtown to see Dad's office on the street level of the Nicollet Hotel at Hennepin and Washington Avenue. Bev had just finished *A Connecticut Yankee in King Arthur's Court*, and would soon be moving on to Mailer. Jennifer's boyfriend Steve had given her a book of poems for her birthday by Takuboku Ishikawa entitled *Poems to Eat*. He had died in 1912 at the age of twenty-six. She said his prevailing mood was depression, aggravated by despair over his inability to truly bond with another. That sounded like a book I would enjoy, especially in the days before I met Bev, and I could see how a young intellectual would give it to his girlfriend to impress upon her the depths of his existential angst. The poems all adhered to an ancient poetic structure of thirty-one syllables known as Tanka, and Bev wrote out twenty-two of them in her letter. She suggested that I think about spending a few days with her in Miami in August during my leave after AIT, an idea that I loved. Then she closed by writing out cummings's *in time of daffodils*, a work far more in tune with her own view of life than the exquisite little jewels of pain from the pen of the morose Ishikawa.

∗∗∗

The most immediately noticeable difference between BCT and AIT was the attitude of the cadre toward the trainees. There was much less harassment and that made everything else more tolerable. We were even allowed to wear civilian clothes when off duty. As in BCT we had PT nearly every day, but by this time I was conditioned to the point where it did not bother me. Also, the exercises were less of a chore without a red-faced DI screaming at you to keep going.

Training began on Monday, May 26, with an orientation session. On Tuesday we learned how to operate several types of radios, including a new model that attached to the operator's helmet. The instructors assured us that we were being trained on all the best and newest equipment. The class included a detailed presentation on all possible means of communication and we learned that even though radio was the least secure, it was the most common one in the RVN. Radio transmissions were often garbled and full of static so one common practice was to spell out important words using the phonetic alphabet, from Alpha to Zulu.

On Wednesday we had a highly detailed class on land navigation and map-reading that started with dead reckoning and then moved on to more precise ways to use a compass, map, and landmarks to move through unfamiliar territory. One method was very similar to the technique we had learned in high school physics of using triangulation to determine distances. On Thursday, after we received our first shots for cholera, the guys went out to the woods to practice some of the things we had covered.

Another difference between BCT and AIT was that now we had to do our own laundry or pay to have it done. We were not confined to barracks nearly as often as in Basic, so I usually did my own at the laundromat, and I went over there on Wednesday night. I had finished *The Rainbow* a couple of days before, and I got a good start on *Tess* while I was waiting for the washer and dryer to finish. I had been saving the Frankl book for when I had a quiet place to think but those were scarce so I figured I would start that after the Hardy.

I had KP on Thursday so I missed the trip out to Pelham Range, but was assigned to help with the first of two meals in the field for the men who were out there. Loading and unloading the mermite cans of food and big containers of beverages from the truck was harder than PT. After lunch we poured out a bunch of potable water to lighten the lifting back into the truck before guys started asking us if we had any to refill their canteens. It was mostly gone by that time and we felt bad about that because it got up to 103 degrees that day. It turned out to be a very good day to miss training because, in addition to the oppressive heat, most of them did not get back from the range until 11:00 p.m. or midnight, and some were out in the woods until 3:00 a.m. I was surprised the cadre kept them out so long because that meant they were up that late themselves as well.

When I got back to the barracks from the mess hall the building was nearly deserted with the troops being out on the navigation exercise. I wrote to Bev that night and it was the first of numerous letters noting how much time I had left. In this case it was a matter of how much I had behind me since I had now passed the one-tenth mark of my two-year enlistment, or seventy-three days. I told her that the word was out we were going to Nam. It was all but certain so I warned her to be prepared. I had already told her that after I learned I was assigned to the infantry I had made the decision to kill rather than be killed if it came to that. I knew that would disturb her so I went on to explain that taking a life was something I would hate to do, and perhaps hate myself for later, but if my own survival was at stake that would be my choice.

Most men wonder at some point in their life what combat would be like and how they would stand up under it. The basic need down through the ages to defend the home territory so that the pack or clan might survive, as well as the desire to expand that territory through attacking adjoining clans, had implanted the warrior mentality somewhere deep in the mind of every male. Tom Barrett and I had talked about these things on bivouac. Hemingway claimed he was never happier than when he was involved in warfare. Mussolini had observed that "war is to men as childbirth is to women." Of course, Papa had been obsessed with death his entire life, and Il Duce was hardly a man I would turn to for any sort of advice. Even so, men hunting men would be an experience like no other, for better or for worse, and I had known guys in BCT who claimed to look forward to it.

I would never have shared these thoughts with my family and perhaps I should not have with Bev either, but my point was that when a man knows he is going to war he cannot help but wonder how he will do and what he will feel. I imagined that raw fear would be a given, but what else might there be? Would it introduce you to a side of yourself that you would rather never know? All in all, instead of reassuring her I probably made the situation worse, but I tried to end on a high note by telling her how excited I was about her suggested visit to Miami in August.

The next day, Friday the 30th, was Memorial Day and we had it off. The idea of a holiday during training was a novel one and I suspect that it was mostly for the benefit of the cadre, but the trainees certainly enjoyed it every bit as much. I got up about 8:00 a.m. and walked around exploring Tigerland. It was bigger than I had thought but the weather was so hot that I did not walk as far as I had planned. You could work up a sweat just walking around the block and I began to feel a strange tingling sensation for the first time in my life that I later learned was "prickly heat." I had breakfast at ten at a nearby drive-in and it was very good. We relished all these little freedoms after the confinement of Basic. I talked with a guy who had just graduated from AIT and he said it gets a little rough but the time went fast because they were so busy. That sounded much like Basic. I had talked with one of the cooks when I was on KP, and he turned out to be another engaged college guy who was drafted out of grad school. He said that the post had a fairly good library, but I decided to save that for another day.

I bought a *Newsweek* and then returned to the barracks to read that and *Saturday Review*, as well as sleeping for about an hour. One thing I learned from the magazines was that Canada was now accepting US deserters as well as draft-dodgers. The heat and inadequate sleep were taking their toll, and many of us spent as much time as possible simply lying around as though we were half sick, usually just in our underwear. *Candy* was showing at the movie theater so I thought I might walk up there and see that later.

I called home and then tried to reach Bev as well, but no one was there. When I tried again later, no one was at our house to verify the charge for a second try at calling Bev. I asked my folks to mail down some of my civilian clothes to wear when I was off duty. I planned to buy a canvas bag for them because my Army duffel bag was already stuffed. They were durable but there were limits and one guy's had split open on the way down from Campbell. I finally got through to Bev and she was in a great, upbeat mood from being outside in the sunny weather. Her enthusiasm was contagious and we had a joking chat that made us forget about the distance between us and the uncertain future. But she was serious when she said that we needed to spend my leave together, whether that was partially in Florida or entirely in Minnesota. It was the perfect end to a great holiday.

I had KP again on Saturday but this time it was much easier because there were no meals out in the field and only two were served in the mess hall on weekends. It was a twelve-hour shift starting at 5:00 a.m. The mess sergeant wanted to keep us busy on a relatively slack day so he had us doing unnecessary tasks such as cleaning all the nooks and crannies of the kitchen, including the narrow area between the big ovens and the wall. I took him at his word and squeezed back in as far as I could, but then realized I could reach even more remote deposits of encrusted grease if I stood on a pipe. It worked at first and I wondered if I was encountering some World War II-era grime, but then a pipe joint gave way under my weight and our senses were assailed by a loud, angry hiss and the unmistakable stink of natural gas. The mess sergeant was a heavyset black guy and I thought his eyes were going to bug out of his face. He yelled for everyone to get outside and, once we were all safely evacuated and the building had not exploded, it took all my concentration to keep a straight face. The fire department soon arrived to shut off the gas and all was back to normal. There were no repercussions. I had not intended for that to happen, but standing on a big gas pipe was not something I would have done in civilian life, and "feet upon the pipes" seemed like a valid variation of "bodies upon the gears." To quote a phrase we had begun using with increasing frequency: "What are they going to do, send me to Vietnam?"

That night I went with three other men to see *Where Eagles Dare*. It was surprising there were any German troops left for the US Army to fight after Richard Burton, Clint Eastwood, and their buddies mowed down so many of them. Squib blood packs exploded by the hundreds, as fans of action cinema had come to expect since the gory climax of *Bonnie and Clyde*. Richard Burton was a great actor who could make any character believable, and Clint was Clint. I would have welcomed them into my outfit. Soldiers always make for a boisterous crowd and there was more noise from the audience than the big speakers. Movies at Fort Mac were a trip. After the show we went bowling. I blew the first game but then rolled my all-time high score in the second. It was not a big night for drinking with all this other activity, and I had only two beers. We also saw a few WACs, a first for all of us.

Sunday, June 1, was another day to take it easy. I had been enjoying spending time with Mike Kemp, the English major from Alabama. His civilian clothes had already arrived so he loaned me a set so we could go around feeling less like soldiers. That night four of us went bowling again, and then up to the Hilltop Service Club. That was a big place with all kinds of facilities and we spent most of our time playing pool. Hilltop had that characteristic southern atmosphere of faded grandeur. It was a place that at one time had been able to affect at least some semblance of class but that now had fallen on harder times and given up all but the most cursory efforts to look presentable. It was a Blanche DuBois of a building that soon became one of my favorite places to spend free time.

The Hilltop had a large ballroom that was now cluttered with a motley collection of worn furniture. Half of its perimeter was a semicircular wall with many windows to catch any passing breeze. There was an evocative quality to this room and I could imagine it during its better days on a Saturday night during World War II filled with soldiers and their girls dancing to the melodies of a big band. The air would be redolent with the scent of magnolia blossoms and the southern belles' perfume. The couples would be taking advantage of any chance to slip out to the adjoining terrace and steal a few kisses under the stars in the sultry Alabama night. Unspoken thoughts of what the next few years might bring would be even more palpable than the melodious strains of foxtrots and waltzes. In those benighted days of strict racial segregation here in the heart of the former Confederacy there would be no black people in the room other than perhaps a few waiters.

Between the three-day holiday weekend and having KP on Thursday, I had gone four straight days without training. One night Doyle brought in a couple of young women from Jacksonville State who wanted to ask us questions in connection with one of their classes. They were not about to get anything out of me, but one of them asked if we think differently now than we had in college. I wrote to Bev about that in my next letter because it was a question I had been contemplating. Certainly my immediate concerns were vastly different. A few months ago my world had revolved around courses, exams, papers, what to do on the weekends, and above all, Bev. I told her how I had her on my mind ever since Phyllis's dinner invitation of November 8. But now my major concern was staying alive for the next year. I knew the odds were vastly in favor of that but, to quote Tom Barrett, they had also been considerably diminished.

But leaving aside these immediate concerns, as well as the fact that I had grown more accepting of the rigors and humiliations of military life, had my fundamental attitudes changed? I liked to think they had not, but it was undeniable that my view of life in the Army was far more realistic now that survival might well depend on our training. This was what I tried to explain to Bev in my letters, but I was also trying to explain it to myself and I was not always satisfied with the answer. I was determined not to become a different man from the one Bev had fallen in love with and, as I told her in nearly every letter, our letters and phone calls were my main lifeline for helping to prevent that.

∗∗∗

Bev wrote on Monday the 26th while enjoying a wonderful spring evening and contemplating the Moon, "that dull gray matter, according to our image-breaking astronauts." The Apollo 10 mission had returned to Earth earlier that day after an eight-day flight that served as a final trial run for the actual lunar landing. The lunar module had flown to within about ten miles of the surface and the stark view of what was in reality a very unromantic freezing gray desert took a bit of the magic out of the Moon's image for many folks, although I thought the whole thing was amazing. At least I knew that Bev would appreciate the names of the command and lunar modules: Charlie Brown and Snoopy. That afternoon she and Joyce C had driven Ed's car out to the Tyrol Hills Clinic for physicals for their summer jobs. They both passed but Joyce gave Dr. Schultz the third degree with questions about such things as where he did his residency, how long he had been practicing, and why he chose to be a general practitioner. He panicked Bev by telling her that she had a split first beat in her heart, but then went on to say it was not a cause for concern. She and Jennifer had walked to Dinkytown after supper and then up East River Road where they saw Baltimore orioles, a rabbit, and a gopher.

That afternoon she had gone down by the river to read, and said that the peaceful environment was a stark contrast to her book, *Why Are We in Vietnam?* She was having trouble understanding it, partly because of Mailer's narrative technique, but mainly because of the mentality of the protagonist. That book reflects Mailer at his hyper-masculine extreme attempting to position himself as Hemingway's heir to the literary heavyweight crown and, even though it offers a realistic portrait of the kind of man who craves the experience of combat, it is far from his best work. I could tell that Bev found it disturbing and I thought that spoke well of her.

The next day was Cap and Gown Day, and she was going through her usual exercise of evaluating a school year as the end approached. She called this one her "Minnesota adventure" because people at home and at Maryville had been astonished that she should move so far away, and especially so far north. She said that, without a doubt, it had been worth it because she had found a much freer academic and social atmosphere at the U and in the Twin Cities than at Maryville. But the most important thing was our meeting each other. That led her to a question that had been troubling her, which was if I would have evaded the draft if it had not been for her. I was uncertain why she thought that might have been the case, but I made a mental note to reassure her in my next letter that it was not.

Bev's next letter on May 28 was on a round piece of stationary divided into twenty-four pie-shaped segments in a sunburst pattern. The design was entitled "The Year of the Sun" and the segments were numbered so that the writer followed them around the circle as she wrote. I had never seen anything like it, and Mike Kemp really went wild when he saw it. I loved the way he got so enthusiastic about things, because it was pretty hard to be glum with a guy like him around. She wrote that while she was walking back from class on Tuesday, Cap and Gown Day, it slowly dawned on her that she loved the U. It was a gorgeous late spring day with kids sitting on the grass on the Mall, riding bikes, waving to friends, and enjoying spirited discussions. She loved the openness of the place because that afforded a freedom that was new to her, especially in the atmosphere of the classrooms. She also said the predicted high for that day was 96 degrees. She had gone to Jane's choir concert at St. Charles the night before along with Mom and Mary. The two girls were "starved" afterwards but at 11:00 p.m. they could not find any places to eat that were still open.

She continued writing the next day, saying that she had her last class with Joe Kwiat. That had been her favorite, especially the half about Twain. She loved my idea of visiting her in Kentucky and said if I came with a buddy she could get him a date as well. She did not know of a nearby motel but said I could stay at camp for free. I had not stopped to consider the difficulty she would have explaining what she was doing spending the night in town with a guy who was not her husband. It was a Girl Scout camp after all, and the counselors would have to keep up appearances. She included a list of the weekends in June and July when there would be no campers around, and closed by describing once again how she often stood on the sundeck of the dorm looking south and wishing we could read each others' immediate thoughts. I think the two of us actually were doing just that more often than either of us realized.

Bev wrote again on Saturday the 31st about how much she had enjoyed our phone conversation the previous evening and then she introduced me to some new characters in her life: it turned out that she had been trying to play the unfamiliar role of matchmaker. She had been attempting to line up Sharyn, one of her friends in Comstock and a nursing student, with a navy man named Jim who was stationed out at the Navel Air Station. Bev would not have known it, but that was one of the places my dad had been stationed during World War II before he was called up for active duty. Jim was the uncle of one of her former roommates and had a heavy Arkansas accent. He had a boat and the previous day had taken Bev and a couple of other women from the dorm water skiing on Prior Lake. Bev got to drive the boat for a while even though she could barely see because she had taken out her contacts for the skiing. She had been impressed by the fancy homes around the shore of the lake.

She was continuing to study for finals and had also made a tape for her folks. A few days later I received a postcard from her dad showing tarpon fishing off Marco Island and saying that the tape had arrived. He welcomed me to the South and said their prayers were with me. I really appreciated the way her parents were reaching out to me and showing their approval of our plans when I had not even met them yet. They were planning to leave for Alaska in the second week of July to visit Bev's oldest sister Sandra and her family in Delta Junction. That would mean they would not be in Miami when I was on leave, so I would not have the chance to meet them before going overseas, but Bev said the two of us could still do some sightseeing around her hometown if I liked that idea. She concluded with a poem by Kahlil Gibran, "Song of the Rain."

Bev wrote on Tuesday, June 3, that the temperature had only been in the forties for the last few days, along with rain and wind. At least it was good weather for studying and people were alternating between doing just that and "going berserk" under the stress of finals. She thought it was hilarious and I remembered how I had always enjoyed the adrenaline rush of finals week, which was actually not bad at all if you were prepared. The night before she had a long discussion with the two girls across the hall, mostly about literature. It started when her neighbors were trying to remember Caddy's name from *The Sound and the Fury* and then, as informal college discussions often do, one subject flowed into another. On Sunday night she had gone to The Embers diner with Jennifer and Steve DeLapp. Steve's future was uncertain; he had just graduated from Carlton and was opposed to the war and determined to find a way to avoid the draft. Bev reflected again on the past year, all the beautiful people she had met in Minnesota, and how many things could have happened that would have prevented the two of us from ever meeting. She wrote out the lyrics to "Thirsty Boots" from her Judy Collins album because it was one of the things that always reminded her of me. The chorus, especially, made her think of how she longed for us to be together so we could soothe each others' troubles.

★★★

Our training week after the long weekend began on Monday, June 2, with a class on the .45 caliber pistol. All mortar men, or 11Cs, had to qualify with that weapon because it was our primary firearm rather than the M16. That was so we would be unencumbered by a rifle when we had to carry the parts of the 81 mm mortar, although the rumor was that most guys carried an M16 anyway. The .45 was a weapon with a long history—it had been the standard US service pistol since the days of World War I. After the class, we went to the range for firing and attempting to qualify. The .45 felt familiar in my hand—Dave and I had a very realistic cap pistol modeled on the same weapon when we were kids. The slug was big with a rounded end rather than the sharp point of the rifle bullet. The kick was far less than I expected but, even so, I found it extremely difficult to hit the target at all. The recoil had a tendency to make your hand jump upwards, but also sideways. The instructor warned us that the weapon was semiautomatic and if we fired rapidly enough the repeated recoils could soon have us pointing it at a 90-degree angle from our initial position, or right at the guy next to us, a mistake he called "blowing your buddy away." I could tell that the cadre was uneasy about being around a bunch of trainees firing such a potent weapon for the first time, and they were also well aware that men who failed to qualify that day would have to return to the range on Saturday along with the instructors. The result was predictable: They passed all of us no matter how wildly off-target our barrages of slugs had been. Even Jim Anderson, who had been on a pistol team for three years, fell twenty points short before his score was "adjusted."

On Tuesday we had classes on land mines, including anti-tank mines, anti-personnel mines, and booby traps. US forces did not use booby traps as such, which were a wide variety of improvised devices placed near frequently travelled routes such as roads and trails and rigged to go off when an unlucky soldier hit the triggering device. These could range in power from a single bullet in a shallow camouflaged hole that would fire upwards through a foot that stepped on it all the way up to an artillery round rigged to explode in a way that would take out a vehicle or an entire patrol if the troops were not spread out enough. One of the most feared was the "bouncing betty," a grenade that would pop out of the ground when triggered and explode at groin level. Others such as punji sticks and spike boards worked without explosives.

Depending upon one's point of view, this unnerving variety of hidden dangers reflected either the ingenuity of gallant guerrilla fighters making do with a fraction of the firepower commanded by their adversaries, or the sinister workings of minds from a strange and devious culture who refused to fight by the "rules" of modern warfare. The later racist-tinged perspective was akin to the American view of the Japanese troops during World War II. The truth was that the VC were fighting in the only possible way that would give them any sort of chance against the world's most powerful military machine, but any admiration we might have had for their resourcefulness was negated by the knowledge that we were training to go into the nerve-wracking hellhole created by the fruits of their inventiveness. Of course, the psychological stress produced by the knowledge that something unseen just around the next bend in the trail could kill you or blow off your foot or your genitals was one of the primary purposes of these devices.

The mine employed most commonly by US troops was the Claymore, which used C-4 plastic explosive to fire 700 steel balls in a well-defined pattern in an arc of about 60 degrees. The statistics were 100% death within 50 meters, 100% casualties within 100 meters, and moderate casualties within 250 meters. The device was directional and the convex side was clearly embossed with the words "FRONT TOWARD ENEMY." One favorite VC tactic was to sneak up to a US unit's perimeter and turn the Claymores around then make some noise so the Americans would detonate them. US policy was that these mines were to be command detonated rather than rigged as booby traps but, like all US ordnance, they could easily be converted to the latter use when acquired by the VC. These parts of the lectures were when eyes started to roll because we all knew that the Geneva Conventions, or any other rules purporting to govern the conduct of modern warfare, had long been abandoned by both sides in Vietnam. A Claymore blast was what had nearly killed Sergeant Seufert, but he never said if it had been enemy or "friendly" fire. The level of exhaustion I was feeling more and more frequently was making it a real effort to stay awake even in classes as graphic and relevant as the one on mines.

    Sergeant Doyle gave us post privileges at seven that evening, so I used the free time for errands. I got a haircut, my first in three weeks, and then did some more laundry. I had decided to save money by doing all of my own laundry, so this time I did the fatigues. The cost of having them done was 85 cents a pair. I figured I would just keep doing my own unless someone complained about all the wrinkles, and I noticed that many of the other guys had made the same decision. I also wrote to Bev that night and told her I was glad she loved the U and felt so at home in Minnesota now. Many places around campus had special meaning for me as well, and I planned to study there again as soon as I got out. She had mentioned being somewhat disenchanted with the educational establishment so I responded that when I was student teaching, the attitudes of many of the career teachers I talked with disappointed me. They seemed very set in their ways and skeptical of innovation of any sort. Some of them, and not necessarily the oldest ones, just seemed to be marking time until they could retire. The uncertainty of the draft and my love of studying literature were the major reasons I went on to grad school, but the attitudes that often prevailed in the teachers' lounges of the schools where I worked was another.

    On Wednesday the 4th we moved on to the M79 grenade launcher. This was a remarkable weapon first used by US forces in Vietnam that looked much like a sawed-off shotgun with an unusually wide barrel diameter, and I was again taken back to the martial toys of my childhood because it reminded me of a ping-pong ball rifle. That similarity was reinforced by its distinctive sound when fired, which was more of a loud "bloop" that a sharp crack. In fact, because of that sound it was often called "the blooper." But the most striking thing about the M79 was that it was a 40 mm weapon with a recoil reduction system that allowed it to be fired from the shoulder. The most common round was the gold one which was a small, high-explosive grenade that, for safety reasons, did not become armed until it had travelled thirty meters. There were several other rounds as well, including illumination and smoke, and even a buckshot round that essentially converted it into the sawed-off shotgun it resembled. I remembered Seufert had said the M79 had been his favorite weapon in Vietnam. After the class we fired them on the range and the recoil was remarkably soft. The unexpectedly moderate report of the weapon being fired was soon followed by the roar of the exploding round.

That afternoon we covered the M72 Light Antitank Weapon (LAW), which was the Vietnam War successor to the old World War II bazooka. This was another tribute to the ingenuity of the weapons industry: an armor-piercing rocket in a single-use fiberglass tube with a total weight of about five pounds. The rocket was unguided, but could pierce any armored vehicle in the world, killing the crew with a lethal blast of hot gas and shrapnel. There was no recoil because the rocket had its own motor and the tube was open on both ends. The essential precaution before firing was to make certain no one was behind you in the back-blast area. We each fired two and, because the M72 is held on the shoulder, the explosion inside the tube was right next to your ear. The instructors did not give us earplugs, maybe based on the idea that we would not be wearing them in combat, and the blasts gave me a terrific pain in my right ear. It felt better in about a half hour and my hearing finally returned to normal. The communists did not have much armor, especially in the southern part of the RVN, but the instructor said the LAW was useful for other purposes as well, especially for blowing snipers out of trees. We finished the day with hand-to-hand combat, a combination of judo and karate that began where we had left off at the end of BCT.

Thursday the 5th was our detail day and I was assigned to weapons cleaning. With all of the firing going on out on the ranges cleaning up the various weapons was a constant chore. Even though the work was easy and out of the sun, it was also boring, and as I serviced one weapon after another I started to reflect on how much time we wasted in the Army. Here was a bunch of men with the ability to make contributions to society, and yet we were sitting there doing mindless rote work instead. The really pathetic thing was that we were glad of it because it was an easy day compared to most of our training. But the worst part was that we were being compelled to go into combat against an "enemy" that had never attacked or even threatened our country. It was not that I thought that college guys like us were too important to waste as cannon fodder. We were no better than any of the other soldiers. I simply did not believe that anybody should be required to fight against their will when our country had not been attacked. That was an abuse of the power of the draft law, a draconian measure under even the best of circumstances.

I wrote to Bev that evening with these thoughts still on my mind, but the first thing I did was to assure her that our relationship and love had not affected my decision to accept being drafted. I had been extremely bitter and conflicted about it the previous summer, but once I had made the decision to go if called up I felt somewhat better about the situation, and that was before the two of us had met. Of course, at that time I had not thought I would end up in the infantry, but the only way to assure an MOS of your choice was to sign up as Regular Army for at least three years, and even then the Army could never guarantee that you would not have to fight anyway if you ended up in Vietnam. I held onto the letter and continued it two days later, assuring Bev that I was not really in such a funk all the time. She had also asked if I could request a transfer out of the infantry, and I said the problem there was that most of the guys in infantry wanted to get out of it so there was really no hope of such a request being granted. I reminded her of Yossarian's futile attempts to be reassigned in *Catch-22*, and to illustrate the absurdity of the Army mentality also told her about the atheist I had been with in Basic who ended up being assigned to chaplain's assistant school.

We were given post privileges on Thursday evening so I went to the movies and saw a World War II drama with Lee Marvin: *Hell in the Pacific*. I had thought that it would deal with the moral dilemma presented by a situation where an enemy soldier you were supposed to kill was also a man you had come to know and grudgingly respect, but Lee Marvin played his part too much for laughs and in the end the director could not decide if he was making a drama or a comedy. The next two features were to be *The Thomas Crown Affair* and *Goodbye, Columbus*. I especially wanted to see the second one because I admired Philip Roth's work.

On Friday the 6th we reviewed communications and first aid. Staying awake through a full day of classroom work was a real exercise in self-discipline. On Saturday we went out to one of the ranges for a weapons demonstration and watched some instructors wipe out a bunch of targets. If Charlie would just cooperate by standing there out in the open he would not stand a chance against American firepower. We got off at 1:00 p.m. so I called home and talked with Mom. She said that Bev had left for camp that morning. I was sorry I had not called her the night before but somehow I thought she was not leaving until Sunday. I already had the camp's phone number and she was going to send me some times when she expected to be able to take a call. I wrote to Bev again about the uncertainty of being able to visit her at Bear Creek with a three-day pass, which would probably be over the Independence Day weekend, one when she was scheduled to be with campers. It did not look as though that was going to work. She had asked again about my leave after AIT and I told her I would love to spend every day of it with her. That could be partially in Miami, especially if her folks were back by then, and the rest in Minneapolis. I said we might be there for the State Fair. After finishing the letter I read *Newsweek*, some *Tess*, and a few poems by Donne.

We were given overnight passes for Saturday night but I had no desire to go into Anniston so I went to see *The Thomas Crown Affair* with my bunkmate, Archie McClanahan from Daytona, Florida. Archie was an easy-going guy who had been working for the railroad when he was drafted. The glider scene with the song "Windmills of Your Mind" was memorable, especially since Steve McQueen just might have been the coolest guy in the world at that time. After the show, Archie went to wash his clothes so I wandered over to a beer joint called Sam's Place. Every company area had a no-frills EM club like Sam's. The beer was the main attraction but there were also snacks, pizza, and a jukebox. I talked with a guy from St. Paul and another one from North Carolina named Jerry. Some of those southern guys really knew how to tell a story, and it reminded me of the American tall-tale tradition and Mark Twain. I especially enjoyed listening to the men from North Carolina, because they sounded like Andy Griffith or Huckleberry Hound. That has to be the world's friendliest-sounding accent. Jerry told us about how he had put a snake in his sister's parakeet's cage and scared it to death and, despite the demise of the hapless bird and the trauma suffered by his bereaved sister, the way he told it just about made me die from laughing. If you ever need someone to deliver bad news in the least upsetting way possible, find a Tar Heel. Once again, alcohol and buddies had proven to be the surest antidote to the GI blues.

***

Bev wrote on Friday the 6th while enjoying a "beautemous" morning, and also exulting in the freedom of having all her work for the quarter completed. She had spent most of Wednesday grading exams with John McNally for English 166. Mom picked her up that evening for a fun night at the house. After a fried chicken supper Bev and Jane played "Concentration" until Mary got home from babysitting. Then the three of them played "I Guess." She said my two sisters were such screams, especially when they talked about school and the people they liked or disliked.

On Thursday morning she took the final for Marty's American novel class, and she enclosed a copy. It included three essay questions with allotted times of fifty, forty, and twenty minutes. Marty's guidelines included dealing with the specific texts and avoiding generalities, and he also cautioned his students not to paraphrase their papers in any of their answers. After that, she worked with McNally until mid-afternoon on grades for his course, and the highlight of the day was that John gave her a corned beef sandwich. Then she took Joe Kwait's final from 4:00 until 6:20 p.m. She described the test, and it was challenging. After that marathon session her back ached from sitting so long in the wooden classroom chairs. That evening Bev, Joyce, and Joyce's cousin ate supper at the Best Steak House in Stadium Village, then walked down to the Erie Plaza Apartments where they were thinking about renting for the following year, and finally finished up with ice cream at Bridgeman's. Joyce was excited about going home to see Doug, the fellow she had been dating for a long time at home. He was now in medical school in North Carolina and with all the doctors in Joyce's family that was bound to be a point in his favor. She and Ed were still good friends but the bad news there was that Ed had failed his prelims and was feeling quite discouraged about it all. Bev wrapped up the day by packing all of her books into boxes.

On Friday Bev completed the task of packing up everything she owned. Jennifer would use and look after the stereo and records over the summer, so that helped a bit. By this time Bev and I were used to the uncertainties of the Army's postal system and she said that my last four letters had all come the day before. At least they got there before she left for camp. She was working on accepting the likelihood I would end up in Nam, and also said that reading Mailer had given her a better understanding of the need some men have to prove themselves in war. Now she was reading *Catch-22* and she planned on taking that and a bunch of other books with her to camp. She hoped to be able to read some each day. She was looking forward to Bear Creek because the life there was so completely different from grad school in the city. They had not even had a radio the previous summer. She enjoyed the break from the pressure of school and also loved concentrating on relating to people of different ages. She had received a letter her mom sent from Germany and it was "a scream" because she always wrote a three- or four-page letter completely in sentence fragments, rather like an extremely long telegram. She had gotten in a little sightseeing and now that baby Becky had arrived she was coming home on Sunday. This three-week trip was the longest that her folks had been apart since they were married, and Bev could tell how much they missed each other. Her dad had been eating out some and also heating up food that her mom had prepared and frozen for him. They had also been sending tapes back and forth.

Her mom was coming up to Minneapolis in October. Bev thought it was good for her mother to get out of her familiar setting sometimes because it gave her a new outlook and made her less shy. She was eager for her folks to have the chance to meet me, but that seemed unlikely now because of their Alaska trip. Her dad had suggested that I come to Miami for the last part of my leave, but Bev knew I would want to say my goodbyes to my family at the end of the leave so it seemed I would not be meeting her folks until I got back from overseas.

Moving on to news around campus, she said that Bob Moore was the new chair of English and Gordon O'Brien the director of graduate studies. The department was in physical disarray because it was being moved from its beautiful home on the mall in Vincent Hall over to space in Main Engineering. Vincent was being given to Math, a unit that was not even in our college. The demoralizing situation was made worse by the fact that the remodeling of the space in Main Engineering had not yet been completed. She closed because she was "approaching the incomprehensible" and enclosed a copy of *The Waking* by Theodore Roethke.

On Saturday the 7th Bev and Joyce had breakfast at the Plantation Pancake House on Hennepin Avenue, and then Joyce drove Bev out to the airport. She had a one-hour flight to St. Louis and then an Ozark flight to Paducah, Kentucky, on a prop plane. The engine noise was distracting and there were lots of kids on the plane, but Bev talked with the lady next to her who was on her way to Clarksville, Tennessee. Her friend Patty, another counselor who was also there for her second summer, picked her up at the airport and drove back to camp slowly to give them more time to talk and get caught up. Bear Creek Girl Scout Camp is on Kentucky Lake, which was formed by a TVA dam on the Tennessee River. Paducah was the nearest major town but the smaller Benton was closer and her letters from camp were always postmarked from there.

She wrote on Sunday that they had swept out all the buildings for the first time, including removing the old rats' nests, washed dishes, and pitched some tents. She said her colleagues on the staff were a riot and she was sure they would enjoy working together. Everyone already had a nickname and Nellie, the director, loved to sing so they had a sing-fest that evening. Her cabin-mates were Freckles, Cricket, Spanky, and Mona, who had such a distinctive name that no alternate moniker was needed in her case. As usual, Bev's nickname was "Beaver." She always loved birds and there were many more there than in the city. Her favorite thing was swimming in the clean lake, especially diving down to the refreshingly cold bottom. As she wrote she was enjoying the crickets and many stars of the woodland night. She closed with love, enjoying the song of a whippoorwill and the insect chorus.

Bev wrote again on Monday the 9th, but with a "?" by the date to indicate that she was already losing track of time out in the wilderness. She was tired from all the physical work and a bit out of sorts because of the lack of privacy. She had trouble sleeping the night before and was awoken at 6:00 a.m. by "the music of hound dogs in the distance." The time before breakfast had been the best part of the day because she was alone except for two laconic cooks and another quiet girl. After breakfast they cleaned the lodge and the "library," which was so dirty that after two sweepings it still looked as if it had not yet been cleaned. It sounded like she had not expected the week's worth of preparation to involve so much cleaning. In the afternoon they moved their belongings to permanent units, planned a game for that night, pitched a huge wall tent, and launched a twenty-one-foot Lightning sailboat. There would be more chores later that day, and she was not in the happiest frame of mind because of physical fatigue and a minor misunderstanding with Patty, who was very quiet and sensitive.

She commented again on how dramatic the switch was from the university to the camp. The two biggest changes were the many physical tasks and the need to relate to people from backgrounds other than academia. For now the counselors and other staff members had the place to themselves, but the biggest change would come on Monday with the arrival of the first group of energetic campers. Bev's unit was the Lion's Den and she would be in charge of eight counselors-in-training (CITs) and about eight Senior Scouts, girls at an age where they were "ingenious, but lazy and crazy." She said the situation was comical in a way, but also so frustrating that she wanted to cry. Since she had been there before and loved the outdoors, I attributed her down mood mainly to physical fatigue and the misunderstanding with Patty. Then

Spartan quarters were a rustic cabin with flimsy screens, a squeaky front door, and an outhouse for a bathroom. Her clothes box was an old orange crate. The cabins and tents had no electricity so she was trying to write in the dim light of a flashlight with weak batteries while the mosquitoes bothered her. She said the drastic change in her environment helped her to understand my feelings when I arrived at Fort Campbell in March. Her need for emotional support caused her to feel the pain of our separation more acutely, but a bit of quiet time to communicate in writing always helped. She loved nature and people so she closed by assuring me, and herself, that she knew things at camp would begin to fall into place for her soon. She enclosed a sketch of her cabin and the central area of the camp, along with a brief poem by Siegfried Sassoon.

On Tuesday the 10th Bev and five others began a lifesaving course. They hoped that their strength would improve with daily swimming. That night they sang while washing the dishes and then some went out for a walk while others, including Bev, stayed in camp and sang folk songs such as "Both Sides Now" and "Scarborough Fair." Mona was trying to provide accompaniment on her guitar. She said that she missed being able to listen to her favorite records but she also loved group singing in camp, especially singing harmonies in rounds by a campfire. That was something I had never experienced. Two of her favorites were "Barges" and "Music Shall Live" in German. She was still feeling out of place because she was a few years older than most of the other girls, but even more so because many of them were rowdy and a few of them swore all the time. I wondered what she meant by "rowdy," and imagined "loud" and "crude." Even so, she thought she would join some of them for cards that night because she had felt lonely by herself the previous evening. She asked if I ever felt alone in a crowd, and I knew she already had the answer to that one.

She asked about what I was up to that week, and wondered if I wore a .45 now. She did not like guns at all. The camp had a rifle range and girls from the seventh grade on up could take instruction that included shooting, but she steered clear of it. She wondered what I was reading and said that she was going to bring her books to the staff house where there were electric lights so that others could use them as well. She was excited about us going to Florida together in August, but agreed that the idea of me coming up to camp on a three-day pass over Independence Day did not make much sense. I had sent home our First Platoon picture from BCT before she left and she had a hard time picking me out, which was not surprising since we all had the same clothing and haircuts.

She said she was sorry I had to accept the Army way of life in order to survive in combat, "but we are all living to survive in our individual ways just as the main characters did in each of the novels we read for Roth." She was right, of course, because challenges and difficult situations were what make life interesting. Writers delved into such dilemmas because that was when people became interesting and revealed their true character, sometimes finding things out about themselves that they had never suspected. That was why the two of us not only loved literature but were obsessed by it. Since all art is an attempt to answer the question of what it means to be human, each encounter with a great work teaches a person a bit more about themselves. I loved how she related the wisdom gained from her studies to what the two of us were experiencing in our relationship and separation. Being apart so soon after we met was not a situation I would ever have dreamed of choosing, but you play the cards you are dealt and hope for a better break on the draw.

On Wednesday evening she played Frisbee with some of her friends in "chigger field" with a champion model that someone had brought. They had a huge bonfire and then she walked down to the shore of the lake and, alone again with the stars and crickets, looked to the south and thought of me. She said she used to imagine that the crickets' singing was the sound of the stars twinkling—a charming thought. Then she went back to the staff house for some card games and more folk songs. On Thursday she received a letter from me with a map I had taken from an issue of *Mad* that gave a facetious view of the hawks' opinion that Vietnam was an integral part of the US. I asked her to "display it proudly" but all that her gang ever said about it was "where did you get that?" She was looking forward to Sunday when the first campers would arrive and I would call. She said calling about 1:00 p.m. would be best because chaos would descend about 2:00 p.m. with the arrival of the younger girls. The phone was in the kitchen, a very public place, and it sounded as though non-emergency personal calls were discouraged, so we would not be able to talk very long, but we still intended to try to connect about once a week.

On Thursday night the entire staff of about thirty camped out in The Land Between the Lakes, an area of federal land between Kentucky Lake and Lake Barkley, both created by TVA dams on the Tennessee and Cumberland Rivers. They had fun canoeing, swimming, and cooking shish kabobs. That night a huge thunderstorm nearly swamped their tents, and when they returned to Bear Creek they found that the roads and paths had been washed out. The sailboat had a big hole in the bow, but the caretaker had already mended that. Part of the dock had blown away but that was recoverable as well. The good part was that all this happened before the campers appeared.

News from the U had arrived in the form of her grade cards and she was disappointed because Marty had given her a C and Kwait a B+. She said that she really did not care because she had learned something in both and especially enjoyed the Whitman/Twain class, but I knew she was disappointed. Even though we both tried not to define ourselves so heavily by the grades we received, that tendency was another thing we had in common. I could not imagine that the C was a fair grade after all the work she had put in, but both of us had bounced back from academic disappointments before. She had also received a letter from the ebullient Sister Paul Mary, the only nun she had ever known. Bev said that they certainly had their share of storytellers at camp, with one from Murray State named Ada Sue topping the list. She claimed to know nothing about everything and told tall tales in a real Southern accent, which was actually the predominant dialect at Camp Bear Creek. Bev was still reading *Catch-22* and seemed to be less entertained than taken aback by Heller's superb portrait of military idiocy and the changes that sane men undergo in order to survive in that surreal and sometimes deadly environment.

***

Down at Fort Mac the weather continued to be hot and humid, a typical Deep South summer, although it would have been even worse if we had not been up in the hills. Like many of the guys, I still felt tired and not completely well so I spent Sunday, June 8, resting. That evening I went up to the theater to see *Goodbye, Columbus* and thought it was great. I loved the way Richard Benjamin and Ali MacGraw portrayed Neil and Brenda's joys and sorrows along the bittersweet journey of their doomed love affair, but I was also fascinated by the depiction of a certain segment of American Jewish culture. That was a world I only knew about from books but I felt that Roth, Bellow, and Mailer had at least given me an introduction to it. The movies at Fort Mac were always especially enjoyable because they were shown in a real theater with a good projection system.

Our training week began on Monday the 9th with a test on everything we had covered so far, including spelling our name using the phonetic alphabet. I ended up getting a perfect score, which surprised me given all the times in class when I had felt semi-comatose. The guys who did not make any mistakes were supposed to be excused from a nine-mile hike, but I figured I would believe that when it actually happened.

On Tuesday I started to feel as though I was getting something worse than a cold, but at least class was interesting—that was the day we began our instruction on the M29 81 mm mortar. This weapon was used to provide firepower in the area between the ranges of small arms and artillery. It actually had a maximum range of about three miles with the most commonly used high explosive round but was most often used against targets much closer than that. It had a total weight of a little less than 100 pounds and broke down into three components that could be carried by individual soldiers: the barrel, the bipod, and the base-plate. The all-important sight was a smaller part that attached to the unit connecting the barrel and the bipod. The weapons platoon was the fifth one of the infantry company, providing fire support to the four rifle platoons. Our platoon would consist of an anti-tank section and an 81 mm mortar section, which included forward observer teams, a fire direction center, and three mortar squads. Each squad included a squad leader, gunner, assistant gunner, ammo bearer, and a soldier who would function where needed as a driver, radio operator, or an additional ammo bearer. One intriguing thing we noticed during the lecture presentations was that the Army's symbol for the mortar was identical to the Mars male gender symbol.

The operation of the weapon was based on three variables: the deflection and elevation of the barrel, and the number of charges on the round. The round did not have a cartridge but instead came with nine pouches of high explosive attached to the narrow area between the main body and the tail fins. Based upon the distance to the target, the crew could quickly strip off pouches to reach the correct charge number. The mortars were muzzle-loaders and when the round was dropped into the barrel a primer on its base struck a firing pin in the bottom of the barrel, igniting the charges. The procedure was to release the round, crouch down, and cover your ears with your hands. There were several types of rounds but the most common was a high-explosive bomb with a bursting area of 25 by 20 meters. It was a devastating weapon used extensively by both sides in the war. For Charlie, the mortar and Soviet bazooka-type or bipod-mounted rockets were also the favorite weapons for lobbing harassing fire into US bases, usually after dark.

We were told that the accuracy was extremely high if the forward observers were able to get into positions to radio back accurate information on the enemy positions. Even without forward observers in place an experienced crew could often quickly sight the weapon onto a target area by firing rounds and making adjustments until they were on target.

For the rest of the week in class we were bombarded with information on the mortar and the various types of rounds. Much of the instruction focused on sighting the weapon and making adjustments based upon the location of the previous rounds. It reminded me of a college math or science class, and I soon realized that we could only absorb a fraction of what they were trying to teach us. Clearly, firing a mortar accurately was a skill that could only be learned well in the field under the tutelage of experienced crewmen, but that was also true to a large extent of everything we were taught in BCT and AIT.

The most common high explosive round weighed over nine pounds, and we already knew that the rate of firing could be rapid. Putting those two facts together gave me some reassurance that the 11Cs really would be spending much of their time toward the rear because there was no way a crew could carry sufficient ammo for an effective barrage very far on foot. That was cold comfort, but any port in a storm. Other than the high explosive (HE), the illumination, incendiary, and smoke rounds were used most frequently and all three relied on white phosphorous as their primary component. Even though the incendiary rounds, like napalm, were not considered antipersonnel weapons, many Vietnamese, soldiers and civilians, suffered horribly from exposure to burning "Willie Peter," just as they did from napalm. The burning particles stick to the skin and often continue to burn their way deeply into the body. If the victims did not die from the burns they might suffer an equally cruel fate by succumbing later to organ failure from phosphorous poisoning caused by the chemical being ingested into their body at the burn sites.

On the morning of Saturday the 14th we had our Brigade Organization Day celebrating the third anniversary of the unit. It was a welcome break from the usual routine, especially after the week of intensive training, but not as exciting as the field day at Campbell. The company commanders had a pie-eating contest, but our Captain McMahon proved to be a light eater. Our First Sergeant put us back into the running by winning the watermelon-eating contest. The weather was oppressive and the main unofficial event was trying to spend as much time as possible standing or sitting in the shade.

There were fifteen events in all and our company came in second out of ten. Events like this were supposed to be good for morale and, even though they may have helped a bit, that was pretty much a hopeless task. It was hard to foster much camaraderie when we knew we were only going to be together for less than two more months, and it was impossible to raise the spirits very high of draftees who were preparing for fighting in Vietnam.

We got off at noon so I ate lunch and then went back to the barracks and slept until 3:00 p.m. My sinuses were stuffed but I still felt as though I was on the road to recovery. I ate supper at the drive-in and then went up to Hilltop where I ran into Larry Anderson from Basic. There were five of us from the old First Platoon at Campbell down at Fort Mac. We played some ping pong and then headed over to the EM Club for some drinking with three other guys that Larry knew. Larry and I were walking ahead and shooting the breeze when we looked back and saw the other guys talking with two black guys and a girl in a car. They called us back and gave all five of us a ride over to the club. It might have seemed a bit foolish for us to accept a ride from total strangers but we had them well outnumbered, and besides, we were trained killers now, so what was the risk? After we got into the club one of Larry's friends said that he had told the folks in the car he would buy some beer for them, but the club had no off-sale and we never saw them again. We sat around drinking beer for a couple of hours and the joint actually had live music, but the band was playing extremely loud discothèque-style numbers and we could hardly hear each other even though we were shouting. We left about 10:00 p.m. and when I got back to the barracks I talked with some of the guys for awhile. The mess hall was right next door and about 10:15 p.m. the MPs caught someone breaking into it. He must have really been drunk to take that kind of risk for some cold Army chow. As soon as I lay down on my bunk I felt exhausted, so I turned in about ten-thirty.

On Sunday the 15th my plan was to wash my clothes and take it easy. Some of the guys got pretty crazy when they drank, especially the ones who had not built up as much of a tolerance for booze as older ones like me, and the results were often hilarious. That morning when one guy looked into the shaving mirror he found that he had "shit hole" written on his forehead with an arrow pointing down his cheek to his mouth.

On days off my thoughts always turned toward home and Bev. I was sure most of the men felt the same way. The night before Larry had told me that his wife was supposed to have their baby in two weeks, but he probably would not be able to go home for it unless the doctor said there was some sort of danger. And then, of course, he would be missing out on the first year of their child's life. That was rough.

One of our NCOs had gone home for the weekend to get married. I knew that was not uncommon and such marriages were always a staple in movies about World War II as well. Every couple had to follow where their love led them, but Bev and I never considered tying the knot before I was a civilian again. It seemed to me that when the guy was shipping out for a combat zone such a ceremony would evoke as much sorrow as joy. I called Bear Creek about 1:00 p.m. but there was no answer so I tried again at 9:30 but there were no lines open then—maybe because it was Fathers' Day. I had sent Dad a card. The PXs were always well-stocked with things like that as a way to help us stay in touch with our families and loved ones, and I always tried to remember birthdays and holidays.

***

Bev wrote on Monday the 16th in the midst of wildly mixed emotions about the situation at Bear Creek. She was asking herself why she took a twenty-four-hour job with poor food, poor pay, poor organization, and terribly frustrated counselors. That was only the first full day of Session I and several counselors and the camp director had already "broken." I assumed that meant breaking down in tears because of overwrought emotions due to severe frustration. I had never gone to an overnight summer camp and I knew it could be difficult for some homesick kids but it had never occurred to me that it could be so traumatic for the counselors. She said she knew the reason she was there was that she loved kids of all ages, but things were in a muddle and she was exhausted from a grueling lifesaving class. By Wednesday afternoon she needed to be able to swim eighteen laps to succeed in the course. She expected to be in a daze the whole time she was there because the normal situation appeared to be one crisis after another.

She went on to describe the good things as well such as talking with the girls in her unit, especially the CITs who would be entering twelfth grade in the fall. They loved discussing books and ideas and were all very sensitive to people and the miracle of living. The girls were having fun singing, doing camp chores, laughing, swimming, and making surprises. Her eight CITs built drainage ditches, a shower, and a table lashed together with twine. She was feeling isolated from the outside world, although she had received a postcard from her mom saying she had arrived home safely from Germany.

She enjoyed the hike to Fossil Point with her girls on Wednesday the 18th. They looked for crinoid stems and had time for long conversations. Some of them were real thinkers but others still accepted ideas they had been taught without much personal questioning. She was impressed by how much all of them had read. Most of them had tried their skill on the rifle range but Bev still had no plans to do that because it frightened her. Back at camp they went swimming after supper and she took advantage of the all-girl environment by skinny dipping. I loved the mental picture that conjured up. Later they packed their food and gear for an overnight trip the next day across the lake to Pisgah Bay for water skiing. Patty was often depressed but she was Bev's best friend at camp and they really understood each others' feelings. In her letter of that day she enclosed a postcard of Tony the Tiger at camp and a poem by Hopkins, "God's Grandeur."

★★★

Back at Fort McClellan on Monday the 16th we practiced more with the mortars, had an armored personnel carrier (APC) demonstration, and went back over quick-kill techniques. The APC weighed eleven tons unloaded and twelve tons combat loaded. It was no tank and its main purpose was to transport troops in a battlefield situation, but its armor was thick enough to deflect fire from rifles and light machine guns. A .50 caliber round could penetrate it. The usual weaponry for the vehicle was a .30 caliber and a .50 caliber machine gun, both mounted. It had a top speed of about forty miles per hour but, unless you were on very smooth and soft soil, anything even approaching that would just about dislodge all the fillings of the troops inside. We rode in one on pavement and the effect was jarring to say the least. For the quick-kill practice my boyhood shoot-from-the-hip BB gun technique served me well and I hit most of the targets. I did not do very well with my M16 when we moved up to that weapon, however, but I felt so out of it that I really did not care.

Some of the other guys had also been complaining about feeling sick for the last week or so. One of the few advantages of my weakened condition was that I could now sleep through almost anything. Guys talking in the barracks and playing their radios did not bother me in the least. The slow but steady onset of exhaustion from weeks of insufficient rest, along with a rigorous physical schedule had begun back in BCT. Seufert used to say he knew that some of us were asleep in class with our eyes wide open, and Larry Anderson swore that I was sleeping once while standing up on KP. It seemed as though the routine would not be getting any easier, because we were scheduled for a five-day bivouac the next week, although we would be coming back and sleeping in the barracks every night. The last two weeks of training was to be intensive RVN training, including sleeping out in the woods for twelve nights.

On Tuesday we had more mortar practice to prepare for the gunner's exam on Thursday. If you flunked, or "boloed" in military parlance, they would give it to you once or twice again. If you still failed you would be assigned the MOS of 11B, rifleman, rather than 11C, mortar man. We had been reminded numerous times that even if you scored a bolo on everything they would still graduate you from AIT. You could not flunk out of the Army, because if that had been the case few of the men I was with would have made the effort to pass.

On Wednesday the 18th I was serving in the chow line out on the mortar range when I almost passed out, something that had not happened to me in years. Sergeant Doyle had me go on sick call and I was admitted to the hospital that night. After running some tests that included blood work and feeling for a swollen spleen, the doctors diagnosed me with mononucleosis and told me I would be sent home for a three-week convalescent leave that would not be counted against my regular leave time. It was a measure of how thoroughly I had been indoctrinated that my first thought was that I would be missing the gunner's exam the next day and maybe end up as a rifleman, but I soon got used to the easy life in the Army hospital and the prospect of three weeks at home. I called my folks to tell them, but I did not have Bev's phone number; I had not realized I would be admitted to the hospital and so had brought nothing with me from the barracks. I finally got some stationary from the Red Cross folks and wrote to her on Monday the 23rd. Sergeant Doyle had come up the same morning to say so long and he also brought my mail, including the first ones from Bev at camp. I explained my situation to her and said that my leave before going overseas would now be in September rather than August since when I returned to Fort Mac I would be resuming my training with another company that was at the point where I had left off. We would have to talk about how that might change our plans for visiting Coral Gables, especially if she was already back in Minneapolis by that time.

Mono seemed like the ideal disease for a reluctant soldier—I did not have any physical discomfort other than persistent fatigue. As soon as a patient with mono tries to exert themselves they get tired out, so no training. I loved the life in the hospital and, even though I was eager to get home, was also sorry to be there for only five days. I got up about 5:45 a.m. and went to bed about 8:30 or 9:00 p.m., with two or three naps in between. The food was good and they provided all you wanted, including juice and ice cream during the day. The only treatment was to eat well and get plenty of rest, and our only work was to change the linen on our beds in the morning. There was a TV in the room and magazines to read so, even though I missed my books, I really could not complain. We had a five-bed room, but the last day I was there was the only one when they were all occupied. There was a sergeant from North Carolina with pleurisy who was also going home on leave, but the other guys just had colds and sore throats. They probably envied the two of us with more serious conditions. One of the nurses said to be sure to rest and not get a summer job like some patients had done on their leaves. I just laughed because that was the furthest thing from my mind. The last time the doctor examined me before I was discharged I asked him to take a look at my right ear, the one that hurt so badly after firing the LAW. He said that a blood vessel had been ruptured by the shockwave of the explosion, but he added that it was healing and that there was no treatment for such an injury.

    On Monday afternoon it was 1:30 p.m. by the time I left the hospital due to all the paperwork. I bought a plane ticket and then went to the barracks to pack up all my gear and turn it in at the supply room. There was more red tape there, but I finally got on the bus to the Anniston airport about 4:45, took a Southern flight to Atlanta, and then a Delta flight to Chicago. I read *Tess of the d'Urbervilles* part of the time and spent the rest watching the beautiful cloud formations. I never have gotten blasé about the miracle of flying but back then I was especially fascinated by it because of how new it was to me. The sun set just before we got to Chicago and I was delayed for two hours at O'Hare, so I read more and tried to rest a bit. I saw a group of guys there who had just been drafted, and I did not envy them because of their Basic Training coming up. I figured the one advantage they had over me was that they would be arriving in Nam two or three months later. The war was beginning to wind down ever so slowly and so any delay in getting there meant an improved chance of surviving. We finally took off at 12:20 a.m. and arrived in Minneapolis at 1:15. The lights of my hometown from above were a beautiful sight. Dad was there to meet me and we finally got home around 2:00. I enjoyed the familiar sights along the drive home, especially Seven Corners and the U.

On Tuesday the 24th I rested, watched TV, and strung my guitar. I was reusing the strings I had taken off before I left and they were too stretched out for me to get them into tune. Uncle Del died that day, just a couple of months after Aunt Tres. I was a pallbearer at his funeral on Wednesday, a quiet affair on a rainy day with few attending. I had some memories of visiting them at their apartment in the city and then later at a place they had up in North Branch. It was a tiny house with a big garden in the back and to city kids like us it was a small farm. He had been ill for a long time and so, as they often say, his passing was a blessing, but it was still a sorrow for Granny to lose another of her siblings.

It was an odd feeling to be back in the old familiar places and it seemed as though I had blinked and time had jumped forward three months. I looked for subtle changes and there were few other than John's new bike and new lights in our alley. I wrote to Bev to update her on everything and also to make sure she knew she could call whenever the time worked for her at camp. Now that I was in a place where she could call me our chances of connecting were much improved.

I told her what I could about my mysterious ailment. I was to report back to Fort Mac on July 14 and if I still had mono they would put me back in the hospital. When my friend Joe Hagan had mono he was in the U Hospital for about six weeks, but there was no way to tell how long mine would last. I still had seven weeks remaining of the ten-week AIT course so that meant I should get my leave sometime in September. I thought Bev would be back in Minneapolis by then so I asked her to think about what that meant for visiting Florida. When I was looking at my brother John's calendar to try to figure out the dates I noticed that for Sunday the 29th, a night with a full moon, he had written "I turn into a wear-wlof." It was fun being around the kids again, especially since they were now home on summer vacation. I closed by encouraging Bev to continue being an inspiration to the girls at camp, because I knew that being around the scouts was what she enjoyed the most.

★★★

Bev wrote on the 24th, still unaware that I was home on leave, to update me on things at camp. She was part of a group that was barbecuing a sheep over an open fire for the entire camp, and it was quite a project. First they had to cut a long pole and two V-shaped pieces to make the spit. Next they salted the mutton and wired it to the spit. Then they had to take shifts watching it roast and turning it occasionally. Her shift had started at 5:00 a.m. that day. A woman named Jane had named the late sheep Emmet, so now everyone was going around asking how Emmet was doing. They were afraid some of the little girls would not eat mutton so the counselors tried to tell them it was a pig, but Bev had doubts about how many of them were really fooled.

One of her friends there had a fellow who had just been classified 1-A so the two of them appreciated being able to share their concerns. In other news, they were celebrating the camp's twenty-fifth anniversary, and so each person was making a present for someone else. Bev painted a rock to look like the face of a sleeping bear for her gift. The counselors were always trying to think up new and interesting activities for the scouts so now they were trying to get permission to take some campers to a ceramic shop. Bev had decided to face up to her fear of guns by shooting five targets at the rifle range, but said that was most likely the end of that activity for her.

She wrote again on Thursday the 26th after receiving my letter about having mono and asked if I might be able to stop in Nashville on my way home on leave. Situations like this came up due to delays in communication by mail because when I had written to her I had not known when I would be leaving Fort Mac and so she assumed I was still down there. The days at camp continued to be a disconcerting ride on an emotional rollercoaster. She had skipped supper the previous night and had a long conversation with Mona about their men, student power, campus riots, and sex education. After that things went downhill fast as some of the counselors again expressed their frustration at disorganization and poor attitudes at camp that session. Some, including Bev, were reduced to tears. It was times like that when one of us was hurting that it was hardest to be apart, and, of course, she was also upset about not being able to be there while I was sick even though I had assured her that I was not in any sort of danger or even physical distress. After the discontentment had been aired, several of them slept out on the point enjoying the moon, stars, and night breezes. It seemed as though the beauties of nature and the youthful enthusiasm of the scouts always helped to restore her spirits before long.

She told me more about the good things at Bear Creek, especially her friends Patty and Sandy and the eight CITs in the unit. Two were from Houston, Texas, one from Missouri, and the other five from Kentucky.

Bev felt they would all make good counselors and, for better or for worse, one thing they were learning was the reality of personality clashes by observing the problems of the senior staff. Bev felt caught in the middle of those situations because her guiding principle was that camp was for the campers to learn and have fun, whereas other staff members attached more importance to rules and sticking to schedules. She felt that the second session would be much better because by then the staff would have made most of the adjustments and compromises needed for them to function as an effective group.

She went on to describe various possibilities for spending my leave between Florida and Minnesota. She was finished with camp on July 25, and thought she would return to Minnesota from Florida by the middle of August. When I got home we could fly to Miami to visit and then return to Minneapolis for the rest of my leave. That all sounded good to me, but, as always during my Army days, the future was uncertain. It is hard to make many plans when you are in the military since most aspects of your life are beyond your control. The situation reminded me of childhood when most of one's life is governed by the decisions of adults, but the crucial difference was that I loved and trusted my parents whereas I was well aware that the military authorities did not have my best interests at heart. We just forged ahead day by day and relied upon love and hope to sustain us. Few letters passed between us without yet another exchange of those thoughts and promises. As was Bev's frequent custom she enclosed a poem. This time one by Hopkins expressing gratitude for the wonders of nature: "Pied Beauty."

In the June 27 issue, *Life* magazine printed photographs of the 242 US troops killed in a single week in Vietnam. It was an average weekly KIA total for mid-1969 and during the 1968 Tet Offensive over twice as many had died within seven days, but this time was different because now millions of readers turned page after page while staring into the eyes of brave young men in their prime who were now dead long before their time. Many of these readers began to question whether anything was being gained that could justify such a tragic price. This stark, graphic, and yet apolitical display of the true cost of the war appearing in such a widely read publication contributed to a more aggressive questioning of our goals by the general public, and our national leaders, even the rabidly law-and-order jackass Spiro Agnew could no longer dismiss this increasingly middle-American discontent as the overwrought ranting of a pack of youthful malcontents.

A slow and unrelenting succession of discouraging events was eroding the public's confidence in the government's assurances that progress was being made: Tet 1968, Khe Sanh, Tet 1969, and most recently Hamburger Hill. The death toll had now reached the 36,000 mark, surpassing that of Korea. Nixon acknowledged the inevitable by announcing the first of the troop withdrawals during a meeting on June 8 with President Thieu on the remote Pacific outpost of Midway Island. Our troop strength was to be reduced by 25,000 by the end of August. To make it clear that this was not a slow-motion surrender he also introduced the policy of "Vietnamization," whereby the Army of the Republic of Vietnam (ARVN) would gradually be assuming greater responsibility for attempting to hold the communists in check. In the combat zone General Abrams abandoned the policy of "maximum pressure" in favor of a more moderate one of "protective reaction." In essence, our leaders were switching our primary strategy from offense to defense. That is nearly always a losing proposition for a military campaign, but it was the only possible middle way between an aggressive stance that was resulting in more casualties than America was willing to bear and the alternative of immediate US withdrawal before the ARVN was sufficiently combat-seasoned to have a fighting chance against the relentless enemy. This was a change that spared the lives of thousands of young Americans in the final four years of our involvement, but, even so, 22,000 more were to die for no good purpose during those years.

Two other events that month were to have lasting significance for the war on the home front. During the SDS convention in Chicago in the middle of June the leadership of the resistance took a radical lurch to the far left when the representatives were unable to come to an agreement on strategy and the Weatherman faction took control. They issued a position paper quoting the concluding line from Bob Dylan's "Subterranean Homesick Blues," and adopted the slogan "bring the war home."

The war had been simmering on the home front for several years now but this was a major escalation, a sort of counterpoint to our military's switch in the other direction to a primarily defensive posture in the RVN. Many of them were self-professed Marxists who viewed US imperialism as the root of all the world's evils and the war in Vietnam as the most outrageous expression of that imperialism. Clearly the Weathermen were far to the left of most of the antiwar activists but, as well as issuing countless fiery proclamations and instigating violence themselves, they also inspired a more radical and uncompromising stance among many others who had run out of patience waiting for the government to listen to reason. As always, that radicalization was matched by an equally enhanced rigidity among their opponents on the right.

The second incident was the Stonewall riots in New York City, which are usually regarded as the beginning of the modern gay rights movement. The last group of oppressed Americans had now reached the breaking point, and inspired by the efforts of racial minorities and women they were finally beginning to demand that their country live up to the founders' vision of equality as one of the natural rights to be protected by the government. Like the other groups demanding change, they had also concluded that the time for mere words had passed.

***

On Friday the 27th I went over to the Twin Cities Draft Information Center on the West Bank where they were renting some second-floor office space at 529 Cedar Avenue near Riverside. Organizations that helped young men deal with the SSS had been around for several years, but I had not made any definite plans to visit one while I was home on leave. I just felt that I was stuck with my situation now that I had accepted enlistment. The suggestion that I visit the center came from a most unexpected source—my Dad. I knew that was tough for him as a World War II vet and I was sure that Mom was the real instigator, but once I thought about it I figured it could not hurt to hear what they had to say. My question for them was not how to get out of the Army, but rather how to go about trying to get my MOS changed. The two men in the office were the ones who advised guys who were not yet in the military, the bulk of their clientele, but they did have a military advisor as well and they suggested I stop back when he was there. I enjoyed the feeling of being back on campus, and noticed that the construction of Koltoff Hall and the addition connecting Vincent and Murphy were both coming along.

I started reading *Mr. Lincoln's Army*, the first volume of Bruce Catton's history of the Army of the Potomac, mostly because I was interested in learning more about the namesake of my base, General George McClellan. Catton portrayed him as a dedicated soldier and honorable man, but one who was often overly cautious and lacking the will to apply the relentless pressure that would be required to wear down the southern forces to the point where they could no longer offer credible resistance. The general considered the

Battle of Antietam a great victory because his army had repulsed Lee's first invasion of the North on September 17, 1862, the bloodiest day in American military history. This particular confrontation was also significant because it lent powerful credence to Lincoln's assurances that the North would prevail as long as it did not lose the will to continue fighting as long as necessary and this bolstering of the public's confidence in an eventual Union victory allowed the president to issue the Emancipation Proclamation. But the president felt that his general should have eliminated Lee's army as a fighting force by capturing it and Catton concurred with this assessment. The Confederates were outnumbered by 20,000 men and McClellan had them trapped on the north side of the Potomac after the battle. Instead of pressing his advantage, McClellan held the Union forces back and allowed Lee's army the time needed to retreat back south across the river.

Catton devoted considerable space to reflections on the relationship between the military and the government in America, a nation where civilian control of the military has been a fundamental principle since the days of the founders. McClellan was deemed too timid, but then there was the case of MacArthur in Korea when Truman dismissed his commander for being overly aggressive. The real offense for MacArthur was failing to follow orders. That is always a serious matter under the UCMJ, but when the President is the one issuing the order it becomes a very grave offense indeed.

This led me to reflect on how the government was using the military in Vietnam and it seemed to me that the Army was being abused by commanders-in-chief who were demanding that it carry out an impossible mission. The military commanders were more than willing to undertake that task because war advanced their careers, and they were also most reluctant to ever report that things were not going as well they had anticipated. Whenever they were forced to make such an admission, the inevitable solution they suggested was more men and armaments. Neither the President nor his commanders could bear to admit that, regardless of whether our intervention might have appeared to make some sense at the beginning, events had now demonstrated that it was a terrible mistake and an unattainable mission.

As always, the ones bearing the burden of that mistake were the troops in the field. If our President and his staff were abusing the military by insisting that it continue to fight a war it could never win, the men at the lower rungs of the military hierarchy were the ones suffering the brunt of that mistreatment. They were the ones killing and being killed and maimed because our leaders were unable to back down. Having more time to think while on leave clearly was doing nothing to improve my state of mind about the war in general and my own situation in particular.

Bev called on the morning of Sunday the 29th and it was great to talk with her in a comfortable place without the background din of other soldiers making their own calls home. Of course, now she was in a similar environment in the camp kitchen with other women around making noise. That also limited the length of our call, but it was still wonderful. After camp was over she was going to visit her friend Patty Harvey's home in Florence, Alabama, on her way down to Florida so she said that might be a chance for us to see each other if I could get a pass then. I told her about reading the Civil War history, and also that I planned to read *2001*. Ever since seeing the film with Dave I had wanted to read Clarke's book for an explanation of what happened in the movie. There were many books on my shelves I had not read yet, so passing the time while I convalesced was never a problem.

Our second car, the Ford, had been acting up so I had not gone back to the draft center yet. I thought I would call and see what they could tell me over the phone. One thing they had not suggested and I never seriously considered was to spend my leave making my mono worse, or at least keeping it active. That was what the nurse had meant when she cautioned me against taking a summer job. I could have eaten very little and ridden my bike every day to the point of exhaustion, but I just did not have it in me to deliberately damage my health. I was uncertain how serious mono could be, and it would have been tough to do those things when I was home with my family. They certainly wanted me out of the Army but they also wanted me healthy. That might have been a golden opportunity to get a medical discharge but, for better or for worse, I did my best to render myself healthy enough for service once again.

***

Bev wrote on Monday the 30th saying that it had gotten even hotter down there. The second session began the day before and was off to a much smoother start than the first one. She was still bothered by feeling isolated and cut off from news of the outside world, but working with the girls made it all worthwhile. During the break between the two sessions the staff had enjoyed some time in town. There was a midnight madness sale in Paducah on Friday night. On Saturday they went water skiing in the Ohio River and then went into Paducah for a late movie, *The Secret War of Harry Frigg* with Paul Newman. She said it was totally predictable and just about the worst movie she had ever seen. That night she and Patty stayed in town with a Jewish family, the Golds. Mrs. Gold, Ursula, was German and still had nightmares about World War II and the Nazis. Bev said she was really a beautiful person.

I wrote to Bev on Tuesday, July 1, telling her more about what I was reading. I sent her some poems by Emily Dickinson and a report on a Gallup Poll showing that, while a slim majority of Americans now favored a truce in Vietnam, a substantial majority also continued to oppose an immediate withdrawal of all troops. The public's approval of a possible truce meant nothing since it was obvious that there were no meaningful terms acceptable to both sides. I also enclosed a brief excerpt from Paul Goodman's *Making Do* that included a description of a small demonstration by a group of progressives:

> These rapidly gathering, rapidly dwindling, demonstrations had become a frequent feature of our cityscape. They meant nothing and they meant everything. They exerted no influence; they meant that people were powerless and at a loss what else to do. But they meant that people had had it and would no longer put up with it, even if all they could do was to carry a sign.

Goodman wrote that in 1962 before the war and the rise of the counterculture, during the doldrums between the Beats and the Hippies when the small minority of young people who were unwilling to accept the prospect of spending a lifetime in a real-world version of a TV family sitcom found themselves with few other prospects beyond living the role of oddball outsiders. Straight society pretty much relegated them to the same category as the wild-eyed misfit of magazine cartoons wearing a prophet's mantle and carrying a sign proclaiming that the world would end soon. No one could have guessed that in a few years people would be challenging all the established institutions as never before but Goodman, like Bob Dylan, picked up on the fact that the times were indeed changing and accurately observed that for a growing number of Americans doing nothing was no longer an option. By 1969 many people were certainly long past the point when they were willing to settle for merely carrying signs.

The most interesting thing I sent Bev, however, was an article from the Minneapolis paper by PFC Tim O'Brien of Worthington, Minnesota, who was serving a tour of duty as an infantryman in Vietnam. We could not have known that he would become one of the greatest writers to bear witness to the American experience in the RVN, but it is remarkable how similar this brief piece is in style and theme to his later works. He started off by observing how much soldiers lie, thereby employing the literary technique of the unreliable narrator by leaving the reader in doubt about the veracity of everything to come. Even though he was serving in combat he said that the soldier's main enemies were boredom and physical misery, which he went on to describe in some detail. He talked about how the enlisted men and lower-ranking officers had lost their willingness to risk their lives for a losing cause, and had instead adopted the strategy of spending most of their time in the field hunkered down in defensive positions.

He went on to offer a vivid description of an incident of abusing Vietnamese civilians, including an old man, in an attempt to get them to divulge information on the local VC. What struck me the hardest was that he cursed himself for accepting enlistment and duty in Vietnam. In Tim's case it was obviously too late to do anything about that, but what about me? Would the day come when I would curse myself? Was it too late for me to do anything about that?

With such thoughts on my mind, on Thursday the 3rd I went back to the Draft Information Center and talked with the military advisor, Alexander (Sandy) Wilkinson, about requesting a change in MOS. Sandy was a well-known figure in the local anti-war and draft-resistance movement as well as a civil right activist, and was awaiting federal prosecution for refusing induction and turning in his draft card the previous year. His family situation was a microcosm of our national divide over the war because his father was a World War II vet; his younger brother Chris had left college and enlisted in the Army the previous year; and Sandy had also dropped out of college to devote all of his time to the draft resistance movement. Despite their strongly differing beliefs on the military and the war, the brothers remained close and respected each other for following their individual consciences. It was especially heartening to hear that their dad also supported both of his sons, and it was clear from his tolerant attitude where his boys had learned to honor beliefs that differed from their own: "They're both right for different reasons."

Sandy gave me some very specific advice. He said the only way to get my MOS changed would be to file for conscientious objector (CO) status and request training and assignment as a medic. I told him my current religious philosophy, which was tepid to nonexistent, but he said the definition for CO purposes was so broad that anyone other than the most militant atheist could qualify. He said that being stubborn was the key and that as soon as you hand the form to your commanding officer you were to be taken off combat training and then they send you down to Fort Sam Houston in San Antonio to begin medic training. It would take anywhere from six weeks to four months for your application to be processed and if it was disapproved you had the options of applying once more, going back to combat training, or going to the stockade. He said if you choose the stockade they will probably just put you back in medic training instead.

It felt good to be taking some initiative toward resolving my dilemma and I appreciated all the help Sandy and the others at the center gave me, but two problems prevented me from experiencing much relief. The first was that I was not a CO according to the military's definition of that term. I was not a pacifist who believed that all war was wrong. All war was tragic, but some had to be fought and won for the greater good and I regarded World War II as one of our country's finest hours.

I firmly believed that Vietnam was a strategic error and morally indefensible, but the CO regulations made no provision for selective objection, because that was regarded as a political position rather than one based upon conscience. To me it was absurd to say that conscience had no role to play in the realm of politics, but the military wrote the rules and I had taken an oath to abide by them. The second problem was that if I was assigned as a medic I would have traded duty as a mortar-man for duty that would almost certainly be even more hazardous. That was a trade-off that could only make sense to men who objected to killing but not to serving in the military. I had the highest admiration for medics, COs or not, but if I was going to be in a combat situation I wanted to be carrying a weapon, not a medical kit. Despite these misgivings I decided to apply for CO status because I could not reconcile myself to doing nothing about my situation. Sandy gave me a booklet to help with my application and said he would review my form before I went back to Fort Mac. The next time I wrote to Bev I asked her to write a letter of support. After I finished up at the Draft Information Center I walked over to Dinkytown and bought a copy of

Marcus Klein's The *American Novel Since World War II* for some additional reading material back at Fort Mac.

We had a family picnic in the backyard to celebrate the 4th and the weather was beautiful. The weather since I got home had been perfect for summer with highs around the low 80s. It was a relief from the heat and humidity of Alabama, and Bev said it had been hot at Bear Creek as well. I went to our family doctor on Monday the 7th and he said that the bleeding in my right ear had all cleared up. I still had mono though and he felt it would take at least two or three more weeks to get rid of it. He also said I was more susceptible to other diseases while my system was weakened by mono, so I hoped they would put me back in the hospital when I returned to Fort Mac, because the communal life of the barracks was notorious for spreading illness. I went to see Zeffirelli's film version of *Romeo and Juliet* that evening, my sister Mary's favorite movie at that time, and enjoyed it. The audience was mostly kids younger than me but they proved to be more mature than the guys at Fort Mac, because I heard no snickering or giggling. On the same day the Zodiac Killer struck for the second time in Vallejo, California, killing one victim and seriously injuring another.

***

Bev wrote on Sunday the 6th. After a late buffet breakfast that morning she helped drive the kids to an outdoor mass. Also that morning, some of the staff and seniors presented a "folk" service, singing "Thank You" and "Clap Your Hands" and then doing a choral reading of cummings's "If up's the word." Later that day she and the senior scouts were going to make a swing but instead ended up jumping rope. The CITs had taken over many of the jobs around camp that session so now Bev had very little to do until nighttime when she was supposed to see that the girls got to bed and to counsel the ones that seemed troubled or depressed. On Saturday she had sailed for the first time that summer, in a Snark with one other girl and then with more of them in a Lightning. She said that sailing made her feel freer than most any other thing. For reading, she had given up for the present on *Catch-22* and begun *The Quiet American* instead. That was the book she had with her when we first talked in Ford Hall back in November.

She was really enjoying working with the girls and joining in on their horseplay and pranks, even though most days she felt as though she was wandering through the hours in a daze. Some of the scouts made a birthday cake for one of the counselors in the shape of an elephant and decorated it with sliced Tootsie Rolls and Fruit Loops. The younger girls, ages nine through twelve, were especially loveable because they looked up to the older ones so much, and Bev did not mind when they hung on her or chased her because she knew they just needed attention. She never lost her sense of wonder at all the different minds and personalities. One thing she missed after spending so many years in a college environment was serious discussions, because the counselors spent most of their free time goofing off or griping to let off steam. Even though she loved the kids, she also wished that she was finished after the current session, especially since most of the CITs were leaving at the end. She would have loved to have all younger girls for the third session, but felt that she had asked Nellie for more than enough favors already.

✸✸✸

On Tuesday the 8th I went back to the DIC and asked Sandy to look over my answers for the CO application. He gave me some suggestions, including emphasizing that I did not become a CO until after I was in the service. That would explain why I had accepted enlistment, but he also gave me a copy of the SSS regulations on CO status that stated a claim "based solely on conscientious objection which existed but was not claimed prior to induction cannot be entertained." He gave me a handout with suggestions for composing letters of support that I sent along to Bev. I felt that the chances of a successful claim were marginal at best but I also felt the need to be doing something about my dilemma other than passively accepting it. Then I went out to the Art Institute to see a special exhibit of French paintings. I enjoyed what was there but it was not as extensive as I had hoped. I was especially interested in the Van Goghs but they only had two and one of them was from the institute's own collection. My folks arranged some nice family activities for my leave and that night we went to the Twins game.

On the 9th I got my plane ticket to return to Mac on Monday the 14th when I was to report for duty by 7:00 p.m. Bev wrote on the same day describing more of the ups and downs of life at Bear Creek. They had visited another camp in southern Illinois that day and then went down to the Murray State Observatory that night. They stopped at Geno's Pizza Place and then received a sharp reprimand for getting back to camp late. She was frustrated by that, as well as the difficulty we had been having connecting by phone. Now that I was home where I could receive calls just about anytime, she was in a place where it was hard to call. There was usually a lot of background noise at camp and one night a storm knocked out their phone service. She was scheduled to take her practical lifesaving test the next day but she still stayed up until 1:00 a.m. to write her letter of support for my CO application. She called on the evening of Friday the 11th so we finally had a chance to talk instead of relying exclusively on the written word. That was always just about the biggest morale booster of all for both of us.

She had been sending me poetry and news items about current events along with her letters, so now that I had more time to read and think I returned the favor. The first of the troop reductions was that month and I sent her a couple of newspaper articles by reporters assigned in-country about that. During the next four years most of these reductions were accomplished by not replacing men who were returning home rather than by sending troops home early. Since an average of well over one thousand men were scheduled to return to the US every day, it did not take long to meet the reduction goals in this way. Keyes Beech wrote a piece on some returning troops of the 9th Infantry Division and a farewell "celebration" held for them by the South Vietnamese government. The men he talked with were cynical and disgruntled about what they saw as the hypocrisy of both the Vietnamese officials and the Army brass. Contrary to the proclamations of the speakers at the event, there was little or no sense of accomplishment among the troops because the war was far from over and all they really wanted was for the interminable ceremony, processing, and baggage inspections to end so that they could escape the stifling heat and board their planes.

The second article was a report by Ronald Ross, the Far East correspondent for the *Minneapolis Tribune*, who also interviewed some departing men of the 9th. He described the same lack of concern for what happened in the RVN after they left, as well as a widespread belief that the ARVN could not defend the south for long against the communists without the support of US forces. One soldier had done his best to avoid being drafted and now that his year was up he offered these reflections.

> You have to come here to see it. You have to see the guys getting their three-day passes for making their kill quotas to believe it could happen. You have to see American GIs torturing Vietnamese, gunning down women. You have to hear colonels refusing to put helicopter gunships into tree lines because they want you to go in there and kill and count the bodies on the ground. What am I going to do when I get home? Go back to school, but not in America.

Some briefer articles also warned of an ARVN "psychological collapse" if the US withdrew too soon, and the strong possibility that parades held in America to honor returning troops would be marred by protests. On a lighter note, I also sent Bev some *Miss Peach* strips describing life at Kamp Kelly because I thought they would be a hit at Bear Creek.

On the morning of Monday, July 14, I boarded my return flight to Alabama with my prospects just as uncertain as when I left for Kentucky four months earlier, and the state of my conscience even less settled.

Chapter 9
AIT AND LEAVE
JULY-OCTOBER 1969

I flew standby on the flight from Minneapolis to Atlanta to save money and the plane was only about half full. They served a great breakfast that included a cheese omelet, Canadian bacon, hashbrown potatoes, cantaloupe, a roll, coffee, and juice. The flight took two hours and then I used my time in Atlanta for reading while I waited for the flight to Alabama. I finished *Tess* and moved on to John Updike's *Couples*. The abrupt change from the world of one writer to another was jarring but refreshing because I had been immersed in Hardy's unrelenting gloom for too long. As always, Updike had me hooked from the first page and it was clear that this was the "big" novel that had been foreshadowed in his earlier works.

Both authors crafted poignant portraits of people struggling through life amid forces and circumstances beyond their control. Tess had the worst of it by far and yet she was the one who knew what she wanted and also possessed the courage to pursue her goals despite having to pay a terrible price. The principal problem the couples of Tarbox faced, on the other hand, was bewilderment over the meaning of their lives amid unprecedented material prosperity while trapped in the stultifying ennui of contemporary suburban America. Their most common attempt at a solution was adultery based on the futile hope that the next affair would somehow begin to fill the spiritual void at the core of their coddled lives. The pill offered the opportunity to indulge in such compulsive behavior with less risk, but sex without love only left them hungering for yet another partner who might finally satisfy their need for true transcendence. I enjoyed the book far more than the Hardy but found myself constantly vacillating between empathizing with Updike's lost souls in the land of freedom and plenty and laughing at them as sybaritic fools, a tension that only a great writer would be able to sustain for a work of nearly five hundred pages. It was no accident that Updike so often presented himself to the camera for his publicity photos with a look of sly bemusement.

The Southern Airlines flight out of Atlanta was on a noisy two-engine prop plane and our first stop was Gadsden. We proceeded from there to Anniston and the entire time from Atlanta was only about an hour. I took the Army bus from Anniston to the base hospital to save cab fare and finally got settled into my room there about 7:00 p.m. When I unpacked my things I was touched to find that Mary had slipped in a card expressing her love and saying she would be thinking about me. As we watched *Gunsmoke* my roommates and I chatted. One man had been sick since April and the docs still could not figure out what was wrong. They speculated that it was some sort of nervous condition and he had already had two convalescent leaves. As long as it was not life-threatening that sounded like the perfect ailment to have in the Army. I wondered why they did not just discharge a guy like that since the draft provided a virtually unlimited supply of troops. For all I know that might have been what happened eventually, but we spent less than one day together and I never saw him again.

They took a blood sample from me on the morning of Tuesday the 15th and then discharged me before the lab examined it. I got the impression that the main concern of the Army medical staff was not the state of my health but getting me back to active duty with my unit. The plan was to put me in a company in their third week of training so I would be picking up where I left off. Bev would be sending me a revised version of her letter of support based upon Sandy's recommendations, and I intended to turn in my CO application when I received that.

I was sitting on a bunk in a vacant barracks that afternoon when a sergeant came in and told me that they would be returning me to Echo Company so I could graduate with my original group of guys. I was already depressed about being back in the prison-like military environment after enjoying the three weeks at home, as well as on edge because of the uncertain future after

I turned in my CO application, but that news made me madder than any of the harassment my buddies and I had been subjected to over the last four months. I had learned to expect the worst from the military but I had not believed that even the Army would send a soldier into a combat zone with only half of the training he was supposed to receive.

I told him I had never even taken the gunner's exam and he said they had me down for a perfect score. So I went over to the orderly room and told the First Sergeant I had not taken the test and did not want to graduate missing a month of training. He agreed when he saw that I would not accept what they were trying to do. I doubted that it was all a mistake, because I knew that they were under pressure from their superiors not to recycle people, which was why they graduated men anyway who had flunked all their tests. Some guys would jump at the chance to get out of an entire month of training so most likely their strategy was to try it and see if the trainee objected. If they had not backed down my next step would have been to go complain to the base Inspector General, but it never came to that.

After that sorry episode I still had no duties so I called home and talked with Dad and Mary. That did nothing to raise my spirits because they said Mom was in the hospital. Her heart rate had been too high and they were performing tests. I could not help but suspect that her health was suffering because of anxiety over the prospect of me going into combat soon. I felt terrible about that even though the situation was not the result of anything I had done, as well as not being able to visit her in the hospital, and the feeling of helplessness about the whole mess left me feeling nearly as frustrated as in the early days of Basic.

On the morning of Wednesday the 16th the Apollo 11 mission lifted off from the Kennedy Space Center. This was the mission the nation had been awaiting most of all because it was to be the first to land men on the Moon, thus fulfilling the goal JFK announced in 1961 of accomplishing that incredible feat by the end of the decade. It felt good for America to be doing something we could be proud of again, but there was also a high level of tension because of concern for the safety of the astronauts. I watched what I could on various TVs around the base, but it was hard to get my mind off of Mom's health as well as my own uncertain status.

★★★

Life at Fort Mac continued to be a quiet affair as I spent most of my time reading *Couples* and relaxing in a deserted barracks. Echo Company was out in the woods for their RVN training so the only ones around were the First Sergeant, a few clerks and cooks, and some other guys who were not well enough for a bivouac. I called home again and found that Mom was doing better. It had been a spell of heart palpitations and they were still performing tests to try to determine the cause. The NCOs in charge must have thought I should at least look as though I had something to do so they assigned me to count some bunks. The weather was even hotter than in June but it was not bad when all I had to do most of the time was sit around indoors.

I felt better after hearing the news about Mom and I wrote to Bev hoping she was in better spirits as well. That was because I had just received one of her letters the day before from back in June during the first session at Bear Creek when things were not going so well. The frequent delays in mail delivery and the glitches with phone calls caused our communications to be out of sync in a way that was almost comical at times, but the hardest part was responding to emotions that we knew the other might no longer be experiencing at the time we were writing back. Love and hope for a better future always sustained us and allowed us to muddle through.

Bev also wrote about our now-moot possible plans for Independence Day in her letter, which brought up the subject again of when we might finally get to see each other. She was coming to Florence to visit Patty after camp, so it was possible I could see her in Anniston if I got an overnight pass. If I got a three-day pass I might be able to fly down to Coral Gables while she was there. At least we knew for sure now that she would be back in Minneapolis by the time I finished training, so we would be able to spend my leave together before I went overseas. It was satisfying to know at least one thing for certain. I tried to call Bev three times that night but the line was busy twice and the third time she was not at the lodge yet. I had to laugh when a girl with a heavy Southern accent shouted to everyone in the building that there was a call for Beaver, her camp name. Bev explained that someone in sixth grade gave her that moniker because of her eagerness and industriousness.

I showed my CO application to Top, the First Sergeant, on the morning of the 17th and he said I should turn it in when I got to my new company. I imagine he was pleased now to be able to pass a problem like me along to another unit. He read it through though, and as I was leaving he sort of grinned and said, "War isn't so bad. It's just a job that has to be done." He was better than the prick who held the position when we had arrived in

May, but that really did not matter to me because I would soon be in another company. They did manage to find something for me to do and I spent the day typing out the 217 graduation certificates for the men in the cycle that was coming to an end soon. After that the small group of us in the barracks was told we had to move to another one. There was no explanation offered, but that was the kind of minor inconvenience we had all learned to accept as a way of life by now, and I had not unpacked much of my stuff anyway.

    I called home that evening and talked with Granny, a rare opportunity that I welcomed. She did not care much for using the phone, but I happened to catch her at a time when she was the only one home. That was John's thirteenth birthday and Dad had taken the kids out to eat and to visit Mom. There was good news, because she was coming home from the hospital the next day. The doctor said it was only a virus, which I guessed was another way of saying the tests showed nothing. I still suspected stress, and one decision I had already made was to be as positive as humanly possible in my letters home while being more realistic in letters to Bev and to Dad at his office. They were under stress as well, of course, but Bev and I had pledged to be honest with each other and I needed to confide in my father. In fact, Dad and I had not told Mom or anyone else in the family about my CO application.

    On Friday the 18th I was reassigned to Charlie Company, another unit in the First Battalion, and got moved in the same day. The barracks were exactly the same style as Echo Company and were down the hill about three blocks away. I made an appointment to see the commanding officer early the next week. On the 19th the Apollo 11 spacecraft entered lunar orbit and began the first of fourteen orbits in preparation for the landing scheduled for the next day. We were given post privileges at noon and the first thing I did was head to the laundromat. I had a big load and since most of it was from before my leave I was glad to have such a poor sense of smell. I was unsure where the EM club was in the new company area and I did not know anyone there yet either, so after I was finished with my clothes I went up to Sam's Place for a rendezvous with the soldier's reliable old buddy, alcohol.

    I was delighted to find a bunch of guys from my old Echo Company 5th Platoon there, and they were shocked to see me. It turned out that after my sudden disappearance in June a rumor started circulating that I had contracted meningitis and died. We had a good laugh over that once I assured them they were not seeing a ghost. They had been out on their twelve-day RVN training but got to come back to the barracks because the next Monday was a half-holiday due to the moon landing. They just about reduced me to hysterics by recounting all the fuck-ups out on their bivouac. The endless series of snafus made it sound like a real-life version of *Beetle Bailey*.

Then I called home and talked with Mom. It was a relief to hear her voice and to know she was feeling better. She said John was mowing the lawn, and I was glad he was old enough to take on that job now that Dave would soon be leaving for Europe.

After that I went over to the old 5th Platoon barracks to see who was around. About six of the guys were there so we went through the same comedy routine as with the group at Sam's about the rumors of my demise. I was glad to be alive and also gratified that they felt the same way about it. They were using my old footlocker as an ice-chest for beer so we drank a few and they treated me to more stories about their farcical misadventures out in the woods.

One of them had a book of Emily Dickinson's poetry and I always appreciated seeing something like that in the violent, hyper-masculine, and misogynistic world of the Army. They were pleased to have only two weeks of training left, whereas I was glad to have had my date for shipping out to Vietnam delayed because of my illness, so everybody was happy.

Sunday the 20th was to be the day for the landing and walk on the Moon so I went up to my old favorite haunt, the Hilltop Service Club, hoping to see some of it on TV. It was scheduled for mid-afternoon so I wrote letters to Bev and my family and then two guys from Basic came in, including my old bunkmate Larry Anderson. His new daughter had arrived and he was given a four-day leave to go home for a visit. The leave was unexpected good news and Larry did not seem to be particularly dismayed about the prospect of being gone for her first year. We played pool for a while and then some men from the old 5th Platoon showed up and we decided to go the movie. It turned out to be a stinker called *On the Way to the Crusades I Met a Girl Who...* with Tony Curtis, but at least it was fun doing things with some buddies who would be gone in a couple of weeks.

The drama continued a quarter of a million miles away as the lunar module undocked from the command module and Neil Armstrong announced "The *Eagle* has wings." Tension was high as the intrepid duo of Armstrong and Buzz Aldrin maneuvered the craft toward the surface while a gauge, later found to be inaccurate, showed fuel needed for the return flight to the command module running desperately low. The suspense intensified as Armstrong reported that the designated landing site was too rocky. The seasoned test pilot switched to manual controls and altered the module's course toward an open expanse of the gray lunar sand. Finally his static-filled message ushered in a new chapter in the history of human exploration: "Houston, Tranquility Base here. The *Eagle* has landed." The module had touched down safely in the Sea of Tranquility.

At home I would have been glued to the TV set watching all of this drama, and I did manage to see most of it on live TV either at the club or back in the barracks where a venerable old portable set was brought in for this unique event. The two astronauts spent two and one half hours walking and running around on the Moon and the way they jumped and bounced around in the reduced gravity even while wearing their heavy spacesuits was unforgettable. They placed scientific measuring devices, collected core samples, and planted the iconic American flag stiffened with wire to make it appear to be waving. They also left a plaque signed by Nixon and the three astronauts with an inscription that concluded "we came in peace for all mankind." Only hours after the *Eagle* blasted off to rejoin *Columbia* for the journey back home to Earth, the USSR's unmanned exploratory craft, *Luna 15*, crash-landed on the surface of the Moon, adding a decisive exclamation point to America's technological victory over our chief rival for world dominance.

After all the science fiction and space movies I had absorbed as a kid, there was a powerful sense of the surreal about this type of adventure actually happening. The war touched everything in those troubled days, however, and I also experienced an overwhelming feeling of poignancy about this crowning achievement coming in the midst of America's greatest debacle. It was the best of times, it was the worst of times; and there were few days without a high level of emotional intensity, nearly as addictive as it was distressing, exacerbated by an almost unbearable need to know what hints of our uncertain future prospects the next day would bring.

On Monday morning I joined the men of my new platoon in their third week of mortar training, which was material I had before with Company E. There was a test on the subject matter of the first two weeks and I scored 140 out of a possible 150. It was another hot and humid day and we had a four-mile forced march from the training grounds back to the company area. I completed that, which made me feel as though I really must have completely recovered. We had Monday afternoon off because of the Moon landing so I went back up to Hilltop and smoked a leisurely cigar that left me pleasantly light-headed without feeling sickly. I was feeling pretty good because some of the guys had told me about the Army's policy of discharging troops with five months or less left to go when they got back from Vietnam. With the delays caused by my illness and some repetition in training that timing would work out well for me, and I felt certain that being in the RVN would be more bearable if I knew I would be a civilian again as soon as I returned. I finished reading *Couples* and recommended it to Bev in my next letter to her. Then I started the Frankl book she had given me.

The rest of the week was more mortar training that I had taken before. On Wednesday we were out in the field and had just gotten our chow when it started to pour, but otherwise the weather continued to be oppressive. Our instructors tended to be a bunch of tightly wrapped guys who would have made excellent subjects for a study of the Type A personality. That would be expected in men who had served in combat in Vietnam but many of them also clearly enjoyed acting like hard-asses to impress the trainees. One black sergeant was the stereotype of Army discipline with a lean muscular build and starched, carefully tailored fatigues. He "had his shit together," as the saying went, and he definitely knew his stuff, but I had trouble keeping a smirk off of my face during his presentation because he invariably pronounced "manipulate" as "man-ip-a-late." This was a word he used often in his tightly clipped speech pattern, often combining it with a series of other m-sounds that resulted in an intriguing example of alliteration. He would spit out instructions on how to "man-ip-a-late the 81 millimeter mortar," sometimes emphasizing that this was to be done in a "military manner."

Another instructor was a red-faced and overweight heart attack waiting to happen. He yelled out his lectures in an agitated and apoplectic style designed to keep even the groggiest recruit from dozing off, but he also warned us that if we did dare to show him disrespect by committing such an infraction he had "boo-coo shit details" to assign as punishment. At first I was puzzled by his pronunciation of "beaucoup," but I soon realized that this was an example of the unique slang employed in the RVN. The biggest challenge in his class was not staying awake but keeping a straight face. When we returned to the company area that afternoon I received a letter from Bev at mail call that included her revised supporting letter.

On Thursday the 24th the Apollo 11 crew splashed down in the Pacific about 1,000 miles southwest of Hawaii. The crew was brought aboard the *USS Hornet* for a heroes' welcome by the crew and a host of news people and dignitaries including Nixon himself. That was but the beginning of a succession of parades and celebratory events crowned by a 45-day "Giant Leap" tour that brought them to twenty-five countries. The tour name was inspired by Neil Armstrong's immortal words as he first stepped onto the lunar surface: "That's one small step for man, one giant leap for mankind." Back in Minnesota one Bloomington city official was so swept up in the national enthusiasm for space travel resulting from the successful landing that he proposed a resolution permitting the construction of rocket-ports in the city, a measure quickly tabled by the city's governing board.

I turned in my CO application on Friday. Both that day and Saturday were devoted to more mortar training, and our gunner's exam was scheduled for Wednesday of the following week. That would bring us up to the point where my training with Company E was interrupted. After we got off duty on Saturday I went up to the service club to escape the heat and write letters. I took a pass on drinking at the EM club that night and stayed at Hilltop to read. I had already finished the Frankl book and found his story of overcoming almost imaginable adversity through faith and will to be most inspiring. That night I finished *Poor Folk*, one of three short novels by Dostoevsky in a book that Dave had given me the previous Christmas. The dour Russian was someone I preferred in limited doses, so I decided to move on to *The American Novel Since World War II* before I read more of him. I got up early the next morning and went over to the mess hall for breakfast. Sunday was the best day for that because we could take our time and eat as much as we wanted since only about half the men got up for it. Then I spent most of the day up at Hilltop again.

* * *

Meanwhile, Bev had been assigned to a group called Pioneer Unit for her last session at Bear Creek. She had girls in her unit ranging in age from to twelve to fifteen, and they were "a real scream." Some had matured physically, some had not, and some were in the process of doing so. Many of them were endearingly awkward as they underwent the transition from being tomboys to young ladies. She wrote on Thursday the 17th about a going-away party the previous night for Trisha Pawley from Houston, the quiet girl with the big eyes who always looked as though she was absorbing everything she saw. She was Bev's favorite CIT and Bev knew she would miss Trisha, but camp was drawing to a close and Bev herself would be finished at the end of the following week. They played games, sang, ate, and slept out on the point under the stars. They also enjoyed some quiet nighttime canoeing, although the waterfront director bawled them out for that the next day. After their night on the point the five of them cooked a breakfast outside of fried eggs, doughnut holes rolled in cinnamon sugar, juice, and hot chocolate. The days continued to be punctuated with more zany high jinks as the end of camp approached, such as whipped cream attacks and moving others' beds out into the middle of Chigger Field.

Trisha was very sensitive and, in anticipation of leaving Bear Creek, she had written a short poem asking whether it was better to make friends or not to do so in order to avoid the hurt that comes in parting. That reminded Bev of how painful it was to leave her college classmates at Maryville, and she said that when she first came to Minneapolis she had told herself subconsciously not to make friends because it hurts too much to leave them. Of course, for a person like her such a resolution was impossible to keep since it was her nature to always welcome others into her life. That was an inspiration for me because I was in almost constant need of an antidote to my natural tendency to retreat inwards and isolate myself. She felt that taking risks and experiencing occasional pain were necessary if one was to experience the joys of living, and that was why she was willing to risk her feelings when we met. She went on to say that she could not be happier with that decision because it had made her more complete than anything else in her experience. I tried to never miss the opportunity to let her know that I felt exactly the same. I was not experiencing many religious impulses in those days so prayers of thanksgiving, or of any sort, were not a part of my routine, but I was certainly eternally grateful for whatever good fortune had brought this wonderful woman into my life, especially at the very time when I was so desperately in need of love and support.

Even though there was no need to do so, she apologized again for the phone situation. The service had been out for three days when she intended to call me while I was at home. I had called the night before when she was not in the lodge, and she said that Anna, the girl from Kentucky who answered it, commented on my "real Northern accent." She was writing to me by candlelight in her tent when Ellen came by and told her that I had called again, so then she felt bad about that and cried herself to sleep. I wished she would not feel that way because I certainly did not expect her to sit next to the only phone in camp every evening, but that was Bev and communications would be better soon.

I endeavored to avoid self-pity by taking these reminders to heart of how difficult the uncertainty of my situation was for my loved ones who had to endure the days between my letters wondering how things were going in the Army. As she often did, she enclosed handwritten copies of some poetry, including one by Rod McKuen from *Listen to the Warm* that began "You won't believe this/but I'm going off to war."

On Friday the 18th Bev led a group of eighteen junior scouts to Fossil Point. The numerous crinoid stems were especially good for stringing into bracelets. They sang going and coming and I found the thought of the chorus of young and innocent female voices in the wilderness to be strangely affecting. I hoped they would never be touched by the pain of war. That night a bunch of them cooked "surprise packages" at the campfire, a mixture of hamburger, onions, potatoes, and carrots wrapped in foil. Dessert was caramel apples. Then the campers cleaned up while the counselors played Frisbee. She had called her folks before they left for Alaska and tried to explain what was going on with me and the Army. I hoped it would not disturb them. She said her dad was in an especially happy mood because he had been looking forward to the trip for so long. Driving from Florida to Alaska and back was certainly the ultimate American road trip.

On Sunday night we finally connected by phone, and she wrote that it made her happy both going to sleep and waking up the next morning. She was a bit giddy from all the usual camp horseplay and it was delightful to find her so relaxed and happy. The preparations for closing down the camp for the season continued as they cleaned up trash and weeds then smashed and burned an old latrine. On Wednesday the 23rd the staff celebrated the upcoming conclusion of the session with a dinner of steak, baked potato, and tossed salad. She was finding time for some reading as well: after finishing *The Art of Loving* she continued with *The Quiet American*. She said she got teased because of all the mail she received, especially one day when she got six letters. In addition to me, Joyce Coulam and my Mom had been frequent correspondents.

On Saturday the 26th Bev and Patty left Paducah and began the drive across Kentucky and Tennessee to Maryville. Leaving camp was traumatic but this time she said that she only cried inside for a change. Friendships formed quickly there, especially for the homesick younger girls, and then were almost as rapidly disrupted by the pain of separation. She had felt more lonely and introspective the entire time than she had the previous summer because of how we missed each other so much and the ambiguity of our prospects over the next year. The two of them enjoyed watching the land become more hilly as they drove east on I-40 from Nashville, arriving at Maryville about 10:00 p.m. They received a screaming welcome from the other four women they had travelled through the West with the previous summer, and the six of them had lunch together the next day along with two other friends, including Marilyn who was leaving in October for a Peace Corps assignment in Kenya.

On Sunday night Bev spent about two hours visiting with another friend, Boyd Daniels, the academic dean. She had been one of his teaching assistants during her senior year and they had developed a close friendship that allowed them to share confidences. Unfortunately, he was feeling down and fearful that Maryville was dying because of all the typical challenges of a small private institution. As always, the common denominator of most of the problems was a shortage of funds, although he was also discouraged by what he saw as a marked deterioration in the tone of the student body. Despite the gloomy subjects, she called their talk the first great one she had in months, even better than the occasional heart-to-hearts at camp. In fact she felt so energized by their visit that she returned to Marilyn's apartment and talked with her friend Carol for two more hours about anything and everything. She shared some of their discussion of faith, including the concept of looking within for God, which reminded me yet again that her beliefs were notably stronger than mine.

Bev and Patty drove from Maryville to Florence, Alabama, for a short stay with Patty's family, and I called her there one night. They had gone to a fabric store and she bought some cotton plaid material with fall colors to make into an A-line dress. She had finished *The Quiet American* and found it sad but seemingly realistic in capturing the struggles in Vietnam toward the end of the French colonial period. The melancholy tale of an American in Vietnam whose good intentions ultimately result in chaos and bloodshed was eerily prophetic considering that the book was published back in 1956. She hoped to read *Couples* since I had enjoyed it so much but first planned to tackle *Giles Goat-Boy*, a postmodern masterpiece that I had also relished. It was no wonder that she received so many letters because she said that she had been writing a few herself nearly every day, especially since camp ended. She wrote one to me from Florence that included a poem by Yevtushenko.

They flew from Florence to Coral Gables on Friday, August 1, and on Sunday they drove to Okeechobee to look for an apartment for Patty for the next school year. After finding her a place, they stopped at Lion Country Safari on the way back to Miami. It was fun keeping house, although it was also strange being there without her parents. After Patty left, Bev planned to spend her time studying, sewing, writing, letters, and reading. Then she would return to Minneapolis in early September and move into the apartment Jennifer had found at 409 University Ave. SE. The two Joyces would not be back yet, so it would be just the two of them until later in the month.

***

I had my interview with the Catholic chaplain, a fat bald Italian priest from New York City, on the evening of Monday the 28th, and we did not hit it off very well. Like the Army doctors, it seemed to me that he ranked the military's priorities above those of his profession, or perhaps he saw serving as a soldier as his primary duty. He read me one of the resolutions from Vatican II in which the good bishops had provided justifications for limited wars, and I knew right then where things were going with our "conversation." What kind of priest would advocate a morality so twisted that he would attempt to use church teaching to justify Vietnam? He questioned me on several points in my application and was not satisfied with most of my answers. He saw right away that my objections were more political than religious, and I could not deny that. The problem was that CO status had to be based on religious convictions, not political beliefs, and that brought us right back to the fact that for military purposes a man recognized as a CO had to have reservations of conscience preventing him from serving in all wars, not just a particular one.

Our interview was discouraging because it made my entire application process seem like an exercise in futility, but before I had a chance to think much about that I decided to try calling Bev in Florence. She was there and we had a wonderful conversation, which included laughing about the fact that we were in the same state for the first time in twenty weeks. One thing we had been talking about for the last two weeks was the possibility that I might be able to get a three-day pass and visit her in Coral Gables sometime in August. It would be great to have the whole house to ourselves but that situation was still very uncertain.

We continued with our mortar training that week and Wednesday the 30th was the first day I had any new training since June 18, the night I was admitted to the hospital. That meant that the leave and overlap in training had delayed the end of my AIT by exactly six weeks. We had night fire training after dark that day, which meant getting to bed much later than usual. On Thursday we had training on the M30 4.2 inch mortar, or the "four deuce." This gun weighed 675 pounds so it was usually vehicle-mounted, and it had a range of up to just over four miles. The lack of portability compared to the 81 mm model meant that the 4.2 inch was not used nearly as much in a war like Vietnam where mobility was often important. The standard organizational configuration was one heavy mortar platoon for each battalion.

On Thursday, Friday, and Saturday we had long lectures on some of the intricacies of the role of the mortar in infantry combat situations such as procedures for forward observers, factors affecting trajectories, spotting, adjusting fire to bring it in on the target without endangering friendly forces, elements of the call for fire, and the Vernier scale. Much of this was quite technical and the classes were designed to give us an overview of the uses of the weapon rather than preparing us to man one immediately. Those more practical skills would be acquired in the only way possible: working with more experienced soldiers in a combat situation.

I took advantage of our improved ability to phone each other since Bev had left camp by calling her again on Thursday evening, her last one in Florence. Not much had happened in two days except for the mortar training, but it was just good to talk. On the night of Saturday, August 2, I had a few beers and went to see the movie *Duffy* with some of the guys. I slept through some of it but liked what I saw. Between being tired out from training and groggy from drinking I rarely saw a film all the way through at Fort Mac, but it was still a diversion to see a movie in a real theater instead of the annoying way they were presented at Fort Campbell.

The practice of assigning all of the college men in the company to the mortar platoon had the unintended result of placing many of the most reluctant and discontented soldiers in the same unit. I was far from the only one who had been called up when the SSS ended deferments for most grad students and anyone who wanted to gripe about the situation was sure to find a willing audience among the men of the Fifth Platoon. The level of discontent in Charlie Company was noticeably higher than it had been in Echo. There was a social worker from New York City named Marty Sheridan who was endearingly bumbling and absent-minded, but appeared totally unfit for the infantry. Another guy from Philadelphia was working on getting a psychological discharge. He seemed perfectly normal when we talked, a little tense maybe, but sometimes he freaked out. That week it happened on the machine-gun range at a time when he was not handling a gun and after that the shrink said to keep him away from weapons. He was the only one who knew how much of this was for real, but I wished him luck in getting out. Another man from Philly was also very uptight about being in the infantry but he had not done anything about it yet. There were more guys from the East Coast in this platoon and many of them talked openly about smoking pot and hash, something I had never experienced.

Another thing I noticed in my new company was a higher level of racial tension. There were many black guys in Charlie but only one in the heavy weapons platoon. This unfortunate situation mirrored that in segregated America as a whole, and I was told that most of the "Negroes" were not very fond of us mortar men. So far there had only been a couple of minor fights but the inevitable reality was that the racial discord in the American civilian world was also reflected in our company.

How could our leaders imagine that situations such as this would not diminish the Army's effectiveness? The attitude of the SSS and the military itself was that a recruit was a recruit. Training would transform this civilian raw material into a uniform product: combat-ready soldiers. It never seemed to occur to "the powers that be" that forcing an increasing number of reluctant recruits into the ranks, especially older men who were more highly educated and accustomed to thinking for themselves, would almost certainly result in a less effective military. I never felt we deserved any special treatment from the SSS because of having more schooling, but the fact was that it was hard to believe we were the kind of men the Army would have preferred to receive. Just as we had no really good options when we were drafted, the Army had no choice but to try to work with the recruits sent to them by the local draft boards.

This was but one of several ways in which the military was misused and abused by the civilian authorities during Vietnam. Our leaders continued to prosecute an increasingly unpopular war that required a heavy reliance upon the draft to maintain troop levels due to an inadequate number of volunteers, the standard one-year tour of duty, and the fear of the political cost that would have resulted from calling up more of the reserves. As with the general population, the war became more and more unpopular with many of the lower-ranking soldiers as it dragged on and on, but the military had no choice but to attempt to carry out the directives of its civilian leaders. The Army, however, was too bound by rigid customs and regulations to adapt successfully to the strange new war it was ordered to fight, and the higher-ranking officers, eager to please their civilian superiors, always reported that things were going much better than they really were. Of course, the inevitable qualification to their optimistic reports was that things could be going even better with a higher troop level. Very few of the men responsible for these disastrous decisions were the ones being killed and maimed and, as the years of conflict ground on, fewer and fewer of the ones put in harm's way were willing to accept the situation in silence.

Nixon, a consummate politician, realized that he needed to do something that at least made it appear he was moving toward ending US involvement in the war, so on July 25 he introduced the Nixon Doctrine at a press conference on Guam. This was a declaration that, while America would provide appropriate aid when requested, our allies bore the primary responsibility for their own defense. The new policy applied to all of our allies but there was no doubt which of them had prompted it and soon the awkward neologism "Vietnamization" began to define the Nixon/Kissinger approach to our long-term strategy in Vietnam. The President then went on to South Vietnam where he met with President Thieu and visited some US military bases.

The following week, Henry Kissinger met secretly with a diplomat from North Vietnam in Paris. It seemed clear to the communists that their willingness to accept massive casualties, combined with growing discontent over the war on the American domestic front, gave them an inevitable advantage that could not be overcome by any amount of American firepower. But the arrogant Kissinger was never one to doubt his own ability to assess a situation. The Harvard academic also fancied himself a master diplomat and negotiator, expressing this view of the situation to his staff: "I can't believe that a fourth-rate power like North Vietnam doesn't have a breaking point."

Even though these initial exploratory talks came to nothing, the protracted four-year poker game known as the peace negotiations had begun with both sides firmly convinced that they held an unbeatable hand and that their bluffing opponent would be the first to fold. That tens of thousands of lives hung in the balance meant nothing to the communists, and that was a price that our President and National Security Advisor were also willing to pay since our huge advantage in firepower ensured that the majority of those causalities would be sustained by the other side. The alternative was the unprecedented humiliation of America losing a war. That was a grim enough prospect for any US president but for an old red-baiter like Nixon who had established his political credentials during the McCarthy era through smearing opponents by accusing them of being "soft on communism" it was difficult to conceive of a calamity greater than meeting defeat at the hands of a bunch of Third World reds. So he almost immediately found himself in the same quagmire that had brought down LBJ. The only respite from the gloomy news was an ongoing mid-summer lull in combat activities. For the last week of July, the weekly totals of combat deaths were the lowest of the year thus far, with 110 US KIAs and 1,963 for the communists.

After my conversation with the chaplain I found myself even more depressed and out of sorts than during the first couple of weeks at Fort Campbell. For the first time since I went into the service I lost my appetite and skipped most meals, but when the weekend came around my thirst for beer was as strong as ever. Now that I had buddies in my new unit I began frequenting our own EM club, Charlie's. This was pretty much a clone of Sam's: a large Quonset hut used as a bar. A bunch of us got drunk there on the evening of Saturday, August 2, and there were some black guys at our table enjoying the boozy revelry as well. One of them commented that socializing with white guys was pretty unusual for him, and I loved the fact that we were all getting on so well. It was a new thought for me that the black troops might feel just as uncomfortable around us as we sometimes did around them. The biggest problem was that so many of us came from civilian environments where the races did not interact very much, but I was skeptical that all this goodwill would still be there when we were sober; we had all heard the stories about serious racial discord among the troops in the RVN.

On Sunday morning I was taking my usual walk up to Hilltop for a day of relaxation when I was hit with the need to have an immediate bowel movement. The suddenness of the impulse was because I had not had one for several days due to eating almost nothing, but the numerous beers from the previous evening obviously broke the logjam. I was near my old

Echo Company area so I ducked into the nearest latrine for an impressively explosive evacuation. As I savored the feeling of relief I found that the toilet I had used was out of order. No matter how many times I tried to flush it there were no results, despite the fact that there had been no "out of order" sign on the door. I quickly washed up and left the empty building before anyone else came in, and as I continued on my way up to the service club I began to imagine the language of the poor guys who were assigned to clean the latrine. The more I thought about it the funnier it seemed and as my spirits rose and the hours passed I slowly began to realize that somehow my monumental purging had been emotional as well as physical. My appetite returned and as I spent the day reading and thinking, I arrived at the decision to withdraw my CO application. Much as I had disliked the chaplain, I had to admit that he was right in saying that my objections to the war in Vietnam did not meet the military's definition of a true CO.

The brief taste of freedom I had on leave had brought home to me how much I hated being in an environment like the Army where we were always being told what to do, and the major attraction of applying for CO status, since it would not exempt me from serving in combat if I was reassigned as a medic, was the feeling that I was finally taking some initiative rather than just constantly following orders. Since it was now all but certain that my application would not have the result I had hoped for, I finally admitted to myself that there was little or no point in doing something that would not accomplish anything for me just for the sake of defying the Army.

★★★

After I resigned myself to going infantry I soon fell back into the familiar routines of Army life. We no longer had Drill and Ceremony just for the sake of practice as in Basic, but we marched at various speeds whenever we were moving on foot between locations, and the old familiar cadence calls are always an evocative thing to anyone who has spent time in uniform. The working day would begin and end with formations where our roster of surnames was read off as we each responded "Here." There was rarely a man missing, and then the officer in charge would yell out "Report," and the NCO taking the roll call would shout out "All present and accounted for, Sir!"

One morning I felt a big fart coming so I let fly right after the "Report" command, which caught the sergeant off guard. There was no way to locate the offender in the middle of a big formation and after a few seconds we were all struggling mightily to keep from snickering. That is the kind of thing that passes for humor in the military. Any successful attempt to defy or mock authority, however minor, was always met with jovial approval.

Another thing that was different about my new unit was that our squad leaders were new sergeants, "shake and bakes," who had been to the NCO school over at Fort Benning, a program the Army instituted due to the need for more NCOs in the war zone. This was a twelve-week program after completion of AIT. When men completed that they were made buck sergeants (E-5) and then they went through AIT again as squad leaders before going to Vietnam. It was sort of strange having NCOs who had not yet been to Nam, but they were much less hard-nosed than some of the uptight and marginally stable Vietnam guys who screamed at us most of the time. On Monday we had a presentation that stressed all the benefits of the NCO school, including higher pay and the chance to develop leadership skills. The advantage that impressed me the most was a six-month delay in going overseas because of the additional training. They were extremely short on mortar NCOs in Nam and so we were encouraged to apply, especially the ones who had gone to college. I decided to give it some thought.

On Tuesday the 5th we had training on the M2 Browning .50 caliber, the standard heavy machine gun for US forces. The instructor talked about the long history of this weapon in the US military in a way that reminded me of my old American military history class in ROTC. It was used on the ground primarily as a defensive weapon because the weight of the gun and tripod, 128 pounds, along with the additional burden of a decent supply of ammo, made it impractical to carry on patrol. In addition, it was employed in groupings of mounted configurations on airplanes, helicopters, ships, and vehicles, and was powerful enough to be an effective anti-aircraft weapon. The bullets were huge, especially compared to those fired by our M16s, and the gun could fire them at up to 1,200 per minute depending on the type being used. A Browning crew with enough ammunition could easily hold off a much larger enemy force.

The instructor's demonstration was impressive as a hail of bullets tore through several old vehicles down range, and then we each had a turn at firing off a burst. The two spade handles and the butterfly trigger made it a comfortable weapon to grasp, and when you pressed down on the trigger with your thumbs the roar of the gun was terrific as the barrel soon began shimmering with the heat. It was exciting at the time to feel the power of the .50 caliber and the cacophony made reflection impossible, but it was also sobering later to contemplate how much death such a gun could dole out. This was a weapon that could mow down many men in seconds and they would not just be shot but literally torn apart.

I continued to find the idea of taking some sort of initiative rather than merely following orders attractive, and so on Wednesday the 6th I withdrew my CO application and signed the papers for the NCO academy, a combination of actions that might easily have made the higher-ups believe I was bucking for a psychological discharge. Sane men forced into an insane situation soon begin to behave in crazy ways as described so masterfully by Joseph Heller, and I believe that coming out of my depression had pushed me over a bit toward the manic side of the mood scale. There were some pretty far out guys in my new platoon and the feeling was contagious. I was starting to wonder if we were beginning to live out our own version of *Catch-22*. A common attitude now that we knew we were headed for the war zone was "What are they going to do—send me to Vietnam?" But if training was getting to be this strange what would Vietnam really be like? The fear of death that was always a possibility there was the common thread running through all the erratic behavior in Heller's novel. That was what really put the men of his 256th Squadron over the edge.

On Wednesday and Thursday we finally had live fire with the mortars. As we approached one of the guns the crew dropped a round into the barrel without alerting us and the unexpected report was quite a jolt. Ed Russell blurted out, "I just about creamed my jeans that time!" Ed was from Out East, but not one of the big cities, and he was one of my favorite buddies. He was just as disgusted about our situation as I was, but he was more vocal about it. I liked his biting sense of humor and we shared a common interest in resisting what the Army was trying to force us to do. We went through many rounds on both days and then on Thursday night we had night fire with illumination rounds. Upon exploding in the air they launched a magnesium "candle" that floated to earth via a small parachute. The portion of the two-day exercise on firing without the aid of a fire direction center seemed like one of the most useful for many combat situations in a guerilla war.

On Thursday after the night firing I was one of the men assigned to the cleanup detail. Our truck driver drove like a maniac and after a stretch of tooth-rattling bumps we heard some sort of explosion in the front of the vehicle, which then slowly coasted to a halt. It turned out that he had blown the engine and by the time they got a replacement out to us and we had brought back the mortars, cleaned them, and then marched back to Tigerland it was 2:30 a.m., only two hours before our standard wakeup time.

On Friday the 8th we had demolitions class. I was selected to push a plunger that set off a charge of 2.5 pounds of TNT but the rest of the class was boring, especially for those of us functioning on two hours of sleep. That afternoon we had a nine-mile march in sweltering heat and by the time we got back our fatigues were so soaked with sweat that it looked as though someone had drenched us with a hose. I took a cold shower after we got off duty and returned to the barracks. I called home that night and told Mom about NCO school. She did not seem to mind, and especially liked the part about the extra half-year in the States. I called Bev also, telling her about NCO school and my decision to withdraw my CO application. I had not mentioned the latter to Mom since she had not known about the application. By that time we had been told that our three-day pass would not be until Labor Day weekend when Bev would already be back in Minneapolis, so there would be no visit to Miami and we would not see each other until my leave after AIT. That was disappointing, but since we had also been told that September 13 was our unit's graduation date at least the two of us did know for sure when we finally would be seeing each other again. The week of training concluded on Saturday with a class on Techniques of Fire, which was scheduled to be our subject for the entire following week.

***

Down in Coral Gables, Patty had left to move into her new place up in Okeechobee and Bev was experiencing some strange sensations triggered by living alone in her childhood home. She said Jennifer had written that her boyfriend Steve had gone for his pre-induction physical at the end of July and was hoping to be classified 4-F, unfit to serve. She did not say what physical or emotional issue might cause him to be disqualified, but I wished him luck.

After the chaos of camp Bev was now enjoying an abundance of time to read and think but, given the uncertainty of what our next year would bring, that was not always such a good thing. Her letters from August often expressed her struggles with religious and philosophical issues. Those are the kind of things that young people, especially students, usually discuss often and at great length, but doing that by mail was almost as unsatisfying as expressing our emotions and feelings for each other by correspondence. We would start writing about our thoughts without really knowing where we were headed, but when the other person was actually there the two of them arrived at a destination by sharing ideas. Two people really cannot do that well when they are apart, but in those days we got by with what we had, which was the mail, the phone, and our thoughts of each other.

Bev's closest friend from childhood and college, Barbara, was also back home just one block away and the two of them were enjoying spending time together again. On the night of Wednesday the 6th they ate supper at the Allyns', the parents of Jack, her sister Annabelle's husband. After eating, Ken and Mable drove them around the city and then over to see the lights on Miami Beach. She was like me in that our unsettled future was causing her to bounce around from one thing to another. She had bought a harmonica for Marilyn, her friend who was going to be teaching in Kenya, and she thought she might get one for herself as well and learn to play. She said that she always felt as though she was expected to go to church when she was home but she stayed home on Sunday the 10th. After attending at the Newman Center and Vince Hawkinson's church, their old pastor at home seemed outdated and irrelevant, but she said she would go the next Sunday to avoid disappointing her parents since they would be back from their long trip by then.

Writing about spiritual matters reminded her that she had received a letter from Sister Paul Mary. She wrote that she likely would never have as strong a religious faith as sister but that she loved talking with her because they shared an optimistic outlook based upon their shared belief in the essential goodness of humanity. I was always pleased to hear her express these views, because I needed that antidote to my own tendencies toward withdrawal and pessimism. I had to work at cultivating hope and her attitude toward life, combined with our love for each other, made that labor much less burdensome, even in such a bleak environment as the military during a time of war.

Bev wrote on Sunday the 10th that our phone call on Friday night had made her so happy that she "bubbled the rest of the night." Sometimes it still amazed me that I could make such a wonderful woman so happy, but I never did get tired of hearing about it. Like Mom, the thing she liked about NCO school was the extra six months before going overseas. She must have sensed that I was not entirely at peace with my decision to apply for the training, but I was grateful that she did not ask much about it. She mentioned that a surprise she had written about in a previous letter had been the idea of renting a car and driving to Knoxville by way of Anniston, but said she would cancel those plans now that we knew for sure when we would be seeing each other. That made sense to me. She was planning to watch *The Agony and the Ecstasy* on the Sunday Night Movie, because the book was one of her favorites. She had now finished the first reel of *Giles Goat-Boy* and, like me, was amazed by Barth's satirical ability and the depth and vividness of his imagination. She enclosed a poem by Amy Lowell and some clippings from *Time* on literary topics and current events.

***

Homicidal madness continued to plague the home front as the Zodiac Killer sent letters to three Northern California newspapers on August 1, each containing one-third of a cryptogram. One week later a couple in Salinas managed to crack the murderer's code and the result was a frightening glimpse into the mind of a madman as he described how he found killing more pleasurable than sex, as well as his belief that in the afterlife his victims would all be his slaves.

But the ravings of Zodiac were quickly forgotten because the day after his puzzle was solved the Manson Family began carrying out their gruesome two-day killing spree in Los Angeles. On the 9th they murdered five people, including the actress Sharon Tate who was expecting her first child in one month, and the next night they killed two more victims, the LaBianca couple, only nine miles away.

It would be several months before detectives solved the horrible crimes and we did not learn all the chilling details of Charles Manson's power over the minds of the members of his "family" until the trial the following year, but we did soon learn the lurid details of the butchery that left the victims with a total of over one hundred stab wounds, as well as messages left in blood on the walls and front doors of their homes. Since the perpetrators were unknown for so long the possible motive was a mystery as well, leaving a shaken public with no clue as to where they might strike next.

With the war continuing to rage in Vietnam and now this mayhem at home it was difficult to avoid the sensation that America was continuing its uncontrolled journey into a strange time of mindless violence.

***

Bev wrote again on Tuesday the 12th about the TV she had been watching. The reception was quite poor because her dad had taken down the aerial on the roof in case a hurricane hit while they were on their trip. The Michelangelo movie had been pretty good but did not really do the book justice. I had introduced her to Johnny Carson and now she really liked *The Tonight Show*. She even watched an old-time comedy. She had gone with Barb to a big bookstore and Barb bought a couple of books. Bev thought about getting *Native Son* but decided that there were already enough unread books for her at her folks' place. The quiet of the house was a dramatic contrast to the chaos of camp and she needed to stay busy to keep from going nuts. She was almost finished sewing her dress and had sent for a book on macramé as well as buying a knitting-fashions book.

She wrote again on the 14th telling more about keeping busy while she rode an emotional rollercoaster, sometimes laughing and then later shedding tears. She shopped that morning, wandering through the Hong Kong Shop and another import store. She found a handbag shop run by a Cuban man who had made purses for forty-eight years, the last two in the Gables. Then in the afternoon she and Barbara ate a submarine sandwich and pizza for lunch before going to see *Romeo and Juliet*. She loved it and understood why Mary liked it so well. The theater was in the Cuban section of town, so there were Spanish subtitles. She closed with two love poems by cummings.

We were enjoying the chance to talk more on the phone, and she wrote on Sunday the 17th after another of our conversations. Her folks had returned, but they both had bad colds so Bev was cooking and doing dishes. That night she fixed a canned ham smothered with crushed pineapple and brown sugar syrup. She liked having a kitchen to cook in again and was also looking forward to doing that in the new apartment. She and her dad had climbed up onto the roof to put back the TV aerial, finishing up just before it began to rain. The next day, she was planning on cutting out the second dress and maybe helping her dad by weeding the flower beds because he had an ear infection as well as a cold. Her folks had loved their trip and her dad took over two hundred slides. They brought her a beautiful pair of slippers made by Eskimos from seal and rabbit fur. She closed with some thoughts about things to do on my leave, including going to Como Park.

✯✯✯

On Monday, August 11, we continued with the new phase of training we had begun at the end of the previous week. Having completed weapons training, we now moved on to "Techniques of Fire," which included the basic formations of a squad in the field, how to assault and defend a position, and some mechanized exercises as well. I wondered how relevant these descriptions of well-orchestrated commands and movements were to the reality of jungle warfare against guerilla insurgents following their own rules on their home turf. On the last three weekdays we stayed out late and ate two meals in the field. It was amazing how dark it was in the woods at night but we soon got used to insects and most of us also learned to stop thinking about snakes all the time. The thought that kept running through our minds, though, was what this would be like if there were enemies out there in the blackness waiting to ambush us when we least expected it. We usually fired our weapons so when we returned to the company area on the late nights we had to clean our rifles before lights-out. The NCOs inspected them carefully so we knew that we might as well do a good job the first time. We ended up getting a total of about eight hours of sleep for the three nights combined. On the third one I heard a sergeant yelling at me and I awoke to discover I had gone to sleep on my bunk in my fatigues and combat boots with my rifle cradled in my arms.

The weather had cooled off somewhat but that was a mixed blessing because we also began to get more rain. Unless there was danger from lightning we just continued with our training so we spent a good deal of time in wet clothes and I soon caught a cold. I only wished I knew how to get mono again. My spirits rose on Saturday because we got Sunday off, and that day we had a mechanized assault exercise where we rode in armored personnel carriers (APCs) manufactured by the Continental Can Company. We also rode back to the company area in the APCs and the noise from the tracked vehicles moving fast on paved roads was deafening, not to mention the jarring vibration.

When I got the chance to contemplate things other than the Army my thoughts were all over the place, just as Bev's were. I wrote her about Unitarianism even though I knew I had no intention of joining any sort of organized church. I also asked her what she thought about living in Canada after I got out of the service. That idea popped into my head because one of the guys in our platoon had gone up to Toronto for a few months after he got drafted, returning when he decided he was not ready to make the commitment to never return to the USA. But he did say he was thinking about moving there after he got out, and another man said that he was planning on doing the same. For obvious reasons, I was down on our nation at the time, but I also knew that I still loved the idea of what America could be too much to ever abandon her. Bev had asked if I had ever tried the harmonica so I told her that I had done that but never gotten very far with it. I also mentioned that when I got out I wanted to get more serious about learning to play the guitar properly. That led me to describe the British and American folk music that I loved and how we could listen to my records together someday. Both of our minds were moving in a million directions because of the stress and uncertainty we were under.

On Saturday night I went to see *The Prime of Miss Jean Brodie*. Maggie Smith was great, but I still slept through about half of it. Rod McKuen was popular then, and he contributed some of the music. I especially liked the title song. On Sunday the 17th I went up to Hilltop to read and write letters while enjoying the air conditioning. Larry Anderson and another guy from Basic showed up and said that they were being held over at Mac as witnesses in a court martial. Anything that delayed going overseas was a good break as long as it did not shorten their post-training leaves. Considering all the unhappy recruits with ready access to deadly weapons, I was surprised there were not more incidents leading to actions under the UCMJ. I asked them if they knew how the film ended but they had not seen it.

After I was done writing to Bev and my family I finished the Klein book, a collection of twenty essays by well-known figures from the worlds of literature and academia. I enjoyed the entire book but found Saul Bellow's essay particularly striking. He observed that "on the whole, American novels are filled with complaints over the misfortunes of the sovereign Self," and also noted that the great writers of the first half of the century provided their post-war successors with "a tonal background of disillusion or elegy." That certainly resonated and it reminded me especially of Hemingway, always one of my favorites, which led me to speculate on how he, Fitzgerald, and Faulkner would view the chaos that was our contemporary America. It seemed to me that Hemingway's young manhood was similar to our own in that a war had transformed both his world and his worldview into ones that were much darker than those of his adolescence. In spite of my strong distaste for military life I took a certain perverse pleasure in imagining I was in a comparable situation because I admired the way he balanced a taste for all the pleasures of life with a world-weary cynicism, making *Ecclesiastes* a perfect source for the title of his first novel. It also worked out well that both inclinations were incentives for heavy drinking.

That was the weekend of Woodstock, although I did not hear about it until I saw the story in a news magazine a week or two later. That delay reflected the way we usually heard about newsworthy events during training because of our physical isolation on the base as well as the fact that we did not hear much news at all except on weekends. There were no TVs in our barracks and the few radios were usually tuned to music stations. I liked to get *Time* or *Newsweek* at the PX and catch up with the news as time permitted, which was usually on Sunday, but that created a curious delay in hearing about all but the most important events. On an Army base, a rock concert was not considered an important event.

Not hearing about events until a week or more after they occurred left me with a strange feeling of my life being out of sync with the civilian world, a sensation much like the way I felt when communicating with Bev and my family by mail, responding to thoughts, feelings, and questions the others had written days before. In fact, "out of sync" is as good a way as any to describe our lives themselves in those days as we struggled with the emotional turmoil of a months-long separation so soon after falling in love, and as I dealt with attempting to come to terms with the abrupt loss of freedom and threat of death or injury in battle that came with being in the Army. With death a daily fact of life in Vietnam and also becoming all too frequent on the home front, it seemed that the nation itself had veered wildly off track. The center was not holding and, since we were deep into unexplored territory, any thoughts about how it might all turn out were mere speculation.

***

And so in the midst of those strange days an equally strange and wonderful event occurred, a happening to end all happenings. Vietnam was the defining event of our generation, but that was never our moniker. No, we were the Woodstock Nation. At the time all I knew down at Fort Mac was that a huge rock concert had taken place but as the months, and then the years, went by the festival continued to grow more and more significant upon reflection until finally arriving at its exalted status as the high watermark of the counterculture. That it became increasingly famous as time passed was due in no small part to the fact that it was so thoroughly documented, with the exhaustive sound and movie recordings eventually yielding five LPs and a well-produced three-hour film. That 400,000 young people could gather for three days to revel in music and peaceful, albeit raucous, fellowship while they shared food and drugs and dealt with rain and mud by celebrating rather than griping about it seemed to validate the promise of the way of life pioneered during the Summer of Love two years earlier out on the other coast. The key moment for me has always been Wavy Gravy's bemused and euphoric spontaneous exclamation in the midst of giving directions on logistics from the stage to the massive assemblage: "We must be in Heaven, Man!" No one even seemed to mind that he was well over thirty.

Of course, the conservative elements of society saw the entire spectacle as nothing but a huge mob of drug-addled hippies reveling like pagans in sexual abandonment to the accompaniment of equally crazed performers, but such reactions were a big part of what the outlandish clothing and behavior were intended to elicit. To have the likes of Nixon, Agnew, or Reagan expressing pleasure at how much fun the young folks were having would have instantly evaporated the essential vitality of the event. The music itself was certainly uneven, but there really was no such thing as a bad performance at Woodstock because, regardless of the technical and artistic quality, all the performers were playing their way into the hallowed realm of legend, although many of them also seemed to be engaged in an informal competition to determine who could get the most wasted and still deliver a credible performance. And how fitting it was that the last artist on Monday morning was Jimi Hendrix, whose soulful and tortured rendition of *The Star-Spangled Banner* so exquisitely captured the mood of America during the days of Vietnam and the culture wars.

In the middle of Woodstock, as I sat up at Hilltop enjoying the respite of a quiet Sunday, Hurricane Camille struck the Gulf Coast, one of only three Category 5 hurricanes to make landfall in the US during the twentieth century. Sustained winds of 190 miles per hour were recorded before the massive storm wiped out the meteorological equipment in its path. The destruction along the Gulf Coast was shocking but, as always, the saddest statistic was the loss of life. The death toll was 256 with nearly half of them caused by flash flooding from torrential rains in Virginia. Camille attracted more attention at Fort Mac than Woodstock since we were in a state on the Gulf Coast but, again, I was not aware of the scope of the damage and death toll until a week or two later when I bought a news magazine featuring the headline "A Killer Named Camille."

★★★

We began our week of patrolling training on Monday the 18th, and this was the start of the newly developed phase of our AIT that was designed to prepare us for combat in Vietnam under conditions as realistic as possible. The week started off on a low note as we sat in class all morning and then went out to the field to form a perimeter, which meant two hours of lying on the ground in the rain. Things picked up on Tuesday and Wednesday because we had night patrols under conditions that seemed realistic: pitch darkness in heavy woods. All of this training was carried out in a big wild area of about 22,000 acres called Pelham Range in the western portion of the base.

Tuesday night was pitch black with clouds obscuring the moon, and we went out to set up an ambush. Nothing special happened at our point but at another point a guy felt two snakes crawl up his leg so he leapt up and immediately ran into a tree in the darkness, then got up again and ran all the way to the road. Another man killed the snakes with blanks, which can cause injury at point-blank range. We never did find out what kind of snakes they were, or if they even existed at all, but it sure made for a funny story. There is no faster rumor mill than a military one and by the time the night was over I had heard at least ten different versions of the story. Of course, the levity was tempered by the knowledge that all four varieties of North American venomous snakes were native to that part of the country, but that factoid was the least of our worries most of the time out in the woods. There was a moon on Wednesday night so that made things easier. We were supposed to walk into an ambush to practice the proper reactions in that situation, but we went through the area one at a time so that if they sprang it they would only "kill" one of us. This seemed to confuse the aggressors since they were waiting for an entire squad to appear and they never sprang it at all.

On Thursday the 21st we threw some hand grenades, but it was hot and my hands were sweaty so one of my grenades fell short. I hit the dirt along with a nearby lieutenant and the explosion brought a rain of mud down on us. It looked like a scene out of a service comedy and when he started swearing it was all I could do to keep from laughing. Soon after that we got thoroughly drenched by a heavy downpour but most of us did not bother to put on our ponchos because we were having a river crossing that evening anyway. Besides, the rubbery ponchos were smelly and miserable to wear in hot, humid conditions.

That night was one of the rites of passage of AIT, Escape and Evasion, a simulation of being caught behind enemy lines. The mission was to travel through about five miles of woods while trying to avoid the aggressors. The soldiers who were captured were taken to a POW camp and sort of beaten up for an hour. The aggressors were "short timers," men back from Nam who had only a little time left in the Army. The word was that they were not about to go through the woods and brush and so they only waited at the roads and firebreaks. To start if off, we had the river crossing, which was using a rope to go hand-over-hand across a dammed-up section of a stream called Cane Creek. But the water was high and the current fairly strong because of the heavy rain, so the operation was taking longer than planned. Then we had a scare when a black guy almost drowned so they called it off for the rest of us. That was a break for those of us who had not crossed yet, even though we were already soaked to the skin from the rain.

We finally arrived at our starting point, got our azimuth, and set out into the woods. Sergeant Ralph, our squad leader, was one of the NCOs from the school where I had applied. I liked him because he was obviously intelligent and there was no air of phony machismo about him. He was like us, a good man caught up in a bad situation, and he always tried to carry out the mission with as little Army BS as possible. I respected him because it was clear that he had our best interests at heart. He broke our squad into two teams and I went with Ralph along with three other men. Our troubles soon started when we discovered that we had a bad compass. In fact, it was worse than useless because, instead of just freezing up, the needle kept pointing us in the wrong direction. Other than being captured, that was about the worst thing that could have happened to us and, of course, we suspected that it was deliberate. Then we found that a low area we needed to pass through was flooded from the downpour. We had to go around it and that completed the job of getting us thoroughly lost.

We crossed two firebreaks without incident and then hit a flooded low section of the woods. Our only choice was to slog through it and it was so dark that we literally could not see our hands in front of our faces. We felt our faces breaking through spider webs at nearly every step and thorns and branches kept lashing at us as well. Ralph took the lead and we each held onto the pack of the man in front of us to form a chain. Suddenly we realized that the other team was no longer there, so the five of us remaining made a pact that we would not be captured. If that did happen, though, it would have to be all of us because we would not allow one or more of us to be caught without doing all we could to free him. We knew that was the way it was in actual combat.

We circled and doubled back to try to get out of the swamp and then finally came to a road. There was a moon that night so once we got out of the trees and brush we could see reasonably well. Sgt. Ralph reconned the road and then motioned us up, but when we all got up onto the road some guys suddenly appeared and yelled "Halt, you're captured." We took off down the road and then crashed into the brush, but when we turned to face our "enemies" they turned out to be some men from another squad who had lost their leader just like the second team from our own squad. Since we had an NCO we had to let them join up with us, and so the nine of us set out again down the road. Even though using the road increased the likelihood of encountering aggressors, we were reluctant to set off through the woods again without a reliable compass. After walking for two or three miles we found ourselves in the middle of a deserted airfield. The moonlight lent a surreal ghostly aspect to the scene as our little column moved across the huge open area. We followed one of the runways to the end of the field and then set off on a path into the woods.

We soon saw a white sign with a big "54" on it: we were on the compass course. That made the going easier because the course was a number of lanes cut through the trees, but it was designed like a huge maze so it was hard to get anywhere. We knew that the course was south of where we were supposed to be so that was at least some useful information, but we were unsure of how to get back on track, especially without a compass. Then we came to another swampy area and this one was infested with clouds of hungry mosquitoes. We continued swatting and slogging along until we realized we were approaching another road. We saw headlights coming and hit the ditch as two POW trucks drove past. After they were gone we listened closely and heard a generator and it dawned on us that we were near the dreaded POW camp. We stayed down and tried to fight off the relentless mosquitoes while Ralph went out to recon again. I respected him for that because he could just as easily have ordered one of us to do it.

Sarge finally returned and we crossed the road and started up a hill, moving away from the enemy camp. We ran into the thickest and thorniest brush yet but just kept pushing on while holding onto each others' packs again. Eventually we were far enough into the woods to be reasonably confident no aggressors would be near such a God-forsaken place and so we stopped to rest and try once again to figure out where we were. We burned a little paper to see our map but still had no way of figuring out our location. So we set off again down the other side of the hill and finally hit another road. We decided once again to choose the risk of encountering aggressors along the road over the misery of wandering through the blackness of the woods, and eventually we saw a light far off through the trees. We hated to go into the woods again but we did not dare approach the camp along the road because we had no idea if it was the friendly one or the POW compound. Ralph reconned yet again and returned to tell us it was the prison camp, so we quietly withdrew and headed back down the road. We came to a dead end so we doubled back and then saw a lone figure coming down the road toward us who turned out to be one of the four men who had joined up with us earlier. He had been the last of our column and we had not even realized that he had fallen about a mile behind.

It was after 1:00 a.m. now and the time for the exercise had expired, so we soon found a main road and walked north. We passed a group of about thirty men and the four we had picked up earlier joined them. After about two miles we saw lights and headed toward them. It was the friendly camp so we signed in, got our C Rations, and boarded a truck. We got back to the barracks about 2:00 a.m. and there were only a few guys there. It turned out that we had caught the second truck back so we felt as though we had done pretty well after all. Taking such a crazy roundabout route had turned out to be a highly effective evasion tactic, so the bad compass might have been a blessing in disguise because it prevented us from following the route the aggressors were expecting. Also, the five of us were all good walkers and we had moved fast the entire night, which was why we kept losing the trailing members of our unit. Our other team evaded capture as well so the entire 4th Squad completed the exercise successfully. The 2nd and 3rd came in later, reporting that they had evaded the enemy as well. The 1st, however, had met with disaster since the entire unit was captured other than one man who was still missing.

When the men from the 1st finally returned they told us that the prison camp was bad. Most of them had been put on the Apache Pole, where they wrap your legs around a pole and then bend you backwards. They really had some big knots on their shins, and one of them admitted that they had all been screaming in pain. While one of them was down a Green Beret poured half a bucket of water down his mouth and nose, and when they let him up he threw the rest of the water on the Green Beret who responded by putting the prisoner's face in the mud and stepping on the back of his head. We heard many tales from the men of the 1st Squad about the miseries of capture, but we all knew that was nothing compared to what would happen to troops taken prisoner in the RVN. Two guys from our platoon managed to escape from the camp, one by running half a mile in his stocking feet. Two sergeants had been captured and the aggressors had been especially tough on them. One of them had a big bruise on his cheek the next day and the other had been knocked unconscious for almost an hour when he was pushed out of a truck with his hands tied. Since prisoners were held for an hour it was nearly time for him to be released when he awoke.

We were told that all the men who had been captured talked except one who was known to be especially stubborn and ill-tempered. That was not surprising but, of course, the other side of the coin was that even the most brutal interrogator rarely has any idea if the information a prisoner is providing is accurate. Their mistake was that they had not even tried to run when the aggressors found them, and that was just stupid. What were they thinking, especially their NCO? I ate my C Rations, took a shower, and got to bed about 3:00 a.m. for a couple hours of sleep. About 7:00 a.m. the missing man from the 1st Squad showed up. When his squad got hit the Green Beret had chased him for a long time, but he was a good runner and managed to evade his would-be captor. He had walked through the woods alone for the rest of the night and found his way back after the sun rose.

On Friday the 22nd everyone was so tired that we felt as though we were moving in slow motion. I almost fell out of the bleachers when I began to doze off during class. There was a model of a Vietnamese village out on Pelham Range and we practiced ambushing that but it was anticlimactic after the previous night in the woods. Most of us had been experiencing prickly heat for weeks but about this time we found out the hard way that in late summer Fort Mac was infested with chiggers, something I had never even known about in Minnesota. The bites of the minuscule pests created a maddening itch far worse than that of a mosquito, and scratching only made it worse.

On Saturday we got our gear ready for the RVN training that would be starting the following week. We were dismissed about midday and given passes, and everyone's main priority was to get drunk. One guy who lived in a nearby town had arranged for a civilian friend to pick him up. They were going into Anniston to buy booze and he said they had room in the car for four more, so I joined that group. We were smart enough not to party in town, and so our plan was to bring our purchases back to the barracks and drink there. I wanted a pint of liquor instead of just beer. It turned out that the county had some sort of strange alcohol control laws that required it to be sold in government-run stores. It was much like a pharmacy in that you went up to a window and told a clerk what you wanted and then he disappeared into the back and returned with your request. They did not seem to have any of my favorite brands and the good old boy in the window and I barely spoke the same language so I ended up with a bottle of orange gin, something I would never have dreamed of drinking back home.

When we finally returned to the barracks and added our purchases to the supply, there were four cases of beer there for communal imbibing as well as many other individual refreshments, such as my pint of gin. Most of us got drunk and then I went up to the movie theater with Marty Sheridan. The power was out there so we went down to the bowling alley and had a few more beers there. Then we tried to bowl without much success, and finally headed back to the barracks for a good night's sleep.

On Sunday morning our quarters were a disaster area, with beer cans and trash all over the place. It was certainly clear that many of the guys would have to do a good deal more drinking before they came up to military standards because they were rank amateurs. One man's bed was covered with vomit and when I went to the front door for a breath of fresh air there was a trail of vomit halfway across the lawn leading right up to the door. I just burst out laughing in spite of myself at the abject misery of some of my hungover comrades. Bev had sent me a box of delicious homemade cookies so I ate some of those for breakfast and then headed up to Hilltop to relax and write letters. I wrote to Bev about our exploits out in the woods and also to let her know that I had asked Dave to get the two of us tickets for the Guthrie for when I was home on leave. It was exciting to know that was less than three weeks away now.

★★★

The excursion into Anniston was the only time I left the base during my time with Charlie Company and it was certainly not necessary to go into town to get alcohol. Charlie's, our EM club, was a short walk from the barracks and it offered all the beer, pizza, and salty snacks an off duty GI could ever desire. I did not smoke myself but that was pretty much a communal affair at Charlie's, because you were immediately engulfed in an acrid cloud of cigarette smoke upon entering the club. I enjoyed the place and the friendship as well because there were a number of guys in our platoon who liked to talk about things in addition to girls, cars, and sports.

The jukebox was always playing and it was usually country so I was unfamiliar with many of the songs, but there were two the guys played so often that to this day I always think of the boozy camaraderie of Charlie's when I hear them. One was Joe South's "Games People Play," with a twangy opening riff that said here comes yet another country track, followed by lyrics that quickly let you know how wrong that first impression was. Rock songs decrying the hypocrisy of the establishment and those in power had been common for several years, but that was a subject country music rarely explored. Like nearly every country artist, Joe bemoaned the fact that relationships so often failed, but, rather than blaming cheating girlfriends and hard-drinking men, he made the far more erudite and self-aware observation that this was due to the universal human failings of overweening pride and an inability to admit when we were in the wrong. He broke new ground for a genre with wide appeal in the Bible Belt by criticizing people who used ersatz religion as a way to cheat folks out of their hard-earned money. Then he wrapped things up with language straight out of a twelve-step program by asking God to deliver him from pride and vanity. Many of us felt that we were being forced to risk our lives because powerful men who had made a terrible mistake could not swallow their pride and admit their error, so that biting condemnation of arrogance and hypocrisy always resonated with the crowd at Charlie's.

The second song, Kenny Rogers' "Ruby," has to be one of the loveliest total downers ever recorded. What a song that was for a bunch of guys headed to Vietnam to hear, and yet they played it for themselves over and over. The song begins with the singer observing that his lady has fixed herself up for a night out, but this man knows that her adornments are not for his benefit. Then the writer employs a sophisticated narrative technique by adopting the speaker's physical perspective. Instead of telling the listener that he is unable to rise and see out the window he relates that he can tell that evening is approaching because of the lengthening shadows on the wall. And then the plaintive chorus follows, sung with beautiful harmonizing, imploring Ruby to stay home at least for that one evening.

The second verse tells us why the speaker has to rely on the angle of the

Sun to know what is going on outside: he is a disabled vet of a war in Asia who had been glad to serve his country when called upon to do so. The song was written about a victim of the Korean War but that was not the conflict on the minds of Americans in 1969. He knows that his injuries prevent him from fulfilling Ruby's needs, but he still longs for her companionship. This would hit home with the troops because what thanks did he get for acting on his belief that it was his duty to fight for his country? He goes on to give a more complete description of his plight, along with the news that his injuries will soon prove fatal, and his pleading reaches a new level of pathetic desperation: Can't you wait until I'm dead to find another man?

Finally, he is reduced to a state of helpless homicidal rage, wishing he was physically capable of murdering his faithless beloved. The chorus repeats for a final time and we are expecting to hear the same familiar line sung one last time, but then the narrator speaks, rather than sings, his final plea to a room occupied only by himself. Despite one hundred betrayals, he cannot stop loving Ruby, and that is the reason that her endless dalliances torture him. Throughout the performance we have gradually become aware that the rhythm section, bass and especially drums, has been evoking the sound of the human heartbeat and the song ends with fifteen seconds of this familiar staccato sound. The speaker, betrayed by both the nation he believed in and the woman he loves, is left alone and bereft with no companionship other than the soon-to-be-silenced beating of his broken heart. The death he is truly longing for is his own, not Ruby's.

We are a universe away from the songbook of World War II that acknowledged the pain of separation while also affirming the righteousness of our cause and the promise of a better life in a world that would be free because of our noble sacrifices. And yet the men preparing to go to a dubious war much like the one that destroyed the man so hopelessly in love with Ruby played the haunting song for themselves over and over. That was Charlie's, and I loved that place.

***

Bev wrote on Thursday the 21st that things were "A-OK" in the Gables, although her patience was wearing thin. She loved her parents very much, of course, but she felt she did not belong there anymore because her way of life was so different from theirs now. She and Barb were still having fun, and the day before they had gone to the beach with three of Barb's former students who were ninth grade girls. Then they went to the zoo where they saw two baby monkeys. Jennifer had written again about how her boyfriend, Steve, was still trying to decide what he would do if was called up. She had enclosed a handwritten copy of Max Ehrmann's beautiful poem "Desiderata", which Bev passed along in her letter to me.

She wrote again on Tuesday the 26th with her mind in a whirl from spending most of the day finishing *Giles Goat-Boy*. Barth's amazing amalgam of history, religion, and myth was truly an intellectual and artistic tour-de-force as well as being immensely entertaining, especially to readers like us since he framed it all in an academic setting. But the fact that such a brilliant mind clearly viewed the world through a lens of nihilism tended to leave the visitor to the universe he conjured up in a state of agitation and vague discontent rather than enjoying the satisfaction and catharsis one hoped for at the conclusion of a long and challenging novel. His self-deprecating humor lightened the gloom at times, but his levity was more often employed in biting satire that readers in an academic environment were often likely to find hitting a bit too close to home. For Minnesota scholars, the titles of East Campus and West Campus were, depending upon one's point of view, disturbingly or hilariously similar to our East and West Banks. That had been a big part of the book's appeal for me, but I could tell that Bev was disturbed by this view of the world so different from her own characteristically optimistic one, because she wrote at some length about the questions running through her mind. I also knew that she was centered enough to soon regain her even keel, which was something I had come to rely upon so heavily in the six months we had been together.

She was nearly finished with her second dress, a blue knit one that she planned to wear on Thursday night to a church dinner in honor of the retiring minister at her folks' church. The TV and hi-fi had both quit working but the audio repairman had come that day and now they could enjoy music again. Her folks had one of the large console-model stereos like the one we had in our home with the big speakers about four feet apart, and in those relatively early days of stereo recordings the two channels often had an exaggerated amount of separation to showcase the effects of the new technology. It was a big advancement over the small mono systems we had grown up with and she was enjoying the *Dr. Zhivago* soundtrack and the newest Peter, Paul, and Mary album with children singing in the choruses.

Jennifer had called to confirm that they could move into the new apartment on the 1st of September, and that was a relief for Bev because now she had a place to live in Minneapolis again. She had written my mom asking if she could stay there for a few days until she got settled, and Kay and Mark were another possibility. She was eager to be back at the U with all the people she had met the previous year and I could tell that the gloomy state Barth's book had left her in earlier in the day was already lifting.

She wrote again on Saturday, August 30, and the Labor Day weekend was to be her last one in Miami. She and her mom had visited their Aunt Neta and Uncle Russell. Neta and Bev's mom sewed while Bev got trapped listening to Russell "expound on the treacherous, conniving nature of the Soviet communists." She did not say if she told him I would soon be fighting the reds, but I imagine he would have approved. She and Barb went to see *2001* at a drive-in the previous night and she found it "amazing, fascinating, but also frightening." The sequence where HAL attempts to take over by killing off the astronauts reminded her somewhat of the power-mad, runaway computer WESCAC's tyrannical rule of West Campus in *Giles Goat-Boy*. The possibility of computers developing wills of their own and becoming more powerful than their creators was irresistible to authors of science fiction, and she and Barb had a discussion on whether that was really possible. Barbara said it was not but Bev still got a bit queasy contemplating all the brave new worlds that scientific advances could introduce.

Before going to the movie she had begun reading *Measure for Measure*, one of the works on the list for the MA exam. I had read it for a Shakespeare class and knew she would enjoy it because neither one of us ever read a work by the greatest writer in English that did not move and change us. She would be flying back to Minneapolis on Tuesday the 2nd, and Mom would pick her up at the airport that evening. Then she would stay at our house for a few nights while she got her stuff moved from storage in Comstock to the new apartment, and Jennifer said she would help with that. She closed with a poem by Emily Dickinson, "Of all the souls that stand create."

On Monday the 1st she celebrated Labor Day by going to the beach with her folks and Barb, getting an early start and leaving by late morning when it began to get crowded. Bev and Barb enjoyed playing beachcombers and watching people. That night her dad took them out to eat. Her father had prime rib, her mother and Barbara had filet mignon, and Bev had lobster tails, "which were scrumptious." She and her dad had talked one night and Bev was afraid she had hurt him by saying that the church in the Gables did not seem like where she belonged any more. She thought that he understood deep down, but it was still hard for a father to accept that his youngest child had outgrown not only the family home but their church as well.

***

Monday, August 25, began our first week of RVN training, and they trucked us out to the area so we could set up camp. We had been told that the cadre would do their best to simulate conditions in Vietnam. The bunkers were already dug, with the ones for the rifle squads around the perimeter and the ones for the mortar squads in the middle. Our bunkers were shaped like the old-time keyhole with a circular shape on top and a rectangle on the bottom. The gun was in the center of the round portion and our sleeping area was in the rectangle. Our preparations that day included building a waterproof roof over our sleeping area and then we rested until dark. We had a couple of fire missions that night, but it was all over by about 10:00 p.m. Then during the night we took turns pulling two-hour guard duty shifts.

One feature of our RVN exercises that reminded us we were not really in the war zone was the daily visit of our faithful sutler in his well-stocked snack truck. As at Fort Campbell, this was a vendor from a company that contracted with the Army for the privilege of offering the troops a variety of sweet or salty snacks for a reasonable price, as well as large paper cups of pop. The food certainly had minimal nutritional value but the laconic driver who usually manned the big van with a sliding side window for serving could never be accused of watering down the pop, or "soda" as most of my non-Minnesota comrades termed it. I still recall the syrupy cola beverage clearly and I usually accompanied my memorably cloying beverage with a frosting-drenched sweet roll or two. I rarely passed up the chance for such an unappetizing snack for the same reason that so many GIs get hooked on cigarettes: When you are bored to death or enduring physical discomfort the chance to enjoy any pleasure, no matter how small or questionable, is not to be ignored. The tobacco especially was irresistible for many out in the field because each C-ration included a pack of four cigarettes along with water-resistant matches. I smoked a few myself, especially on guard duty during the lonely nights when thoughts of home were the strongest, but somehow managed to avoid becoming addicted to nicotine.

On Tuesday we went out on a recon patrol, and on Wednesday an ambush patrol. It was mostly just tramping through the pine forests and brush and now that we were doing it in broad daylight I noticed that some areas did look almost tropical. I even saw bamboo growing along the creek, although I had no idea if that was a native species or something planted to make things look more like Southeast Asia. On Thursday the Charlies got to sit around the base camp while the Bravos went out on patrol again. On Friday morning they trucked us back in, but they did not let us off duty until noon on Saturday. That night I went up to the theater with a couple of other guys to see *Arabella* with Virna Lisi and Terry Thomas then came back and slept for about thirteen hours. That was the longest and best night's sleep I had been able to get since I returned to Fort Mac in July.

About this time I was informed that my application to the NCO school had been rejected because of having had mono. That was probably true because I doubt if my CO application ever made it into my file since I had withdrawn it. I did not mind being turned down since it was highly unlikely I would have finished or even begun the course anyway. Given the way I felt about the war, it really made no sense for me to seek a position involving any sort of leadership.

On Sunday the 31st I went to see *Dr. Zhivago*. I had seen it before but had enjoyed it so much that I wanted to see it again. That night I called both Bev and my family. She had asked if they delivered mail to us out in the field because she wanted to send some more goodies, and I assured her that they did and that we would love that. Mom said they were going to the traditional Labor Day picnic at Bud and Ruth Brodie's home in Robbinsdale. Dad and Bud had been friends since they grew up together on the North Side, and we had been going to their place on Labor Day for years. Thinking about that made me kind of homesick. I used to get down in the dumps coming home from Brodie's when I was in grade school at St. Charles because school was starting the next day, but I never minded it as much in my De La Salle days because the last part of summer got quite boring for me as an adolescent. When I was in college I looked forward to going back because I usually enjoyed my classes whereas working full-time, even my favorite summer job of carrying mail, began to get tedious after three months.

Monday, September 1, was Labor Day. We got up at 5:30, ate breakfast, and cleaned the barracks. We were done with that by about 8:00 and then they gave us post privileges for the rest of the day. I went up to Hilltop and wrote a letter to Bev while sitting at a table on the patio before the place opened. My plan for the day was to read and watch TV. The post had a decent library, so I had been spending some off-duty time there as well as at the service club. One nice thing about the library was that it was invariably nearly empty.

Our second week of RVN training began on Tuesday and it was more interesting than the first one because we moved every day. As with the first week, we had good luck with the weather. The only rain we had was on Wednesday and that was actually fortunate because the water truck missed us that day. We made shelters with our ponchos to stay dry and filled our canteens from the rivulets of rainwater running off of them. We had a hard march that day also. The distance was only about 6.5 miles but it was over steep hills and we were carrying the mortars, which meant an added burden of about forty pounds for each of the mortar-men. Workouts like that made me realize that all the PT had paid off. I hated to admit that the Army had done me any good at all, but I was almost certainly in the best physical condition of my adult life up to that point. We were supposed to have trucks but our platoon DI said we would have to walk in Nam so we might as well walk here as well.

Friday the 5th was a good day because we came back in that morning, cleaned our equipment and weapons, and then goofed off for the rest of the day. Mail call brought a cake that Bev baked for me, and a bunch of us enjoyed that. That night I went to see *The Valley of the Gwangi* staring James Franciscus, my old English teacher idol from *Mr. Novak*, except this time he was getting chased around by dinosaurs down in Mexico. The great special effects by Ray Harryhausen were the one redeeming feature in an otherwise absurd film. I had always loved his science fiction movies as a kid, and begged my folks to bring me to them.

On Saturday night I went to see *The Night They Raided Minsky's*, which was enjoyable, and on Sunday I took in *Number One*, starring Charlton Heston in an unconvincing performance as an aging quarterback. I also called home on Sunday, and Bev was there, too, because the phone in the new apartment was not connected yet. We were all excited because I would be there in person in only six days.

As with the last week of BCT, the final week of AIT was mostly just busy work and practicing for our "graduation ceremony." It was clear that discipline was slacker as even our sergeants' cadence calls became less an encouragement to be enthusiastic about being in the Army and going to war and more a reflection of our true attitudes:

Sergeant, Sergeant, this is it.
One more week of this here shit!

One more week of polishing brass,
Then Fort Mac can kiss my ass!

On one of our last days of training we were given the option of going through the big obstacle course. Such courses had been a part of our exercises for the last six months but this one was far more imposing than the ones we had been using. It had the tall towers and climbing walls like the ones they always feature in movies about military training. About half of us chose to do it, and I joined those opting out. That we were given a choice was another reflection of the more lax attitude since we returned from our field exercises. One man fell off of an obstacle and broke his collarbone. It was impossible to say if he did it deliberately but at least he certainly succeeded in delaying his trip to the RVN. During our final week we received the last of the series of three inoculations for plague, the seventeenth shot since induction.

Everything was overshadowed by the knowledge that we would be in a combat zone within a month, and that it was unlikely all of us would be coming back alive one year later. But even that bitterness was heavily mitigated by the certainty of three weeks back at home with our families and loved ones. Ho Chi Minh died at the age of 79 on September 2, but this seemed unlikely to have any effect on the communists' conduct of the war. If anything, his final apotheosis as a national hero in death might well stiffen the enemy's resolve.

On the 5th Lt. William Calley was charged with six counts of premeditated murder for the My Lai Massacre the previous year, and a number of other officers and enlisted men were soon to be charged with related crimes. But since these proceedings were conducted under the military judicial system the Army was still able to keep them secret from the general public and we had no knowledge of them at that point.

✲✲✲

Dave left New York on Wednesday, August 27, on a Holland America Lines ship bound for Holland for a year of study abroad focusing on photography and glass blowing. Bev flew back to Minneapolis on a Northwest flight with a stopover in Atlanta on Tuesday the 2nd, enjoying some unusual cloud formations as well as views of Miami, Miami Beach,

Nashville, the Tennessee River, Louisville, and Rochester. The approach to the Minneapolis airport was spectacular because they could see the shadow of the plane as well as the city's chain of lakes. Mom, Mary, and Jane met her at the airport. That night they enjoyed Johnny and Ed cutting up on *The Tonight Show*.

On Wednesday Mom drove Bev to the bank to deposit her money, and then to her new home. Bev liked it but said that it did need much cleaning. It was set up for budget-conscious students with accommodations for four in a one-bedroom furnished apartment. There was a fairly large living room separated from the kitchen by a sliding door. The bedroom was also large and was furnished with two bunkbeds. The place had two large closets and a linen closet, so storage would be adequate if limited. Bev and Jennifer were going to start cleaning and making things look homier that night.

Bev was spending a few days at our house until the apartment was organized and she was able to move her things over there from Comstock. While she was writing to me on the 3rd Mary came home from her new high school, Grace up in Fridley, and Bev said she looked nice in her uniform. Jane seemed a bit lost because she only had a half day of school that day and then sat around the house the rest of the time. After John came home from swimming class he and Jane "sat glued to the TV" for *Dark Shadows*. That cracked me up because I remembered how much they loved that crazy show.

On Thursday the 4th she took the bus to campus to register for her fall classes, choosing Tom Clayton's "Classics of Literary Criticism" and Ted Wright's "Poetry of W. B. Yeats." They both met on Monday-Wednesday-Friday so that would cut down on the number of times she had to walk the mile or so from the apartment to campus, although she said that she would probably try to go to the library on the other days anyway. The English Department began its long exile in the Institute of Technology area that year, and "after much sleuthing" she found the departmental office in 207 Main Engineering. Like their apartment, it was quite spacious but not yet cleaned or arranged. She was planning to move the next day but said again how much she loved being with my family. She had good conversations with Mom and enjoyed being around the kids as well.

On Sunday the 7th Bev wrote when she returned to the apartment from my family's house after our phone conversation. She had her stereo and records again and was listening to Judy Collins sing "Tomorrow is a Long Time." She was feeling a bit sad after the days with her family and mine and felt there were things she would have liked to have said to Mom but somehow was not able. The plan had been for her to spend the day at our house, and that morning in bed she was thinking that she should call before they came after her. The lack of a phone was a burden. Then soon after she crawled down from her upper bunk Mary and Jane knocked on the door. After the ride home, she played Concentration, Sorry, and Rack-O with Jane. Then when John got back from swimming, they all played Scrabble, with Mary winning.

That evening Bev, Mary, and Jane rode around on bikes and stopped at the Dairy Queen over in the St. Anthony Village shopping center before coming home. Jane was back to being her usual extroverted self and Bev told her about camp because she asked what it was like. She said that Jane would love it. In closing she reflected once again on the inadequacy of words to express her true feelings. I always felt that frustration as well, and it seemed like such a curious thing for two people for whom words were such a vital part of life, but that was one reason why we both felt the need to read and study literature. The great writers often expressed things we were feeling, and reading them helped us to clarify our own thoughts and feelings, as well as introducing us to ones we had failed to consider on our own. Actually, I always felt that she did a most eloquent job of telling me how she felt, and those words meant the world to me, especially while I was in the emotionally stifling environment of an Army training camp.

On Tuesday the 9th Bev sent me a collage of interesting faces she had cut out of magazines. She had not gone out much that day because of "Brr" weather, but she was certainly getting things done. She had marked some hems and bought a few things for the kitchen along with some yarn, a pattern for a sweater for her mother, "and other piddly things." Mom and John had helped her move a trunk and large suitcase from Comstock, and the place was getting to look more like home. Her books were piled on the coffee table and floor because she had not been able to get her bookcase yet from a friend of Jennifer who had kept it for her. She was now reading *The Winter's Tale* and thought she would move on to Donne's poetry after that. The much-awaited telephone was scheduled for installation on Thursday, and she was planning on taking the bus downtown to buy a few more things on Wednesday. Her letter concluded with another construction paper cutout, this time of a peace symbol. I drew that on most of my letters and envelopes as well. It was everywhere in those days.

She wrote again on the 11th with the big news that their phone had just been connected. They had both been going nuts without one and one night Jennifer exclaimed "We could die and no one would know it!" The previous night two friends, Helen and Kathy, had come over for supper and then the four of them went out to George's in the Park, a popular nightspot for young people in St. Louis Park. Bev wanted to get out of the apartment and watch people, whereas the others were planning on dancing, having a few drinks, and hopefully meeting some guys. She said the people-watching was good but the band was so loud that it was hard to hear what anyone was saying. She listened to a few guys who just wanted to talk with someone, including a social welfare grad student who just returned from South America. He considered not coming back because of the draft but then returned anyway. They talked about such things as politics, the economy, and the nature of people. Like many young people in those days, he cited Camus for his philosophy of living. She never learned the guy's name.

She had started to reread John Donne the day before, another title on the list for the MA exam, and was reminded that, in spite of some of his convoluted conceits, his subjects and opinions were most relevant to the world of today. She was so anxious for me to be back home that she felt as though she was walking around in a daze. She closed with a poem by Emily Dickinson, "Hope is the thing with feathers."

***

Saturday, September 13, finally arrived and I bid farewell to Fort McClellan for the last time. As much as I despised being forced under threat of prison to fight in a war in which I did not believe, I did have to admit that I certainly could have ended up on much worse AIT bases than Fort Mac. But now all thoughts were of home. I took the familiar connecting flight to Atlanta and then the long one back to Minneapolis. Dad and Bev met me at the airport and when Bev and I fell into each others' arms it felt as though all was finally right again with the world. It was strange to think that we had been apart far longer than the brief time we had known each other, and yet we had gotten so close through our letters and phone conversations that we had no doubts that we were meant for each other. And so there I was back in the old home again just two months after I had left at the end of my leave in July.

Bev, my family, and I seemed to have a mutual unspoken agreement to avoid talking much about the Army or the prospects for the next year.

We took things easy and enjoyed each others' company for three wonderful weeks, even though I know that none of us could avoid thinking about where I would be in a month. Bev's mom came up for a PEO convention so I got to meet her—a lovely, quiet, and very traditional kind of lady but not without a sly sense of humor and a strong competitive streak when it came to games. I found Marcia delightful and I also got the chance to talk with Bev's father Bob by phone for the first time while I was home. Fall quarter classes started on Monday the 29th, and Joyce Coulam had moved into the apartment by then. In anticipation of being joined by Joyce Rolla, she had cut out an article title from a magazine, "Take Your Joyce," and taped it to the linen closet door. It was great to see JC again, the very personification of the adage "still waters run deep," and it was fun to see how the three of them enjoyed each others' company so much as they organized their new home.

✱✱✱

The normal excitement of the start of a new academic year on our campus was enhanced by a convergence of issues and events relating to our national struggles. Controversy erupted even before classes began over "co-ed" arrangements at Freshman Camp, leading to a series of assurances from harried administrators that the term did not refer to the sleeping quarters. Welcome Week was more memorable than usual because of the activities of a new student organization known as Fight Repression of Erotic Expression (FREE). Its members passed out literature and greeted freshman by explaining their goals of educating the campus community about "erotic minorities" and protesting the "legislation of sexual morality."

Even a bit of the Apollo Mission found its way to our campus as two professors in the Institute of Technology received about 1.5 ounces of "moon dust" to study, representing our share of the forty-eight pounds of dust and rock the astronauts had gathered from the Sea of Tranquility. Two new departments, Afro-American Studies and American Indian Studies, began offering courses. Both units were established following negotiations begun after the Morrill Hall occupation. The trial of three of the protestors was scheduled to begin on the 20th, and the Liberation Coalition announced plans to march in their support.

The primary focus of attention as students returned to campuses across the country was the antiwar movement, and the first important event was a national Moratorium to be held on October 15. Nixon had been in office for nine months now and few of those opposing the war felt that his reductions in troop levels and draft calls were an adequate response to what they saw as a grave national crisis. But the deep division between Americans on this issue was made clear by the fact that, despite the intensity of the anti-war sentiment on many campuses, Nixon's Vietnam policy earned an approval rating of 71 percent in a national poll. The unrest and militancy of the previous year led one VP at a Midwestern university to remark "a lot of college administrators are returning to campus with the same feelings generals must have returning to battle."

About twenty-four organizations on our campus had a full schedule of activities planned for Moratorium Day, with the main event being a rally in front of Coffman followed by a march downtown to the Federal Office Building. About 250 faculty members took out a full-page ad in the *Daily* expressing support and calling for the assistance of President Moos and his staff. This immediately resulted in yet another controversy as a VP announced that all classes must be covered. On Thursday, September 2, Moos welcomed students and faculty to campus at the annual convocation ceremony in Northrop with a speech entitled "Reaching for the Rainbow of the New World," inviting them to "be inspired by possibility rather than depressed by reality." Pep talks have their place but it was pretty hard for many of us to be chasing rainbows that fall.

Other notable events while I was home on leave included the beginning of the trial of the Chicago Eight on September 24 on charges relating to the disturbances at the Democratic National Convention in August 1968. Judge Julius Hoffman was soon to become a hated symbol of the establishment among progressives, especially after he reacted to Bobby Seale's frequent courtroom outbursts by ordering him bound and gagged, eventually reducing the defendants to the Chicago Seven by sentencing Seale to an unprecedented and draconian four years in prison for contempt of court. On the 26th, the Beatles released their magnificent swan song *Abbey Road*, although I was not to hear it until later in Vietnam. The next day the Zodiac Killer struck again in Northern California when he brutally knifed a young couple who had been picnicking, one of whom survived. This latest outburst of random violence was especially unnerving to Californians since the gruesome Tate and La Bianca murders were still unsolved.

***

Bev and I did our best to concentrate on each other and neither of us could recall a happier time in our lives than those three weeks in September and early October. By the end of my leave we considered ourselves married in every respect except the paperwork. It was inevitable that things would begin to get tense and hectic as the time remaining grew shorter and emotions became rawer and more difficult to repress. During the last weekend joy was largely overshadowed by stress and melancholy. Friday the 3rd was my 23rd birthday, and the next day was to be my last at home.

I had been sleeping on a bed in the amusement room in the basement because I did not want John to have to move out of my old room on the main floor. It was hard to sleep much on the last night as my mind raced through all the memories of the twenty years I had lived in that house beginning when I was three years old, as well as all the hopes Bev and I shared for the future. A new chapter of life would begin the next morning and, even though I knew the odds were very strong that I would survive the next year, the chance that I would not was the specter that had haunted all of us since it had become clear that I was going to Vietnam to fight. I hated the thought of the pain that possibility was causing Bev, Mom, Granny, and the others, especially since there was really nothing much I could do to alleviate it. Bev and I would rely on love and hope. I was not one to pray in those days, but I knew that my family would be doing that every day, probably the rosary, and that thought did provide me with a measure of comfort. I hoped their faith would help to soothe their anxiety. Sometime in the middle of the night I finally drifted off into a troubled sleep.

The story continues in
*In Liberating Strife: A Memoir of the Vietnam Years,
Volume II: In Country*

Glossary

AIT: Advanced Individual Training

AAAC: Afro-American Action Committee

APCs: armored personnel carriers

ARVN: Army of the Republic of Vietnam

BCT: Basic Combat Training

CBR: chemical, biological, and radiological

COC: Code of Conduct

CEWVN: Committee to End the War in Vietnam

CLA: College of Liberal Arts

CMU: Coffman Memorial Union. The main student union building on the campus of the University of Minnesota, and thus an important center of student life and campus events.

CO: conscientious objector

COC: Code of Conduct

Counterculture: A broad-based term for the cultural movement that emerged in the 1960s due to widespread dissatisfaction, primarily among young adults, with the predominant conservative, middle class American way of life that had emerged in the years following World War II. It was expressed by a fervent dedication to progressive or even anarchic political views, but also distinctive music, art, clothing, and slang. It was thus regarded by many of its devotees as a new and more enlightened world view and way of life, not merely a novel style or fad. A notable characteristic was a predilection for illegal mood-altering substances such as marijuana, in contrast to the more accepted and legal intoxicant, alcohol. The term "Counterculture" is usually considered more broad than "The Resistance," referring to the movement against the war in Vietnam as well as opposition to racial injustice in American society, although the later term is certainly an integral component of the former.

CQ: charge of quarters

De La Salle, or "De:" a Catholic high school on Nicollet Island in downtown Minneapolis

DI: drill instructor

EM: Enlisted Men's (Club)

Forward observer: a soldier located near the target area designated for a mortar or artillery attack with the duty of communicating the coordinates of the target's location back to the fire crew

FREE: Fight Repression of Erotic Expression

HE: high explosive

HHH: Hubert H. Humphrey

ICBM: intercontinental ballistic missile

KIA: killed-in-action

KP: kitchen patrol

LAW: Light Antitank Weapon

Merchant Marine: the sailors and fleet providing auxiliary support to the US armed services during time of war

MCLU: Minnesota Civil Liberties Union

MOS: Military Operating Specialty

MSA: Minnesota Student Association. An official University body elected by the students and therefore constituting an important voice, but with little actual power beyond that.

NCO: non-commissioned officer

NG: National Guard

NSA: National Student Association

NVN: North Vietnam

PT: physical training

PO: post office

PX: post exchange

RNA: ribonucleic acid

ROTC: Reserve Officers' Training Corps

RVN: Republic of Vietnam (South Vietnam)

"SAN": "The Student as Nigger"

SASS: Students Against Selective Service

SDS: Students for a Democratic Society

SSS: Selective Service System

STRAP: Students for Racial Progress

TA: teaching assistant

The Bomb: a generic term for an atomic or hydrogen bomb

TVA: Tennessee Valley Authority

UCMJ: Uniform Code of Military Justice

UM: University of Minnesota

URI: upper respiratory infection

VC: Viet Cong

VD: venereal disease

W.E. B. Dubois Clubs: left-leaning young peoples' organizations of the 1960s organized by the Communist Party USA

WIA: wounded-in-action

About the Author

Steve Atkinson was born in Minneapolis and has lived there for most of his life. After returning from Vietnam in 1970, he enrolled in the Graduate School at the University of Minnesota on the GI Bill, earning an MA in English and History, and an MBA in Accounting. He retired in 2009 after a career in financial services, a welcome change that has allowed him to devote more attention to his first loves of reading and writing. He and Bev, his wife of 46 years, also spend time on such favorite activities as traveling and volunteering, but they agree that the best job of all is grandparenting. They live in Minneapolis within a mile of their son and his family.

www.ingramcontent.com/pod-product-compliance
Lightning Source LLC
Chambersburg PA
CBHW042227010526
44113CB00044B/2736